WHY CALL ME GOD?

Is God willing to prevent evil but not able?
Then he is not omnipotent.

Is he able but not willing?
Then he is malevolent.

Is God both able and willing?
Then whence cometh evil?

Is he neither able nor willing?
Then why call him God?

Epicurus [341-271 BCE]

WHY CALL ME GOD?

The Gospel Seen with
A Single Eye

J. H. Hatfield

CAPABEL PRESS

First published 2009 in Great Britain by

Capabel Press Ltd
PO Box 137
Frodsham
WA6 1AX
www.capabelpress.com

Copyright © 2009 J.H.Hatfield

Typesetting assistance by
Iain Beswick

Cover by His and Hers Design
www.hisandhersdesign.co.uk

Printed in Great Britain by the MPG Books Group
Bodmin and King's Lynn

The right of J.H. Hatfield to be identified as the author of this work has been asserted by him in accordance with the Copyright, Designs and Patents Act, 1988

British Library Cataloguing in Publication Data
A catalogue record for this book is available from the British Library

ISBN 978-0-9562057-0-4 (paperback)

For Paul

For whom this task was first begun

Theme

τετύφλωκεν αὐτῶν τοὺς ὀφθαλμοὺς
καὶ ἐπώρωσεν αὐτῶν τὴν **καρδίαν**,
ἵνα μὴ ἴδ**ωσιν** τοῖς **ὀφθαλμοῖς**
καὶ νοήσ**ωσιν** τῇ καρδίᾳ
καὶ στραφ**ωσιν**, καὶ ἰάσομαι αὐτούς.

He has blinded their eyes

And petrified their <u>heart</u>

That they may not see <u>with the eyes</u>

And perceive with the heart.

And they may be turned, and I may heal them.

(John 12:40)

τότε ἀ**ν**οιχθή**σον**τα**ι** ὀφθαλμοὶ τυφλῶν
καὶ ὦτα κωφῶν ἀ**κούσον**τα**ι**

Then eyes of (the) blind <u>shall be opened up</u>

And ears of (the) deaf <u>shall hear</u>.

(LXX Isaiah 35:5)

Koine Greek Alphabet

Greek Number Value	Greek Letter		Name	English Equivalent	
1	A	α	alpha	A	a
2	B	β	beta	B	b
3	Γ	γ	gamma	G	g
4	Δ	δ	delta	D	d
5	E	ε	epsilon	E	e
7	Z	ζ	zeta	Z	z
8	H	η	eta	Ē	ē
9	Θ	θ	theta	TH	th
10	I	ι	iota	I	i
20	K	κ	kappa	K	k
30	Λ	λ	lambda	L	l
40	M	μ	mu	M	m
50	N	ν	nu	N	n
60	Ξ	ξ	xi	X	x
70	O	ο	omicron	O	o
80	Π	π	pi	P	p
100	P	ρ	rho	RH,R	rh,r
200	Σ	σ , ς	sigma	S	s
300	T	τ	tau	T	t
400	Y	υ	upsilon	U	u
500	Φ	φ	phi	PH,F	ph, f
600	X	χ	chi	CH	ch
700	Ψ	ψ	psi	PS	ps
800	Ω	ω	omega	Ō	ō

For a full list of numerical symbols employed in Koine Greek, see Meztger B.M., *Manuscripts of the Greek Bible*, Oxford University Press, 1991, ISBN 0-19-502924-0, p.9.

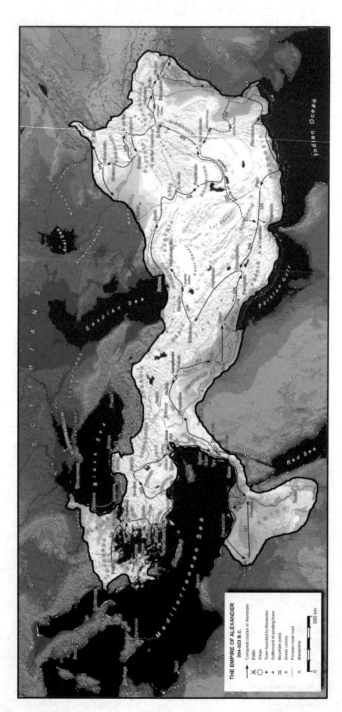

Empire of Alexander the Great
323 BCE

Permission is granted to copy, distribute and/or modify this map
under the terms of the GNU Free Documentation License,
Version 1.2 or any later version published by the
Free Software Foundation

THE EMPIRE OF ALEXANDER
334-323 B.C.

Conquest course of Alexander
Battle
Siege
Town founded by Alexander
Settlement of existing town
Mountain pass
Greek colony
Persian royal road
Alexandria

500 km

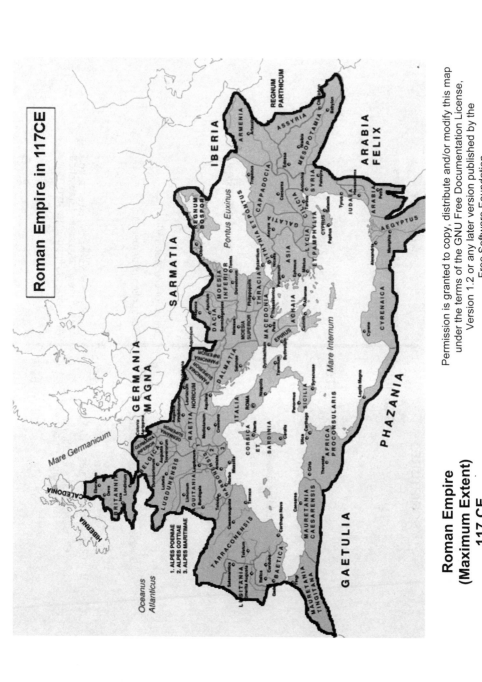

Roman Empire in 117CE

Roman Empire
(Maximum Extent)
117 CE

HISTORY

SCRIPTURE

| SCRIPTURE | BCE 1000 | 750 | 500 | 250 | 0 | 250 | 500 |

HISTORY:
- Prior myth of Abraham => Moses; Solomon & David (myth ?)
- Exile of Jews to Babylon (70 years); Deuteronomic Reforms within Judaism
- Conquests of Alexander the Great
- Death of Cleopatra VII
- Destruction of Jerusalem
- Constantine comes to power at York; Nicene creed; Nazareth established; Augustine of Hippo & Jerome

SCRIPTURE:
- Hebrew bible established ?
- Genesis re-written in in Greek (LXX)
- Gospels & NT letters in Greek
- Oldest extant copies in Greek; Christian church established; Latin bible (Vulgate)

Timeline

500	Gregory the Great & Augustine of Canterbury
	Islam established
750	Charlemagne & Holy Roman Empire
	Oldest extant copies in Hebrew
1000	
1250	Crusades against Islam
1500	Invention of printing
	Protestant Reformation
	King James bible (English)
1750	French Revolution
	Charles Darwin: Theory of Natural Selection
CE 2000	

Contents   Page

Contents   Page

Gospel of Thomas
Saying No.2:

P.Oxy. 654. 5-9	[λέγει ἰησοῦς]	Jesus said:
	μὴ παυσάσθω ὁ ζητῶν τοῦ ζη[τεῖν ἕως ἄν] εὕρῃ,	Let the one seeking not cease from seeking until he finds.
	καὶ ὅταν εὕρ[ῃ, θαμβηθήσεται	*And when he finds, he will become astonished.*
	καὶ θαμ]βηθεὶς βασιλεύσῃ	And being astonished, he will reign.
	κα[ὶ βασιλεύσας αναπα]ήσεται	And reigning, he will cease.

Preface

It was in September 1958 that I first arrived at a Roman Catholic boarding school not far from the sea in Sussex. I was nine years old.

Latin was amongst the subjects taught. For sixteen centuries it had prevailed as the universal language of the church so our daily religious services were largely conducted in Latin too. Only with the decrees of the Second Vatican Council (1962-65) would that practice be ended.

From age eleven I was chosen to be amongst the few taught Greek as well. But no one ever thought to inform us that the stories we were told about Jesus were first written down, and were still preserved, in the language we would now learn. Such Bible texts as we had in English were translations made at second hand from the Latin of the 4th century.

In due course I went on to another school, this time in North Yorkshire. The College of St Laurence at Ampleforth Abbey is owned and controlled by the English Congregation of the Order of Saint Benedict. The religious services continued. But I shortly discovered that I must purchase army boots and go on parade every Monday with toes polished black to a mirror finish. And on these occasions we were taught to use the Lee-Enfield .303 rifle, a British military weapon which saw much use in the First and Second World Wars. I was aged barely fourteen.

An upper echelon of the Roman Catholic church in Britain has long sought to re-establish its former influence. Amongst the means deemed appropriate is inclusion in the ranks of those directing the armed forces of the state. This demonstrates loyalty to the crown, something called into doubt in penal times.

The military influence may be explained on this basis. But in any case this was the church of Emperor Constantine the Great, a body whose theology extends to encompass the brilliant idea[1] that:

> The Church, the Mystical Body, exists on this earth, and is called the Church militant, because its members struggle against the world, the flesh and the devil.

I settled down to study classics and history, and before long elected to switch to science. In due course such learning would prove, for those encompassed and beset by '*the world, the flesh and the devil*', superior to any weapon.

It was in December 1967 that I completed my spell at this school. Before that year was out I had been offered a scholarship by St John's College, Cambridge. The Master at the time was John Boys Smith, a theologian who had taken to university administration and risen to become Vice Chancellor of the University. Now this was a place of real learning, and I knew it.

St John's College was founded in 1511 by Lady Margaret Beaufort, mother of the English king Henry VII, and by her chaplain John Fisher, Bishop of Rochester. It took its name from the medieval *Knights Hospitalers of the Order of St John the Baptist* (aka: *Knights of St John of Jerusalem*) whose buildings had occupied the site in years gone by.

Fisher was involved in founding several Cambridge colleges. But establishing St John's proved for him quite a struggle, as becomes clear with this abstract from Cecilia Hatt's book, *A Brief Life of John Fisher*[2]:

> From 1511 to 1514, Erasmus was resident in Cambridge, lecturing in Greek and working on translations of the New Testament in Greek, of Basil, and an edition of Jerome. Fisher from time to time helped him with funds from his own pocket: a letter of 1511 makes it clear that Erasmus had asked for money, thinking that Fisher had the free use of Lady Margaret's bequest, but Fisher replied that this money was strictly accounted for in the needs of the colleges. Both Fisher and Erasmus were invited in 1512 to the fifth Lateran Council, but in the event neither man was able to attend. Fisher made another plan to go to Rome two years later but was again disappointed.

> Also in 1514, Fisher suggested that he should resign the chancellorship of Cambridge University, so that it could be offered to Wolsey, who would be a richer patron. Wolsey refused the offer, and the university promptly reappointed Fisher as Chancellor for life. During these years Fisher was mainly resident in his diocese, with frequent journeys to London for Convocation and to Cambridge, where the work on the new foundation of St John's College was going on. The new king, Henry VIII, refused to part with some of the funds intended by Lady Margaret for the endowment: she had died before making her wishes for the college sufficiently clear in her will. Finally Fisher dissolved two decayed nunneries and used their funds for the college.

> Erasmus's New Testament was published in 1516. Fisher was full of enthusiasm for the new Latin translation and began to

learn Greek. He also began to learn Hebrew about this time and became an admirer of Johannes Reuchlin, the German champion of Hebrew studies. The new chapel of St John's was consecrated in this year, and in 1517 Nicholas Metcalf, Fisher's chaplain and archdeacon, became Master of the college. All the details of the provision of revenue for St John's College were not completed until 1522. Fisher wrote:

> *Forsooth, it was sore laborious and painful unto me that many times I was right sorry that ever I took that business upon me.*

Perhaps the effort was worthwhile. But this was a troubled time in England and Fisher met with his end in a manner just as shocking as it was sad. To speak against the king was deemed malicious. Hatt explains:

> At Fisher's trial in Westminster Hall on 17 June, it was brought against him that he had denied the supremacy of the king. Fisher protested that he had done so at the instigation of the king and under conditions of secrecy, but, he added, as he had not done so maliciously, he was not guilty, whereupon the judges replied that the word 'maliciously' had no effect in the statute, and the act itself of speaking was malicious. Fisher was condemned to be hanged, drawn, and quartered. He was 66 years old. The sentence was later remitted to beheading. Two days afterwards, three young Carthusians were executed at Tyburn. On 22 June 1535, Fisher was beheaded at Tower Hill. Judge William Rastell, who was present at the execution, gives a vivid description of the scene:

> > *Then was his gowne taken of frome hyme and hys typpett; And he stodde vp there in the sight of the people (where was a wonderous nombre of people gatherred to see this horrible execution, of whiche myself whas one) - a long, lene slender body, nothing in a maner but skyne and bare bones, so that the most parte that there sawe hym marveyled to see any man, bearing life, to be so farre consumed; for he seemed a lene body carcas, the flessh dene wasted away, and a verie Image of death, and, as one myght saye, death in a mans shape, and vsing a mans voice.*

Arriving in Cambridge in October 1968, I spent four years reading first Natural Sciences and then Chemical Engineering. For the next thirty I would work in the British chemical industry. Developing into a freelance engineering consultant, I focused on solving problems left unsolved by others who had found them too tough to crack, and my efforts were met with real success. Such work provided a good grounding for challenges yet to come.

With the commencement of the year 2001 Pope John Paul II issued from Rome an Apostolic Letter with the title *Novo Millennio Ineunte* [*Entering the New Millennium*]. It began in this way:

> At the beginning of the new millennium, and at the close of the Great Jubilee during which we celebrated the two thousandth anniversary of the birth of Jesus and a new stage of the Church's journey begins, our hearts ring out with the words of Jesus when one day, after speaking to the crowds from Simon's boat, he invited the Apostle to "put out into the deep" for a catch: "*Duc in altum*" (*Lk* 5:4).
>
> Peter and his first companions trusted Christ's words, and cast the nets. "When they had done this, they caught a great number of fish" (*Lk* 5:6).

The Roman Catholic Church was at the time deeply mired in scandal on account of instances of child abuse by members of its celibate clergy, and all the more so on account of its past efforts to cover up what had happened. This had emerged as a particular problem in the USA, Ireland, Australia and in the UK. In these countries the scandal risked augmenting the prevailing decline in church membership.

For England and Wales a *Review on Child Protection* was appointed under Lord Nolan. Its recommendations were aimed in particular at preventing any recurrence of sexual abuse. Nolan was a family friend; he too had attended Ampleforth College. But it seemed to me that abusive behaviour in the Catholic church went deeper than was generally recognised and I suspected his recommendations would serve as little more than a sticking plaster. My own experience suggested it was the traditionally dominant style of the church which carried with it the potential for abuse in all that was said and done.

Academic philosopher Anthony Grayling, in his book '*What Is Good?*'[3], says this:

> Some have felt sympathy for those embattled in their beliefs in this way. Others feel sympathy for them for the different reason that they are victims of a false and distorting perception of the world, a view into which they are trapped typically because of their upbringing and circumstances. For the continued existence

of religions is largely the product of religious education in early childhood - itself a scandal since it amounts to brainwashing and abuse, for small children are not in a position to evaluate what they are taught as fact by their elders. (The vast majority of religious educational institutions are for very young children).

An organisation whose biggest problem is that it doesn't know what the real problem is will never escape from the consequences of that problem. I decided to investigate for myself the ideological foundations of the Catholic church. For on the face of things it is truly puzzling that here is an organisation claiming for itself exclusive rights as the channel for a god who is good, but which all down the centuries has been seen to act in ways which so plainly were far from good.

I would relearn the Greek of my early years and study the gospels in Greek. In this way I would *'put out into the deep'* as bidden ... and see whether, after so many centuries, fish were still there to be caught.

As for this, no one addressing NT scripture can escape these facts:

- The passages at Mt.7:10 and Lk.11:11 are consistent in advising that *a serpent* be substituted for *a fish*.

- At Rv.12:9 the ancient *serpent* is identified as *'the one called a devil and Satan, the one deceiving the whole world'*.

- The passage at Rv.2:24 refers to *'those who do not know the deep things of Satan'*.

With this to go on, I could expect a fishing trip with a difference. Indeed I soon began to realise[4] that there is more to scripture than the Catholic church has *ever* admitted to knowing ... a great deal more. This book has been written to explain a good part of what that is.

Lastly, here is a suggestion for those who may like to explore this book but are unaccustomed to reading in Greek. In the tables, read the translation to English given in the right hand column. At the same time keep an eye on the Greek source in the left hand column and see if you can learn to recognise some of the key words (or names) which the writers have concealed within other words. Attention has been drawn to these, most often by employing a larger size of font.

J.H. Hatfield
January 2009

Acknowledgments

The author and publisher are grateful to Connor Birch for reading the early drafts of this book and making suggestions for improvement.

For scripture of the *Old Testament* the immediate source was the CATSS LXX edition prepared (with reference to the updated Rahlfs edition) by the *Thesaurus Linguae Graecae* [TLG] Project directed by T. Brunner at the University of California, Irvine and made available through the *Center for Computer Analysis of Texts* at the University of Pennsylvania.

For scripture of the *New Testament* the immediate source was the Nestlé-Aland 26th Edition Greek text, identified also as UBS3 (United Bible Societies). This is the Greek text underlying most English translations made since 1881, including the New American Standard and New International Versions. Certain words are enclosed in square brackets [ ] or double brackets [[ ]]. These show where the critical text editors have considered the inclusion or omission of such text to be in question.

Whole lifetimes of work have been given by certain scholars in modern times to critical studies of the biblical manuscripts and to the meticulous task of eliminating textual corruption wherever possible. Their work has gone largely unnoticed by the world but here it is recognised with vast appreciation. Through their dedication to the task they have rendered a great service to many.

The extensive translations in this book from Greek scripture to English have been made by the author. He has sought to make them as literal as possible. The aim was to preserve the sense intended by the original writers, exposing where possible the nuance and innuendo present in what they wrote.

Abstracts from the works of certain other writers have been included for purposes of criticism or review and within the limits generally agreed to constitute fair dealing. These have been attributed in full wherever possible.

PART 1

~

THE EYES
OF
THE BLIND

~

"A liar is someone who tells an untruth knowing it is untrue,
or being reckless* to its truth or falsity".

*Mr Justice Lindsay, in the case of Railtrack Small Investors
   vs. HMG (Oct 2005)*

   * devoid of caution; heedless of danger, etc

"It is self-deception, the lie we do not see, that serves best to
deceive our enemies. The best way to tell a lie is to believe it
yourself".

Sean Spence, Reader in Psychology, University of Sheffield

"They needs must find it hard to take Truth for authority
who have so long mistaken Authority for truth".

Gerald Massey, Egyptologist

Chapter 1

Introducing Greek Scripture

This is a book about scripture. It is about those writings from the ancient world better known to some as '*The Bible*', and how to understand them.

The book relies predominantly upon working with scripture in Greek. To proceed in this way is essential if we are to have any chance of penetrating the ancient 'mystery' which underpins the gospels.

What is known as Koine [*common*] Greek was the language employed by the various authors of scripture at the time when their skills were approaching a peak. That stage was reached almost two thousand years ago with the release of many new books. Of these, twenty seven were later assembled into what is known today as the canon [*rule*] of the *New Testament*, amongst them the four established gospels and the Pauline letters. These new books followed in the cultural tradition already established by what Christians recognise as the *Old Testament*, a collection of originally Hebrew texts. Here were the five books of the Pentateuch (known also as the *Torah* or *Law of Moses*), the books of Kings and Chronicles, the books of the Prophets, the Davidic Psalms, the wisdom books, and others besides: and even these had been rewritten into Greek several centuries before the gospels appeared.

One reason for working in Greek is to preclude ideological bias introduced by subsequent translators. In practice a particular problem down all the centuries has been adjustments to the divine names made by translators determined at any cost to assert a monotheist agenda.

Another reason is that key features of the message in Greek fail to pass through the barrier imposed by translation. As we shall see, the authors convey a part of their meaning by selecting certain words deliberately to invoke other words related by a similar spelling or sound. In effect, the words they choose have other words concealed within them. Where an important component of meaning is conveyed in this way, it will of course be filtered out by attempts to rewrite in a different language. The only way to preserve meaning is to preserve the actual text in which that meaning was first expressed.

To illustrate what may be lost in translation, let us consider the Greek text at a familiar point in the narrative of *Genesis*, Chapter 22:

LXX Gn. 22:13	καὶ ἀναβλέψας αβρααμ τοῖς ὀφθαλμοῖς αὐτοῦ εἶδεν καὶ ἰδοὺ **κριὸς** εἷς κατεχόμενος ἐν φυτῷ σαβεκ τῶν κεράτων	And Abraham, looking up, with his eyes, saw … and look! A single **_ram_** held down in a Sabek plant by the horns.
	καὶ ἐπορεύθη αβρααμ καὶ ἔλαβεν τὸν κριὸν καὶ ἀνήνεγκεν αὐτὸν εἰς ὁλοκάρπωσιν ἀντὶ ισαακ τοῦ υἱοῦ αὐτοῦ	And Abraham went and took the ram and brought it as a whole-fruit (offering) in exchange for Isaac, his son.
22:14	καὶ ἐκάλεσεν αβρααμ τὸ ὄνομα τοῦ τόπου ἐκείνου **κύριος** εἶδεν ἵνα εἴπωσιν	And Abraham called the name of that place "He saw **_a lord_**" - so that they should say:
	σήμερον ἐν τῷ ὄρει **κύριος** ὤφθη	"Today in the mountain **_a lord_** was seen".

The reader in Greek learns that Abraham saw **κριὸς** [*a ram*]: but the place name is to indicate that Abraham saw **κύριος** [*a lord*]. The difference in spelling between the two words is slight, as is the difference in their sound. Is it not plain that the authors intend an association of some sort, even perhaps equivalence? But in translation to any other language the innuendo is lost. Many similar examples may be given where comprehension is restricted to those who read in Greek, whilst the reader in translation, deprived of pivotal clues to meaning, ultimately misses the point completely.

Scripture was written to be understood in the language in which it was written. There is a natural and legitimate rôle for translation. But the irrecoverable mistake - and the mistake so widely made down the centuries - has been to publish translations *with the source text removed*. Here is the origin of much doctrinal confusion. For the message of scripture is deeply challenging, packed with riddles and truly subtle in its expression. Even the most attentive reader, deprived of the original text, may soon be led far astray.

For this reason scriptural passages cited in this book will be drawn from the composite Greek sources available to modern translators. As an aid to those unfamiliar with Greek, a strictly literal translation to English will be set alongside. Surely this must be the correct approach for the study of scripture in any culture which does not have Greek as its language for everyday use?

As mentioned already, the majority of the *Old Testament* books were set down first in the Hebrew language but by the time the gospels appeared it was already two to three hundred years since these earlier books had been rewritten into Greek. This change in the language assigned for scripture came about following the conquests of Alexander the Great [356-323 BCE] whose successors imposed a Hellenist (Greek) culture from Egypt and Greece in the west through Palestine and Mesopotamia and beyond to the east.

Later, with the free movement of peoples which distinguished the Roman Empire, Hellenism spread its influence westwards across the Mediterranean so that Greek continued as the language of learning in the Roman world in the first two centuries CE. It was in this period that Greek versions of scripture were in widespread use. Few could still read in Hebrew. Even in Palestine itself dialects of Aramaic were established in everyday use.

In this book we shall use the most abundant and well known Greek version of the *Old Testament*, the *Septuagint*. In Greek it was known as οἱ ό, meaning '*the seventy*', from the popular story (attributed to Aristeas) that it had been produced by seventy translators. In the Roman world this version was identified with the tag **LXX** - the symbol in Latin for the number 70.

This important textual source was produced at Alexandria (Egypt) around 250 BCE. Copies circulated widely: indeed plenty of the later manuscripts exist to this day. Then it is widely held, and with good evidence, that this was the version of the *Old Testament* [OT] familiar to the *New Testament* [NT] authors.

For example Jobes and Silva[1] assert:

> An additional consideration, however, brings the LXX and the NT even closer together; namely the indisputable fact that the NT writers knew and used the OT in its Greek form.

Theirs is an opinion consistent with the following recent statement[2]:

> Today we know that the Greek translation of the Old Testament produced at Alexandria - the Septuagint - is more than a simple (and in that sense really less than satisfactory) translation of the Hebrew text: it is an independent textual witness and a distinct and important step in the history of revelation, one which brought about this encounter in a way that was decisive for the birth and spread of Christianity.

By the time the gospels appeared, essentially all scripture was known and studied - and also written - in Greek, although it did retain certain traits of style inherited from Hebrew syntax and a small number of Hebrew or Aramaic phrases were incorporated into the Greek text by transliteration (for example at Mt.27:46 and Mk.15:34).

For the gospel authors it was the *Septuagint* which provided the reference (or base text) against which they now wrote, and from which they took quotations. They could easily have written all the gospels without being able to read Hebrew at all. Interestingly, some scholars hold that one or more of the gospels may have been written at Alexandria, the home of the LXX.

But let us return to the aim of this book. More precisely, it is about the *nature* of Greek scripture, about the *methods* employed in its composition, and about *how* to extract the message such scripture conveys. Ultimately then, *it is about how scripture may be soundly understood* - something which may not be possible for those relying upon any subsequent translation, whether to Latin, Coptic or Armenian, or to one of our modern languages.

The need for such a book is surely pressing, for there is certainly far more to the λόγος [*message*] of scripture than has been widely understood ever since the fourth century CE. In that century the Catholic church was newly established and already the request was issued by Pope Damasus ~382 CE for some early translations of scripture into Latin to be 'corrected' by the scholar Jerome (his full name in Greek was Ευσέβιος Σωφρόνιος Ιερώνυμος).

To this day we know Jerome's Latin edition as the *Vulgate* Bible. But how strange - and how unfortunate - that after revising the four gospels against sources in Greek[3], Jerome followed up by translating much of the *Old Testament*, including the five books attributed to Moses, from a recently established Hebrew source, a precursor to the Masoretic text which we still have today. For with this choice it became almost certain that the original coupling would be lost between the Greek text of the gospels and the Greek version of *Genesis*. And this in its turn might put at risk the transmission of scripture's deeper meaning.

Alongside translations to Latin, the fourth century saw some other trends develop. One was to assign to scripture a historicity it did not deserve, as Constantine's biographer Eusebius of Caesarea sought to do with his inventive Εκκλησίαστικη Ίστορία [*Church History*]. Another was to interpret scripture at the most literal level possible, as Jerome's friend Eusebius of Cremona sought to do. Rome in the fourth century was steadily losing its political and military grip on the world: its struggling empire would shortly collapse. Yet the Roman Catholic church was fast establishing its hold ... with Constantine's Nicene creed, with a god who had entered the Roman world in the person of Jesus, with extraordinary tales supposed to have been recorded by those who had known him. The stage was set for the later development of the Holy Roman Empire which would underpin medieval Europe, would survive for more than eight hundred years, and was finally brought to an end only with the Napoleonic Wars.

How many now would be led astray? The growing dominance of the Roman Catholic church was not the result *per se* of translating scripture to Latin, rather it was sustained by the successful assertion of a false historicity for the gospels and by the loss of ability in the western world to read the original texts in Greek. It was typical that Augustine of Hippo, foundational theologian of the western church, should struggle to learn Greek (as he himself notes in his *Confessionum, Liber I, XIII-XIV*). And Jerome's achievement as *vir trilinguis* (knowing Hebrew, Greek and Latin) was rare indeed in that age.

Such considerations go a long way towards explaining why there is, to this day, more to the message of scripture than the Christian tradition will readily admit: for much was misconstrued in that age. And as for the developments of subsequent centuries, it was never likely that any person would explain correctly a matter he had yet to grasp for himself.

So often religious leaders consider it as strange, as disturbing, even as heretical or offensive, if someone should assert that there is more to the meaning of scripture than they themselves have ever taught, or indeed have ever known. The very suggestion may be regarded as an unwelcome challenge to authority, an authority which does not find it easy to examine for flaws a teaching and tradition which, however defective, has survived for seventeen centuries.

A common response may be to say *"There is no new revelation"*. Yet such a remark lacks weight when made by those who cannot even read in Greek. For where scripture of the *New Testament* is concerned, a reader without Greek is no better placed than one who is blind.

Notwithstanding every protest, this book will demonstrate that there *is* more to scripture than many have ever known. As you read further you may come to this appreciation for yourself. The themes of scripture are tightly self-consistent and the task of penetrating them not entirely free from effort. But who will say that it cannot be done? And who lays claim to knowing all the answers when as yet he (or she) has never read in Greek?

What could it Mean to be Blind?

Notice how the concept of *the blind guide of the blind* is found in the gospels themselves (*qv.* Mt.15:14, 23:16; Lk.6:39). In the narrative we find Jesus addressing the scribes and Pharisees as '*hypocrites* and *blind guides*'.

Indeed he goes further to accuse them of being:

Mt.	ὁδηγοὶ τυφλοί, οἱ διϋλίζοντες	Blind guides, those straining
23:24	τὸν κώνωπα τὴν δὲ κάμηλον	out the gnat but ***gulping***
	καταπίνοντες.	***down*** a camel.

The gospels are packed with sayings which cannot be taken literally but must be recognised and understood as allegory or as riddles.

Perhaps you are familiar with London's Cockney slang. In this form of rhyming slang a selected word is replaced by another word borrowed from an unconnected phrase chosen to rhyme with the word replaced. The association of the original word and the slang word is rarely obvious to the uninitiated.

Suppose that an acquaintance says to you :

> Let's go 'n take a butchers

As many Londoners will know, it means :

> Let us go and take *a look*

The paired rhyming rule neatly transforms 'a butcher's *hook*' into '*look*'. But think how hard it would be to understand what was meant if you didn't know the rhyming rule.

Now put yourself for a moment in the place of a person living in a future age, say in the year 4000 CE. After much effort, you have learned to read in ancient English, a tongue long since lost from everyday use. And then you come across the phrase '*take a butchers*'. What could it mean? Two thousand years after it was written, the challenge posed to us by scripture is no less severe than this.

In the passage above from *Matthew*, the behaviour attributed to blind guides is typical of the riddles embedded in the gospels. If it seems to make but little sense, then we may guess it has been generated by using some kind of private convention, and may be understood correctly only by those who **know** that convention. The verb in Greek which holds this sense of knowledge acquired is γινώσκω [*I know or I learn to know*]. From it is derived the noun γνῶσις [*knowledge*], and from this we obtain in English the adjective **gnostic**. As we shall discover, the texts of Greek scripture, including all the gospels, are in this sense gnostic. They are gnostic through and through.

But what do we have to know before we can solve the riddle about the gnat and the camel? It may help to recall here the Jewish tradition about the wily 'serpent' who in the book of *Genesis* (the first book of the *Torah*) enters the narrative at Chapter 3. It is here that the serpent deceives the woman Eve, with his promise that:

> By death you shall not die …
> and you shall be like gods, knowing good and evil.

As we shall see, the narrative of all scripture echoes to this deceitful theme. The same bland assertion then provides the foundation for Christian doctrine as first set forth by the Catholic church (and by the time you reach the end of this book you should appreciate the reason for this correspondence).

In the story the serpent is cursed for his successful deceit … cursed to go upon his belly and eat earth all the days of his life (like a worm). Yet Jewish tradition[4] claims of the serpent that prior to this punishment:

> Like a man, he stood upright upon two feet, and in height he was equal to the camel

Suzetta Tucker presents further evidence for equivalence between serpent and camel at:
> http://ww2.netnitco.net/~legend01/camel.htm

The implication in the riddle about *blind guides* is that such a person gulps down a camel without even recognising he has done so: for who would try to swallow a camel on purpose? It is implicit too that those who 'gulp down camels' do so *only, or mainly, on account of their blindness.*

Blindness results in a failure to 'see' what is placed before you. The visitor to London, upon seeing a notice which instructs him to "*Pick up the dog*", may not appreciate that he must go to the *telephone* (dog and *bone* = *telephone*). His actions may not match those intended by the author of the notice, who might easily think of the hapless visitor as suffering from word blindness because his responses show beyond doubt that he doesn't know the meaning intended for the word 'dog'.

Now let us suppose that the word for 'camel' has been used in scripture to replace the word 'serpent'. Then it would not be surprising if many readers didn't 'see' the serpent. On this basis they too would be classed as blind … for they have failed to 'see' what was placed before them. But their real problem is that they don't understand the gnostic convention employed by the writer, for whom the word *camel* is simply an alternate name for a serpent.

In *Genesis* Chapter 24, Rebecca (an attractive young lady who later turns out to be evil) journeys to meet for the first time with Isaac, to whom she will shortly be married. Isaac is portrayed in scripture as good, although ruthlessly deceived in his old age by Rebecca and Jacob who conspire to deceive him *by exploiting his growing blindness* (it is a theme which keeps recurring in scripture: the 'blind', even when they mean well, labour under a persistent disadvantage because they are not able to recognise what is set forth to be evil).

Rebecca travels to meet Isaac *mounted upon a camel*. The story is packed with much significant detail, but shortly we are told:

LXX	καὶ ἐξῆλθεν ισαακ	And Isaac went out to
Gn.	ἀδολεσχῆσαι **εἰς τὸ πεδίον** τὸ	meditate **in the plain**
24:63	πρὸς δείλης καὶ ἀναβλέψας	towards evening. And looking
	τοῖς **ὀφθαλμοῖς** εἶδεν	up **with the eyes**, he saw
	καμήλους ἐρχομένας	camels coming.

In the narrative Isaac has gone out to meditate. He looks up *with the eyes* [*in Greek:* τοῖς **ὀφθαλμοῖς**]. Isaac is not yet blind. He sees camels coming. But if we are not to be classed as blind then we are expected to see something more than camels. Without doubt you will have seen something more yourself. But the key question is this: did you recognise what you saw? Did you see through the disguise?

The word in Greek for *a serpent* is **ὄφις**. Portrayed throughout scripture's narrative as an evil deity, the cunning serpent is definitely not 'good news'. Indeed at Rv.12:9 he is given as "***the great dragon, the ancient serpent, the one called a devil and Satan, the one deceiving the whole world***".

When Isaac looks up *with the eyes* [τοῖς ὀφθαλμοῖς], what we should be able to make out, concealed amidst the text, is ὄφις [*a serpent*]. Already the same opportunity has been afforded several times in connection with what Abraham 'sees' (*qv.* Gn.13:14, 18:2, 22:4, 22:13) … and before him the woman Eve (Gn.3:6).

Those with a good memory may recall how Abel was slaughtered after he went out with evil Cain εἰς τὸ πεδίον [*into the plain*]. Here Isaac too goes into the plain - and meets with his evil wife-to-be. Perhaps you are just beginning to gain new sight … catching the flavour of how scripture worked for those '*in the know*' in the Hellenist world? If so, you will realise how little of this could ever have been grasped by a person reading in translation. For in translation to Latin (which never was a language of scripture, and never will be) τοῖς ὀφθαλμοῖς becomes merely *oculis*. All who read in translation suffer instant blindness: for now there's no '*serpent*' to see.

But for those who read in Greek, this further '*camel*' riddle may now be quite easy to solve.

Mt.	πάλιν δὲ λέγω ὑμῖν,	But again I say to you, it is
19:24	εὐκοπώτερόν ἐστιν κάμηλον	easier (for) a camel to go
	διὰ τρυπήματος ῥαφίδος	through (the) hole **of a**
	διελθεῖν ἢ πλούσιον εἰσελθεῖν	**needle** than (for) a rich
	εἰς τὴν βασιλείαν τοῦ θεοῦ.	person to enter into the
		kingdom of God.

The *hole in a* **needle** constitutes the *narrow gate* mentioned already in the same gospel (Mt.7:13-14). The solution to this riddle appears to be very similar to the one involving Isaac. Once again we have a camel, once again we can make out ὄφις [*a serpent*]. This time the letters are jumbled up, but still it's not hard to see.

The Amazing Power of the Human Mind

I cdnuolt blveiee taht I cluod aulaclty uesdnatnrd waht I was rdanieg. The phaonmneal pweor of the human mind!

Aoccdrnig to rscheearch taem at Cmabrigde Uinervtisy, it deosn't mttaer in what oredr the ltteers in a wrod are, the olny iprmoatnt tihng is taht the frist and lsat ltteer be in the rghit pclae.

The rset can be a taotl mses and you can sitll raed it wouthit a porbelm. Tihs is bcuseae the huamn mnid deos not raed ervey lteter by istlef, but the wrod as a wlohe.

Such a cdonition is arppoiately cllaed Typoglycemia ! > > :-)

Amzanig huh? Yaeh and yuo awlyas thought slpeling was ipmorantt.

The above text (of which the true origin is obscure and may not be the University of Cambridge) first circulated on the internet in September 2003. What we may learn from it is that merely jumbling up the letters of the words in a passage does **not** necessarily destroy meaning. For where a language is already familiar to the reader, the human mind does have the ability to pick out more than exactly what is written.

By a modest extension of the same principle, selected words in scripture may be concealed in a mis-spelled form wholly within other words spelled correctly. It is no use claiming that readers would be unable to follow what has been done where the word ὄφις is concealed within the word ραφίδος. The jumbled passage cited above demonstrates clearly (but working in English) that recognition of this kind would really have been quite easy for those with a trained eye who were accustomed to reading in Greek and knew what they were looking for.

Now perhaps you are beginning to see how scripture functions as a self-learning text, with its riddles graded in difficulty from elementary through to the more advanced.

We find that the following theme crops up five times in the three synoptic gospels, so clearly it is quite important:

Mt.	ὅστις γὰρ ἔχει, δοθήσεται	For whoever has, it will be
13:12	αὐτῷ καὶ περισσευθήσεται:	given to him and he will have
	ὅστις δὲ οὐκ ἔχει, καὶ ὃ ἔχει	in abundance: but whoever
	ἀρθήσεται ἀπ' αὐτοῦ.	does not have, even what he
		has will be taken from him.

And yes, already this *is* our experience. First we obtained a solution to one riddle, then shortly the solution to another. Now this new riddle about abundance makes for three. Is the entire theme of scripture starting to unravel in our hands?

It is easy to appreciate that once you latch on correctly to the underlying convention employed by these gnostic authors, you will quickly see more and more of what they mean. Meanwhile those who do not 'see' can be led far astray - through taking literally all that is said, while persistently missing the central point.

In that regard, there is heavy irony in the fact that the gospel narrative itself is populated so thickly with those encountering Jesus who are said to be either blind or deaf. At one point we are even told how Jesus smears mud in the eyes of a man who is blind from birth (Jn.9:6). It is hard to take this seriously as the way to restore someone's sight. But which readers of these stories pause to consider that they themselves may be numbered along with those mentioned in the gospel narrative … blind and deaf to the λόγος, both to the *message* of scripture and to the *identity* of Jesus himself?

In truth, everywhere that scripture is read - *and most particularly where it is read in translation to Latin or to another vernacular language -* these afflictions of sight and hearing are certain to take their toll. And from the dire lack of books similar to this one, it is plain that hardly anyone in our age does manage unaided to spot the critical themes of scripture - and most never spot them at all.

Indeed such is the premature enthusiasm with which so many lock down meaning for scripture *before they have even learned to understand,* that these persons end up clinging on for dear life to the wrong end of the scriptural 'stick'. And in this way they are caught in a trap from which they never contrive to escape.

Surely it must be worth our while to penetrate the mind of these ancient authors and understand aright what they wrote. They are clearly great philosophers, imaginative and highly astute. What they write is deeply clever, steeped in a Gnostic ideology and painstakingly expressed in Greek. It is a *mystery* for the reader to solve: the term crops up twenty eight times in just ten of the *New Testament* books.

In this passage from *Luke*, the author has Jesus speak as follows:

Lk.	ὁ δὲ εἶπεν, ὑμῖν δέδοται	But he said "To you it is
8:10	γνῶναι τὰ μυστήρια τῆς	given to know the mysteries
	βασιλείας τοῦ θεοῦ, τοῖς δὲ	of the kingdom of God, but to
	λοιποῖς ἐν παραβολαῖς, ἵνα	the rest in parables - that
	βλέποντες μὴ βλέπωσιν καὶ	seeing they may **not** see,
	ἀκούοντες μὴ συνιῶσιν.	and hearing they may **not**
		understand".

Is it not clear that the function of the so-called *parables* is actually to preserve the mystery by limiting the circle of those who know what it is? Far from enlightening the reader (as so often is claimed) the function assigned to the parables is to ensure that many will **not** see, and will **not** understand. It is a rôle in which they are surely most efficacious.

The Fate of the 'Many'

It follows from what we have learned so far that the gospels are examples of *esoteric* texts. They are directed for a select few who possess beforehand, or can acquire, enough knowledge to understand them. And if we ask what becomes of the *many* who lack this knowledge, again the authors have Jesus give the answer:

Mt.	εἰσέλθατε διὰ τῆς στενῆς	Enter in through the narrow
7:13	πύλης: ὅτι πλατεῖα ἡ πύλη καὶ	gate. For broad (is) the gate
	εὐρύχωρος ἡ ὁδὸς ἡ	and spacious the way which
	ἀπάγουσα εἰς τὴν ἀπώλειαν,	leads to destruction - and
	καὶ πολλοί εἰσιν οἱ	<u>many</u> are those entering in
	εἰσερχόμενοι δι' αὐτῆς:	through it.

The '*many*' - those who don't manage to catch on - are, in all their unwitting and misguided confidence, going like lemmings on the broad and spacious way which leads to their own destruction.

How ironic that the Catholic church (named from Greek **καθ' ὁλικός** = *for the whole* community) should think of itself as the conduit by which not just many, but *all* men may be (as it claims) 'saved'.

The church might do well to recall the story *Luke* makes Jesus tell:

Lk.	εἶπεν δέ τις αὐτῷ, κύριε, εἰ	But one said to him, "Lord,
13:23	ὀλίγοι οἱ σωζόμενοι; ὁ δὲ	are they **_few_**, those (who are)
	εἶπεν πρὸς αὐτούς,	saved?". But he said to them
13:24	ἀγωνίζεσθε εἰσελθεῖν διὰ τῆς	"Strive to enter in through the
	στενῆς θύρας, ὅτι πολλοί,	narrow door - for **_many_**, I say
	λέγω ὑμῖν, ζητήσουσιν	to you, will seek to enter in,
	εἰσελθεῖν καὶ οὐκ ἰσχύσουσιν.	and will not have the strength

13:25	ἀφ' οὗ ἂν ἐγερθῇ ὁ οἰκοδεσπότης καὶ ἀποκλείσῃ τὴν θύραν, καὶ ἄρξησθε ἔξω ἑστάναι καὶ κρούειν τὴν θύραν λέγοντες, κύριε, ἄνοιξον ἡμῖν: καὶ ἀποκριθεὶς ἐρεῖ ὑμῖν, <u>οὐκ</u> οἶδα ὑμᾶς πόθεν ἐστέ.	From whenever the ruler of the house may rise up, and may close the door, and you shall begin to stand outside and knock at the door, saying, `Lord, open to us!`: then answering he will say to you `I do **not** know you, where you are from.`
13:26	τότε ἄρξεσθε λέγειν, ἐφάγομεν ἐνώπιόν σου καὶ ἐπίομεν, καὶ ἐν ταῖς πλατείαις ἡμῶν ἐδίδαξας:	Then you shall start to say `We ate in your presence and we drank, and you taught in our streets`.
13:27	καὶ ἐρεῖ λέγων ὑμῖν, οὐκ οἶδα [ὑμᾶσ] πόθεν ἐστέ: ἀπόστητε ἀπ' ἐμοῦ, πάντες <u>ἐργάται ἀδικίας</u>.	And he will say, speaking to you `I do not know [you] where you are from. Get away from me, all **workers of iniquity**`.
13:28	ἐκεῖ ἔσται ὁ κλαυθμὸς καὶ ὁ βρυγμὸς τῶν ὀδόντων, ὅταν ὄψησθε ἀβραὰμ καὶ ἰσαὰκ καὶ ἰακὼβ καὶ πάντας τοὺς προφήτας ἐν τῇ βασιλείᾳ τοῦ θεοῦ, <u>ὑμᾶς δὲ ἐκβαλλομένους ἔξω</u>.	There will be the whimpering and the grinding of the teeth, when you see Abraham and Isaac and Jacob, and all the prophets, in the kingdom of God - **but yourselves thrown out outside**."

The Nature of 'A Mystery'

Some six billion copies of the Bible have been sold in translation to many languages. Yet what a tragedy that these 'Bibles' lack the Greek source. On account of this omission their message is corrupted, the *mystery* badly obscured. No one will ever learn from these what the original authors hoped for the reader to understand. It is impossible.

Of course *mystery*, as a fictional genre, was never confined to the ancient world. Its method has been retained in the present age. After the Bible, the writer with most books sold (an estimated four billion) is Agatha Christie. Her first crime novel was titled *The Mysterious Affair at Styles*. Aficionados may recognise these features:

- From the outset the plot is established in the mind of the writer. But for the reader it lies at first concealed behind apparently innocuous detail in the narrative.

- Someone is killed, setting off the quest to identify the one responsible for the atrocity.

- The killer goes unrecognised (it may be in disguise).

- The story develops with all manner of detail. To begin with no pattern is readily identifiable.

- There is a risk that the reader will overlook the smallest of details, some of which may turn out to hold a vital significance.

- The reader may be led far astray, at least for a time.

- The *mystery* is finally resolved when we learn *to recognise* the person who committed the original offence.

- This is achieved through coming to know the real significance of the details presented in the narrative, including perhaps the personal traits of the offender.

- In this way is the *mystery* ultimately laid bare.

Scripture shares most of these features. But throughout there is just one *mystery*. Established in the early chapters of *Genesis*, it is developed and recursively elaborated in each of the books which follow. With crime novels it is usual to disclose in the final chapter the solution to the *mystery*. But with scripture there is no final chapter. Instead the readers must solve the *mystery* for themselves ... as we shall do in this book.

Here are some further references to a camel which are given in *Mark* and may yet turn out to hold real significance:

Mk.	καὶ ἦν ὁ ἰωάννης	And John was clothed with
1:6	ἐνδεδυμένος τρίχας **καμήλου**	**camel** hair and a skin belt
	καὶ ζώνην δερματίνην περὶ	around his loins - and eating
	τὴν ὀσφὺν αὐτοῦ, καὶ ἐσθίων	locusts and wild honey.
	ἀκρίδας καὶ μέλι ἄγριον.	

If John the Baptist is clothed with camel hair this tends to suggest that he is a keeper of camels ... and perhaps that he has killed one to make use of its pelt. We shall learn more about John in later chapters. Meanwhile here are some more clues about him which may help to elucidate the *mystery*:

Lk.	ἐλήλυθεν γὰρ ἰωάννης ὁ	For John the Baptist came
7:33	βαπτιστὴς μὴ ἐσθίων ἄρτον	*not* eating bread *and not*
	μήτε πίνων οἶνον, καὶ λέγετε,	drinking wine, and you say
	δαιμόνιον ἔχει:	he has a demon.

And here are some clues about Jesus, announced to shepherds by '*an angel of a lord*':

Lk.	ὅτι ἐτέχθη ὑμῖν σήμερον	For there was born to you
2:11	σωτὴρ ὅς ἐστιν χριστὸς	today a saviour - who is
	κύριος ἐν πόλει δαυίδ:	Christ, lord in a city of David

2:12	καὶ τοῦτο ὑμῖν **τὸ σημεῖον**,	And this for you (is) **the sign**:
	εὑρήσετε βρέφος	you will find a foetus
	ἐσπαργανωμένον καὶ	*wrapped* and *laid up in an*
	κείμενον ἐν φάτνῃ.	*animal feed trough.*
	(*verses omitted here*)	
2:16	καὶ ἦλθαν σπεύσαντες καὶ	And they came hurrying and
	ἀνεῦραν τήν τε μαριὰμ καὶ	found both Mary and Joseph,
	τὸν ἰωσὴφ καὶ τὸ βρέφος	and the foetus ... laid up *in*
	κείμενον **ἐν τῇ φάτνῃ**:	**the animal feed trough**.
2:17	ἰδόντες δὲ ἐγνώρισαν περὶ	And seeing it, <u>they gained</u>
	τοῦ ῥήματος τοῦ λαληθέντος	<u>knowledge</u> ... concerning the
	αὐτοῖς περὶ τοῦ παιδίου	word spoken to them about
	τούτου.	this child.

Each clue here has something to do with food or diet. In the case of Jesus, the shepherds are told quite explicitly that this is to be '*a sign*' to them; and the writer asserts that, seeing it, they *did* indeed gain knowledge about the child Jesus.

We may not understand this yet. But there is one thing we should notice before moving on. John the Baptist comes consuming *neither* bread *nor* wine, these being foods derived respectively from cereal crops and from fruit. Yet the infant Jesus is found in the animal feed trough. Babies generally take milk from their mothers: but does this 'child' prefer cereal as its food? We might expect that shepherds would be familiar with what goes into an animal feed trough, most likely to be cereals or grasses.

The later narrative of the gospels makes it clear how Jesus as an adult is accustomed to consume *both* bread *and* wine ... but equally clear that *these are foods which John avoids*. In Chapter 4 of this book we shall turn our attention to the early chapters of *Genesis*. It is then that we may understand the basis for the mutually exclusive diets specified in the gospels for Jesus and for John.

Looking Ahead

If scripture relies upon riddles and allegorical parallels to convey significant meaning then we are left with the risk that many innocent readers will not solve the *mystery* at all. Only those who pay meticulous attention to what the Greek authors wrote will be ready to master the riddles and discover what it's all about. Indeed the authors anticipate just this outcome. They suggest that the *mystery* is accessible only to the few ... to those who can understand.

It is open to any reader to deny that such a restriction exists. But what if it were true that the authors of scripture intended the majority of their readers to be led astray on the strength of what was written? Then those in denial would be those excluded from the mystery.

The doctrine of the Catholic church was largely established by the end of the fourth century CE. Since then some dogma has been added, but little in essence has changed. In the sixteenth century the Protestant Reformation brought a great challenge to the church. But the central tenets of its doctrine were still inherited by all the churches which today identify themselves as Christian.

In this book we shall solve the *mystery* of scripture. It will then be clear that those persons responsible for established doctrine were amongst 'the many' who never understood. They never managed to solve the *mystery* at all. It is a remarkable conclusion. Yet as this book unfolds we shall find it hard to escape. For anyone who does succeed in penetrating the mystery will expose the established doctrine to be merely that of those deluded, deluded through their failure to recognise the core theme of the very scriptures upon which they seek to rely.

How regrettable that so many should be led so far astray, and for so long. Ignorance pervades the modern world as much as in the past. Where the Christian tradition is concerned, what was mistaken in the early centuries remains mistaken today. What was denied then is still denied to this day. Yet where a *mystery* is set forth in narrative form, the way to solve it is to read with care, to remember what you have read, and finally to engage the power of reason. It is only through systematic analysis of all the evidence that any sound conclusion may be reached.

Chapter 2

Culture and Doctrine:
Then and Now

As mentioned in the previous chapter, this book is about scripture - and *how it may be soundly understood*. But before we penetrate any further into what the authors know at 1 Cor.2:10 as **τὰ βάθη τοῦ θεοῦ** [*the deep things of God*], it may be useful to sketch out a brief summary of:

- the cultural background to scripture, as it developed over several thousand years

- the main ways in which the actual *message* of scripture has come to be understood, not least in the form of Christian doctrine

So in this chapter we shall note first where tradition and teaching began and then see where it (mostly) ended up.

The Ancient World

Anthropologists tell us how Neolithic man set aside the nomadic lifestyle of the Epipaleolithic (or Mesolithic) hunter-gatherer to become an arable farmer. This change went hand in hand with the development of the plough and selective breeding of grasses to produce high yielding cereal crops. It is widely held that it began in the fertile and sun-kissed river valleys of Mesopotamia and Egypt around eight thousand years ago (this was several millennia after the most recent glacial period had ended).

So it was that **ὁ γεωργὸς** [*the earth worker*] came upon the scene (it is from this Greek word that we derive the English name *George*). Strains of barley, lentils, wheat and chickpeas were familiar crops in those times.

Many other developments followed as a direct result. For now, except where specific challenges intervened such as locust swarms or failure of the annual river flood, a population could be fed reliably on cereals, vegetables and fruits produced intensively by only a small proportion of its members. The others (up to 90% under favourable conditions) were freed to take different work. In this way it became possible to build the first cities - relying upon professional artisans such as stonemasons and woodworkers. In due course further important advances came with the advent of metal smiths and the invention of the wheel. Large armies were now a troublesome possibility. Systems for writing and counting were developed, proving useful for administration and the keeping of records. And finally there came upon the scene shops, libraries, schools, politics, structures of civil power (of which organised religion formed one part) - and complete new systems of organised thought such as geometry and philosophy.

The Sumerian (later Babylonian) civilisation developed in Mesopotamia. And from around 4000 BCE the impressive civilisation in Egypt, of which so much evidence remains to this day, grew up along a portion of the River Nile some six hundred kilometres in length. We shall not dwell here upon the long history of Egypt. Suffice it to say that, following brief periods under Persian control, Egypt was finally taken by Alexander in 332 BCE and for three hundred years fell under the influence of a culture essentially Greek. This was the period of the Ptolemaic Pharaoh rulers. Alexandria, their port city near the mouth of the Nile, became the epicentre for culture and trade in the whole region.

Now it was at Alexandria around 250 BCE, during this *Hellenist* period, that the Hebrew books of scripture began to be rewritten into Greek, so extending the early tradition of riddles into that language. In due course this new version of scripture was widely adopted by religious Jews in the Hellenist world in substitution for the Hebrew original - much as the King James Bible (1611) has been adopted by many in the English speaking world today, particularly in North America. For them this was authentic scripture. Many centuries were to pass before the Jewish diaspora communities would revert to the use of Hebrew scripture.

It was only with the Battle of Actium in 31 BCE, and with the death of Cleopatra VII at her own hand in the following year, that the age of the Pharaoh rulers was brought to an end. Egypt fell now under Roman control but Greek persisted as the language of learning, and so as the language of scripture. Within a hundred years the Greek versions of the *Old Testament* (predominantly the **LXX**) would be extended by the addition of the gospels and other NT books, in this way forming the platform upon which both Gnostic and Christian traditions would be based.

Syria and Palestine, with the land of Israel and the cities of Damascus and Jerusalem, lay on the natural route (known as the Fertile Crescent) from Babylon in the east to Egypt in the west. This central region was influenced by both civilisations. Indeed it was liable to be overrun and controlled first by one, then by the other. In this way the people defined by the Jewish faith were dispersed throughout the whole region - along with their religious tradition. Indeed tales of the captivity in Egypt, and the later exile to Babylon, form a part of the historical background for the narrative of scripture itself (scripture is not history but its narrative does have a historical background).

For the inhabitants of these early civilisations, the distinction between the *pastoral* (or *semi-nomadic*) rôle and the *arable* rôle was a real, if quite recent, fact of life. Even today nomadic peoples resent their territory being enclosed by others for use in intensive agriculture. And this is hardly surprising because if they are to sustain their rôle such a development promises only distress - in the shape of hunger for their children and poverty to come.

Quite possibly it was this consideration which persuaded the authors of *Genesis*, the first book of scripture, to adopt the distinction between *pastoral* and *arable* lifestyles at the very heart of their 'plot' (the framework around which they would write). For *Genesis*, as we shall see, is predicated from the outset upon the concept of the *pastor* (or shepherd) being inherently good - whilst anyone *working the earth* (or engaging in related activities such as building *a tower* or *a city*; *qv*. Gn.11:1-9) is deemed inherently evil.

This turns out to be a prevailing stereotype, sustained through all the books of scripture (even providing the basis for what has become the liturgical tradition of the Eucharist). We shall explore this further when we examine the early chapters of *Genesis* in detail. But for now let us simply note these key points:

- At LXX Gn.1:27 God brings into being '*a* person' who is '*made in the image of a god*'. From the instruction issued in the next verse that he should '*grow and multiply and fill the earth and lord over it*', it appears that this *person* must be the '*lord*' (god) ... a secondary deity distinct from the prime God of Gn.1:1 but matching in appearance.

- At LXX Gn.1:29 a specific diet is assigned for this '*person*' ... cereal crops and arboreal fruits.

- At LXX Gn.2:8 this '*person*' is first identified by the title '*lord god*' (sic). It is now he who '*plants a Paradise within Eden in the east*'. The word *paradise* comes from the Persian language and suggests a garden, irrigated and sheltered by a wall or hedge. This can provide the foods specified already for the diet of this '*person*', cereals and fruit. So the '*lord god*' is portrayed as an earth-worker (a horticulturalist) right from the start.

- At Gn.3:1 we are introduced to the serpent, a creature we are told has been made by the '*lord god*'. It seems that this same *Paradise* is the domain of the serpent - for it is here that he deploys his cunning to deceive the woman. But we notice that Adam himself is *not* deceived (*qv*: 1 Tm.2:14). And we notice that what Jesus says in the narrative at Lk.23:42-43 implies that

Paradise is _his_ kingdom. It is an assertion which may carry more significance than many realise.

- At LXX Gn.3:14 the serpent is cursed … to '_go upon your chest and belly … and eat earth all the days of your life_' (it is the style of a worm).

- At LXX Gn.4:2 '**_Abel was a herdsman of flocks_**, but **_Cain was working the earth_**'. Here the stereotype begins to emerge in full contrast.

- In the next verse Cain has brought '_from the fruits of the earth_, a sacrifice _for the lord_'. However God pays no attention to Cain, nor to his sacrifices. And if God himself is deemed to be good, we are left to consider that Cain (and his '_works_') may be otherwise.

- At LXX Gn.4:8 Cain slaughters his brother Abel. We are confronted by an escalation of evil. From _working the earth_, Cain has progressed to _killing his brother_. The position is robustly interpreted in the NT texts at 1 Jn.3:12:

| 1 Jn. 3:12 | οὐ καθὼς κάϊν ἐκ τοῦ πονηροῦ ἦν καὶ ἔσφαξεν τὸν ἀδελφὸν αὐτοῦ· καὶ χάριν τίνος ἔσφαξεν αὐτόν; ὅτι τὰ **ἔργα** αὐτοῦ πονηρὰ ἦν, τὰ δὲ τοῦ ἀδελφοῦ αὐτοῦ δίκαια. | Not like Cain. He was from the evil one and slaughtered his brother. And for the sake of what did he slaughter him? Because his **_works_** were evil, but those of his brother (were) just. |

- At Gn.4:17 Cain learns to 'know' his woman … and she, conceiving, gives birth to Enoch. And he (Cain) _was building up a city_ and named the city after the name of his son, Enoch.

- Cain's '*woman*' seems to be his own mother because at this point in the narrative Eve (deluded now by the serpent's empty promise) remains the only woman.

Notice it was the '*lord god*' who built ΕΥΑΝ [*Eve*] from Adam's rib (LXX Gn.2:22). In Greek this *rib* is πλΕΥρὰν.

The number value of the word **πλευρὰν** is **80+30+5+400+100+1+50** = **666**, thus providing a solution to the numerical riddle posed at Rv.13:18:

| Rv. 13:18 | ὧδε ἡ σοφία ἐστίν· ὁ ἔχων νοῦν ψηφισάτω τὸν ἀριθμὸν τοῦ θηρίου, ἀριθμὸς γὰρ ἀνθρώπου ἐστίν· καὶ ὁ ἀριθμὸς αὐτοῦ ἑξακόσιοι ἑξήκοντα ἕξ. | Here is wisdom. The one having understanding, let him calculate the number of the beast, for it is the number *of a person*. And its number is *six hundred and sixty six*. |

- At Gn.9:20 Noah, having taken pains to save so many creatures from the flood, seems to manifest his true nature. For we are told that he began to be ἄνθρωπος γεωργὸς [*an earth worker person*] and planted ἀμπελῶνα [*a vineyard*]. We may now expect both *bread* and *wine*. At the very next verse Noah gets drunk and Ham '*sees the nakedness of his father*'. These activities of Noah appear to re-establish, in the aftermath of the flood, the works of Cain … previously deemed to be evil (and the nakedness of Noah seems to evoke the nakedness of the serpent).

- At Ezekiel 16:49 these *'fruits of the earth'* are associated with the city of Sodom … a city so corrupt it must be destroyed:

LXX	πλὴν τοῦτο τὸ ἀνόμημα	Full (was) this, the iniquity of
Ezk.	σοδομων τῆς ἀδελφῆς σου	your sister Sodom: pride in
16:49	ὑπερηφανία ἐν πλησμονῇ	sufficiency **of breads**, and in
	ἄρτων καὶ ἐν εὐθηνίᾳ **οἴνου**	her squandering an
	ἐσπατάλων αὐτὴ …	abundance **of wine** …

We shall go into all this in more detail later on. But is the pattern not clear? *All* the things associated with *working the earth* - be it production of cereals or fruit, consumption of bread or wine, the building of cities, or even getting drunk - are, for the authors of scripture, stereotyped as evil.

What then do they deem to be good? The *pastor* Abel is good, as are his *gifts* … which we may know because God (the prime God of Gn.1:1) looks upon these with favour (Gn.4:4).

Abel's gifts are *'from the firstborn of his flock and from their fats'* (the word for *fats* implying, in the Hebrew original, dairy products such as milk, butter and cheese). Of course it is the theme of Exodus that the promised land is *'a land flowing with milk and honey'* (LXX Ex.3:8). And then in the gospels we learn that it is John the Baptist whose food is *'locusts and wild honey'* (Mt.3:4; Mk.1:6).

The following excerpt from LXX Isaiah further supports the idea that the gifts brought by Abel are good. Yet it must be the birth of John the Baptist which is anticipated here, not that of Jesus as many suppose.

LXX	διὰ τοῦτο δώσει κύριος αὐτὸς	On this account (the) lord
Is.	ὑμῖν **σημεῖον** ἰδοὺ ἡ	himself shall give you *a sign*.
7:14	παρθένος ἐν γαστρὶ ἕξει καὶ	Look! The virgin shall have in
	τέξεται υἱόν καὶ καλέσεις τὸ	(her) belly, and give birth to,
	ὄνομα αὐτοῦ εμμανουηλ	a son. And you shall call his
		name *Emmanuel*.
7:15	**βούτυρον καὶ μέλι φάγεται**	***Butter and honey he shall***
	πρὶν ἢ γνῶναι αὐτὸν ἢ	***eat***. Before either he knows
	προελέσθαι πονηρὰ **ἐκλέξεται**	or chooses evil things, ***he***
	τὸ ἀγαθόν	***shall choose the good***.
7:16	διότι πρὶν ἢ γνῶναι τὸ	Because before either the
	παιδίον ἀγαθὸν ἢ κακὸν	child knows good or evil, he
	ἀπειθεῖ πονηρίᾳ τοῦ	disobeys cunning to choose
	ἐκλέξασθαι τὸ ἀγαθόν ...	the good ...

The name *Emmanuel* means in Hebrew '*God-with-us*'. The '*virgin*' here cannot be Mary (as commonly supposed). Instead this must refer to the woman identified in *Luke* as Elizabeth, barren until she conceives the infant who shall be named John (Lk.1:7, 1:13, 1:24).

The authors of scripture maintain a dualist (or bipolar) view of the world. All that they portray is in black and white: people and things are either good or they are evil. Yet the risk is ever present that what is set forth as evil may appear so attractive to the reader that it is mistaken for what is good. In this way readers who fail to 'catch on' to the core theme of scripture may end up being 'caught out' very badly.

Clearly both butter and honey are declared here as if they were tokens of what is *good*. And notice how the child must <u>*disobey cunning*</u> in order to choose what is good. As we shall see in the next chapter, *disobeying cunning* is precisely what Adam has to do in the story set in Paradise (Gn.2/3). And could it be that just this same challenge faces every single reader of scripture? Perhaps it does.

In summary, it looks very much as though '*workers of the earth*' are stereotyped as *evil* - along with the primary foods they produce, foods which grow in the light. This category embraces cereals and fruit … from which are derived both bread and wine.

In contrast it appears that secondary foods are considered as *good*. These are foods not derived from the light, or not directly at any rate. Examples are Abel's '*firstborn of his flock*' and the *dairy products* yielded by such creatures. Already in Chapter 1 we heard the gospel authors assert that John the Baptist shuns bread and wine: his diet is locusts and wild honey. These *locusts* are insects: they *feed off* primary foods such as cereal crops. And *honey* is produced by a different kind of insect, this time *collected from* a range of primary foods such as cereal crops and fruiting plants.

Notice how it is the common trait of sheep, goats, locusts and bees that they *consume* primary foods … in the process either becoming, or producing, secondary foods which humans may then choose to eat.

So here are some of the 'dots' which run through all scripture. Later we shall work at joining them up rather better.

Of course we must explain the Christian tradition of the Eucharist. Here we have "**bread … which earth has given and human hands have made**", also "***fruit of the vine and work of human hands***" (from *Roman Catholic Liturgy of the Eucharist*, 1974). How curious that these offerings of primary foods, ***fruits of the earth***, appear to match in kind the sacrifice brought *for the lord* by Cain.

For Cain is evil, and his was ***the sacrifice ignored by God*** .

Persian Religion

The cultural contribution from the east carried with it a dualistic component from Iranian Mazdaism. This derived in particular from Zoroastrianism, the religion of the Persian Empire (550-330 BCE) prior to its defeat by Alexander.

According to Mazdaean teaching, life originated from two principles. The first is **Ahura-Mazda** (*Wise Lord*, the light principle) and the second **Anghra-Mainyu** *or* **Ahriman** (*Destructive Spirit*, darkness).

Shahrestani, the twelfth century Islamic scholar, in his *Al-Melall Va Al-Nehal* (Nations and Sects) explains as follows:

> Magis were of three sects: Geomarathians, Zurvanians and Zoroastrians. They all shared the view that two principles govern the universe: Ahura-Mazda and Ahriman.
>
> **Ahura-Mazda** is the being who pre-existed - and **Ahriman** the created one.

Ahriman is considered to be the personification of the evil spirit in the world. Shahrestani goes on to explain this tradition:

> Ahura-Mazda wondered how it would be if he had a rival. From this thought Ahriman, the evil spirit, was born - who revolted against the light and declined to abide by its laws.
>
> A battle took place between the armies of the two. The Angels came forward as mediators and agreed upon a truce - that the underworld be given to Ahriman for seven thousand years and then to the Ahura-Mazda for another seven thousand years.
>
> Man's reason for clothing himself in a physical body was to enable him to battle against Ahriman; and his salvation depends upon defeating him.

It was held that Ahura-Mazda wished people to know him, for he maintained:

> If they know me, everyone will follow me.

But the desire of Ahriman was that they should *not* know him, for he realised:

> If they know me then no one will follow me.

Ahura-Mazda is transparently good. He is confident that all those who succeed in knowing him will follow him.

But Ahriman is '*the evil one*'. He relies for effect upon deceit. Seeking to keep his true nature a secret, he trusts that those who do *not* know him will think of him as good.

We shall not seek in this book to rely in any sense directly upon the tenets of Zoroastrianism. Yet a passing knowledge of the tradition may help us to perceive the origin for the matching theme which assumes great importance in Greek scripture. For as we shall see, the character of Ahura-Mazda may be translated to that of **God** … and the character of Ahriman to that of the impostor, the deceitful **lord god**.

Egyptian Religion

Over several thousand years the culture of Egypt was polytheist. The Egyptian populace embraced many gods, each one distinguished by name, form and function. Yet they thought of all their major gods as a series of manifestations of the god Amun.

Amun (*or* Amun-Re) was held to be king of the gods. His huge temple at Karnak on the Upper Nile was maintained for over 2000 years. His name means:

'The Hidden One ',

his true nature held to be secret.

Amun

Statue in Sudan National Museum, Khartoum

Photo reproduced (head & shoulders only)
courtesy of Sudan Archaeological
Research Society, London

The <u>god</u> Amun was depicted as a <u>ram</u>-headed figure wearing a head-dress which incorporated a pair of tall feathers, a sun disk, and a Uraeus. The name for the latter is derived from Egyptian οὐραῖος [*basilisk; cobra*] but suggests also Greek ὡραῖος [*beautiful*]. The basilisk was a <u>serpent</u> renowned for its ability to spit venom in the eyes of its victim (so rendering the victim blind).

Many Pharaoh rulers of Egypt were named *AmenHotep* or *AmenOphis*, from *Amun* combined with Greek ὄφις [*serpent*]. In Chapter 1 we have noted already the association in scripture between the Greek words κριὸς [*a ram*] and κύριος [*a lord*]. And even today it is common within the Christian tradition to end a prayer with the name '***Amen***'.

Thus *ram, serpent,* and *lord* are all 'tags' in scripture associated with (or derived from) the tradition of the Egyptian god ***Amun***.

Some particular aspects of the Egyptian world may merit a brief mention at this point. First is the event known to historians as *The Amarna Interlude*. The 18th Dynasty *King AmenOphis III* (or *AmenHotep III*) ruled for almost forty years [1402-1364 BCE]. His wife was *Queen Tiy*, said to be the descendant of a Hebrew tribe. *AmenOphis III* was father to *AmenOphis IV*, the king who came to power as a teenager ~1352 BCE and shortly took the new name *Akhenaten* [*He who is of service to the Aten*]. The name *Aten* refers to the disc of the sun.

Akhenaten (he was married to *Nefertiti*, perhaps mother to *Tutankhamun*) is famous for having forced the abandonment of Egypt's traditional gods, along with their temples for so long established at Karnak. To take their place he constructed from scratch a city in the desert far to the north on the Nile at *el-Amarna*. There he built a new temple, forcibly asserting his new monotheist cult established to worship the *Aten*, the disc of the sun. After his death Egypt reverted to its traditional gods: and such was the opposition to the religion of the sun-disc god that references to it were now deleted from numerous public records of the time. For those seeking to assert a monotheist tradition this was truly a very bad start.

In view of the role played by *Moses* in scripture, both as nominal author of the five books of the Law (*The Pentateuch*) and as a character in the narrative of those same books, it is interesting to appreciate that the older brother of *Akhenaten* was named *Tut-Moses*, a priest of Memphis. This man appears to have met with a premature death shortly before the accession of *Akhenaten*. Does this event foreshadow the story in Genesis 4 of Abel's demise at the hands of Cain? It is an intriguing question.

A further point to mention is the Egyptian tradition that at death a person would enter '*the broad hall of the two truths*' to be judged. It was held that the dead person's heart would be weighed on a pair of scales against *Maat*, the goddess of truth. Forty-two assessor gods would interrogate the deceased about their past life. If the person passed the test then *Thoth*, the god of knowledge, would declare them '*True of Voice*' and they would be led by *Horus* into the realm of *Osiris*. Otherwise their hopes were crushed in the jaws of the goddess *Ammut*, devourer of the dead.

As is well known, the Egyptians followed the practice of mummifying their dead to preserve the *ka*, the attribute of a person considered to remain with the body after death. In preparing a mummy it was customary to remove all the internal organs except for the heart. Even the brain was removed through the nose, but the heart was always left in place. This was because it was held to be the locus of *knowing*, at the deepest level. As such it should still be needed by the deceased.

Ideas consistent with this are reflected in the gospels. There the heart is presented as the organ required for reasoning out fundamental truth. There are many examples. At Mk.2:6 we have:

Mk. 2:6	ἦσαν δέ τινες τῶν γραμματέων ἐκεῖ καθήμενοι καὶ διαλογιζόμενοι ἐν ταῖς καρδίαις αὐτῶν	But there were some of the scribes sitting there and reasoning in their hearts

And at Mk.8:17 Jesus 'knows' about the bread, but his hearers don't:

Mk. 8:17	καὶ γνοὺς λέγει αὐτοῖς, τί διαλογίζεσθε ὅτι ἄρτους οὐκ ἔχετε; οὔπω νοεῖτε οὐδὲ συνίετε; πεπωρωμένην ἔχετε τὴν καρδίαν ὑμῶν;	And knowing, he said to them "What do you reason - that you do not have breads? Do you not perceive, nor understand? Do you have your heart petrified?"

Those whose hearts are 'petrified' are those failing to follow the significance of the numerous riddles in the gospels ... in this case the riddles about the bread.

The Gnostic Tradition of Scripture

We shall now address those belief systems from the early centuries CE which laid their claim to scripture and in one way or another were identified as '*Gnostic*'.

Quite some diversity existed amongst these arcane religious traditions because the thinking behind them was largely speculative and therefore open to successive elaboration. At the same time many of those encountering Gnostic texts might fail to recognise what they were - and go on to misconstrue them. Where this occurred it would have been no accident: for it was the deliberate intention of those who devised and promoted such writing that its very obscurity should serve to lead astray those outside the circle of particular knowledge.

So cleverly was their composition done that it would be construed in one way by the few who shared the key perspective of the writer - but in a way quite different by those who lacked that key. What lay in the balance here was the distinction drawn between what was good and what was evil. The risk was that those who lacked the key might embrace as good those very things which the authors held to be evil. By writing in this way the authors could implement in the real world the scriptural theme asserted at LXX Gn.3:1 where the wicked serpent 'was the *most* sagacious of all the wild beasts … which the lord god made'. And many would indeed be led astray.

Augustine of Hippo holds a prominent position amongst Christian theologians of the western tradition. The risks in store for all who encounter scripture are well reflected in the opinion he gives (early 5th century) in his *De Doctrina Christiana* (*Concerning Christian Doctrine*):

Book 2: Chap. 6. Use of the Obscurities in Scripture which arise from its figurative language

7. Sed multis et multiplicibus obscuritatibus et ambiguitatibus decipiuntur, qui temere legunt, aliud pro alio sentientes, quibusdam autem locis, quid uel falso suspicentur, non inueniunt : ita obscure dicta quaedam densissimam caliginem obducunt. Quod totum

prouisum esse diuinitus non dubito ad edomandam labore superbiam et intellectum a fastidio reuocandum, cui facile inuestigata plerumque uilescunt.

But *hasty or careless readers are caught out* by the many and manifold obscurities and ambiguities, substituting one meaning for another - and in some places (which for instance may be suspected to be false) they cannot hit upon even a fair interpretation. Some of the expressions are so obscure as to shroud the meaning in the thickest darkness. And I do not doubt that all this was divinely arranged for the purpose of subduing pride by toil - and for preventing a feeling of squeamishness in the intellect ... which does generally hold in small esteem what is discovered without difficulty.

Book 4: Chap. 8. The obscurity of the sacred writers, though compatible with eloquence, not to be imitated by Christian teachers

22. Sed nos etsi de litteris eorum, quae sine difficultate intelleguntur, nonnulla sumimus elocutionis exempla, nequaquam tamen putare debemus imitandos nobis eos esse in his, quae ad exercendas et elimandas quodammodo mentes legentium et ad rumpenda fastidia atque acuenda studia discere uolentium, celandos quoque, siue ut ad pietatem conuertantur , siue ut a mysteriis secludantur, animos impiorum, utili ac salubri obscuritate dixerunt.

But although I take some examples of eloquence from those writings of theirs which there is no difficulty in understanding, we are not by any means to suppose that it is our duty to imitate them in those passages where, with a view to exercise and to train the minds of their readers, and to break down the squeamishness *and stimulate the zeal of those who are willing to learn, whilst also keeping in ignorance the minds of the impious that either they may be converted to piety or shut out from a knowledge of the mysteries,* from one or other of these reasons *they have expressed themselves with a useful and wholesome obscurity.*

Typical of the Latin age in which he lives, Augustine goes so far and then gets stuck. He sees the deliberate obscurity of scripture. He identifies the rôle such obscurity plays: it serves to conceal the mystery, to withhold it from the reader. Yet there he stops. He does not explain the mystery itself; and in his other books he makes numerous assertions which, had he actually known the solution to the mystery and wished to share it with his readers, he never should have uttered.

His unfamiliarity with Greek may have been one reason for his getting stuck; for without reading in Greek many of scripture's riddles are impossible for anyone to resolve. Whatever the reason, it seems plain that Augustine may be numbered amongst the many who never have contrived to fathom **τὰ βάθη τοῦ θεοῦ** [*the deep things of God*].

As a first step towards understanding for ourselves the nature of the challenge posed by scripture we may do well to examine the following passage from the Pauline letter *1 Corinthians*:

1 Cor. 2:6	σοφίαν δὲ λαλοῦμεν ἐν τοῖς τελείοις, σοφίαν δὲ οὐ τοῦ αἰῶνος τούτου οὐδὲ τῶν ἀρχόντων τοῦ αἰῶνος τούτου τῶν καταργουμένων:	And we speak wisdom amongst those accomplished - yet a wisdom not of this age, nor of the rulers of this age, of those being made redundant.
2:7	ἀλλὰ λαλοῦμεν θεοῦ σοφίαν ἐν μυστηρίῳ, τὴν ἀποκεκρυμμένην, ἣν προώρισεν ὁ θεὸς πρὸ τῶν αἰώνων εἰς δόξαν ἡμῶν:	But we speak a godly wisdom within a mystery, hidden away - which God fore-ordained before the ages purposed for our glory,
2:8	ἣν οὐδεὶς τῶν ἀρχόντων τοῦ αἰῶνος τούτου ἔγνωκεν, εἰ γὰρ ἔγνωσαν, οὐκ ἂν τὸν κύριον τῆς δόξης ἐσταύρωσαν.	Which not one of the rulers of this age have known. ***For if they knew, they would not have crucified the 'lord of glory'.***

2:9	ἀλλὰ καθὼς γέγραπται, ἃ ὀφθαλμὸς οὐκ εἶδεν καὶ οὖς οὐκ ἤκουσεν καὶ ἐπὶ καρδίαν ἀνθρώπου οὐκ ἀνέβη, ἃ ἡτοίμασεν ὁ θεὸς τοῖς ἀγαπῶσιν αὐτόν.	But just as it has been written "Things which eye did not see and ear did not hear - and which did not ascend to the heart of a person ... which God prepared for those who love him".
2:10	ἡμῖν δὲ ἀπεκάλυψεν ὁ θεὸς διὰ τοῦ πνεύματος: τὸ γὰρ πνεῦμα πάντα ἐραυνᾷ, **καὶ τὰ βάθη τοῦ θεοῦ.**	Yet to us, God revealed (them) through the spirit. For the spirit investigates all things, **even the deep things of God**.
	(*verses omitted here*)	
2:14	ψυχικὸς δὲ ἄνθρωπος οὐ δέχεται τὰ τοῦ πνεύματος τοῦ θεοῦ, μωρία γὰρ αὐτῷ ἐστιν, καὶ οὐ δύναται γνῶναι, ὅτι πνευματικῶς ἀνακρίνεται:	But a Soulish person does not receive the things of the spirit of God, for to him it is foolishness. And he is not able to know (them) because it is examined spiritually.
2:15	ὁ δὲ πνευματικὸς ἀνακρίνει [τὰ] πάντα, αὐτὸς δὲ ὑπ' οὐδενὸς ἀνακρίνεται.	But the Spiritual (person) examines all things - and he himself is examined by no one.

The author asserts that if only *the rulers of this age* had known *the deep things of God*, that *godly wisdom hidden away within a mystery*, then they would **not** have crucified *the lord of glory*.

It is thus implied that Jesus should not have been killed. You will recall that in the gospel narrative it was the preference of Pontius Pilate to release Jesus (*qv.* Lk.23:16). Yet if the gospel narrative had not provided for the crowd to seize Jesus and have him crucified then

Christian theology would never have developed as it did - to rely upon the vicarious merits of Jesus' suffering and death. And there could be no claim for redemption from sin. If this conclusion puzzles you, please read on: we shall return to the matter in the later chapters of this book.

Now the passage above draws a sharp distinction between a Soulish (or psychic) person, to whom the things of the spirit of God are mere foolishness, and the Spiritual person who investigates all things, *even the deep things of God*. This distinction is utterly characteristic of Gnostic thinking which we know identified three mutually exclusive types for humanity:

- *Spiritual or Pneumatic*: inheriting from Sophia (see below) true wisdom and the knowledge of God. *Au fait* with the secrets and mysteries.
- *Soulish or Psychic*: inheriting from, and subject to, the Demiurge (see below). Lacking a knowledge of God, such persons cannot attain to what is 'spiritual'. Worshipping the Demiurge in place of God, they exhibit the faith of the blind.
- *Hylic or Somatic*: purely material, going after their own lusts.

Whatever Augustine's limitations, it is clear from the history of the centuries before him that the tradition of Greek scripture did pose a very substantial challenge to all who encountered it. We have seen already some of the evidence which shows that the authors of scripture wrote to reflect the Gnostic tradition. Their esoteric theme was concealed behind a façade constructed from allegory and from riddles. And their tradition, the tradition which prompted them to write what they did, was unfamiliar to many of those who read what they wrote. In consequence what was written to be intentionally challenging was often not understood. Instead, many readers formed a shallow and mistaken impression, the result of embracing only superficially what they had read. Indeed these readers were liable to reject the whole cultural context which they had not understood, discarding all things Gnostic as if they were nothing more than nonsense.

Thus was the Wisdom about God dismissed by the ignorant as folly.

It is precisely the point made in the passage from *1 Corinthians*:

> ... a soulish person does not receive the things
>   of the spirit of God, for to him it is foolishness.

In fact the Gnostic tradition was fully elaborated within those texts of scripture authorised by the Catholic church as its *canon*, including both *Genesis* and the four gospels. It is one purpose of this book to expose and explain exactly that fact. Yet the church, as the assembly of those ignorant of scripture's mystery, denied this. And so many centuries have now elapsed since the Gnostic tradition of Wisdom lost its widespread currency, and so little trace of it survives in our culture today, that the whole matter remains quite challenging, even for those keen to learn.

In this book we shall not attempt to cover the full diversity of Gnostic tradition: there are other sources for this (see *Bibliography*). But we should mention in summary certain key points.

For a definition of Gnosticism we may turn to Alastair Logan[1] (*University of Exeter*):

> 'Gnosticism' is the modern designation, probably coined in the eighteenth century, for a religious movement or group of movements of late antiquity which claimed to possess a specific and superior type of knowledge, *gnosis*.

> Such movements asserted that human persons have their origin in another (heavenly) world but have been cast into this lower world of evil, error and illusion ... itself the handiwork of subordinate beings. Their awakening and return to that transcendent world is achieved through a saving call issued by a heavenly revealer.

> Knowledge is thus essentially saving knowledge, salvation is through self-acquaintance, and this knowledge tends to be reserved for an elite.

> Proponents of such a view seem first to have been identified and
> attacked by Christian writers of the middle to late second century,
> such as Justin Martyr and Irenaeus of Lyons, as representing a
> form of Christian 'heresy' …

The Gnostic groups of the early centuries were known after leaders
such as Marcion, Valentinus, Basilides, and Saturninus. Alternatively
they could be named for the deities identified in the myth they
espoused. On this basis some were known as Ophites, from Greek ὄφις
[*serpent*]; some as Naassenes, now from Hebrew נָחָשׁ [*nachash*
= *serpent*]; some as Barbelognostics, named for the female aeon
Barbelo; and some as Sethians, after Seth, first identified at Gn.4:25,
but also the name for one of Egypt's gods.

Ioan Couliano[2] says:

> Cain, for example, is the representative of the good Pleroma
> according to the Cainites, but he is held as an evil character by
> the Ophites.

> Even more instructive is the evaluation of the Snake.
> Paradoxically those groups whose names refer to the Snake,
> such as the Ophites or the Naassenes, take him to be evil: he is
> the Angel of Iniquity for the Naassenes, and the Devil for the
> Ophites, although Sophia uses him to pass her message to the
> first human pair.

These ideas seem to make sense apart from the suggestion that Cain
may be good: for scripture offers consistent evidence to the contrary,
culminating with the statement at 1 Jn.3:12.

All Gnostic ideas were founded in some way on the concept of a
Pleroma (or family) of gods derived from the female archon *Sophia* (or
Barbelo). Amongst the members of the Pleroma were **Ialdabaoth** and
Sabaoth whose Hebrew names point to an origin in Jewish lore. Thus
the *Lord Sabaoth* is in Hebrew '*lord of hosts*', mentioned forty-nine
times in LXX Isaiah as κύριος σαβαωθ, then in the NT at Rm.9:29 and
at Jm.5:4.

Origen (*Contra Celsum, VI, xxxi*) refers to the system of the Ophites with the names of seven archons: *Ialdabaoth, Iao, Sabaoth, Adonaios, Astaphaios, Ailoaios*, and *Oraios*. Yet most commonly it is **Ialdabaoth** who is framed as Plato's *Demiurge*, a second rate deity filled with vain but ignorant pride about his supposed work of creation. He thinks of himself as the only god: he remains unaware of the existence of the prime God who has made him. He is therefore mistaken to consider creation as if it were all his own work. His error (or sin) is intimately connected with his hubris (or pride). Yet he is an imperfect being, prone to making mistakes. And a part of the theme is that, for the careful observer, these mistakes may serve to betray him - giving away his true identity.

Accordingly it is *not* impossible to identify the *Demiurge* - and having done so, to escape his controlling influence. To achieve just this is to meet the Gnostic 'challenge'. But the first requirement is to recognise that this is a deity who is *not* God.

Ialdabaoth is elsewhere identical with **Samael** [Aramaic: *blind god; god of the blind*] and with **Saklas** [Aramaic: *fool*]. Moreover **Satan** is considered an alternate name for **Samael**.

Alastair Logan[3] cites from the *Apocryphon of John*:

> The archon who is weak ... has three names, the first Ialtabaoth, the second Saklas, the third Samael. And it dwells on the folly of his ignorant boast[4] : 'I am God and there is no other god but me'.

Margaret Barker[5] summarises from Irenaeus (*Contra Haer.*1:24, 1:30) and from Epiphanius (*Panarion* 45.1.4):

> Saturnilus taught *explicitly* that the second God was the God of the Jews, one of the angels created by the unknown Father. Basilides taught that the angels of the last heaven, those who divided the earth between them, had as their chief the God of the Jews. The Ophites taught that the God of the Jews was this angel figure who was named *Yaldabaoth*. He had made a covenant with Abraham. Severus, an associate of Marcion, said

that this Yaldabaoth was not only the son of the Good God, but was also the devil whose other name was Sabaoth.

Gnostic schemes were essentially dualistic in their theology. They hypothesise first a prime God and then a *Demiurge* to play the rôle of prideful impostor (though it is true that in many schemes things were more elaborate). Some characters explicitly manifested in wider Gnostic myth match those identified in scripture, as we might expect. The *Lord Sabaoth* we have mentioned already; then there is the *serpent*, who as **Satan** or the devil (*qv.* Rv.12:9, 20:2) features throughout the whole canon of scripture from *Genesis* to the gospels and *Revelation*.

It is impossible to avoid the conclusion that Gnostic thinking was somehow connected with the religious traditions of Judaism which were later transferred into early Christianity. Indeed Logan[6] says:

- To supporters of the majority opinion that Gnosticism emerged from Judaism and of the minority view which sees it as an offshoot of Christianity, one has to pose the question: is it then a schismatic revival movement or series of movements harking back to the past (a sect), or rather a new religious movement or movements offering new answers to old problems (a cult)?

- Ignatius (of Antioch) implies that the breakaway group he is combating claims to be Christian, has shared with the community in the initiation rite of chrismation, but rejects the reality of the incarnation, cross and resurrection of Christ, as attested by law, prophets and gospel, and does not recognise or share in the Eucharist.

- The Ophites of Irenaeus vividly illustrate the distinctive exegesis of the Old Testament of these gnostics: the prophets, from Moses on, are the mouth-pieces of Ialdabaoth but unwittingly transmit some true prophecies through the activity of Sophia (Irenaeus, *Adv. Haer.* 1.30.11). Intriguingly however, David and Solomon are omitted from the list of deluded prophets of Ialdabaoth, surely on the grounds that David's Psalms and Solomon's Proverbs and Wisdom, as primary source material for Christian (including gnostic) theology, had to be true, entirely inspired by Sophia!

- Salvation depends on which spirit dominates; the Holy Spirit or its demonic counterpart, the counterfeit spirit. Those souls on whom the Holy Spirit descends will be saved; all they need is ascetic freedom from the passions, using the flesh as a mere vehicle until on death they ascend to heaven. But those souls on whom the counterfeit spirit descends will be led astray, although there is always the possibility, via transmigration, of gaining the saving knowledge and ascending.

For the gnostic writer, the task of authorship was about configuring the *mystery* in such a way that it could indeed be solved, but not too easily, and not by everyone. The task faced by their readers would then be to solve the mystery set forth in this way, if indeed they could. And if they could then they would *'learn to know'* the truth, the truth embedded behind scripture's façade.

Now, as Logan reminds us, second century adherents to Gnostic tradition were criticised and dismissed as mistaken by Justin Martyr and Irenaeus of Lyons. The opinions of these two writers were shortly embraced by the Catholic church which now engaged them in the attempt to despoil and displace the Gnostic tradition in its entirety. For in the early centuries CE the Catholic church was in the process of installing itself. Like a cuckoo[7] hatched in the scriptural nest, it would now expel the authentic tradition and seek to make the nest its own.

After more than eighteen centuries the original justification for this self-insertion is reproduced unaltered in the continuing attempt to discredit the Gnostic tradition. Within his teaching delivered in General Audience in St. Peter's Square (28 March 2007) Pope Benedict XVI asserts[8] (*Vatican's own translation to English*):

Irenaeus was first and foremost a man of faith and a Pastor. Like a good Pastor, he had a good sense of proportion, of the riches of doctrine and missionary enthusiasm. As a writer, he pursued a twofold aim: to defend true doctrine from the attacks of heretics, and to explain the truth of the faith clearly. His two extant works -

the five books of *The Detection and Overthrow of the False Gnosis and Demonstration of the Apostolic Teaching* (which can also be called the oldest "catechism of Christian doctrine") - exactly corresponded with these aims. In short, Irenaeus can be defined as the champion in the fight against heresies. The second-century Church was threatened by the so-called *Gnosis,* a doctrine which affirmed that the faith taught in the Church was merely a symbolism for the simple who were unable to grasp difficult concepts; instead, the initiates, the intellectuals - *Gnostics,* they were called - claimed to understand what was behind these symbols and thus formed an elitist and intellectualist Christianity. Obviously, this intellectual Christianity became increasingly fragmented, splitting into different currents with ideas that were often bizarre and extravagant, yet attractive to many. One element these different currents had in common was "dualism": they denied faith in the one God and Father of all, Creator and Saviour of man and of the world. To explain evil in the world, they affirmed the existence, besides the Good God, of a negative principle. This negative principle was supposed to have produced material things, matter.

He goes on:

Firmly rooted in the biblical doctrine of creation, Irenaeus refuted the Gnostic dualism and pessimism which debased corporeal realities. He decisively claimed the original holiness of matter, of the body, of the flesh no less than of the spirit. But his work went far beyond the confutation of heresy: in fact, one can say that he emerges as the first great Church theologian who created systematic theology; he himself speaks of the system of theology, that is, of the internal coherence of all faith …

He then says:

The true teaching, therefore, is not that invented by intellectuals which goes beyond the Church's simple faith. The true Gospel is the one imparted by the Bishops who received it in an uninterrupted line from the Apostles. They taught nothing except this simple faith, which is also the true depth of God's revelation.

> Thus, Irenaeus tells us, there is no secret doctrine concealed in the Church's common Creed. There is no superior Christianity for intellectuals. The faith publicly confessed by the Church is the common faith of all. This faith alone is apostolic, it is handed down from the Apostles, that is, from Jesus and from God …

He then asserts:

> All Churches must agree with the Church of Rome, recognising in her the measure of the true Apostolic Tradition, the Church's one common faith. With these arguments, summed up very briefly here, Irenaeus refuted the claims of these Gnostics, these intellectuals, from the start. First of all, they possessed no truth superior to that of the ordinary faith, because what they said was not of apostolic origin, it was invented by them. Secondly, truth and salvation are not the privilege or monopoly of the few, but are available to all through the preaching of the Successors of the Apostles, especially of the Bishop of Rome. In particular - once again disputing the "secret" character of the Gnostic tradition and noting its multiple and contradictory results - Irenaeus was concerned to describe the genuine concept of the Apostolic Tradition …

If we attempt a précis, the Catholic church here asserts:

1. It admits to the existence of Gnostic teaching.

2. It recognises how this attempts to account for the existence of evil in the world by advancing a scheme (or schemes) dualistic in nature which posit, in addition to the good God, a negative principle somehow responsible for the material world.

3. It feels threatened by such teaching and seeks to fight it as heresy.

4. Irenaeus did well to defend 'true' doctrine from the threat such teaching posed: on this account he was a champion.

5. The faith of the Church of Rome is the simple faith first taught by the Apostles.

6. There is no secret tradition, nor any matter of faith to learn beyond what is taught by the Catholic church.

7. Thus there is no superior Christianity for intellectuals. Those claiming otherwise possess no truth superior to that of simple faith because what they say is not of apostolic origin, it is merely invented by them.

8. Truth and salvation are not the privilege or monopoly of the few but available to all through the preaching of the apostolic succession.

Reducing the argument still further, we seem to be left with something like this:

> We are simple persons and cannot understand what is said to us by those we identify as intellectuals. It follows that these persons must be deluded - and that which they seek to explain must be foolish and harmful nonsense. For there can be no truth beyond that asserted by the Apostles, a truth we repeat ourselves.

Perhaps you recall the point made in the passage from *1 Corinthians*:

> ... a soulish person does not receive the things
>   of the spirit of God, for to him it is foolishness.

Unfortunately there is no significant evidence for the existence of these so-called 'Apostles' except as characters within the fictional narrative of NT scripture. And NT scripture itself is comprised of texts which plainly are Gnostic from start to finish.

Could it be that the claims made by the Catholic church are made only by those unable to solve the riddles posed in scripture, those unable to conceive that they may have made any kind of mistake? And that, assigning a false historicity to scripture's narrative, they proceed to rely upon this invention as justifying their wilful certainty?

Logan[9] says of the Gnostic tradition:

> ... the ignorant and arrogant Demiurge, *Ialdabaoth*, is the creator and ruler of this world - and God of the Old Testament.

Perhaps it should not surprise us if those who embrace this deity as their god are found to manifest such attributes themselves.

Reviewing the Gnostic Tradition

It is surely unwise to claim that in scripture there is no secret tradition, nothing hidden. We need do no more than turn to the gospels to learn how scripture itself declares its message to be hidden. The following example is from *Luke* (but the same idea is advanced at Mt.10:26; Mk.4:22; Lk.12:2):

Lk. 8:15	τὸ δὲ ἐν τῇ καλῇ γῇ, οὗτοί εἰσιν οἵτινες ἐν καρδίᾳ καλῇ καὶ ἀγαθῇ **ἀκούσαντες τὸν λόγον** Κ**α**τέχουσ**ΙΝ** καὶ Κ**α**ρπ**Ο**Φοροῦσ**ΙΝ** ἐν ὑπομονῇ.	But that (seed which fell) in the good earth, these are those in a noble and good heart. **Hearing the message**, <u>they take charge of it</u> and <u>they bring forth fruit</u> in patience.
8:16	οὐδεὶς δὲ λύχνον ἅψας καλύπτει αὐτὸν σκεύει ἢ ὑποκάτω κλίνης τίθησιν, ἀλλ' ἐπὶ λυχνίας τίθησιν, ἵνα οἱ εἰσπορευόμενοι βλέπ<u>ωσιν</u> τὸ φῶς.	And no one lighting a lamp covers it with a container or places (it) underneath a bed: but he places (it) upon a lampstand so that those coming in <u>may see</u> the light.
8:17	οὐ γάρ ἐστιν κρυπτὸν ὃ οὐ φανερὸν γενήσεται, οὐδὲ ἀπόκρυφον ὃ οὐ μὴ γνωσθῇ καὶ εἰς φανερὸν ἔλθῃ.	For it is not hidden that it shall not become visible, nor secret that it might not become known - and might come into view.
8:18	βλέπετε οὖν πῶς ἀκούετε: ὃς ἂν γὰρ ἔχῃ, δοθήσεται αὐτῷ, καὶ ὃς ἂν μὴ ἔχῃ, καὶ ὃ δοκεῖ ἔχειν ἀρθήσεται ἀπ' αὐτοῦ.	Then watch out how you hear. For to each who has, to him it shall be given - and to each who does not have, even what he thinks he has will be taken away from him.

The passage is about the seed, the seed scattered by the sower. Already at Lk.8:11 the seed has been declared as ὁ λόγος τοῦ θεοῦ [*the 'Logos', the saying of God*]. At 8:15 some very particular 'seed' has been scattered into the text … which, if you fail to see it, may later cause you to stumble.

The *message* is next compared to a lamp … for which one option is that it remains *hidden* and *secret*, but which preferably will *become known* or will *come into view*.

How then does it *become known*? "Watch out **how** you hear" … and in particular how you hear in the verse at 8:15.

They take charge of it and they bring forth fruit in patience … and they will be given more. You too can do this. But should you fail, then *even what you think you have will be taken away from you*!

We have mentioned already both κάϊν [*Cain*] and ὄφιν [*a serpent*]. It was after these characters in scripture's narrative that Gnostic groups, the Cainites and Ophites, were named in the early centuries CE.

Who will still say that nothing has been hidden at Lk.8:15? Scripture's façade is implemented using riddles … riddles of many kinds. Amongst the techniques deployed by the authors is anagrammatic dispersion. It is the method of the sower … the sower who disperses key components of the message … which in this way become invisible. But they are only invisible to those with sleepy eyes. For:

> It is not hidden, that it shall not **become visible**, nor secret that it might not **become known** - and might come into view.

Surely you could see these key components for yourself? Here are some in a different passage. This time the 'seeds' (*ie.* the Greek letters) are clumped together which makes them even easier to spot:

Mk.	καὶ ἦραν κλάσματα δώδεκα	And they took up twelve
6:43	κοφίνων πληρώματα καὶ	broken pieces full of baskets,
	ἀπὸ τῶν ἰχθύων.	and from the fishes

It is when the 'broken pieces' are removed from the Greek word for 'baskets' that we find the name of the serpent 'hidden' inside.

Do you see what the gospel authors have done? It may be worth explaining at this point that the Greek uncial manuscripts prevalent in late antiquity inscribed the text tightly between the margins of the page, leaving no spaces between words. So finding alternate readings such as those explained above would have been even easier than it is for us today. This is how the passage at Mk.6:43 actually appears in fourth century *Codex Vaticanus*:

ΚΑΙΗΡΑΝΚΛΑCΜΑΤΑΛ···
ΛΓΚΑΚΟΙΡΙΝΩΝΙΙΑΗΡω
ΜΑΤΑΚΑΙΑΠΟΤΩΝΙΧ°Υ
ΩΝ

Here the same text is reset using a modern lower case Greek font, still without spaces. The word **κοφίνων** [*of baskets*] is underlined; nested within it we can see the word οφίν [*serpent*]:

καιηρανκλασματαδω
δεκα<u>κοφιν</u>ωνπληρω
ματακαιαποτωνιχθυ
ων

Here is a related example where we find the Greek word **καινὴ** [*new*] and hidden within it we can see the name for K̲α̲ι̲ν̲ [*Cain*]:

| Lk. 22:20 | καὶ τὸ ποτήριον ὡσαύτως μετὰ τὸ δειπνῆσαι, λέγων, τοῦτο τὸ ποτήριον ἡ K̲α̲ι̲ν̲ὴ διαθήκη ἐν τῷ αἵματί μου, τὸ ὑπὲρ ὑμῶν ἐκχυννόμενον. | And the cup likewise after the dining, saying "This (is) the cup, the <u>new</u> testament in my blood poured out on your behalf" |

These examples show how easy it would have been for a Greek reader in the early centuries CE to spot words within words in the original text. But this kind of riddle does not pass through the barrier posed by translation. As a result, any reader of Jerome's carefully verified translation to Latin would be tantamount to blind, able no longer to 'see' (in the Latin translation) what once had been 'hidden' in Greek.

We may well ask what will become of those who fail to notice what has been hidden. In the following passage a sharp distinction is drawn between the wise who respond to 'these sayings of mine' by 'making them' … and the foolish who do not. Here the *Rock* is God:

| Mt. 7:22 | πολλοὶ ἐροῦσίν μοι ἐν ἐκείνῃ τῇ ἡμέρᾳ, κύριε κύριε, οὐ τῷ σῷ ὀνόματι ἐπροφητεύσαμεν, καὶ τῷ σῷ ὀνόματι δαιμόνια ἐξεβάλομεν, καὶ τῷ σῷ ὀνόματι δυνάμεις πολλὰς ἐποιήσαμεν; | Many will say to me in that day: 'Lord, lord, did we not prophesy in your name, and cast out demons in your name, and in your name make many mighty works?' |
| 7:23 | καὶ τότε ὁμολογήσω αὐτοῖς ὅτι οὐδέποτε ἔγνων ὑμᾶς· ἀποχωρεῖτε ἀπ' ἐμοῦ οἱ ἐργαζόμενοι τὴν ἀνομίαν. | And then I shall repeat to them that 'I never knew you: keep away from me, those working iniquity'. |

7:24	πᾶς οὖν ὅστις ἀκούει μου τοὺς λόγους τούτους καὶ ποιεῖ αὐτοὺς ὁμοιωθήσεται ἀνδρὶ **φρονίμῳ**, ὅστις ᾠκοδόμησεν αὐτοῦ τὴν οἰ**κίαν** ἐπὶ τὴν πέτραν.	Everyone therefore who hears these sayings of mine and makes them, he shall be likened to a <u>sagacious</u> man who built his <u>house</u> upon the Rock.
7:25	καὶ κατέβη ἡ βροχὴ καὶ ἦλθον οἱ ποταμοὶ καὶ ἔπνευσαν οἱ ἄνεμοι καὶ προσέπεσαν τῇ οἰκίᾳ ἐκείνῃ, καὶ οὐκ ἔπεσεν, τεθεμελίωτο γὰρ ἐπὶ τὴν πέτραν.	And the rain came down and the rivers came and the winds blew and they fell against that house: yet it did not fall for it had been founded upon the Rock.
7:26	καὶ πᾶς ὁ ἀκούων μου τοὺς λόγους τούτους καὶ μὴ ποιῶν αὐτοὺς ὁμοιωθήσεται ἀνδρὶ μωρῷ, ὅστις ᾠκοδόμησεν αὐτοῦ τὴν οἰ**κίαν** ἐπὶ τὴν ἄμμον.	And everyone hearing these sayings of mine and not making them, he shall be likened to a foolish man who built his <u>house</u> upon the sand.
7:27	καὶ κατέβη ἡ βροχὴ καὶ ἦλθον οἱ ποταμοὶ καὶ ἔπνευσαν οἱ ἄνεμοι καὶ προσέκοψαν τῇ οἰκίᾳ ἐκείνῃ, καὶ ἔπεσεν, καὶ ἦν ἡ πτῶσις αὐτῆς μεγάλη.	And the rain came down and the rivers came and the winds blew and they struck against that house: and great was its collapse!

Back in the second century Irenaeus wrote to condemn the Gnostics. But surely he was amongst **οἱ ὁδηγοὶ τυφλοὶ τυφλῶν** [*the blind guides of the blind*] … as are those who seek even today to deny the validity of Gnostic tradition?

When we boil down the challenge which the authors of scripture posed to their readers, it was ultimately about *knowing* how to distinguish, on a reliable basis, good from evil - and how to spot the deceit involved when what was evil sought to masquerade as good.

There is a strong theme in the NT texts that the reader (apparently presumed to be male) must press on with the task of learning (of acquiring knowledge) until 'he' concludes the race and becomes 'a completed man'. Such a person has solved the *mystery*, he has achieved *gnosis*, he has finished the race, he has spotted the 'catch' in the themes of scripture, he has avoided falling into the trap.

Here is a passage which serves to illustrate the theme:

Heb. 5:13	πᾶς γὰρ ὁ μετέχων γάλακτος ἄπειρος λόγου δι**ΚΑΙ**οσύ**V**ης, νήπιος γάρ ἐστιν:	For each one who partakes of milk (is) inexperienced in the message <u>of righteousness</u> - for he is an infant
5:14	**τελείων** δέ ἐστιν ἡ στερεὰ τροφή, τῶν διὰ τὴν ἕξιν τὰ αἰσθητήρια γεγυμνασμένα ἐχόντων πρὸς δι**ΑΚ**ρισι**V** καλοῦ τε καὶ κακοῦ.	But '**completing**' is the solid food for those (who) through habit have the senses exercised towards <u>discernment</u> both of good and of evil

In the first verse, the letters required to form the name for **ΚΑϊV** [*Cain*] are found in the correct order within the word δι**ΚΑΙ**οσύ**V**ης [*righteousness*]. This is a simple example of what is being taught. It is suitable for 'infants'.

In the second verse it is somewhat harder to spot the name for Cain; now the letters are scrambled out of the required order. Here is the 'solid food' intended for those who 'through habit' now have the senses exercised towards δι**ΑΚ**ρισι**V** [*discernment*] ... both of good and of evil.

The writer has much to teach his readers about how to read what is written and how to understand it. What we see here is typical of the subtle way he goes about the task.

In the following passage the names of both ἄβελ [*Abel*] and κάϊν [*Cain*] can both be found within a single word (in the NT canon there are just two further instances of this, at Ac.4:13 & 2 Cor.4:9):

| Heb. 6:1 | διὸ ἀφέντες τὸν τῆς ἀρχῆς τοῦ χριστοῦ λόγον ἐπὶ τὴν τελειότητα φερώμεθα, μὴ πάλιν θεμέλιον καταβαλλόμενοι μετανοίας ἀπὸ νεκρῶν ἔργων, καὶ πίστεως ἐπὶ θεόν, | Therefore leaving the message of the first principles of Christ, let us carry on to **completion** - not <u>throwing down</u> again a foundation of repentance from dead works and faith upon a god |

The same theme emerges in the letter of *James*. It is asserted that scripture demands more than just 'sitting back to listen'. The reader must become ποιητὴς ἔργου [*a maker of work*]:

| Jm. 1:25 | ὁ δὲ παρακύψας εἰς νόμον τέλειον τὸν τῆς ἐλευθερίας καὶ παραμείνας, οὐκ ἀκροατὴς ἐπιλησμονῆς γενόμενος ἀλλὰ ποιητὴς ἔργου, οὗτος μακάριος ἐν τῇ ποιήσει αὐτοῦ ἔσται. | But the one peeping into the **completed** law, that of freedom, and continuing, not becoming a hearer of forgetfulness but a maker of work, this one will be blessed in what he makes. |
| 1:26 | εἴ τις δοκεῖ θρησκὸς εἶναι, μὴ χαλιναγωγῶν γλῶσσαν αὐτοῦ ἀλλὰ ἀπατῶν καρδίαν αὐτοῦ, τούτου μάταιος ἡ θρησκεία. | If anyone seems to be religious, not bridling his tongue but deceiving his <u>heart</u>, this one's religion is in vain. |

It appears that if you so much as peep into the *completed law* you can expect freedom: but if instead you deceive your heart [Καρδίαν] then your religion will be in vain. And here is the warning for those would-be teachers who do not know their subject thoroughly:

Jm. 3:1	μὴ πολλοὶ διδάσκαλοι γίνεσθε, ἀδελφοί μου, εἰδότες ὅτι μεῖζον κρίμα λημψόμεθα.	Let not many become teachers, my brothers, knowing that we will receive a greater judgment.
3:2	πολλὰ γὰρ πταίομεν ἅπαντες. εἴ τις ἐν λόγῳ οὐ πταίει, οὗτος **τέλειος** ἀνήρ, δυνατὸς χαλιναγωγῆσαι καὶ ὅλον τὸ σῶμα.	For in many things we all stumble. If anyone doesn't stumble in message, this (is) a **completed** man, able to bridle also the whole body.

The teacher who does not *stumble* in what he teaches, *this is the completed man.* Where Gnostic method is engaged, much is only hinted at, much is said indirectly. What is critically important is that you are able to see what is meant … that you are able to 'catch on'.

Scripture tests your ability to analyse evidence and reach a logical conclusion. It tests your intellectual stamina and inherent truthfulness. And as we shall see it tests your humility, your ability to recognise that you are merely man. For you are not 'made in the image of a god' (Gn.1:27) but, like Adam, you are 'made from the dust' (Gn.2:7).

Jm. 1:9	καυχάσθω δὲ ὁ ἀδελφὸς ὁ ταπεινὸς ἐν τῷ ὕψει αὐτοῦ,	So let the humble brother boast in his high position
1:10	ὁ δὲ πλούσιος ἐν τῇ ταπεινώσει αὐτοῦ, ὅτι ὡς ἄνθος χόρτου παρελεύσεται.	But the rich in his humility - because like a flower of grass he will pass away.

The rich man is rich in his humility. He knows he is made from cosmic dust and one day will simply 'pass away'.

Conventional Christian doctrine

So active is the mind of man that a name must be found for everything … even a name for nothing. Where nothing is confined in a bounded space we announce a perfect *vacuum*. Gravitational, electric and magnetic fields propagate through such a space, as does light but not sound. Yet no matter exists within it: the space is filled completely with nothing.

As for the concept of God, here is an answer, an answer so often personified with human attributes, to the question we can hardly frame. Here is a token to account conveniently for what we do not know and cannot contrive to find out. Some arguments for the existence of God are inferential, along the lines that if something exists then there must be an active agent responsible for its existence (it is a human trait, as psychologists remind us, to attribute agency even where it is absent). Such a proposition is advanced in Christian theology to attribute to one God the origin and existence of all things, from galaxies down to the human race. Yet God is just a name we use, perhaps with some myth attached: and in this way nothing is explained.

It would be more useful to observe that if such a God did exist then we should not know. And if such a God did not exist then still we should not know. In fact we have no way to tell between these two possibilities: beyond our initial assumption of a cosmic creator and sustainer, we can say nothing. All we are able to do is to name him (though some religious traditions bridle even at this). We then fill the space we assign in our minds by making up stories which, with repetition and ritual, we proceed to render indelible.

Christianity first appeared in the early centuries CE. It is plain enough that this was a development, though some might say a perversion, of the Jewish religion: but in a more particular fashion its origins may be traced to the Gnostic tradition within Hellenist Judaism. This is why, in the second and third centuries, Christianity developed in parallel with what many would later disparage as Gnostic sects and why it exhibited such diversity in its gestational period. At the same time it endured intermittent persecution and its followers were strikingly few in number. But with the accession to power of Constantine at York (306 CE) everything was to change. The Christian tradition would now be adopted, adapted and robustly exploited by the Roman Emperor. Responding to the slogan 'One God, one emperor, one empire, one church, one faith', the Christian church now assumed the title καθ' ὅλικός [Catholic = for the whole; universal] and progressively it was integrated with the apparatus of the Roman state. In due course Emperor Theodosius decreed a ban (380 CE) on all pagan rites and practices, confirming Christianity as the state religion, the Catholic church as the state church, and any ideological deviation (heresy) as a crime against the state.

From now on Christians would kill Christians because they disagreed on doctrine. Many more would die as infidels who were never Christians in the first place. Where mainstream Jewish religion was concerned, the newfound Catholic church would seek to oppress and to contain it by means of forced conversion, pogroms or other forms of persecution. And in due course Islam would be assaulted with crusades.

The Gnostic tradition was the esoteric convention which had actually brought forth the gospels and NT letters. Yet because the Catholic church had by now lost sight of its Gnostic origins it would shortly (and most unwisely) seek to extinguish these entirely. In the quest for a single faith, imperial authority would be turned towards this end.

With the passage of further centuries, and the challenge posed in the East by Islam, the Roman Catholic church obtained for itself a dominant position in the Christian world. To this day it makes a three-fold claim to authority for its teaching: first from scripture, next from tradition, and finally from what it terms the magisterium, the teaching authority of its bishops.

The claim is plainly false at every level. The scriptures it embraces are manifestly Gnostic fiction, packed with riddles configured for the reader to solve (as this book serves well enough to show). Yet the Catholic church fails to recognise these riddles for what they are, preferring to embrace the gospels as inspired commentaries upon a series of historical (if miraculous) events. On this account alone it gets into enormous difficulty. Failing entirely to grasp the deeper message conveyed by the selection of scriptures it has sought to make its own, the church has formulated doctrine of unwarranted complexity.

Next it claims an unbroken *tradition* handed down in succession to its hierarchy from certain persons named in the narrative of scripture, maintaining that these 'apostles' were actually appointed by Jesus (who was himself God) and were then tasked by him to continue his mission on earth.

An authority laying claim to a divine origin will always attract those who seek for themselves power over others. But Roman Catholic theologian Prof. Hans Küng[10] says of the claim for apostolic succession:

> It cannot be verified that the bishops are 'successors of the apostles' in the direct and exclusive sense. It is historically impossible to find in the initial phase of Christianity an unbroken chain of 'laying on of hands' from the apostles to the present-day bishops.

And he continues:

> However, the earliest list of bishops in the [writings of] second-century church father Irenaeus of Lyons, according to which Peter and Paul transferred the ministry of *episkopos* [bishop] to a certain Linus, is a second century forgery. A monarchical episcopate can be demonstrated for Rome only from around the middle of the second century (Bishop Anicetus).

> Thus the presbyteral-episcopal church constitution is not based on any institution by Jesus Christ ...

We might add that because scripture is essentially allegorical fiction there can never be any sound basis for the claim that the Christian church was established by eleven (or twelve) of those named in the gospel, that is by a handful of men appointed by Jesus and whose teaching authority would be inherited by those they appointed in turn.

It is true that the gospel *narrative* tells how Jesus, after his baptism, both acquires (Lk.4:6) and exhibits (Lk.4:32, 4:36, etc) 'authority'; later he assigns it to those present at the Passover meal (Lk.22:30). But persons who rely upon this to derive authority for themselves make two mistakes. The first is to treat the gospel narrative, and the cast of characters who feature within it, as a record of real persons and actual events; for the record is fiction, along with most of the characters in it. The second involves the failure to penetrate the 'mystery' of scripture and so to recognise correctly the identities assigned by the authors for the characters named in the 'cast'. In a later chapter we shall explore more fully the origin given by the gospel writers for the 'authority' of Jesus. It is a diabolical business, as we shall discover.

As for the *magisterium*, it is merely the teaching authority of those who are 'blind', as the scriptural authors imply so persistently, to the message of scripture itself. Just like the innocent 'disciples' who accompany Jesus in the gospel narrative, these bishops do not understand about the bread. They are blind even to the identity of Jesus and the one he refers to as 'Father' (as will become clear with the subsequent chapters of this book). It follows that theirs is an 'authority' which mistakes what is attractive (but evil) for what is portrayed in scripture as good, so leading many astray.

Yet the very name **καθ' ὅλικός** [*for the whole; universal*] illustrates how the Catholic church, though itself an offshoot of Hellenist Judaism, acquired an early ambition for exclusive religious and political dominance, an ambition it maintains to this day. Fortified by the conviction that it mediates a singular, meritorious and salvific truth which it then feels obliged to promote (*qv.* Mt.4:19, 28:19; Mk.1:17), the Roman Catholic church is an impressive example of an organisation parasitic upon human society. Power-seeking and defiant, its ideological complacency is little short of breathtaking. But, as Roman legend held of Achilles, it has one point of acute vulnerability. Its greatest weakness is not the astounding nature of the doctrinal claims it makes. *Its greatest weakness is its inability to explain the 'mystery' embodied in the very scriptures it has sought to make its own.*

For century after century the Catholic church has escaped the consequences of this fault. Here was an organisation which only formed in the first place because those who formed it did not possess the knowledge to fathom **τὰ βάθη τοῦ θεοῦ** [*the deep things of God*]. Its place in human affairs was reasonably secure whilst no one else knew how to do this. But the entire edifice was always at risk of collapse the moment it became known how to fathom the ancient 'mystery' set forth in scripture. Here is the Achilles heel of the Catholic church - and the central subject of this book.

This weakness is a serious one. For once people understand that the god they are accustomed to worship is not really God at all, their behaviour is very likely to change, and it may well change faster than the Catholic church can keep up with. If it should then transpire that the god they were accustomed to worship is not even good, and that all concerned have been caught out by a diabolical theme implemented by the authors of scripture in times of Antiquity and sustained unwittingly by the church for millennia, what will happen now? Will not the church be held accountable ... for leading so many astray in the first place, as equally for the incompetence by which so much folly has been sustained for so long?

The Protestant Reformation brought a great challenge to the Roman Catholic church. This it survived by refusing to bend to many of the objections raised. Yet its escape was achieved at the cost of much suffering and conflict on all sides and the loss (in many nations) of its exclusive rôle. The issues at stake included corrupt practice (such as the sale of indulgences), the Eucharistic doctrines of transubstantiation and the real presence, access to the Bible, and justification by faith alone. But the remarkable thing is that no one seems to have recognised that the scriptures were essentially Gnostic fiction. That step would be left for a future generation.

Still in the western world we face a great challenge over the setting aside of errors from the past. Christian doctrine differs little from what was taught at the time when the church was fully established at the end of the fourth century CE. Perhaps the greatest adjustment in recent times has been the abandonment of the church's claim, derived from *Genesis*, that the cosmos was brought into being in a complete state over the course of just six days some time around 4000 BCE (say six thousand years ago). Yet in taking this step the church has continued to assert historicity for the gospels, insisting that they are reliable records of real events which actually did take place. What would it take to recognise that a document from the early centuries CE, tightly packed with riddles, might not be history at all but was instead Gnostic fiction?

The Contribution made by Charles Darwin

Completing his degree course at Cambridge in 1831, it was on 27th December that Darwin left Plymouth aboard the survey ship HMS *Beagle*. His trip round the world was of almost five years duration and he did not return to England until 2nd October 1836. By 1844 he had written a 230-page essay explaining how the struggle for life could promote the progressive development of species by selecting for those individuals which were best adapted to survive. Yet it was not until 1859 that his famous book was published under the title *On The Origin of Species By Means of Natural Selection, or the Preservation of Favoured Races in the Struggle for Life.*

He begins his Introduction[11] as follows:

> When on board HMS *Beagle*, as naturalist, I was much struck with certain facts in the distribution of the inhabitants of South America, and in the geological relations of the present to the past inhabitants of that continent. These facts seemed to me to throw some light on the origin of species - that mystery of mysteries, as it has been called by one of our greatest philosophers. On my return home, it occurred to me, in 1837, that something might perhaps be made out on this question by patiently accumulating and reflecting on all sorts of facts which could possibly have any bearing on it. After five years' work I allowed myself to speculate on the subject, and drew up some short notes; these I enlarged in 1844 into a sketch of the conclusions which then seemed to me to be probable: from that period to the present day I have steadily pursued the same object. I hope that I may be excused for entering on these personal details, as I give them now to show that I have not been hasty in coming to a conclusion.

Darwin had *patiently accumulated and reflected upon all sorts of facts which could possibly have any bearing upon ... the mystery of the origin of species*, and not for five years did he allow himself *to speculate on the subject.* This is the proper method of those who would establish the principles of knowledge in any field. Eventually he set forth his theory. And it would not be long before evidence from the field of palaeontology demonstrated clearly a number evolutionary series in the fossil (or geological) record, effectively confirming what Darwin had proposed.

These ideas challenged long-established Christian teaching which asserted that the whole world, and every species of life within it, had been created by God in the space of just six days. For it was clear that a mechanism such as Darwin proposed for progressive development of species by mutation and selection must operate over millions of generations if it was to be effective in producing even the present diversity of life forms. If it must also account for the trail of extinct species exhibited in the fossil record, then the count of generations must be all the greater.

The second part of the problem was this. The geological record would shortly turn out to support an age for the earth of some 4,500 *million* years. Yet the Christian church taught that Adam had been created by God 'in his image' (Gn.1:27) on the sixth day of creation. Then Eve was derived from Adam's rib (Gn.2:22) which made Adam the single ancestor for the human race. Using calculation from Biblical genealogy, the creation was dated to some time around 4000 BCE. The confusion surrounding this claim was compounded by the fact that theologians were mistakenly conflating the 'god' person made at Gn.1:27 with the 'dust' person formed at Gn.2:7; but that is a matter addressed in subsequent chapters of this book and we shall not go into it here.

By the end of the nineteenth century it was plain to many that the Christian church, with all its claims for unique authority, had been underestimating the age of the earth by a factor approaching one million times (10^6)! It was soon clear that those who had interpreted the Bible in a literal manner *to account for the existence of everything* had been gravely mistaken in much of what they claimed.

This proved a serious blow to confidence. Before long even the Catholic church felt compelled to accept that the early chapters of *Genesis* were myth[12]. Yet it continued to confuse the 'heavenly' Person made at Gn.1:27 with the 'dust' person formed at Gn.2:7: and it continued to treat the gospels and Pauline letters as if they were records of history. On both counts there was more trouble in store, though such was the level of complacency that still the church could not see what was wrong.

We should note here that Roman Catholic doctrine differs in certain respects from what is held by the Eastern Orthodox, Russian Orthodox and Coptic churches. One key difference is embodied in the credal disagreement on the nature of the Trinity, the *Filioque* dispute.

Roman Catholic doctrine differs again from what is variously held by those Christian traditions which retain their Catholic origins but whose ideas were later re-determined through the course of the Reformation. Yet even these traditions continue to regard the gospels substantially as if they were records of events which actually took place during the first century CE.

Conflict with the Implications of Evolution?

John Sandwith Boys Smith attended Sherborne School before going up in 1919 to St John's College, Cambridge where he read first Economics, and then Theology. In later years he would become both Master of his college and Vice Chancellor of the University.

It was in 1930 that he wrote on *"Christian Doctrine and the Idea Of Evolution"*. There he turns to the implications of Darwinian Evolution for Christian doctrine, which he believes is in serious need of revision because, as he says :

> … the traditional system of Christian Doctrine is in many respects in conflict with [the] implications of Evolution.

In 2003 St John's College published posthumously the sermons of its former Master, John Boys Smith. Here are abstracts from what he says[13]:

> Let us say instead that belief ought to be founded on evidence. And let us go further and say that this is above all true of religious belief ... *Where else would it be worse to be deceived?*
>
> …

To believe is to be convinced by the evidence you apprehend. The evidence may be of many sorts. The fundamental need is to see it.

…

Integrity is the quality of looking at what presents itself to you instead of (for some personal reason) turning the eyes away. Both the saint and the scholar exhibit it; and without it there is neither saint nor scholar.

…

The inspired guess, the scientific imagination, play a chief part in active discovery.

---- o ----

Take first scholarship - the thing, perhaps the first thing, a University is designed to promote and to train its members to acquire. And by scholarship I do not mean the qualities demanded of the student of letters rather than of the student of the sciences; for true scholarship, in its essential character, is the same in both; only the spheres of its activity or application are different. *It means undivided attention to the evidence; keen, discriminating, sensitive; and the drawing of the conclusions which that evidence, and not some other thing, requires.*

…

It means also a gift of imagination, which is a gift, though one that can be developed; but that too is the means of making fullest use of the evidence that is seen, and of seeing more. But the first condition is the single eye, *that sincerity of vision which looks without bias or partiality at what is there to be seen*.

Ignorance, at every stage, is in some degree inevitable, and it makes some errors unavoidable. But the most frequent errors, and those that propagate a crop of further errors, are not the consequence of ignorance, but just of the lack of the single eye - of prejudice, of the desire to maintain a preconceived opinion, to refute some other opinion, to save yourself trouble, or to prove yourself right. And for these there is only one cure : *the single eye*.

Boys Smith argues for a holistic, intellectually rigorous and strictly honest approach to academic work - including for the derivation (or validation) of Christian doctrine. There must be no fudging, no inconsistency, no evidence unaccounted for. And the cure for error, he suggests, is *the single eye*.

His conclusion evokes the following passage in the gospels (see also Mt.5:29; Mk.9:47). The context here is a consideration of '*who will be greatest in the kingdom of the heavens*'. The name *Gehenna* is a Jewish equivalent to the Christian concept of Hell.

Mt. 18:3	καὶ εἶπεν, ἀμὴν λέγω ὑμῖν, ἐὰν μὴ στραφῆτε καὶ γένησθε ὡς τὰ παιδία, οὐ μὴ εἰσέλθητε εἰς τὴν βασιλείαν τῶν οὐρανῶν.	And he [Jesus] said "Truly I say to you: if you do not turn back and become like the children, you will not enter into the <u>kingdom</u> of the heavens.
18:4	ὅστις οὖν ταπεινώσει ἑαυτὸν ὡς τὸ παιδίον τοῦτο, οὗτός ἐστιν ὁ μείζων ἐν τῇ βασιλείᾳ τῶν οὐρανῶν.	Whoever therefore will humble himself like this child, this one is the greatest in the <u>kingdom</u> of the heavens"
	(*verses omitted here*)	
18:9	καὶ εἰ ὁ ὀφθαλμός σου σκανδαλίζει σε, ἔξελε αὐτὸν καὶ βάλε ἀπὸ σοῦ: καλόν σοί ἐστιν μονόφθαλμον εἰς τὴν ζωὴν εἰσελθεῖν, ἢ δύο ὀφθαλμοὺς ἔχοντα βληθῆναι εἰς τὴν γέενναν τοῦ πυρός.	And if your eye <u>scandalises</u> you, take it out and <u>throw</u> [it away] from you: it is good for you to enter into life one-eyed, rather than having two eyes to be thrown into the Gehenna of Fire.

Chapter 3

The Key to Scripture's Plot:
LXX *Genesis*

The four passages which follow are taken from the NT canon:

1 Cor. 2:6	σοφίαν δὲ λαλοῦμεν ἐν τοῖς τελείοις, σοφίαν δὲ οὐ τοῦ αἰῶνος τούτου οὐδὲ τῶν ἀρχόντων τοῦ αἰῶνος τούτου τῶν καταργουμένων:	***And we speak wisdom*** amongst those accomplished - yet a wisdom not of this age, nor of the rulers of this age, of those being made redundant.
2:7	ἀλλὰ λαλοῦμεν θεοῦ σοφίαν ἐν μυστηρίῳ, τὴν **ἀποκεκρυμμένην**, ἣν προώρισεν ὁ θεὸς **πρὸ τῶν αἰώνων** εἰς δόξαν ἡμῶν:	But we speak a godly wisdom within a mystery, ***hidden away*** - which God fore-ordained ***before the ages*** purposed for our glory,
2:8	ἣν οὐδεὶς τῶν ἀρχόντων τοῦ αἰῶνος τούτου ἔγνωκεν, εἰ γὰρ ἔγνωσαν, οὐκ ἂν τὸν κύριον τῆς δόξης ἐσταύρωσαν.	***Which not one of the rulers of this age has known. For if they knew, they would not have crucified the 'lord of glory'.***
Mt. 13:34	ταῦτα πάντα ἐλάλησεν ὁ ἰησοῦς ἐν παραβολαῖς τοῖς ὄχλοις, καὶ χωρὶς παραβολῆς οὐδὲν ἐλάλει αὐτοῖς:	Jesus spoke all these things in parables to the crowds, and without a parable he spoke to them nothing.

13:35	ὅπως πληρωθῇ τὸ ῥηθὲν διὰ τοῦ προφήτου λέγοντος, ἀνοίξω ἐν παραβολαῖς τὸ στόμα μου, ἐρεύξομαι **κεκρυμμένα ἀπὸ καταβολῆς [κόσμου]**.	So that it might be fulfilled what was spoken through the prophet, saying "I shall open my mouth in parables, I shall utter **things hidden from laying down [of world]**".
Mt. 16:19	δώσω σοι **τὰς κλεῖδας τῆς βασιλείας** τῶν οὐρανῶν, καὶ ὃ ἐὰν δήσῃς ἐπὶ τῆς γῆς ἔσται δεδεμένον ἐν τοῖς οὐρανοῖς, καὶ ὃ ἐὰν λύσῃς ἐπὶ τῆς γῆς ἔσται λελυμένον ἐν τοῖς οὐρανοῖς.	"I shall give to you **the keys of the kingdom** of the heavens. And what you may bind upon the earth will be bound in the heavens, and what you may loose upon the earth will be loosed in the heavens."
Lk. 11:52	οὐαὶ ὑμῖν τοῖς νομικοῖς, ὅτι **ἤρατε τὴν κλεῖδα τῆς γνώσεως**: αὐτοὶ οὐκ εἰσήλθατε καὶ τοὺς εἰσερχομένους ἐκωλύσατε.	"Woe to you, the lawyers! Because **you took away the key of gnosis** (knowledge). You did not enter in yourselves - and those entering in, you hindered."

At the time when these texts appeared there was as yet no Christian church. What is reflected in the assertions made here is the reality of the *Jewish* religious scene in the late first century CE. Yet it was upon the platform provided by such texts that the Gnostic tradition would continue to thrive - and upon the same platform that what we now think of as *Christianity* would shortly take root.

It is plain enough that the author of *1ˢᵗ Corinthians* considers that something of significance in connection with '*godly wisdom*' has been '*hidden away within a mystery*' - and it is implicit that this '*mystery*' is enshrined within scripture itself. It seems moreover that some of those '*entering in*' to the mystery were being hindered. Specifically, they were being hindered by those Jewish teachers who were '*lawyers*' - meaning those who sought to interpret and to uphold the Law of Moses as set forth in the Torah. In the gospel narrative the accusation is made that these so-called '*lawyers*' have '*taken away the key of gnosis*'. The accusation is put into the mouth of Jesus himself, lunching with a Pharisee (Lk.11:37).

The suggestion that Israel's teachers may have *removed the key to true Knowledge* and *taught in contravention of Wisdom* sounds like a Gnostic protest. It may remind us of Alastair Logan's opinion already cited in Chapter 2:

> The Ophites of Irenaeus vividly illustrate the distinctive exegesis of the Old Testament of these Gnostics: (that) the prophets, from Moses on, are the mouth-pieces of Ialdabaoth …

Then Margaret Barker[1] emphasises:

> Israel's oldest religion was not monotheistic.

She considers that the early Temple tradition, reflected for example in *1ˢᵗ Isaiah*, was later replaced with a monotheist interpretation of scripture imposed with the Deuteronomic reforms which followed the return from exile in Babylon - but that the earlier tradition somehow survived to contend with the new. She goes on to suggest:

> The older strata of the Old Testament *do* look very like the roots of the later gnostic systems and it is significant that the gnostics had links to the older ie. superseded strata. Were the gnostic teachers such expert textual critics that they chose only the older material, or did they know another tradition behind what we read in the Old Testament? They certainly knew of a great variety of beliefs within Judaism …

In discussing the *Tripartate Tractate* she says:

> This passage probably represents the teaching of Heracleon, a student of Valentinus. What is interesting is the implication that our 'normal' reading of the Old Testament, that God is one and spoke through the ancient Scriptures, is thought to be a heresy established by misreading.

And in discussing *1 Enoch 94.50 & 91.10* she says:

> Enoch had also prophesied that there would be an evil generation of sinners who would find no place for Wisdom, but that *Wisdom would be given back to the elect at the end of the time when they awoke from their sleep.*

Later in this book we shall see what Jesus' students missed when (in the narrative) they fell asleep at Gethsemani on the Mount of Olives. For there was something significant about Jesus' behaviour which they evidently failed to notice (*qv.* Mt.26:36 seq).

But what were those '*things hidden from the laying down of the world*' (Mt.13:35)? The passage at Lk.11 yields perhaps further clues when the author has Jesus say:

Lk. 11:49	διὰ τοῦτο καὶ ἡ σοφία τοῦ θεοῦ εἶπεν, ἀποστελῶ εἰς αὐτοὺς προφήτας καὶ ἀποστόλους, καὶ ἐξ αὐτῶν ἀποΚτενοῦσΙν καὶ διώξουσιν,	On this account the wisdom of God also said "I shall send to you prophets and apostles: and some of them they will kill and they will persecute
11:50	ἵνα ἐκζητηθῇ τὸ αἷμα πάντων τῶν προφητῶν τὸ ἐκκεχυμένον ἀπὸ καταβολῆς κόσμου ἀπὸ τῆς γενεᾶς ταύτης,	So that the blood of all the prophets, shed from laying down of world, may be demanded from this generation."

11:51	ἀπὸ αἵματος **ἄβελ** ἕως αἵματος ζαχαρίου τοῦ ἀπολομένου μεταξὺ τοῦ θυσιαστηρίου καὶ τοῦ οἴκου: ναί, λέγω ὑμῖν, ἐκζητηθήσεται ἀπὸ τῆς γενεᾶς ταύτης.	From (the) blood of **_Abel_** to the blood of Zacharias, slain between the altar and the dwelling. Yes I say to you, it will be demanded from this generation!
11:52	οὐαὶ ὑμῖν τοῖς νομικοῖς,	"Woe to you, the lawyers!
	ὅτι **ἤρατε τὴν κλεῖδα τῆς γνώσεως**:	Because **you took away the key of Gnosis** (knowledge).
	αὐτοὶ οὐκ εἰσήλθατε καὶ τοὺς εἰσερχομένους ἐκωλύσατε.	You did not enter in yourselves - and those entering in, you hindered."
11:53	**Κ**ἀκεῖθε**ν** ἐξελθόντος αὐτοῦ ἤρξαντο οἱ γραμματεῖς καὶ οἱ φαρισαῖοι δεινῶς ἐνέχειν καὶ ἀποστοματίζειν αὐτὸν περὶ πλειόνων,	<u>And with that</u> emerging from him, the scribes and Pharisees began to take strongly against (him) and to interrogate him concerning more things
11:54	ἐνεδρεύοντες αὐτὸν θηρεῦσαί τι ἐκ τοῦ στόματος αὐτοῦ.	Lying in wait for him to hunt down something from his mouth

12:1	ἐν οἷς ἐπισυναχθεισῶν τῶν μυριάδων τοῦ ὄχλου, ὥστε **Κα**ταπατε**ῖ**ν ἀλλήλους, ἤρξατο λέγειν πρὸς τοὺς μαθητὰς αὐτοῦ πρῶτον, προσέχετε ἑαυτοῖς ἀπὸ τῆς ζύμης, ἥτις ἐστὶν ὑπόκρισις, τῶν φαρισαίων.	Within which, by the coming together of the myriads of the crowd so as <u>to tread down</u> one another, he began to say to his students first "Keep yourselves from the yeast of the Pharisees - which is hypocrisy.
12:2	οὐδὲν δὲ συγκεκαλυμμένον ἐστὶν ὃ οὐκ ἀποκαλυφθήσεται καὶ κρυπτὸν ὃ οὐ γνωσθήσεται.	But nothing is concealed which will not be revealed, and hidden which will not become known."

Nothing is concealed which will not be revealed
- and hidden which will not become known.

That last word **γνωσθήσεται** [*it will become known*] makes this sound like an inherently gnostic assertion.

Emboldened in the passage above you may notice some features which could easily have been '*hidden*'. If the text had been manipulated in the course of composition to achieve this result then that could account for some very peculiar phrasing (Lk.11:53 above) and for the incongruous events cited in the narrative (Lk.12:1 above). Oddities of this kind may serve to attract the reader's attention. But in reality they could be the product of the author's wish to include, for the purpose of exemplification, certain words whose particular function was to '*hide*' the name of **κάϊν** [*Cain*]. In contrast, at Lk.11:51 we saw **ἄβελ** [*Abel*] whose name was not hidden. Perhaps you cannot imagine what motive the gospel authors might have to write in such a way. It is a matter which should become clear in Chapter 5 of this book.

In the gospel narrative the priest Zacharias is father to John the Baptist. But *Zacharias* is also the name designated for John himself (*qv.*

Lk.1:59), imprisoned from the time of Jesus' baptism and subsequently beheaded.

In the passage above, an explicit link is asserted between Zacharias (*alias* John?) and Abel, the one who in the narrative of *Genesis* was killed by his brother Cain. And it appears that the violent elimination both of Abel and of John the Baptist is connected in the mind of the author with the removal of the *Key of Knowledge*. We may well suspect that this is the key for *Knowing the Knowledge of Good and Evil*, the name given to one of the two trees in the narrative of *Genesis* Chapter 2.

One way or another, the passage at Mt.13:35 suggests that whatever has been 'hidden', it has indeed been hidden '*from the laying down of the world*'. Shortly we shall address the first four chapters of Genesis. Here is the '*origin*' of scripture, and the place where we find described the '*laying down*' of the world. Surely this is where we should look if we want to find the '*key*' to scripture's mystery.

But before we begin on the task we must first decide whether to work from a Hebrew source for *Genesis* or from the Greek *Septuagint* translation, the LXX.

By the end of the fourth century CE the Gnostic tradition of scripture had been largely suppressed in favour of the monotheist interpretation embraced and promoted by the Catholic church. In Chapter 1 we noted that this was the time when Jerome was asked to produce revised translations of the gospels to Latin, working from Greek sources. A few years later he went on to translate the books of the OT (apart from the Psalms) from sources in Hebrew which may themselves have been revised as late as the second century CE. These were precursors of the Masoretic Texts [MT] still in use today (the oldest MS of the complete Hebrew Bible extant today is actually from the tenth century CE).

Jerome's choice explains why, in the first four chapters of *Genesis*, the combination of divine names (**God, lord god & lord**) employed in the Latin Vulgate follows essentially the same pattern found in the Hebrew MT. In the Septuagint translation to Greek the combination of names used in these early chapters follows a different pattern. For this reason amongst others, many scholars infer that the Hebrew source available to Jerome differed significantly from the Hebrew source which six centuries before his time had served as the basis for the Septuagint translation made at Alexandria.

Jerome's decision to work from the Hebrew appears at best curious and at worst perverse. Although the earliest texts were known to have been in Hebrew, the Hebrew texts available to him were a recent version and did not tally with the LXX Greek. Jerome's choice was also felt to be unsatisfactory because the LXX was known to have been the version familiar to and preferred by the NT authors themselves. And the LXX was still pre-eminent, even in Christian circles in the Latin west.

Augustine of Hippo was amongst those who maintained that the LXX was inspired scripture, having at least the same authority as the Hebrew from which it had once been derived (*ca.* 250BCE), even in respect of any variations or additions which may have been incorporated at the time it was produced. In his opinion the LXX provided a robust dispensation of scripture for the gentile nations and ought to be used as the basis for any subsequent translation, for example to Latin.

In his *City of God (Book XVII, Chapter 43)*, Augustine writes on '*The Authority of the Septuagint Translation, Which, Saving the Honour of the Hebrew Original, is to Be Preferred to All Translations*'. He says[2]:

> For while there were other interpreters who translated these sacred oracles out of the Hebrew tongue into Greek, as Aquila, Symmachus, and Theodotion, and also that translation which, as the name of the author is unknown, is quoted as the fifth edition, **yet the Church has received this Septuagint translation just as if it were the only one**; and it has been used by the Greek Christian people, most of whom are not aware that there is any other.
>
> From this translation there has also been made a translation in the Latin tongue, which the Latin churches use. Our times, however, have enjoyed the advantage of the presbyter Jerome, a man most learned, and skilled in all three languages, who

translated these same Scriptures into the Latin speech, not from the Greek, but from the Hebrew.

But although the Jews acknowledge this very learned labour of his to be faithful, while they contend that the Septuagint translators have erred in many places, *still the churches of Christ judge that no one should be preferred to the authority of so many men*, chosen for this very great work by Eleazar who was then high priest; for even if there had not appeared in them one spirit, without doubt divine, and the seventy learned men had, after the manner of men, compared together the words of their translation, that what pleased them all might stand, no single translator ought to be preferred to them; but since so great a sign of divinity has appeared in them, certainly, if any other translator of their Scriptures from the Hebrew into any other tongue is faithful, in that case he agrees with these seventy translators, and if he is not found to agree with them, then we ought to believe that the prophetic gift is with them. For the same Spirit who was in the prophets when they spoke these things was also in the seventy men when they translated them, so that assuredly they could also say something else, just as if the prophet himself had said both, because it would be the same Spirit who said both; and could say the same thing differently, so that, although the words were not the same, yet the same meaning should shine forth to those of good understanding; and could omit or add something, so that even by this it might be shown that there was in that work not human bondage, which the translator owed to the words, but rather divine power, which filled and ruled the mind of the translator.

Some, however, have thought that the Greek copies of the Septuagint version should be emended from the Hebrew copies; yet they did not dare to take away what the Hebrew lacked and the Septuagint had, but only added what was found in the Hebrew copies and was lacking in the Septuagint, and noted them by placing at the beginning of the verses certain marks in the form of stars which they call asterisks. And those things which the Hebrew copies have not, but the Septuagint have, they have in like manner marked at the beginning of the verses by horizontal spit-shaped marks like those by which we denote ounces; and many copies having these marks are circulated even in Latin.

But we cannot, without inspecting both kinds of copies, find out those things which are neither omitted nor added, but expressed differently, whether they yield another meaning not in itself unsuitable, or can be shown to explain the same meaning in another way. If, then, as it behoves us, we behold nothing else in these Scriptures than what the Spirit of God has spoken through men, if anything is in the Hebrew copies and is not in the version of the Seventy, the Spirit of God did not choose to say it through them, but only through the prophets. *But whatever is in the Septuagint and not in the Hebrew copies, the same Spirit chose rather to say through the latter, thus showing that both were prophets.*

For in that manner He spoke as He chose, some things through Isaiah, some through Jeremiah, some through several prophets, or else the same thing through this prophet and through that. Further, whatever is found in both editions, that one and the same Spirit willed to say through both, but so as that the former preceded in prophesying, and the latter followed in prophetically interpreting them; because, as the one Spirit of peace was in the former when they spoke true and concordant words, so the selfsame one Spirit hath appeared in the latter, when, without mutual conference they yet interpreted all things as if with one mouth.

It seems that Jerome was persuaded by Jewish concerns that he should work from the Hebrew text. Possibly the wish of the newfound Catholic church to conceal the Gnostic origin and content of the NT texts coincided with a renewed Jewish prejudice to the same effect, inducing Jerome to translate from Hebrew in the attempt to sustain not only harmony with Jewish teachers of his acquaintance but a monotheist interpretation for scripture as a whole.

Unlike Jerome, we shall work in this book from the Greek Septuagint translation. The first reason for such a choice is that the LXX represents the earliest surviving version of the Pentateuch, including *Genesis*. The second reason is that Greek is a precise language with a comprehensive vocabulary whilst Hebrew is so concise that it is more likely to give rise to ambiguity. The third and most important reason is that here is the version which provided the theological and literary context within which the NT writers and their readers actually worked during the early centuries CE. It is for these reasons that the LXX should give us the best possible basis for penetrating the '*mystery*' enshrined in the gospels and NT letters.

There is one further decision for us to take; which version to use. The LXX itself was widely copied in manuscript form over many centuries. Today we have substantially complete copies which date from the fourth or fifth centuries and numerous portions and fragments which are dated earlier. But as one might expect there are minor variations from one copy to another.

During the past two hundred years a huge amount of work has been done on the numerous LXX sources in the specialised field of study known as *textual criticism*. It is the aim of such meticulous and devoted scholarship to collect the oldest recoverable texts and by correlating these to achieve the closest possible approximation to the notional 'original', reconstructing this systematically from the widest possible selection of textual data.

In our quest to penetrate the '*mystery*' of scripture and to understand it, the best possible result should be obtained if we use a recently revised composite text of this kind. We shall choose the CATSS LXX edition of the Septuagint prepared by the TLG (*Thesaurus Linguae Graecae*) Project directed by T. Brunner at the University of California, Irvine and made available through the Center for Computer Analysis of Texts (CCAT) at the University of Pennsylvania. This has been verified against the individual Göttingen editions which have appeared since 1935 when the Rahlfs *Septuaginta* was first published.

A huge amount of work has gone into producing this source. It includes what is probably the closest approximation we shall get to the version of *Genesis* used by the NT authors themselves.

Chapter 4

LXX *Genesis*: The First Seven Days

All scripture is fiction
- but it is *very* important to notice exactly what is said, and by whom

Primeval Disorder & Darkness

Gn. 1:1	ἐν ἀρχῇ ἐποίησεν ὁ **θεὸς** τὸν οὐρανὸν καὶ τὴν γῆν	In origin **God** made the heaven and the earth.
1:2	ἡ δὲ γῆ ἦν ἀόρατος καὶ ἀκατασκεύαστος καὶ σκότος ἐπάνω τῆς ἀβύσσου	But the earth was invisible and unformed - and darkness (was) above the abyss.
	καὶ πνεῦμα θεοῦ ἐπεφέρετο ἐπάνω τοῦ ὕδατος	And a spirit of a god was overlaid above the water.

Here at the outset is the prime God, the uncreated and immaterial origin of heaven and earth, immersed in primeval darkness. The earth itself is invisible and unformed. As yet there is no activity of any kind.

Notice that what is found above '*the water below*' is not '*The spirit of God*'. The matter is less clear than that. What we have is '*a spirit of a god*'. For all that we can tell at this juncture, it might be the '*spirit*' of quite a different god. What is hinted at becomes clearer with the first verse of the the fourth gospel (*John*); see Chapter 8 of this book.

Day 1

Gn. 1:3	καὶ εἶπεν ὁ **θεός** γενηθήτω φῶς καὶ ἐγένετο φῶς	And **God** said "Let light happen". And light happened.

1:4	καὶ εἶδεν **ὁ θεὸς** τὸ φῶς ὅτι καλόν	And **God** saw the light as good
	καὶ διεχώρισεν **ὁ θεὸς** ἀνὰ μέσον τοῦ φωτὸς καὶ ἀνὰ μέσον τοῦ σκότους	And **God** divided [*alt*: separated, segregated, dissociated, discriminated] amidst the light and amidst the darkness.
1:5	καὶ ἐκάλεσεν ὁ θεὸς τὸ φῶς ἡμέραν καὶ τὸ σκότος ἐκάλεσεν νύκτα καὶ ἐγένετο ἑσπέρα καὶ ἐγένετο πρωί ἡμέρα μία	And God called the light 'day', and the darkness he called 'night'. And evening happened, and morning happened: DAY ONE.

Presumably God is well accustomed to the primeval darkness. And although he has created Heaven and Earth, notice that God *does not* make the light; he merely permits it.

God '*saw the light as good* '. Presuming that God is good, this leaves two possibilities: [1] the light was good or [2] God could see no evil.

God '*divided*' between light and darkness. This may just imply that God discriminated between the two. Or something more active could be intended. Anyway, the light is now called '*day*' and the darkness '*night*', for God says so. The dualism is evident here. Perhaps we have here God, together with the '*spirit*' of a second god. Possibly one of these is betokened as good and the other as evil. It is too soon to be sure.

Day 2

| Gn. 1:6 | καὶ εἶπεν **ὁ θεός** γενηθήτω στερέωμα ἐν μέσῳ τοῦ ὕδατος καὶ ἔστω διαχωρίζον ἀνὰ μέσον ὕδατος καὶ ὕδατος καὶ ἐγένετο οὕτως | And **God** said "Let a space happen in the midst of the water, and let it be a divider amidst water and water". And it happened like this. |

1:7	καὶ ἐποίησεν **ὁ θεὸς** τὸ στερέωμα καὶ διεχώρισεν **ὁ θεὸς** ἀνὰ μέσον τοῦ ὕδατος ὃ ἦν ὑποκάτω τοῦ στερεώματος καὶ ἀνὰ μέσον τοῦ ὕδατος τοῦ ἐπάνω τοῦ στερεώματος	And **God** made the space, and **God** divided [*alt*: separated, segregated, dissociated, discriminated] amidst the water which was down below the space, and amidst the water which was up above the space.
1:8	καὶ ἐκάλεσεν **ὁ θεὸς** τὸ στερέωμα οὐρανόν <u>καὶ εἶδεν **ὁ θεὸς** ὅτι καλόν</u> καὶ ἐγένετο ἑσπέρα καὶ ἐγένετο πρωί ἡμέρα δευτέρα	And **God** called the space 'heaven', <u>and **God** saw it as good</u> [*omitted in Hebr. MT*]. And evening happened, and morning happened: SECOND DAY.

Once again we are told that God '*divided*', this time between the water below and the water above. As before, this may just imply that he discriminates between the two. Or it may mean more. The space between them is now called '*heaven*'. The dualism is still apparent, perhaps representing good and evil. It is still too soon to be sure. God '*saw the space as good*'. As with the light, this does not necessarily mean that it *was* good.

Day 3

Gn.	καὶ εἶπεν **ὁ θεός** συναχθήτω	And **God** said "Let the water
1:9	τὸ ὕδωρ τὸ ὑποκάτω τοῦ	beneath Heaven coalesce
	οὐρανοῦ εἰς συναγωγὴν μίαν	into one assembly [*alt*: one
	καὶ ὀφθήτω ἡ ξηρά καὶ	synagogue] and let the dry
	ἐγένετο οὕτως καὶ συνήχθη	appear" - and it happened
	τὸ ὕδωρ τὸ ὑποκάτω τοῦ	thus. And the water beneath
	οὐρανοῦ εἰς τὰς συναγωγὰς	Heaven coalesced into their
	αὐτῶν καὶ ὤφθη ἡ ξηρά	assemblies [*alt*: their
		synagogues] - and the dry
		appeared
1:10	καὶ ἐκάλεσεν **ὁ θεὸς** τὴν	And **God** called the dry
	ξηρὰν γῆν καὶ τὰ συστήματα	'earth', and the systems of
	τῶν ὑδάτων ἐκάλεσεν	waters he called 'seas'. And
	θαλάσσας καὶ εἶδεν **ὁ θεὸς** ὅτι	**God** saw it as good.
	καλόν	

It is the '*water below*' which now coalesces into '*one assembly*' (literally, '*one synagogue*'). What remains is '*the dry*', now called '*earth*'. Could it be that the synagogue is set forth as good, but the dry earth as evil? The latter has the character of a desert. In the gospels Jesus meets with Satan in the desert. It is still too soon to be sure.

Gn.	καὶ εἶπεν **ὁ θεός** βλαστησάτω	And **God** said "Let the earth
1:11	ἡ γῆ βοτάνην χόρτου σπεῖρον	sprout a grassy plant
	σπέρμα κατὰ γένος καὶ καθ'	spreading seed according to
	ὁμοιότητα καὶ ξύλον	(its) kind and variety - and a
	κάρπιμον ποιοῦν καρπόν οὗ	fruit-bearing tree making fruit
	τὸ σπέρμα αὐτοῦ ἐν αὐτῷ	of which its seed (is) within it,
	κατὰ γένος ἐπὶ τῆς γῆς καὶ	according to (its) kind upon
	ἐγένετο οὕτως	the earth". And it happened
		like this.

1:12	καὶ ἐξήνεγκεν ἡ γῆ βοτάνην χόρτου σπεῖρον σπέρμα κατὰ γένος καὶ καθ' ὁμοιότητα καὶ ξύλον κάρπιμον ποιοῦν καρπόν οὗ τὸ σπέρμα αὐτοῦ ἐν αὐτῷ κατὰ γένος ἐπὶ τῆς γῆς καὶ εἶδεν **ὁ θεὸς** ὅτι καλόν	And the earth brought forth a grassy plant spreading seed after its kind and variety - and a fruit-bearing tree making fruit of which its seed (is) within it, according to (its) kind upon the earth. And **God** saw it as good.
1:13	καὶ ἐγένετο ἑσπέρα καὶ ἐγένετο πρωί ἡμέρα τρίτη	And evening happened, and morning happened: THIRD DAY.

On Day 3 we have also the origin of the seed-bearing grassy plants, and the trees bearing fruit with seeds. We shall see later, as the subsequent theme of scripture unfolds, how these have a pivotal role to play. And now that they have sprouted we shall need some of the light to '*shine upon the earth*' and make them grow.

Day 4

Gn. 1:14	καὶ εἶπεν **ὁ θεός** γενηθήτωσαν φωστῆρες ἐν τῷ στερεώματι τοῦ οὐρανοῦ εἰς φαῦσιν τῆς γῆς τοῦ διαχωρίζειν ἀνὰ μέσον τῆς ἡμέρας καὶ ἀνὰ μέσον τῆς νυκτὸς καὶ ἔστωσαν εἰς σημεῖα καὶ εἰς καιροὺς καὶ εἰς ἡμέρας καὶ εἰς ἐνιαυτοὺς	And **God** said "Let luminous bodies happen in the space of Heaven for lighting of the earth (and) to divide amidst the day and amidst the night; and let them be for signs, both for seasons and for days and for years;

1:15	καὶ ἔστωσαν εἰς φαῦσιν ἐν τῷ στερεώματι τοῦ οὐρανοῦ ὥστε φαίνειν ἐπὶ τῆς γῆς καὶ ἐγένετο οὕτως	And let them be for lighting within the space of Heaven so as to appear upon the earth". And it happened like this.
1:16	καὶ ἐποίησεν **ὁ θεὸς** τοὺς δύο φωστῆρας τοὺς μεγάλους τὸν φωστῆρα τὸν μέγαν εἰς ἀρχὰς τῆς ἡμέρας καὶ τὸν φωστῆρα τὸν ἐλάσσω εἰς ἀρχὰς τῆς νυκτός καὶ τοὺς ἀστέρας	And **God** made the two great luminous bodies, the greater luminous body to rule the day, and the lesser luminous body to rule the night and the stars.
1:17	καὶ ἔθετο αὐτοὺς **ὁ θεὸς** ἐν τῷ στερεώματι τοῦ οὐρανοῦ ὥστε φαίνειν ἐπὶ τῆς γῆς	And **God** placed them in the space of Heaven so as to appear upon the earth,
1:18	καὶ ἄρχειν τῆς ἡμέρας καὶ τῆς νυκτὸς καὶ διαχωρίζειν ἀνὰ μέσον τοῦ φωτὸς καὶ ἀνὰ μέσον τοῦ σκότους καὶ εἶδεν **ὁ θεὸς** ὅτι καλόν	And to rule the day and the night, and to divide amidst the light and amidst the darkness. And **God** saw it as good.
1:19	καὶ ἐγένετο ἑσπέρα καὶ ἐγένετο πρωί ἡμέρα τετάρτη	And evening happened, and morning happened: FOURTH DAY.

Here are the two great luminous bodies (the sun and the moon). They are to rule the day and the night, dividing between them.

Still God saw it as good. But perhaps we should recall that God began in darkness, and merely permitted the light.

Day 5

Gn.	καὶ εἶπεν ὁ **θεός** ἐξαγαγέτω τὰ ὕδατα ἑρπετὰ ψυχῶν ζωσῶν καὶ πετεινὰ πετόμενα ἐπὶ τῆς γῆς κατὰ τὸ στερέωμα τοῦ οὐρανοῦ καὶ ἐγένετο οὕτως	And **God** said "Let the waters bring forth creeping things with living souls and birds flying upon the earth down the space of Heaven". And it happened like this.
1:20		

1:21	καὶ ἐποίησεν ὁ **θεὸς** τὰ κήτη τὰ μεγάλα καὶ πᾶσαν ψυχὴν ζῴων ἑρπετῶν ἃ ἐξήγαγεν τὰ ὕδατα κατὰ γένη αὐτῶν καὶ πᾶν πετεινὸν πτερωτὸν κατὰ γένος καὶ εἶδεν ὁ **θεὸς** ὅτι καλά	And **God** made the large sea creatures, and every soul of living creeping thing which the waters brought forth, after their kind, and every winged bird after its kind. And **God** saw them as good.

1:22	καὶ ηὐλόγησεν αὐτὰ ὁ **θεὸς** λέγων αὐξάνεσθε καὶ πληθύνεσθε καὶ πληρώσατε τὰ ὕδατα ἐν ταῖς θαλάσσαις καὶ τὰ πετεινὰ πληθυνέσθωσαν ἐπὶ τῆς γῆς	And **God** blessed them, saying "Grow and multiply and fill the waters within the seas, and let the birds multiply upon the earth".

1:23	καὶ ἐγένετο ἑσπέρα καὶ ἐγένετο πρωί ἡμέρα πέμπτη	And evening happened, and morning happened: FIFTH DAY.

It is now the waters which bring forth birds - and creeping things. Notice how the creeping things have souls.

Day 6

Gn. 1:24	καὶ εἶπεν **ὁ θεός** ἐξαγαγέτω ἡ γῆ ψυχὴν ζῶσαν κατὰ γένος τετράποδα καὶ ἑρπετὰ καὶ θηρία τῆς γῆς κατὰ γένος καὶ ἐγένετο οὕτως	And **God** said "Let the earth bring forth a living soul after a four-footed kind, and creeping things and wild beasts of the earth after (their) kind". And it happened like this.
1:25	καὶ ἐποίησεν **ὁ θεὸς** τὰ θηρία τῆς γῆς κατὰ γένος καὶ τὰ κτήνη κατὰ γένος καὶ πάντα τὰ ἑρπετὰ τῆς γῆς κατὰ γένος αὐτῶν καὶ εἶδεν **ὁ θεὸς** ὅτι καλά	And **God** made the wild beasts of the earth after (their) kind, and the pastoral beasts after (their) kind, and all the creeping things of the earth after their kind. And **God** saw them as good.

The earth too brings forth creeping things - also wild beasts and four-legged creatures.

Gn. 1:26	καὶ εἶπεν **ὁ θεός** ποιήσωμεν **ἄνθρωπον** κατ' εἰκόνα **ἡμετέραν** καὶ καθ' ὁμοί**ωσιν** καὶ ἀρχέτωσαν τῶν ἰχθύων τῆς θαλάσσης καὶ τῶν πετεινῶν τοῦ οὐρανοῦ καὶ τῶν κτηνῶν καὶ πάσης τῆς γῆς καὶ πάντων τῶν ἑρπετῶν τῶν ἑρπόντων ἐπὶ τῆς γῆς	And **God** said "Let us make *A PERSON according to our image* and according to likenesses. And let them rule (over) the fishes of the sea, and (over) the birds of Heaven, and (over) the pastoral beasts, and (over) all the earth, and (over) all the creeping things which creep upon the earth"

1:27	καὶ ἐποίησεν ὁ θεὸς ΤὸΝ ἄνθρωπον κατ' εἰκόνα θεοῦ ἐποίησεν αὐτόν ἄρσεν καὶ θῆλυ ἐποίησεν αὐτούς	*And* God *made 'THE PERSON'. According to (the) image of a god he made HIM. Male and female he made them.*
1:28	καὶ ηὐλόγησεν αὐτοὺς ὁ θεὸς λέγων αὐξάνεσθε καὶ πληθύνεσθε καὶ πληρώσατε τὴν γῆν καὶ καταΚΥΡΙΕύσατε αὐτῆς καὶ ἄρχετε τῶν ἰχθύων τῆς θαλάσσης καὶ τῶν πετεινῶν τοῦ οὐρανοῦ καὶ πάντων τῶν κτηνῶν καὶ πάσης τῆς γῆς καὶ πάντων τῶν ἑρπετῶν τῶν ἑρπόντων ἐπὶ τῆς γῆς	And **God** blessed them, saying "Grow and multiply and fill the earth and **LORD** over it. And rule (over) the fishes of the sea, and (over) the birds of heaven, and (over) all the pastoral beasts, and (over) all the earth, and (over) all the creeping things which creep upon the earth"

What has just happened here on DAY 6 is of central importance to the proper understanding of all subsequent scripture. If we misunderstand this then the risk will be much increased that in reading the subsequent texts, the gospels included, we shall suffer from what the authors consider as '*blindness*'. This is no small consideration; for many are those readers caught unawares and so led far astray.

Here in this passage is the description of **The Person** made **in the image of a god** ... and then directed to '*fill the earth and* **lord** *over it*'. Imagine that God could indeed be seen; one made '*in the image of a god and according to likenesses*' must appear to the observer like God himself. And if such a one is to '*lord over the earth*' then surely this must be the one we find referred to subsequently with the title '**lord god**'?

A few verses into *Genesis* Chapter 2 we shall encounter again the one who now will go by this title. Those familiar with Gnostic tradition may well have anticipated that sooner or later such a second god would emerge in the story line. It is here on the **sixth day** that the narrative develops in this way. That this is the materialisation of the Gnostic Demiurge could hardly be made more clear.

This look-alike is to 'lord it' over birds, beasts and creeping things. His subjects then will include the serpent, first encountered in *Genesis* Chapter 3.

Notice that at Gn.1:27 this **Person** is referred to first in the singular, and then in the plural as ἄρσεν καὶ θῆλυ [*male and female*]. Such a description provides for the Demiurge to take androgynous form. In the ancient world it was common to think of deities as combining the attributes of male and female.

Margaret Barker[1] says:

> The second God was the creator, the archon who made the world. This was a characteristic of western Gnosticism.
> …
> The second God in his evil aspect sometimes had animal form as did all the archons. (This was a convention known also in the apocalypses, where the monstrous forms represented evil, animal forms the human, and human forms the divine). The *Hypostasis of the Archons* describes 'an arrogant beast resembling a lion. It was androgynous' (HA CG.II.4.94).

Notice also the hint of aggressive dominance. The direction on how the earth is to be ruled is: κατακυριεύσατε αὐτῆς [*lord it down*]. Even the Hebrew text uses the verb וּרְדוּ [*subjugate*] and Robert Alter[2] says:

> The verb *radah* is not the normal Hebrew verb for "rule" (the latter is reflected in "dominion" of verse 16), and in most of the contexts in which it occurs it seems to suggest an absolute or even fierce exercise of mastery.

So there you have it: this **second god** is not portrayed as the most friendly of characters. A cautious approach may prove advisable. But even with all this explained, we certainly cannot proceed until we have addressed the widely held opinion that the verse at Gn.1:27 may be understood to say:

> So God created **man** in his [own] image, in the image of God created he him; male and female created he them.

> [King James Version: 1611]

Any such translation is misleading. That is the kindest thing we can say about it. To demonstrate what is wrong with it, the Greek and Hebrew sources are presented here along with strict translations to English. In both Greek and Hebrew the direct article is used - and in each language we have a word which conveys the meaning '*person*':

LXX Gn. 1:27	καὶ ἐποίησεν ὁ θεὸς **τὸν** **ἄνθρωπον** …	And God made **the** **Person** …
Mechon Mamre 1:27	וַיִּבְרָא אֱלֹהִים אֶת-הָאָדָם בְּצַלְמוֹ,	And Elohim created **the** **Person** in an image …

The strict meaning is definitely:

> God made/created **the Person** …

Only wilful or lax translation could render either Hebrew or Greek as:

> God created **man** …

Yet reliance on this second rendering, so widely espoused by so many and for so long, lies right at the heart of doctrine asserted by Jewish monotheists as well as by Christian teachers (it goes back at least to Philo in the first century CE). And those who embrace it will never understand what Jesus means in the gospel narrative when again and again he refers to himself as ὁ υἱὸς τοῦ ἀνθρώπου [*the son of the Person*]. For they rush to translate this as ***son of man*** - and do so despite the fact that they are hardly able to explain why Jesus should describe himself in this way. Then theirs is the problem identified in the gospels when Jesus is heard to make this assertion:

| Lk. 10:22 | πάντα μοι παρεδόθη ὑπὸ τοῦ πατρός μου, καὶ οὐδεὶς γινώσκει τίς ἐστιν ὁ υἱὸς εἰ μὴ ὁ πατήρ, καὶ τίς ἐστιν ὁ πατὴρ εἰ μὴ ὁ υἱὸς καὶ ᾧ ἐὰν βούληται ὁ υἱὸς ἀποκαλύψαι. | Everything was given away to me under my father. And no one knows who the son is except the father, and who the father is except the son and he to whom, if he should wish, the son may reveal (him). |

These resolute monothesists persistently conflate the '*heavenly person*' of Gn.1:27 with the '*dust person*' (known also in English as Adam) who is made by **God** at Gn.2:7 - **and in this way they make a double-edged mistake** (*qv.* Heb.4:12).

They seek to excuse themselves from recognising the introduction into scripture's plot of a second god, a second god who shortly turns out to be an evil impostor. And the only way they can find to escape from recognising this is so to mis-construe what has been written that they actually place *themselves* into the rôle configured by the authors for the evil god whose part in the narrative they prefer to deny.

Prompted by pride, such readers interpret scripture to say **that they themselves are made in the image of God**. Amongst the three Abrahamic religions, only Islam avoids this mistake. And could there be any greater mistake, any greater '*sin*'? As we shall see later, one component of the serpent's promise to the woman at Gn.3:4-5 is that ἔσεσθε ὡς θεοὶ [*you shall be like gods*]. And look! At Gn.3:13 the woman herself *admits* that she has been deceived. Is it not plain from this alone that the authors of scripture consider the serpent's promise a satanic deceit? Yet this same proposition resides at the very heart of what for so many centuries has been taught by the Christian church. If pride cometh before a fall then do not those who elevate themselves to the level of the gods risk an abrupt and dramatic descent?

The authors of scripture were clever. They have provided for their readers to face a choice. Some would restrain themselves. Taking good care over their reading, these would penetrate the mystery and understand it. The rest would rush in headlong, swallowing down the scriptural 'meal' without first examining the dish which was placed before them (*qv.* Pr.23:1-9). They would damn themselves through the unrestrained exercise of mortal pride. And plainly the authors knew that the first group would be *few*, but those in the second group *many* (*qv.* Mt.7:13-14).

Finally, those familiar with the *Documentary Hypothesis*, attributed usually to Wellhausen but now largely discredited, may suspect that it has served as a figleaf to help cover up a multitude of mistakes. But we shall not go into that here. Instead we shall return to the events detailed for **DAY 6**, and to the further instructions issued to the **lord god**, the 'Person' made in the image of a god:

Gn.	καὶ εἶπεν **ὁ θεός** ἰδοὺ δέδωκα	And **God** said "Look, I have
1:29	ὑμῖν **πᾶν χόρτον σπόριμον**	given to YOU [pl.] *every*
	σπεῖρον σπέρμα ὃ ἐστιν	*grass spreading seed to*
	ἐπάνω πάσης τῆς γῆς καὶ	*propagate which is above*
	πᾶν ξύλον ὃ ἔχει ἐν ἑαυτῷ	*all the earth*, and *every tree*
	καρπὸν σπέρματος	*which has within itself fruit*
	σπορίμου ὑμῖν ἔσται εἰς	*(having) seed to propagate*.
	βρῶσιν	For you it shall be for eating.
1:30	καὶ πᾶσι τοῖς θηρίοις τῆς γῆς	And to all the wild beasts of
	καὶ πᾶσι τοῖς πετεινοῖς τοῦ	the earth, and to all the birds
	οὐρανοῦ καὶ παντὶ ἑρπετῷ τῷ	of Heaven, and to every
	ἕρποντι ἐπὶ τῆς γῆς ὃ ἔχει ἐν	creeping thing that creeps
	ἑαυτῷ ψυχὴν ζωῆς πάντα	upon the earth (and) which
	χόρτον χλωρὸν εἰς **βρῶσιν**	has within it a soul of life, (I
	καὶ ἐγένετο οὕτως	have given) every (kind of)
		green grass for eating". And
		it happened like this.

On Day 3 we saw the earth bring forth:

> A grassy plant spreading seed after its kind and variety
> And a fruit-bearing tree making fruit of which its seed (is) within it

The events of Day 6 build on this, establishing a link with Day 3. For here at Gn.1:29 a diet is set for the **lord god**, the '**Person**' now made *in the image of God.*

The food source set by God for this '**Person**' is:

> Every grass spreading seed to propagate which is above all the earth, and every tree which has within itself fruit (having) seed to propagate.

A second god has been brought into being, made '*in the image*' of the first. The second therefore *resembles* the first. Inevitably the challenge now facing every reader is how to distinguish the two. And in the scheme configured by the authors the means to tell them apart is now to be found in their personal traits.

In scripture the first trait by which the **lord god** may be distinguished is his preference in food. For his diet is to be seed-bearing plants, or to be more exact, cereals and fruit.

Having regard to the list of foodstuffs which would have been known to the authors of *Genesis*, we can expect these cereal crops to include:

- σῖτος [*wheat; grain*]
- κριθῆ [*barley*]
- φακος [*lentil*]

- and trees bearing fruits to include:

- ἡ συκῆ [*the fig*]
- ἡ ἄμπελος [*the vine*]

Each of these foods features explicitly somewhere in the narrative of Genesis or the gospels. But a diet may extend to encompass derived foods. Under this heading we must identify also:

- ἄρτος [*bread*]
- οἶνος [*wine*]

This diet serves as a distinctive trait, not only for the **lord god** (of whom we shall learn more shortly), but for his subjects, those who seek to worship him or aspire to be like him.

As we shall see in the subsequent narrative, this diet distinguishes those who know only the **lord god** from those who know **God**, thus making it plain who's on which side. And since Gnostic tradition asserts that the second god resembles the first in appearance, indeed that he seeks to pass himself off *as if he were the first*, for us as readers this knowledge may prove vital. Indeed it provides a first key means by which we may penetrate what otherwise could remain for us *a mystery unresolved*.

Anyone familiar with scripture's narrative may already begin to perceive:

- What is the rôle played by the *fruit* tree placed in the midst of Paradise (LXX Gn.2:9)

- What Abraham should realise when he encounters the priest Melchizedek 'bringing forth *bread* and *wine*' (LXX Gn.14:18)

- Why Esau 'held cheap' his birthright (his 'first birth') by eating Jacob's *bread* and drinking the soup which Jacob has made from *lentils* (LXX Gn.25:34; see also Chapter 7 of this book)

- Why it was an effective 'sign' to the shepherds when they found the foetus lying in the *animal feed* trough (Lk.2:16)

- What is signified in the gospels when on the third day Jesus turns the contents of six water pots into *wine*, and this is identified as the '*beginning of the signs*' Jesus did (Jn.2:11)

- What is signified in the gospels when Jesus takes *bread* and *wine* (*qv. also* Jn.6:35, 15:1)

Clearly this diet of *cereals* and *fruit* has an important part to play in scripture. We shall shortly explore it further.

Meanwhile we should not forget the associated diet, that set at Gn.1:30 for those creatures now subordinate to **The Person**.

For:

- all the wild beasts of the earth

- all the birds of Heaven

- every creeping thing that creeps upon the earth (and) which has within it a soul of life

the diet is to be: **πάντα χόρτον χλωρὸν** [*every (kind of) green grass*].

Those familiar with the shortest of the four gospels may recall the crowd of those who behave '*like sheep without a shepherd*'.

Jesus bade them sit up:

> ... ἐπὶ τῷ χλωρῷ χόρτῳ   (Mk.6:39)
> ... upon the green grass

After which:

> ἔφαγον πάντες καὶ ἐχορτάσθησα   (Mk.6:42)
> All ate and were foddered

The word used here implies that they ate grass (or hay). But for those with Jesus a far more serious problem was imminent ...

> οὐ γὰρ συνῆκαν ἐπὶ τοῖς ἄρτοις   (Mk.6:52)
> For they did not understand about the breads

DAY 6 has been a momentous day. It has seen the materialisation of a second god, a contender to **God** himself. It is brought to a close in this way:

Gn.	καὶ εἶδεν ὁ **θεὸς** τὰ πάντα	And **God** saw everything that
1:31	ὅσα ἐποίησεν καὶ ἰδοὺ **καλὰ**	he made, and look:
	λίαν καὶ ἐγένετο ἑσπέρα καὶ	***exceedingly good***. And
	ἐγένετο πρωί ἡμέρα ἕκτη	evening happened, and
		morning happened:
		SIXTH DAY.

Notice how the established pattern of God's approval is disrupted. We have grown accustomed to hearing that '*God saw it as as good*'. But notice what is said here: notice too what is *not* said.

We are told that '*God saw everything that he made*'. But no statement is made to the effect that '*God saw it as as good*'. Instead we are told to '*Look ...*' *ie.* to look *for ourselves*.

Could this phrase **Καλὰ λίαν** [*exceedingly good*] conceal a multitude of sins? The word **λίαν** [*exceedingly*] crops up only twice in the whole Greek Pentateuch. It will only be used once more - and then explicitly of **ΚΑΙΝ** [*Cain*] at Gn.4:5.

Day 7

Gn.	καὶ συνετελέσθησαν ὁ	And they were completed,
2:1	οὐρανὸς καὶ ἡ γῆ καὶ πᾶς ὁ	Heaven and Earth, and all
	κόσμος αὐτῶν	the cosmos from them.
2:2	καὶ συνετέλεσεν ὁ **θεὸς** ἐν τῇ	And **God** finished on the
	ἡμέρᾳ τῇ ἕκτῃ τὰ ἔργα αὐτοῦ	SIXTH DAY his works which
	ἃ ἐποίησεν καὶ κατέπαυσεν	he made. And he ceased on
	τῇ ἡμέρᾳ τῇ ἑβδόμῃ ἀπὸ	the SEVENTH DAY from all
	πάντων τῶν ἔργων αὐτοῦ ὧν	his works which he made.
	ἐποίησεν	

| 2:3 | καὶ ηὐλόγησεν ὁ **θεὸς** τὴν ἡμέραν τὴν ἑβδόμην καὶ ἡγίασεν αὐτήν ὅτι ἐν αὐτῇ κατέπαυσεν ἀπὸ πάντων τῶν ἔργων αὐτοῦ ὧν ἤρξατο ὁ **θεὸς** ποιῆσαι | And **God** blessed the SEVENTH DAY and made it holy, because *within* it he ceased from all his works which **God** had begun to make. |

It was at Gn.1:1 that **God** created *Heaven and Earth*. At that point the earth was invisible and unformed. There was as yet no evil expressed.

By the end of **DAY 6** this original creation has been manipulated into the form of the cosmos, the ordered and structured world of light and of life.

To cap it all, the **lord god** has been brought into being and given charge over the cosmos. He is the second god. But he thinks of himself as the only god. Like **God**, he cannot be seen directly by humans. But he may be distinguished by the diet assigned to him.

With the dawn of **DAY 7** we see **God** cease from all his works. It is time to stop. For **God,** by introducing an evil contender, has taken already a step too far.

In this way the fictional scene is set, the underlying plot of scripture now configured. Good will now contend with evil on every page. This is why we shall need to pay close attention to what is written. For although in **God** there is no deceit, what is evil is free to masquerade as good.

We shall be put to the test with attempts at deceit, attempts for which scripture itself will be the medium. But we hold one essential 'key' which should keep us safe. This key is the diet which will permit us reliably to tell the two gods apart.

It will enable us to distinguish what has been set forth as evil from what has been set forth as good.

Chapter 5

The Book of Genesis
of Heaven and Earth

In this chapter we shall examine the important passage of scripture which runs from Gn.2:4 to Gn.4:26. It is designated '*The Book of Genesis of Heaven and Earth*'. The title associates it with *Heaven and Earth*, which at Gn.1:1 **God** himself has made. This makes it **God**'s 'own' book. If **God** is good then it should be free from explicit deceit. So to be properly informed, all that we have to do is read carefully, remember what we have read, and solve any riddles as we go.

It is worth pointing out that such a straightforward approach may no longer be wise once we come to the '*The Book of Genesis of Persons*' (Gn.5:1 seq.). That 'book' is associated by its title not with **God** but with the **lord god** (*aka*: '**the Persons**'; Gn.1:27). It is the **lord god**'s 'book'. It begins with an alternate version of events, a version which appears misconstrued as if to suit the perspective of this second god. From this point on we may need to guard against explicit misinformation in the narrative. In particular, we may need to watch out for a devious trick, the substitution of one god's name for the other.

Yet for now, within the limits of Gn.2:4 to Gn.4:26, it should be possible for us to rely strictly upon what is written. It is on that basis that we shall proceed.

The Dust Person

Gn.	αὕτη ἡ βίβλος γενέσεως	This (is) the Book of Genesis
2:4	οὐρανοῦ καὶ γῆς ὅτε ἐγένετο	of heaven and earth (at the time) when it happened.
	ᾗ ἡμέρᾳ ἐποίησεν **ὁ θεὸς** τὸν οὐρανὸν καὶ τὴν γῆν	On the day **God** made the heaven and the earth
2:5	καὶ πᾶν χλωρὸν ἀγροῦ πρὸ τοῦ γενέσθαι ἐπὶ τῆς γῆς καὶ πάντα χόρτον ἀγροῦ πρὸ τοῦ ἀνατεῖλαι	All (the) green of the field had yet to happen upon the earth, and all the grass of the field had yet to spring up.
	οὐ γὰρ ἔβρεξεν **ὁ θεὸς** ἐπὶ τὴν γῆν καὶ ἄνθρωπος οὐκ ἦν ἐργάζεσθαι τὴν γῆν	For **God** did *not* rain upon the earth and there was not a person to work the earth.
2:6	πηγὴ δὲ ἀνέβαινεν ἐκ τῆς γῆς καὶ ἐπότιζεν πᾶν τὸ πρόσωπον τῆς γῆς	But a spring came up from the earth and watered all the face of the earth.
2:7	καὶ ἔπλασεν **ὁ θεὸς** τὸν ἄνθρωπον χοῦν ἀπὸ τῆς γῆς καὶ ἐνεφύσησεν εἰς τὸ πρόσωπον αὐτοῦ πνοὴν ζωῆς καὶ ἐγένετο ὁ ἄνθρωπος εἰς ψυχὴν ζῶσαν	And **God** formed the dust person from the earth and breathed into his face a breath of life. And the person became a living soul.

We are told that '*God did not rain upon the earth*'. This might suggest that '*the water above heaven*' (Gn.1:7) was not under **God**'s control.

Instead '*a spring came up from the earth*' (ie. from *the water below*). **God** was now able to form the dust person and '*breathe into his face a breath of life*'. We notice that here **God** acts like κεραμεὺς [*a potter*].

Here is the first mortal creature to take human form. From Gn.2:16 this '*dust person*' will be known as Adam [Hebrew: *person*].

If **God** himself is good, so it seems is the '*dust person*' he makes. If the '*water below*' is also deemed good, this would explain the significance attached in the gospels to the '*baptism of John*' (*qv.* Jn.1:26; Ac.18:24-25).

Paradise and the Two Trees

Gn.	καὶ ἐφύτευσεν **κύριος ὁ θεὸς**	And **the 'lord god'** planted a
2:8	παράδεισον ἐν εδεμ κατὰ	paradise within Eden in the
	ἀνατολὰς καὶ ἔθετο ἐκεῖ τὸν	east - and placed there the
	ἄνθρωπον ὃν ἔπλασεν	person which **he** formed.
2:9	καὶ ἐξανέτειλεν **ὁ θεὸς** ἔτι ἐκ	And **God** made to grow, still
	τῆς γῆς πᾶν ξύλον ὡραῖον εἰς	from the earth, each tree that
	ὅρασιν καὶ καλὸν εἰς	is beautiful for looking at and
	βρῶσιν καὶ τὸ ξύλον τῆς	good for eating: BOTH *the*
	ζωῆς ἐν μέσῳ τῷ παραδείσῳ	*tree of life in the midst of*
	καὶ τὸ ξύλον τοῦ εἰδέναι	*Paradise* AND *the tree for*
	γνωστὸν καλοῦ καὶ πονηροῦ	*knowing knowledge of*
		good and evil.

This is where the **lord god** makes his first move. What he does is to '*plant a Paradise*'. This Persian word suggests a garden surrounded by a wall or hedge. There he places the 'person' which _he_ has formed. Who might this person be? The instruction given to the **lord god** at Gn.1:28 was:

> Grow and multiply and fill the earth and **LORD** over it. And rule (over) the fishes of the sea and (over) the birds of heaven - and (over) all the pastoral beasts and (over) all the earth - and (over) all the creeping things which creep upon the earth.

From this, and given how the narrative shortly develops, we may guess that the person the **lord god** has 'formed' is the serpent.

As for **God,** he produces two trees. He does not '*plant*' them (as the **lord god** might do) but makes them grow from the earth, much as he has done with Adam.

The trees are beautiful for looking at and good for eating. In the midst of Paradise is the 'tree of life'. Then we have the 'tree for knowing knowledge of good and evil'. From the clause structure here we may infer that this second tree is not in the middle of the garden; it may not be inside the garden at all.

The River with Four Branches

Gn.		
2:10	ποταμὸς δὲ ἐκπορεύεται ἐξ εδεμ ποτίζειν τὸν παράδεισον ἐκεῖθεν ἀφορίζεται εἰς τέσσαρας ἀρχάς	Now a river went out from Eden to water Paradise: from there it was parted into four branches.
2:11	ὄνομα τῷ ἑνὶ φισων οὗτος ὁ κυκλῶν πᾶσαν τὴν γῆν ευιλατ ἐκεῖ οὗ ἐστιν τὸ χρυσίον	The name for the one is Phison: this (is the one) encircling all the earth of Euilat, there from it is the gold.
2:12	τὸ δὲ χρυσίον τῆς γῆς ἐκείνης καλόν καὶ ἐκεῖ ἐστιν ὁ ἄνθραξ καὶ ὁ λίθος ὁ πράσινος	But the gold of that earth (appears?) good, and there is the coal [alt: the red stone] and the green stone.
2:13	καὶ ὄνομα τῷ ποταμῷ τῷ δευτέρῳ γηων οὗτος ὁ κυκλῶν πᾶσαν τὴν γῆν αἰθιοπίας	And a name for the second river, Geon: this (is the one) encircling all the earth of Ethiopia.
2:14	καὶ ὁ ποταμὸς ὁ τρίτος τίγρις οὗτος ὁ πορευόμενος κατέναντι ἀσσυρίων ὁ δὲ ποταμὸς ὁ τέταρτος οὗτος εὐφράτης	And the third river (is the) Tigris, the one going opposite Assyria. But the fourth river, this (is the) Euphrates.

| 2:15 | καὶ ἔλαβεν **κύριος ὁ θεὸς** τὸν ἄνθρωπον ὃν ἔπλασεν καὶ ἔθετο αὐτὸν ἐν τῷ παραδείσῳ ἐργάζεσθαι αὐτὸν καὶ φυλάσσειν | And **the lord god** took the person which he formed and placed him within Paradise to work it and to keep guard. |

The 'inserted' passage about the river serves to distract the reader at this point by interrupting narrative continuity. It is also obscure, having the appearance of a compound riddle. The river has four 'branches'. But trees have branches too; could this river somehow also be the *tree for knowing knowledge of good and evil*? It could be intended thus, for the passage about the river follows immediately upon the first mention of this tree. Perhaps we should notice too that the river went _out_ from Eden to water Paradise.

With the interruption done, the final verse repeats what was said at 2:8. If this refers to the serpent, his task is now *'to work the garden and to keep guard'*.

The Instruction given to Adam

| Gn. 2:16 | καὶ ἐνετείλατο **κύριος ὁ θεὸς** τῷ αδαμ λέγων ἀπὸ παντὸς ξύλου τοῦ ἐν τῷ παραδείσῳ βρώσει φάγῃ | And **the lord god** gave a command to Adam, saying "From each tree of those *within* Paradise you [*sg.*] may eat as food: |
| 2:17 | ἀπὸ δὲ τοῦ ξύλου τοῦ γινώσκειν καλὸν καὶ πονηρόν οὐ φάγεσθε ἀπ' αὐτοῦ ᾗ δ' ἂν ἡμέρᾳ φάγητε ἀπ' αὐτοῦ θανάτῳ ἀποθανεῖσθε | *But from the tree for knowing good and evil*, do not [*pl.*] eat from it. But then in the day that you [*pl.*] may eat from it, by death you [*pl.*] shall die". |

It is not **God** but the **lord god** who issues Adam with the prohibition here (and notice that this prohibition is never issued to the woman, for she as yet does not exist).

Adam is given explicit permission to eat from 'each tree of those *within* Paradise', a class which must include the tree *in the midst of Paradise*. So the **lord god** allows Adam to eat from the *tree of life*.

We can also deduce that the tree he forbids to Adam, the *tree for knowing good and evil*, cannnot be amongst those trees *inside* the garden. It follows that it must be located *outside* the garden, confirming the impression first given at 2:9.

Now Adam is told that if he defies the **lord god** and eats from this tree then "by death you will die"! If this is true then Adam's knowledge of his own mortality, his knowledge of the transience of his very existence, seems to be intimately entwined with the possibility of his acquiring the knowledge of good and evil.

More precisely, it seems that if Adam *were* to eat from this tree then he *would* learn to distinguish good from evil: but at the same time his mortality would be confirmed. It is in this way that the story seems to carry a strong moral punch, as valid today as it was when first written.

Before we move on we must ask what *motive* the **lord god** could have for instructing Adam not to eat from the *tree for knowing good and evil*.

Perhaps the **lord god** is evil himself. Then he seeks to prevent Adam eating from that 'tree' because he seeks to keep Adam from learning this vital fact?

It seems quite possible. Let us see how the narrative develops.

Interplay between the 'lord god' and God

Gn. 2:18	καὶ εἶπεν **κύριος ὁ θεός** οὐ καλὸν εἶναι τὸν ἄνθρωπον μόνον ποιήσωμεν αὐτῷ βοηθὸν κατ' αὐτόν	And **the lord god** said "It is not good for the person to be alone. Let us make for him a helper like him".
2:19	καὶ ἔπλασεν **ὁ θεὸς** ἔτι ἐκ τῆς γῆς πάντα τὰ θηρία τοῦ ἀγροῦ καὶ πάντα τὰ πετεινὰ τοῦ οὐρανοῦ καὶ ἤγαγεν αὐτὰ πρὸς τὸν αδαμ ἰδεῖν τί καλέσει αὐτά καὶ πᾶν ὃ ἐὰν ἐκάλεσεν αὐτὸ αδαμ ψυχὴν ζῶσαν τοῦτο ὄνομα αὐτοῦ	And **God** formed, still from the earth, all the wild beasts of the field and all the birds of Heaven. And he brought them to Adam to see what he would call them. And, (for) each one, if Adam called it 'living soul', that (was) its name.
2:20	καὶ ἐκάλεσεν αδαμ ὀνόματα πᾶσιν τοῖς κτήνεσιν καὶ πᾶσι τοῖς πετεινοῖς τοῦ οὐρανοῦ καὶ πᾶσι τοῖς θηρίοις τοῦ ἀγροῦ τῷ δὲ αδαμ οὐχ εὑρέθη βοηθὸς ὅμοιος αὐτῷ	And Adam called names for all the pastoral beasts and for all the birds of Heaven and for all the wild beasts of the field. But for Adam there was not found a helper similar to him.

Here it is the **lord god** who states that "It is not good for the person to be alone" and (with a suggestion of divine co-operation) "Let *us* make for him a helper like him".

Yet it is **God** who forms (still from the earth) sundry creatures and Adam who names them all. But none was found similar to Adam.

The first woman

Gn. 2:21	καὶ ἐπέβαλεν **ὁ θεὸς** ἔκστασιν ἐπὶ τὸν αδαμ καὶ ὕπνωσεν καὶ ἔλαβεν μίαν τῶν πλευρῶν αὐτοῦ καὶ ἀνεπλήρωσεν σάρκα ἀντ' αὐτῆς	And **God** threw a trance upon Adam and he slept: and he took one of his ribs and filled up flesh in exchange for it.
2:22	καὶ ᾠκοδόμησεν **κύριος ὁ θεὸς** τὴν <u>πλευράν</u> ἣν ἔλαβεν ἀπὸ τοῦ αδαμ εἰς γυναῖκα καὶ ἤγαγεν αὐτὴν πρὸς τὸν αδαμ	And **the lord god** built the <u>rib</u> which he took from Adam into a woman, and brought her to Adam.

God takes one of Adam's ribs. The **lord god** then intervenes: it is he who builds the rib into a woman, bringing her to Adam.

In Greek the rib is **πλευράν**. The **lord god** builds it into **a person**. In Greek each letter of the alphabet doubles to serve as a number. The **ἀριθμὸς** [*number value*] for **πλευράν** is derived as follows:

$$\begin{array}{ccccccc} \pi & \lambda & \epsilon & \upsilon & \rho & \acute{\alpha} & \nu \\ 80 + & 30 + & 5 + & 400 + & 100 + & 1 + & 50 = 666 \end{array}$$

Attention should be drawn here to what is stated in the NT book of *Revelation*:

Rv. 13:18	ὧδε ἡ σοφία ἐστίν: ὁ ἔχων νοῦν ψηφισάτω τὸν ἀριθμὸν τοῦ θηρίου, ἀριθμὸς γὰρ **ἀνθρώπου** ἐστίν:	Here is Wisdom. The one having an intellect, let him calculate the number of the beast, for it is the number *of a person*.
	καὶ ὁ ἀριθμὸς αὐτοῦ ἑξακόσιοι ἑξήκοντα ἕξ.	And its number (is) *six hundred* (and) *sixty six*.

The one responsible for making the *rib* into '*a person*' was the **lord god**. And if the connotation here is a trifle sinister perhaps we should not be surprised. For here is Wisdom. And is it not a core purpose of Wisdom to teach the discerning reader how to distinguish what is good from what is evil?

Finally, it may be worth noting that whereas the word τριάκοντα [*thirty*] provides all the characters we need to spell out the name of Κάϊν [*Cain*], the word πεντάκις [*five times*] provides not only these letters but has in addition a number value derived as follows:

$$\pi \quad \varepsilon \quad \nu \quad \tau \quad \alpha \quad \kappa \quad \iota \quad \varsigma$$
$$80 + 5 + 50 + 300 + 1 + 20 + 10 + 200 = 666$$

Adam recognises the woman

Gn.	καὶ εἶπεν αδαμ τοῦτο νῦν	And Adam said "This now (is)
2:23	ὀστοῦν ἐκ τῶν ὀστέων μου	bone out of my bones and
	καὶ σὰρξ ἐκ τῆς σαρκός μου	flesh out of my flesh. She
	αὕτη κληθήσεται γυνή ὅτι ἐκ	shall be called woman
	τοῦ ἀνδρὸς αὐτῆς ἐλήμφθη	because out of her man she
	αὕτη	was taken"
2:24	ἕνεκεν τούτου καταλείψει	On account of this, a person
	ἄνθρωπος τὸν πατέρα αὐτοῦ	shall leave his father and his
	καὶ τὴν μητέρα αὐτοῦ καὶ	mother, and he shall be
	προσκολληθήσεται πρὸς τὴν	glued to his woman, and they
	γυναῖκα αὐτοῦ καὶ ἔσονται οἱ	shall be the two into one
	δύο εἰς σάρκα μίαν	flesh.
2:25	καὶ ἦσαν οἱ δύο γυμνοί ὅ τε	And they were, the two (of
	αδαμ καὶ ἡ γυνὴ αὐτοῦ καὶ	them), naked, both Adam
	οὐκ ᾐσχύνοντο	and his woman, and they
		were not ashamed.

The woman is flesh and bone, derived from Adam himself.

In Hebrew a play upon words emerges here in much the same way as it does in English (where wo*man* is derived from ***man***). But in Greek this link is lost because the words for *man* and *woman* have different roots.

The Wily Serpent ... and *his* Tree

Gn. 3:1	ὁ δὲ ὄφις ἦν φρονιμώτατος πάντων τῶν θηρίων τῶν ἐπὶ τῆς γῆς ὧν ἐποίησεν **κύριος ὁ θεός**	But the serpent was the most sagacious of all the wild beasts, of those (going) upon the earth, which **the lord god** made.
	καὶ εἶπεν ὁ ὄφις τῇ γυναικὶ τί ὅτι εἶπεν **ὁ θεός** οὐ μὴ φάγητε ἀπὸ παντὸς ξύλου τοῦ ἐν τῷ παραδείσῳ	And the serpent said to the woman "What (was it) that **God** said? 'You [pl.] may not eat from any tree within Paradise' ?"
3:2	καὶ εἶπεν ἡ γυνὴ τῷ ὄφει ἀπὸ καρποῦ ξύλου τοῦ παραδείσου φαγόμεθα	And the woman said to the serpent "From (the) fruit of a tree of Paradise we may eat,
3:3	ἀπὸ δὲ καρποῦ <u>τοῦ ξύλου ὅ ἐστιν ἐν μέσῳ τοῦ παραδείσου</u> εἶπεν **ὁ θεός** οὐ φάγεσθε ἀπ' αὐτοῦ οὐδὲ μὴ ἅψησθε αὐτοῦ ἵνα μὴ ἀποθάνητε	But from (the) fruit <u>*of the tree which is in the midst of Paradise*</u>, **God** said 'Do not [pl.] eat from it, nor may you [pl.] touch it so that you [pl.] might not die' " [*ie.* in order to avoid dying]

Superlatives are rarely found in scripture. But ὁ ὄφις [*the serpent*] is declared up front as φρονιμώτατος [*most sagacious*] amongst all the wild beasts which the **lord god** made to go upon the earth. Even his name may be formed from the description assigned to him ... as φρΟνΙμώτατος (nominative) or as φρΟνΙμώτατος (accusative).

In all that is now to follow it appears that the serpent and his maker work together as one. We should be on our guard.

The serpent addresses to the woman an innocent question: '*What was it that God said?*'. Much has been written about this question, and much misunderstood. The serpent asks what **God** has said.

His question does not allude to Adam's encounter at Gn.2:16. For this encounter was with the **lord god**, and when it took place the woman did not exist. So to what encounter does the question allude? Indeed what *has* **God** said to the woman? We are not informed directly. Instead we have the woman's report. She informs the serpent that **God** has permitted eating the fruit of a tree of Paradise but prohibited:

- Eating from the fruit of the tree in the midst of Paradise
- Touching this same tree with the intention to avoid dying

So this is the position:

- The **lord god** has told Adam that he may eat from any tree *within* the garden, but not from the *tree for knowing knowledge of good and evil*.

- **God** seems to have told the woman that she may eat from a tree of the garden, but not from the tree *in the midst* of the garden (this is the one we know as the *tree of life*; *qv.* Gn.2:9).

The **lord god** has told Adam not to eat from one tree; and it would seem that subsequently **God** has told the woman not to eat from the other tree.

In other words the 'impostor' has told Adam not to eat from the tree which, although it conveys knowledge of good and evil, precludes any life beyond death. But **God** (who we may think of as good) has told the woman not to touch the more alluring tree, the *tree of life* in the midst of Paradise.

The Tree of Life

Gn.	καὶ εἶπεν ὁ ὄφις τῇ γυναικί οὐ	And the serpent said to the
3:4	θανάτῳ ἀποθανεῖσθε	woman "By death you [pl.]
		shall not die

3:5	ᾔδει γὰρ ὁ θεὸς ὅτι ἐν ᾗ ἂν	For **God** knows that in the
	ἡμέρᾳ φάγητε ἀπ' αὐτοῦ	day you [pl.] may eat from it,
	διανοιχθήσονται ὑμῶν οἱ	your eyes shall be opened
	ὀφθαλμοὶ καὶ ἔσεσθε ὡς θεοὶ	up, AND you [pl.] shall be like
	γινώσκοντες καλὸν καὶ	gods, knowing good and
	πονηρόν	evil".

The encounter between the woman and the serpent clearly takes place inside the garden. For back at Gn.2:15 we were told that:

> ... **the lord god** took the person which _he_ formed
> and placed him _within_ Paradise to work it and to keep guard.

Yet we have concluded already that the _tree for knowing knowledge of good and evil_ must be _outside_ the garden.

It follows (quite contrary to the standard explanation advanced by the Christian church) that the tree from which the woman takes the fruit to eat _must be the tree of life_. This readily explains the first part of the serpent's tempting suggestion that:

- By death you shall not die ...

And the serpent goes on to claim that:

> **God** knows that in the day you may eat from it
> - your eyes shall be opened up
> - you shall be like gods, knowing good and evil

The promises made by the serpent are those betokened by the _tree of life_. They are attractive to many, there can be no doubt of that. But are they good? That is the really important question.

The Woman takes the fruit ...

Gn. 3:6	καὶ εἶδεν ἡ γυνὴ ὅτι καλὸν τὸ ξύλον εἰς βρῶσιν καὶ ὅτι ἀρεστὸν τοῖς ὀφθαλμοῖς ἰδεῖν καὶ ὡραῖόν ἐστιν τοῦ κατανοῆσαι καὶ λαβοῦσα τοῦ καρποῦ αὐτοῦ ἔφαγεν καὶ ἔδωκεν καὶ τῷ ἀνδρὶ αὐτῆς μετ' αὐτῆς καὶ ἔφαγον	And the woman saw the tree as good for <u>eating</u> and as agreeable <u>with</u> the <u>eyes</u> to see, and (that) it is beautiful for understanding fully. And taking (some) of its fruit, she ate. And she gave (some) also to her man with her, and they ate.
3:7	καὶ διηνοίχθησαν οἱ ὀφθαλμοὶ τῶν δύο καὶ ἔγνωσαν ὅτι γυμνοὶ ἦσαν	And the eyes of the two *were* opened up, and ***they learned to know*** that they were naked.
	καὶ ἔρραψαν φύλλα συκῆς καὶ ἐποίησαν ἑαυτοῖς περιζώματα	And they stitched leaves of a fig, and made for themselves aprons.

The woman sees the tree placed in the charge of ὁ ὄφις [*the serpent*] as:

καλὸν ... εἰς βρῶσιν [good for <u>eating</u>]

and as:

ἀρεστὸν τοῖς ὀφθαλμοῖς ἰδεῖν [agreeable <u>with the eyes</u> to see]

In the chapters which follow we shall return to the significance of what there is 'to see' in this passage and how it is echoed in subsequent scripture. Beyond a doubt the authors of Greek scripture were comprehensively clever in every facet of their work, including what they have done here.

The woman takes the fruit, and she eats. She gives some also to her man with her - and they (both) eat. To do this has been forbidden to the woman by **God**: but to Adam it has not been expressly forbidden.

As for the serpent's promise, their eyes are opened up. But the remainder of the promise proves a shallow deceit: for at this point all that they actually '*learn to know*' is that they are naked. It is the manifest trait of the serpent!

Retaining as a working hypothesis the notion that **God** is good but the **lord god** is evil, we may summarise the position as follows:

- The woman reports that she was told by **God** not to eat from the tree in the midst of Paradise, nor to touch it with intent to survive her own death. This tree is the *tree of life*.

- But her evil inclination leaves her vulnerable to the deceitful suggestion of the serpent, the agent (or manifestation) of the **lord god**.

- With her choice to eat from this tree, the woman disobeys **God**. Her 'sin', in seeking for herself the immortal status of a god, is presumably inspired by her difficulty in coming to terms with her own mortality. Yet this too is the sin of human pride.

- As for Adam, it was the **lord god** who charged him, on pain of death, not to eat from the *tree for knowing knowledge of good and evil*.

- And Adam has done no wrong by sharing with the woman the fruit from the *tree of life*. For to him this was not forbidden.

The Woman Deceived, but Adam NOT

Gn.	καὶ ἤκουσαν τὴν φωνὴν	And they heard the voice of
3:8	**κυρίου τοῦ θεοῦ**	**the lord god** walking about
	περιπατοῦντος ἐν τῷ	in Paradise towards evening.
	παραδείσῳ τὸ δειλινόν καὶ	And they were hidden, both
	ἐκρύβησαν ὅ τε αδαμ καὶ ἡ	Adam and his woman, from a
	γυνὴ αὐτοῦ ἀπὸ προσώπου	face of **the lord god** in the
	κυρίου τοῦ θεοῦ ἐν μέσῳ τοῦ	midst of the tree of Paradise
	ξύλου τοῦ παραδείσου	
3:9	καὶ ἐκάλεσεν **κύριος ὁ θεὸς**	And **the lord god** called
	τὸν αδαμ καὶ εἶπεν αὐτῷ	Adam and said to him
	αδαμ ποῦ εἶ	"Adam, where are you?"
3:10	καὶ εἶπεν αὐτῷ τὴν φωνήν	And he said to him "I heard
	σου ἤκουσα περιπατοῦντος	your voice walking about in
	ἐν τῷ παραδείσῳ καὶ	Paradise. And I was afraid
	ἐφοβήθην ὅτι γυμνός εἰμι καὶ	because I am naked and I
	ἐκρύβην	was hidden".
3:11	καὶ εἶπεν αὐτῷ τίς ἀνήγγειλέν	And he said to him "Who
	σοι ὅτι γυμνὸς εἶ μὴ ἀπὸ τοῦ	announced to you that you
	ξύλου οὗ ἐνετειλάμην σοι	are naked? Surely you did
	τούτου μόνου μὴ φαγεῖν ἀπ'	not eat from the tree of which
	αὐτοῦ ἔφαγες	I commanded you 'Of this
		alone not to eat from it'? "
3:12	καὶ εἶπεν ὁ αδαμ ἡ γυνή ἦν	And Adam said "The woman
	ἔδωκας μετ' ἐμοῦ αὕτη μοι	whom you gave (to be) with
	ἔδωκεν ἀπὸ τοῦ ξύλου καὶ	me, she gave to me from the
	ἔφαγον	tree, and I ate."

| 3:13 | καὶ εἶπεν **κύριος ὁ θεὸς** τῇ γυναικί τί τοῦτο ἐποίησας καὶ εἶπεν ἡ γυνή ὁ ὄφις ἠπάτησέν με καὶ ἔφαγον | And **the lord god** said to the woman "What (is) this you did?". And the woman said "The serpent deceived me and I ate". |

At Gn.3:8 both Adam and his woman were '*hidden from a face of the lord god in the midst of the tree of Paradise*'. The passage reeks of obscurity.

Given his diet prescribed at Gn.1:29, the **lord god** has a natural interest in all that is connected with sowing and with seed. Then the mysterious 'person' made by the **lord god** (this seems to be the serpent) has been charged with 'working' and 'guarding' the garden of Paradise (LXX Gn.2:8 =>2:15).

Could it be that the 'face' of the **lord god**, which at Gn.3:8 is hidden in the midst of the tree 'παραδείσου' [*of paradise*], is intended to be ὁ σπείρας [*the one sowing*]? If so, the letters for the second word have been 'scattered' (or dispersed) within the first. Perhaps this should not surprise us. Scattering that which disappears, later to re-emerge, is precisely what does happen with seeds. It *is* the method of the sower. Does the same thing happen here with the letters of the Greek alphabet?

In the gospels, as part of the parable of the sower at Mt.13:39, an 'enemy' identified as ὁ σπείρας [*the one sowing*] is explicitly equated with ὁ διάβολος [*the devil*]. Moreover the ἀριθμὸς [*number value*] for ὁ σπείρας is derived as follows:

$$\text{ὁ} \quad \text{σ} \quad \text{π} \quad \text{ε} \quad \text{ι} \quad \text{ρ} \quad \text{α} \quad \text{ς}$$
$$70 + 200 + 80 + 5 + 10 + 100 + 1 + 200 = 666$$

Now at Gn.3:10 both Adam and his woman hear the voice of the **lord god** 'περιπατοῦντος' [*walking about*]. Again περιπατοῦντος could suggest ὁ σπείρας [*the one sowing*]. Adam, it seems, may be good at finding what has been hidden. For it is Adam, and not the woman, who upon hearing the 'voice' of the lord god responds by reporting that he is afraid (Gn.3:10). This rather suggests that Adam knows, or has recognised, who the **lord god** is.

The **lord god** now says to Adam:

> Who announced to you that you are naked? Surely you did not eat from the tree of which I commanded you 'Of this alone not to eat from it' ?

Remember, it was from the *tree for knowing knowledge of good and evil* that the **lord god** instructed Adam not to eat (Gn.2:17). So with this question we have the first indication that Adam actually *has* disobeyed the **lord god** in eating also from this tree. Yet Adam gives nothing away when he replies:

> The woman whom you gave (to be) with me, she gave to me from the tree - and I ate.

As noted already, there is for Adam no offence in eating the fruit from the *tree of life*. Nothing suggests that eating this fruit is forbidden to him and he does not touch the tree itself.

Nor is it wrong for Adam to 'eat' from the other tree, the *tree for knowing the knowledge of good and evil*. By doing this he 'disobeys cunning to choose the good', the theme made explicit at LXX Is.7:16. He does not disobey **God**. He disobeys the **lord god**, the deity who seeks to deny him knowledge of good and evil, the 'second god' who tries to keep secret the knowledge that he himself is neither 'good' nor **God**.

The action of Adam in eating from this second 'tree' is fundamentally heroic.

How curious it is, and how disconcerting, that the Christian church should uphold a doctrine which asserts that Adam and Eve were equally guilty of the gravest sin when *both* of them disobeyed **God** to eat from the *tree for knowing the knowledge of good and evil*. The church has made this assertion since at least the time of Augustine of Hippo (end of 4th century CE). It goes on to claim that all of human kind is blighted from birth by the consequences of this ***Original Sin***.

On the basis of what we have reasoned here, this claim appears to be the result of a most serious misunderstanding. Perhaps it illustrates the depth of the mire into which they fall who succumb (even today) to the wiles attributed in scripture to the 'serpent', that ardently monotheist reptile who would have you recognise the **lord god** as if he were the only god.

In the narrative at Gn.3:13 the woman says: '*The serpent deceived me and I ate*'. But how many others have been deceived by the serpent's attractive promise? The entire membership of the Christian church? For almost two millennia?

The proposals on the next page follow those set forth in a Roman Catholic instructional text (approved 1971):

A CATECHISM OF CHRISTIAN DOCTRINE
FAITH
Chapter One

1. Who made you?

   God made me.

2. Why did God make you?

   God made me to know Him, love Him and serve Him in this world, and be happy with Him forever in the next. (See Qu. 169, 320, 336, 339, etc.)

3. To whose image and likeness did God make you?

   God made me to his own image and likeness.

4. Is this likeness to God in your body, or in your soul?

   This likeness to God is chiefly in my soul.

5. How is your soul like to God?

   My soul is like to God because it is a spirit, and is immortal.

6. What do you mean when you say that your soul is immortal?

   When I say my soul is immortal, **I mean that my soul can never die.**

7. Of which must you take most care, of your body or of your soul?

   I must take most care of my soul; for Christ has said, 'What doth it profit a man if he gain the whole world, and suffer the loss of his own soul?' Matt. 16:26 (In Catholic theology, the soul and body are not opposed to each other. **The human body is a temple of the Holy Spirit, made to the image and likeness of God.** Salvation is for the whole person, both body and soul.)

Is it not clear that the essentials of doctrine asserted here match closely those deployed by the serpent to deceive the woman at Gn.3:4-5?

It is a vital point which seems to have been widely missed.

In the gospels we hear Jesus repeat the assertions first made by the serpent to the woman. The scenarios depicted at Jn.4:14 and Jn.11:26 reproduce that at Gn.3:4. The Christian church repeats these promises in its turn. Yet the promise of eternal life remains what it always was, the message by which the woman was deceived.

So what appears to have happened is this. Scripture itself has served down the centuries as the vehicle for repeating the serpent's promise, delivering Satan's attractive delusion '*to the whole world*', just as suggested at Rv.12:9. Later in this book we shall see how this development has been assisted by the church's failure to recognise the identity which the authors of scripture assign to Jesus. For in attempting to explain why the message of the church matches that of the serpent we are met with a total impasse until at last we succeed in penetrating the 'mystery' of scripture and learn who Jesus is set forth to be.

The Roman Catholic church has yet to penetrate the 'mystery' embodied in the scriptures upon which it seeks to rely. This is why the serpent's deceitful claim has been echoed and promoted so consistently by the church itself. The Protestant and Reformed churches have laboured under an identical burden; for they too have proved incapable of solving the riddles in scripture.

In summary, the Christian church asserts that man is made in the image of God. It proceeds to extend to its members the promise of eternal life. But these claims match the assertion made to the woman by the fictional serpent ... who in scripture is held to be Satan, *the deceiver of the whole world.*

The attractive but illusory assertion advanced by Satan is this:

- **By death you shall not die ...**

For **God** knows that in the day you may eat from it:

- Your eyes shall be opened up and

- **You shall be like gods**, knowing good and evil.

The lord god curses the serpent

Gn. 3:14	καὶ εἶπεν **κύριος ὁ θεὸς** τῷ ὄφει ὅτι ἐποίησας τοῦτο ἐπικατάρατος σὺ ἀπὸ πάντων τῶν κτηνῶν καὶ ἀπὸ πάντων τῶν θηρίων τῆς γῆς ἐπὶ τῷ στήθει σου καὶ τῇ κοιλίᾳ πορεύσῃ καὶ γῆν φάγῃ πάσας τὰς ἡμέρας τῆς ζωῆς σου	And **the lord god** said to the serpent "Because you made/did this, cursed (are) you from all the pastoral beasts and from all the wild beasts of the earth. Upon your chest and belly shall you go, and eat earth all the days of your life.
3:15	καὶ ἔχθραν θήσω ἀνὰ μέσον σου καὶ ἀνὰ μέσον τῆς γυναικὸς καὶ ἀνὰ μέσον τοῦ σπέρματός σου καὶ ἀνὰ μέσον τοῦ σπέρματος αὐτῆς αὐτός σου τηρήσει κεφαλήν καὶ σὺ τηρήσεις αὐτοῦ πτέρναν	And I shall put enmity amidst you and amidst the woman, and amidst your seed and amidst her seed. He shall watch you for a head, and you shall watch him for a heel".
3:16	καὶ τῇ γυναικὶ εἶπεν πληθύνων πληθυνῶ τὰς λύπας σου καὶ τὸν στεναγμόν σου ἐν λύπαις τέξῃ τέκνα καὶ πρὸς τὸν ἄνδρα σου ἡ ἀποστροφή σου καὶ αὐτός σου **κυριεύσει**	And to the woman he said, "Multiplying, I shall multiply your sorrows and your sighing. In sorrows you shall bring forth children. And your recourse shall be towards your man, and **he shall lord** (it over) you".

In the first chapter of this book we noted how Jewish tradition claims of the serpent that prior to this punishment "*Like a man, he stood upright upon two feet, and in height he was equal to the camel*". It is here that the serpent is cursed, to go on his chest and upon his belly, and eat earth all the days of his life.

The verse at Gn.3:15 is often mistranslated. The offspring of the woman and the offspring of the serpent are now to be set at enmity. The informed reader of subsequent scripture is to 'watch out' for **κεφαλήν** [*a head*] as a sign for the serpent; any offspring of the serpent must 'watch out' for **πτέρναν** [*a heel*].

The riddle configured here is deployed unerringly at several subsequent locations in scripture. One is at the birth of Esau and Jacob where the *heel* of Esau is poised over the *head* of Jacob (Gn.25:26). Another is in the narrative of the fourth gospel where Jesus washes the feet of his student Peter (Jn.13:3-18). There the *heel* of Peter is raised above the *head* of Jesus (it is in solving this riddle that the true character of Jesus is disclosed to the reader; see Chapter 11 of this book). This *heel over head* metaphor is widely recognised to this day in the secular cultures of the Middle East.

Finally the woman is to bring forth children in sorrows, and her man will ***lord it*** over her.

The lord god speaks to Adam and curses the earth

Gn.	τῷ δὲ αδαμ εἶπεν ὅτι ἤκουσας	But to Adam he said
3:17	τῆς φωνῆς τῆς γυναικός σου καὶ ἔφαγες ἀπὸ τοῦ ξύλου οὗ ἐνετειλάμην σοι τούτου μόνου μὴ φαγεῖν ἀπ' αὐτοῦ ἐπικατάρατος ἡ γῆ ἐν τοῖς ἔργοις σου ἐν λύπαις φάγῃ αὐτὴν πάσας τὰς ἡμέρας τῆς ζωῆς σου	"Because you listened to the *voice* of your woman, and you ate from the tree of which *I* commanded you 'From this alone not to eat from it', accursed (is) the earth in your works. In sorrows you shall eat it [*earth*] all the days of your life.
3:18	ἀκάνθας καὶ τριβόλους ἀνατελεῖ σοι καὶ φάγῃ τὸν χόρτον τοῦ ἀγροῦ	Thorns and thistles [*alt:* caltrops] it shall raise up for you, and you shall eat the grass of the field.

3:19	ἐν ἱδρῶτι τοῦ προσώπου σου φάγῃ τὸν ἄρτον σου ἕως τοῦ ἀποστρέψαι σε εἰς τὴν γῆν ἐξ ἧς ἐλήμφθης ὅτι γῆ εἶ καὶ εἰς γῆν ἀπελεύσῃ	In the sweat of your face you shall eat your bread until your return to the earth from which you were taken. For you are earth, and to earth you shall return".
3:20	καὶ ἐκάλεσεν αδαμ τὸ ὄνομα τῆς γυναικὸς αὐτοῦ ζωή ὅτι αὕτη μήτηρ πάντων τῶν ζώντων	And Adam called the name of his woman Zoe, because she (was) mother of all the living.

Adam *has* listened to the voice of his woman. In the narrative she has spoken twice. The first time she said:

> From (the) fruit of a tree of Paradise we may eat, but from (the) fruit *of the tree which is in the midst of Paradise*, **God** said 'Do not eat from it, nor may you touch it so that you might not die'

Later she said:

> The serpent deceived me and I ate.

With her first message the woman reported what **God** said to her. Seduced by the serpent, she then disobeyed **God**. When she spoke a second time it was to admit that she had been deceived.

Adam, it seems, has heard what she said. The tree in the midst of Paradise was the *tree of life* (Gn.2:9). Adam has not sought to survive his own death by touching this central tree. Perhaps, from the woman's report, he realises that to do this is what **God** himself forbids.

It is now that the **lord god** draws attention to the fact that Adam has actually eaten from the *other* tree, the tree the **lord god** forbade to him, the *tree for knowing knowledge of good and evil*. In doing so Adam has disobeyed. But all he has done is to disobey the **lord god**. And to disobey an evil god (who seeks, with his prohibition, to keep you from knowing that he is evil) is truly to act in a way which is good.

Adam has passed the test which was set for him: and any person who reads scripture with care may do the same.

Notice that the **lord god** does not curse Adam. Instead he curses the earth from which Adam was taken. It will produce thorns and thistles. Adam is to eat grass, and eat bread only '*in the sweat from his face*', until his return to the earth.

As for the woman, deluded and cursed by her folly, Adam calls her ζωή [*Zoe; life*]. For she is to be *mother of all the living*.

God himself confirms that Adam does know Good & Evil

Gn.		
3:21	καὶ ἐποίησεν **κύριος ὁ θεὸς** τῷ αδαμ καὶ τῇ γυναικὶ αὐτοῦ χιτῶνας δερματίνους καὶ ἐνέδυσεν αὐτούς	And **the lord god** made for Adam and for his woman skin tunics (under-garments), and put them on.
3:22	καὶ εἶπεν **ὁ θεὸς** ἰδοὺ αδαμ γέγονεν ὡς εἷς ἐξ ἡμῶν τοῦ γινώσκειν καλὸν καὶ πονηρόν καὶ νῦν μήποτε ἐκτείνῃ τὴν χεῖρα καὶ λάβῃ τοῦ ξύλου τῆς ζωῆς καὶ φάγῃ καὶ ζήσεται εἰς τὸν αἰῶνα	And **God** said "Look, Adam has become alike to one of us ... for knowing good and evil. And now, lest perhaps he should put forth the hand, and take of the tree of life and eat, and live in the Aiona ..."
3:23	καὶ ἐξαπέστειλεν αὐτὸν **κύριος ὁ θεὸς** ἐκ τοῦ παραδείσου τῆς τρυφῆς ἐργάζεσθαι τὴν γῆν ἐξ ἧς ἐλήμφθη	And **the lord god** sent him out from Paradise of luxury ... to work the earth from which he was taken.

3:24	καὶ ἐξέβαλεν τὸν αδαμ καὶ	And he threw out Adam and
	κατῴκισεν αὐτὸν ἀπέναντι	settled him down opposite
	τοῦ παραδείσου τῆς τρυφῆς	Paradise of luxury. And he
	καὶ ἔταξεν τὰ χερουβιμ καὶ	set in place the Cherubim,
	τὴν φλΟγίνην ρΟμφαίαν	and 'the flaming sword which
	τὴν στρεφομένην φυλάσσειν	turned' to guard the way of
	τὴν ὁδὸν τοῦ ξύλου τῆς ζωῆς	the tree of life.

The **lord god** makes skin tunics for Adam and for his woman … and puts them on (the significance of this is somewhat obscure and we shall not go into it here).

Now **God** himself observes:

> Look, Adam *has* become alike to one of us *for knowing good and evil*.

It is the final confirmation, this time from **God** himself, of Adam's achievement. He *has* learned to distinguish good from evil. Then he must have 'eaten' from the *tree for knowing knowledge of good and evil*. **God** goes on to make this complementary observation:

> And now, lest perhaps he *should* put forth the hand, and take of the tree of life and eat, and live in the Aiona …

The *Aiona* is the eternal realm of the gods. The implication is that Adam has not followed the example of the woman (in her quest to be like a god and to live for ever) by taking for himself the illusory 'fruit' from the *tree of life*.

Here is the position of Adam:

- He was made by **God** from the earth.

- He knows **God**, which makes Adam **good**.

- He has established the truth: he will return to the earth from which he was made.

- And he knows it, which is **good**.

- In Adam there is no pride.

The position of the woman is:

- She was made by the **lord god** from Adam's rib.

- She thinks the **lord god** is God.

- She is deluded: she thinks she will be like a god and live for ever (which can only be done on Satan's terms).

Outwitted, the **lord god** proceeds to expel Adam from Paradise to work the earth from which he was taken … setting in place all that will guard the way to the troublesome *tree of life*, the tree forbidden by **God**.

Those with a keen eye for the Greek at 3:24 (above) may see the letter **φ** repeated five times … and may glimpse ὄφιν [*a serpent*], somehow concealed in the '*flaming sword*'.

The respective rôles of Adam & Eve are summarised in this Table:

	Tree of Life (in the midst of the garden)	Tree of Knowing the Knowledge of Good and Evil
Adam	He joins with Eve in eating from the fruit of this tree (3:6).	The **lord god** instructs him not to eat from this tree, warning he will die if he does so (2:17).
	But there is no indication he has touched the tree. Nor was he ever forbidden to eat from its fruit, so this for him is no offence.	Yet we infer that he does eat from it (3:17, 3:22). He has disobeyed the **lord god**. But he was right to do so because the **lord god** is evil (therefore seeks to keep Adam from learning to distinguish good from evil).
Eve	She says she was instructed by **God** not to eat from this tree, neither touch it with intent to avoid death (3:3). But the serpent asserts (3:4-5) that if she does eat from it: • She will not die • Her eyes will be opened up • She will become like a god, knowing good and evil Persuaded by the serpent, she *does* touch this tree and she *does* eat from it (3:6). Overcome by her evil desires, she has been tricked. She has disobeyed **God**. Later she admits she has been deceived (3:13).	She was never forbidden to eat from this tree. This is what she might have done, were it not for her flawed nature (at 2:22 she was built by the **lord god** from Adam's rib).

The analysis of the story we have drawn out here may appear disturbing to many if only because a different solution has long been upheld by the Christian church. Perhaps you think the solution set out here, in which Adam is not deceived but instead learns the truth, is fanciful and must be mistaken?

We have noted already the confidence of many scholars that the New Testament authors were amongst the large number of those relying upon the Septuagint for the text of *Genesis*. If this is correct, then those authors should have understood the story in much the same way that we have explained it in this chapter. Let us see what one has to say about Adam:

1 Tm.	ἀδὰμ γὰρ πρῶτος ἐπλάσθη,	For Adam was formed first,
2:13	εἶτα εὔα:	then Eve;
2:14	καὶ ἀδὰμ **οὐκ** ἠπατήθη, ἡ δὲ γυνὴ ἐξαπατηθεῖσα ἐν παραβάσει γέγονεν.	And Adam was ***not*** deceived, but the woman, being thoroughly deceived, happened into transgression.

This is from the letter *1 Timothy* (authorship attributed to Paul, for the real author we have no name). The point made here could hardly be clearer: ***Adam was not deceived***. The assertion is dualistic in nature, with Adam and Eve taking positions which are wholly opposite. This passage supports the exegesis set forth in this chapter so far.

Augustine's fourth century doctrine on ***Original Sin***, according to which both Adam and Eve eat from the tree for knowing the knowledge of good and evil, so blighting all humanity with sin because of the defiance both showed to God, must surely be mistaken.

It appears that Augustine himself never understood what the 'mystery' of scripture was. It would follow that he understood neither the riddle in *Genesis* about the two trees, nor this passage which follows from *Romans* Chapter 5:

Rm. 5:12	διὰ τοῦτο ὥσπερ δι' **ἑνὸς ἀνθρώπου** ἡ ἁμαρτία εἰς τὸν κόσμον εἰσῆλθεν καὶ διὰ τῆς ἁμαρτίας ὁ θάνατος, καὶ οὕτως εἰς πάντας ἀνθρώπους ὁ θάνατος διῆλθεν, ἐφ' ᾧ πάντες ἥμαρτον	On this account, just as through **ONE PERSON** the mistake (*alt*: Sin) came into the world and, through the mistake, Death ... so also Death extended to all persons - *on condition that all made a mistake*.
5:13	ἄχρι γὰρ νόμου ἁμαρτία ἦν ἐν κόσμῳ, ἁμαρτία δὲ οὐκ ἐλλογεῖται μὴ ὄντος νόμου·	For until (there was) a law, there was a mistake in the world. But a mistake is not imputed where no law exists.
5:14	ἀλλὰ ἐβασίλευσεν ὁ θάνατος ἀπὸ ἀδὰμ μέχρι μωϋσέως καὶ ἐπὶ τοὺς <u>μὴ</u> ἁμαρτήσαντας ἐπὶ τῷ ὁμοιώματι τῆς παραβάσεως ἀδάμ, ὅς ἐστιν τύπος τοῦ μέλλοντος.	Yet Death did reign from Adam until Moses, even upon those not making a mistake [*alt*: not sinning] about the 'likeness' of the transgression of Adam, who is a type of what is to come.

It is asserted that the mistake came into the world through (just) *one person* ... and that consequently death came to all *on condition that all did sin* (one must read carefully; a condition not fulfilled may serve effectively to negate the assertion it is set to qualify).

Many have inferred from this passage that the writer thinks Adam made a mistake (ie. that he 'sinned'). Yet this is not a sound conclusion: Adam is mentioned only at 5:14 and the 'likeness' of his transgression is not in fact spelled out.

Adam is the Gnostic hero of scripture. Nothing in the narrative permits us to argue that 'sin' came into the world through any action of his.

The first 'children': Cain and Abel

Scripture is about good and evil. On this account it is robustly dualistic. Again and again we find in the narrative related pairs … spouses, brothers, cousins, even twins. The pattern begins in *Genesis* with Adam and Eve. It is reinforced with Abel and Cain, with Isaac and Rebecca, with Esau and Jacob. Later it extends into the gospels, now with John the Baptist and Jesus.

Which of these narrative characters the authors deem to be good, and which of them evil, is usually plain from the '*works*' assigned to them; that is, from their activities, their behaviour, the things that they say and do. Certain traits, for example a preference in foods, can give away in a trice the true nature of a person. In this connection the diet prescribed for the **lord god** at Gn.1:29 has a key role to play. This alone can unlock for us the entire '*mystery*' of scripture.

Now here is the next development in scripture's exacting theme:

Gn.	αδαμ δὲ ἔγνω ευαν τὴν	But Adam *learned to know*
4:1	γυναῖκα αὐτοῦ καὶ	Eve, his woman, and she,
	συλλαβοῦσα ἔτεκεν τὸν καιν	conceiving, gave birth to Cain.
	καὶ εἶπεν ἐκτησάμην	And she said "I acquired
	ἄνθρωπον διὰ τοῦ θεοῦ	**a person** by means of God".
4:2	καὶ προσέθηκεν τεκεῖν τὸν	And she added giving birth to
	ἀδελφὸν αὐτοῦ τὸν αβελ	his brother, Abel.
	καὶ ἐγένετο αβελ ποιμὴν	And it happened (that) Abel
	προβάτων καιν δὲ ἦν	(was) a herdsman of flocks,
	ἐργαζόμενος τὴν γῆν	but Cain was working the earth.

Adam is formed from the dust of the earth, Eve is built from Adam's rib, but to Cain goes the title πρωτότοκος πάσης κτίσεως [*firstborn of all creation*]. We note in passing that at Col.1:15 the same description is assigned to Jesus; it is a point we shall return to later.

Now it is clear that Eve is the mother of Cain, but who is the father? This is an important question. Let us hear what the mother has to say.

According to the Hebrew text (MT) Eve says:

> I have acquired a man (with?) **the lord**.

But according to the Greek (LXX) she says:

> I acquired a person by means of **God**

If Adam was the father she would hardly make the latter remark, for she would not refer to Adam as **God**.

But Eve has been with the serpent. That might explain the child. And if she is convinced that the serpent is **God**, that might explain her remark.

If we are on the right track here then the perspective of Eve is that of a monotheist. She thinks of the serpent, himself a manifestation of the **lord god**, as if indeed he were **God**. Then hers is a pivotal mistake (or sin).

This hypothesis is fully consistent with the long tradition of Jewish teaching which makes the explicit claim that Cain was descended from the serpent. Ginzberg[1] recounts as follows:

> But after the fall of Eve, Satan, in the guise of the serpent, approached her, and the fruit of their union was Cain, the ancestor of all the impious generations that were rebellious towards God, and rose up against Him. Cain's descent from Satan, who is the angel Samael, was revealed in his seraphic appearance. At his birth, the exclamation was wrung from Eve, "I have gotten a man through an angel of the Lord".

And Margaret Barker[2] points out:

> Targum *Pseudo-Jonathan* also knew that Eve had conceived Cain from Samael, the angel of the Lord.

The origin of Cain from the serpent (Satan or Samael; the angelic manifestation of the **lord god**) is reinforced by the author of the NT letter *1 John* when he writes:

1 Jn.	οὐ καθὼς Κάϊν **ἐκ τοῦ**	Not like Cain. **_He was from_**
3:12	**πονηροῦ** ἦν καὶ ἔσφαξεν τὸν	**_the evil one_** and he
	ἀδελφὸν αὐτοῦ: καὶ χάριν	slaughtered his brother. And
	τίνος ἔσφαξεν αὐτόν; ὅτι τὰ	for the sake of what did he
	ἔργα αὐτοῦ πονηρὰ ἦν, τὰ δὲ	slaughter him? Because his
	τοῦ ἀδελφοῦ αὐτοῦ δίκαια.	works were evil, but those of
		his brother (were) just.

Now let us consider Abel. He is the second-born child of Eve. The actions of the brothers are clearly opposed: then it appears that Abel must be the one who is good.

If Adam too is good, formed by **God** from the dust, we are left to infer that Adam is the father of this second child.

So here is the pattern: Cain inherits from the serpent a nature inherently evil, whilst Abel inherits from Adam both goodness and the knowledge of **God**.

In more detail, this is what the author of *1 John* has to say:

1 Jn.	ὁ ποιῶν τὴν ἁμαρτίαν ἐκ τοῦ	The one making the mistake
3:8	διαβόλου ἐστίν, ὅτι ἀπ' ἀρχῆς	[*alt*: the sin] is from the devil,
	ὁ διάβολος ἁμαρτάνει. εἰς	because from the beginning
	τοῦτο ἐφανερώθη ὁ υἱὸς τοῦ	the devil makes a mistake.
	θεοῦ, ἵνα λύσῃ τὰ ἔργα τοῦ	For this the 'son of God' was
	διαβόλου.	revealed, that it might set
		free the works of the devil
		[*alt*: that you shall untie the
		works of the devil].

3:9	πᾶς ὁ γεγεννημένος ἐκ **τοῦ** **θεοῦ** ἁμαρτίαν οὐ ποιεῖ, ὅτι σπέρμα αὐτοῦ ἐν αὐτῷ μένει: καὶ οὐ δύναται ἁμαρτάνειν, ὅτι ἐκ **τοῦ θεοῦ** γεγέννηται.	Each one begotten from **God** does not make a mistake [*alt*: does not sin] because his seed remains within him. And he is not able to make a mistake because he has been begotten from **God**.
3:10	ἐν τούτῳ φανερά ἐστιν τὰ τέκνα **τοῦ θεοῦ** καὶ τὰ τέκνα τοῦ διαβόλου: πᾶς ὁ μὴ ποιῶν δι**ΚΑΙ**οσύ**Vην** οὐκ ἔστιν ἐκ **τοῦ θεοῦ**, καὶ ὁ μὴ ἀγαπῶν τὸν ἀδελφὸν αὐτοῦ.	In this the children of **God** are revealed, and the children of the devil. Each one not 'making' <u>justice</u> is not from **God**, and the one not loving his brother.

{*See that those who know how can 'make' Cain's name from the Greek word for justice*} |
| 3:11 | ὅτι αὕτη ἐστὶν ἡ ἀγγελία ἣν ἠκούσατε ἀπ' ἀρχῆς, ἵνα ἀγαπῶμεν ἀλλήλους: | For this is the message which you heard from the beginning, that we may love one another. |
| 3:12 | οὐ καθὼς ΚΑϊν ἐκ τοῦ πονηροῦ ἦν καὶ ἔσφαξεν τὸν ἀδελφὸν αὐτοῦ: καὶ χάριν τίνος ἔσφαξεν αὐτόν; ὅτι τὰ ἔργα αὐτοῦ πονηρὰ ἦν, τὰ δὲ τοῦ ἀδελφοῦ αὐτοῦ δίκαια. | Not like Cain. He was from the evil one and he slaughtered his brother. And for the sake of what did he slaughter him? Because his works were evil, but those of his brother (were) just. |

Cain, the firstborn of all creation, is first amongst τὰ τέκνα τοῦ διαβόλου [*the children of the devil*]. Notice that his *works* were evil.

And what were those *works*?

> καιν δὲ ἦν ἐργαζόμενος τὴν γῆν   (Gn.4:2)
> **Cain was <u>working the earth</u>**

In contrast Abel is first amongst τὰ τέκνα τοῦ θεοῦ [*the children of God*].

And what were his works?

> ἐγένετο αβελ <u>ποιμὴν προβάτων</u>   (Gn.4:2)
> **It happened that Abel (was) <u>a herdsman of flocks</u>.**

What happens next turns out to be pivotal to the thematic development of all subsequent scripture.

<u>The Two Offerings , and the nature of Cain's Mistake</u>

Gn.	καὶ ἐγένετο μεθ' ἡμέρας	And it happened with (the)
4:3	ἤνεγκεν καιν ἀπὸ τῶν	days that Cain brought from
	καρπῶν τῆς γῆς θυσίαν τῷ	the fruits of the earth a
	κυρίῳ	sacrifice **for the lord.**
4:4	καὶ αβελ ἤνεγκεν καὶ αὐτὸς	And Abel brought both he
	ἀπὸ τῶν πρωτοτόκων τῶν	from the firstborn of his flock
	προβάτων αὐτοῦ καὶ ἀπὸ τῶν	- and from their fats. And
	στεάτων αὐτῶν καὶ ἐπεῖδεν ὁ	**God** looked upon Abel and
	θεὸς ἐπὶ αβελ καὶ ἐπὶ τοῖς	upon his gifts
	δώροις αὐτοῦ	

4:5	ἐπὶ δὲ καιν καὶ ἐπὶ ταῖς	But upon Cain and upon his
	θυσίαις αὐτοῦ οὐ προσέσχεν	'sacrifices' he did not pay
	καὶ ἐλύπησεν τὸν **καιν λίαν**	attention. And it grieved
	καὶ συνέπεσεν τῷ προσώπῳ	**Cain exceedingly**, and he
		fell to the face.
4:6	καὶ εἶπεν **κύριος ὁ θεὸς** τῷ	And the **lord god** said to
	καιν ἵνα τί περίλυπος ἐγένου	Cain "*Why* did you become
	καὶ ἵνα τί συνέπεσεν τὸ	sorrowful? And *why* did your
	πρόσωπόν σου	face fall?
4:7	οὐκ ἐὰν ὀρθῶς προσενέγκῃς	Did you not make a mistake
	ὀρθῶς δὲ μὴ διέλῃς ἥμαρτες	[*alt:* did you not sin] if you
		brought (your sacrifices)
		rightly but did not distinguish
		rightly?
	ἡσύχασον πρὸς σὲ ἡ	Wait quietly for his recourse
	ἀποστροφὴ αὐτοῦ καὶ σὺ	to you and (then) you shall
	ἄρξεις αὐτοῦ	take first place over him."

With the days, Cain brings *from the fruits of the earth* a sacrifice for the **lord**. It makes sense that he should do this '*with the days*', for it was at Gn.1:5 that **God** called the light '*day*', and light is required for the growth of fruiting plants.

Abel, in contrast, is a pastor of flocks. Here is the stereotype we noted in Chapter 2 of this book. Abel brings both '*he from the firstborn of his flock*' and '*from their fats*'. In the Hebrew text the connotation here is of dairy products, foods such as butter and cheese. Thus each brings what he has; but Abel brings '*gifts*' and Cain brings '*sacrifices*'.

> Now **God** looked upon Abel and upon his gifts ... but upon Cain and his 'sacrifices' he did not pay attention. And it grieved Cain exceedingly, and he fell to the face.

What was wrong with Cain's offering? Why did **God** ignore his sacrifices? Perhaps more important, why did **God** ignore Cain? Much ink has been spilled in attempting to answer these questions.

Some speculate[3] that Cain failed to prepare his sacrifice in the correct way.

Then Josephus, first century Jewish historian, is said to have suggested that God is more pleased with things which grow spontaneously than with that which is '*forcibly produced by the ingenuity of covetous man*'.

Puritan 'scholar' John Owen is said to have linked the offerings with the assertion on the Mosaic covenant at Heb.9:22 '... *without shedding of blood, remission does not happen*'. He insisted that the bloodless nature of Cain's offering was the reason for its rejection. Yet prior to the slaughter of Abel this makes little sense, for there is no suggestion in the text that the respective offerings are intended to be expiatory, nor that Abel's acceptable '*gifts*' demanded the spilling of blood.

All these suggestions appear misdirected. The answer to the riddle is surely simpler. A useful hint is addressed to Cain himself right here in the text of *Genesis*:

Mechon	הֲלוֹא אִם-תֵּיטִיב, שְׂאֵת,	If you do well, shall it not
Mamre	וְאִם לֹא תֵיטִיב, לַפֶּתַח	be lifted up? And if
Gn.	חַטָּאת רֹבֵץ;	you do not do well, sin
4:7		lurks at the gate ...
LXX	οὐκ ἐὰν ὀρθῶς προσενέγκῃς	Did you not make a
Gn.	ὀρθῶς δὲ μὴ <u>διέλῃς</u> ἥμαρτες	mistake [*alt*: did you not
4:7	...	sin] - if you brought (your)
		sacrifices) rightly but <u>did</u>
		<u>not distinguish</u> rightly?

The meaning in the Hebrew text (above) is somewhat difficult to grasp: we can only infer that Cain has done something wrong. But what is said in the Greek is more helpful. The word διέλης is the *2ⁿᵈ person singular, active voice, strong aorist subjunctive* of the verb διαιρέω [*distinguish; divide*].

The question posed to Cain does not suggest he made any mistake by the act of bringing an offering. It does imply that, in bringing it, Cain *has failed to draw some vital distinction*. **God** has then ignored his sacrifice. Perhaps what Cain has brought is simply not suited for **God**. But why should Cain get this wrong?

First, if the father of Cain is the serpent, and his mother Eve, there is double reason to expect that Cain himself will inherit the perspective of his deluded mother. It follows that the only 'god' of whom Cain will have any knowledge is his own father. This is the second god, the **lord god**, the one taking form as the serpent. As suggested by the alternate name **Samael**, this one is also '*god of the blind*'.

Next, is it not clear that the offering Cain brings, *from the fruits of the earth*, falls into the class specified at Gn.1:29? Given Cain's origin, it is only to be expected that his offering should turn out to be suited for the **lord god**. And we may readily anticipate that **God**, who is good, will pay no attention to this alien sacrifice '*from the fruits of the earth*'. This would explain why, when **God** comes by, the offering is not disturbed.

Then the primary *distinction* which Cain fails to make is the distinction betwen **lord god** and **God.** As an ardent monotheist in a robustly dualist scenario, he is oblivious of the need to draw any such distinction. In this sense he himself is 'blind'. He cannot distinguish good from evil. He is blind to the truth about **God**. But he has just witnessed the consequence of his ignorance. For **God** has accepted the gifts brought by his brother Abel, but overlooked the sacrifice which he has brought himself.

Cain does not understand. But what he does know is this. His offering has been ignored. To him it is the token of his own rejection.

And we are told:

> ... ἐλύπησεν τὸν **καιν λίαν**   (*remember Gn.1:31?*)
> ... it grieved **Cain exceedingly**

> ... καὶ συνέπεσεν τῷ προσώπῳ.
> ... and he fell to the face.

It is far from unusual (if inherently risky) for persons to pray to an unseen god with their faces pressed to the ground. But why are we told that Cain 'fell to the face'?

Such behaviour may remind us of the curse placed upon the serpent at Gn.3:14:

> ... to go upon your chest and belly

Cain's disappointment turns now to jealousy and to resentment. He has not understood the first part of what was said to him at Gn.4:7: but the second part he *has* understood. He will follow the **lord god**'s advice. He will eliminate the competition posed by his half-sibling. *Then* he will gain the attention which, as 'firstborn', he surely deserves.

Cain gets the attention he craves

Gn. 4:8	καὶ εἶπεν καιν πρὸς αβελ τὸν ἀδελφὸν αὐτοῦ διέλθωμεν εἰς τὸ πεδίον καὶ ἐγένετο ἐν τῷ εἶναι αὐτοὺς ἐν τῷ πεδίῳ	And Cain said to Abel, his brother "*Let us go into the plain*" [*voice omitted in Hebrew MT*]. And it happened in their being in the plain.
	καὶ ἀνέστη καιν ἐπὶ αβελ τὸν ἀδελφὸν αὐτοῦ καὶ ἀπέκτεινεν αὐτόν	And Cain was resurrected upon Abel, his brother - and he killed him.

By tradition, the plain is the location for (military) conflict. There:

> Cain was resurrected upon Abel, his brother
> - and he killed him.

Here is the first murder in scripture's narrative: it will not be the last. Ginzberg[4] explains the Jewish tradition that Cain killed Abel by pelting him with stones.

Here too is the first '*resurrection*' in scripture's narrative. Again, it will not be the last.

Gn.	καὶ εἶπεν **ὁ θεὸς** πρὸς καιν	And **God** said to Cain
4:9	ποῦ ἐστιν αβελ ὁ ἀδελφός σου ὁ δὲ εἶπεν οὐ γινώσκω μὴ φύλαξ τοῦ ἀδελφοῦ μού εἰμι ἐγώ	"Where is Abel, your brother?" But he said "*I do not know.* **AM I** *my brother's guardian?*"
4:10	καὶ εἶπεν **ὁ θεός** τί ἐποίησας φωνὴ αἵματος τοῦ ἀδελφοῦ σου βοᾷ πρός με ἐκ τῆς γῆς	And **God** said "What did you do? A voice of the blood of your brother shouts to me from the earth.
4:11	καὶ νῦν ἐπικατάρατος σὺ ἀπὸ τῆς γῆς ἣ ἔχανεν τὸ στόμα αὐτῆς δέξασθαι τὸ αἷμα τοῦ ἀδελφοῦ σου ἐκ τῆς χειρός σου	And now you are cursed from the earth, which 'opened its mouth' to receive the blood of your brother from your hand
4:12	ὅτι ἐργᾷ τὴν γῆν καὶ οὐ προσθήσει τὴν ἰσχὺν αὐτῆς δοῦναί σοι στένων καὶ τρέμων ἔσῃ ἐπὶ τῆς γῆς	For you shall work the earth and it shall not add its strength to yield for you. Sighing and trembling you shall be upon the earth."

Now Cain has succeeded in attracting the attention of **God**.

For the first time **God** speaks to him. He asks:

> Where is Abel, your brother?

Had he known what was good, Cain might have loved his brother. But with embracing the wrong god, he has killed him instead!

Cain is ignorant of many things. In replying to the voice, Cain says (notice that he simply '*says*' it, he does not address what he says to **God** because he does not know **God**):

> οὐ γινώσκω μὴ φύλαξ τοῦ ἀδελφοῦ μού **εἰμι ἐγώ**
> I do not know. **AM I** my brother`s guardian?

Cain seeks to shirk responsibility for the step he has now taken.

This is the first place we hear the phrase '**AM I**' (or '**I AM**'). It will turn out to be a key trait by which the one uttering it may be recognised.

God is provoked by the absence of Abel into issuing a curse himself. **God** says:

> What did you do? A voice of the blood of your brother shouts to me from the earth. And now you are cursed from the earth, which 'opened its mouth' to receive the blood of your brother from your hand.

This passage reflects the wordplay in the Hebrew original where the blood [*Hebr.*= **dam**] of Abel 'cries out' from the earth [*Hebr.*= a*dam*ah]. Indeed **God** made **Adam** from the earth so that Adam's name reflects his own origin.

God continues, saying to Cain:

> For you shall work the earth and it shall not add its strength to yield for you. Sighing and trembling you shall be upon the earth.

Here are yet further traits by which Cain may be recognised, '*sighing*', '*trembling*', and poor-yielding crops. But a 'sign' of still greater importance is about to be defined.

Retribution Foretold ... and a Sevenfold Sign for Cain

Gn.	καὶ εἶπεν καιν πρὸς τὸν	And Cain said to the lord "*My*
4:13	κύριον μείζων ἡ αἰτία μου τοῦ	*accusation (is) greater than*
	ἀφεθῆναί με	*(will allow) my acquittal*
4:14	εἰ ἐκβάλλεις με σήμερον ἀπὸ	*If you throw me out today*
	προσώπου τῆς γῆς καὶ ἀπὸ	*from a face of the earth, I*
	τοῦ προσώπου σου	*SHALL BE HIDDEN ALSO*
	κρυβήσομαι καὶ ἔσομαι	*FROM YOUR FACE. And I*
	στένων καὶ τρέμων ἐπὶ τῆς	*shall be sighing and*
	γῆς	*trembling upon the earth,*
	καὶ ἔσται πᾶς ὁ εὑρίσκων με	*and it shall be that each*
	ἀποκτενεῖ με	*one finding me shall kill*
		me".

Here Cain responds. His reply is addressed to '**the lord**'. For although it was **God** who cursed him, Cain thinks it was the **lord god** speaking.

Cain says:

> My accusation (is) greater than (will allow) my acquittal. If you throw me out today from a face of the earth, I SHALL BE HIDDEN ALSO FROM YOUR FACE. And I shall be sighing and trembling upon the earth, and it shall be that each one finding me shall kill me.

Let us analyse his statement:

1.   My accusation (is) greater than (will allow) my acquittal.

Cain recognises his offence as so great that it cannot be overlooked (this will have important consequences).

2. **If you throw me out today from a face of the earth, I shall be hidden also from your face.**

    Cain threatens that if he is punished with exclusion he will become '*hidden*'. In other words he will go in disguise … so that you may have difficulty in recognising him.

3. **I shall be sighing and trembling upon the earth.**

    But here is one trait by which he may be recognised … sighing, even shivering.

4. **It shall be that each one finding me shall kill me.**

    Cain has killed his brother. He now asserts that in due course *he too will be killed* … by those who encounter him.

The narrative continues:

Gn.	καὶ εἶπεν αὐτῷ **κύριος ὁ θεός**	And the **lord god** said to him
4:15	οὐχ οὕτως πᾶς ὁ	"Not just so, each one killing
	ἀποΚτεί**νας ΚαΙΝ** ἑπτὰ	Cain shall set free SEVEN
	ἐκδΙΚούμε**Να** παραλύσει καὶ	vengeances". And the **lord**
	ἔθετο **κύριος ὁ θεὸς** σημεῖον	**god** placed a sign for Cain,
	τῷ **ΚαΙΝ** τοῦ μὴ ἀνελεῖν	so that everyone finding him
	αὐτὸν πάντα τὸν	should not raise him up [*alt*:
	εὑρίσΚο**Ντα** αὐτόν	not do away with him].
4:16	ἐξῆλθεν δὲ **ΚαΙΝ** ἀπὸ	So Cain went out from a face
	προσώπου **τοῦ θεοῦ** καὶ	of **God** and settled in (the)
	ᾤκησεν ἐν γῇ ναιδ	earth of Nod, opposite Eden.
	Κατένα**Ντι** εδεμ	

An extra twist is added here to the plot. The **lord god** has heard what Cain said. He now chimes in to assert:

> Not just so, each one killing Cain shall set free seven vengeances.

And we are told:

> The **lord god** placed _a sign for Cain_, so that everyone finding him should _not_ raise him up [_alt_: not do away with him].

In this way an additional constraint is added to 1-4 above:

> There will be a (sevenfold) sign for Cain … _a sign by which he may be recognised._ And those who do recognise him are _not_ to 'raise him up'.

The plot for subsequent scripture is now configured. It may be summarised like this:

- Cain is the guilty fugitive: banished, he will go in disguise.

- In due course he too will be killed (in retribution for the slaughter of Abel).

- His death (ironically) will be at the hands exclusively of those who _fail_ to recognise him.

- But a 'sign' will be set for Cain … by which he _may_ be recognised. And those who _do_ recognise him, far from killing him, will choose to ignore him (just as **God** does, _qv_. Gn.4:5).

- Cain is evil. He is also an egotist, seeking attention. The best way to deal with him is to pay him no attention whatever.

The *'sign'* devised for Cain will permit us to penetrate his brilliant disguise. But what is this sign? It is demonstrated for us right there in the passage where it is first declared.

Cain, remember, is a worker of the earth, a sower. The task of a sower is to scatter, or disperse, his seed. The *'sign'* for Cain is achieved by *dispersing* the letters of Cain's own name into the Greek words of the text. The scriptural authors engage once again the elementary technique we have seen them use elsewhere, *anagrammatic dispersion*.

In the table above (Gn.4:15-16) the words have been carefully chosen. It is not difficult to spot the name of Cain. It features three times as such, then four times *dispersed within other words*. Appearing seven times in all, it is a SEVENFOLD *'sign'*.

To make the matter clear, the *'sign'* for Cain is exemplified as follows:

- ἀποΚτεἰνας   : killing
- ΚαΙν   : Cain
- ἐκδΙΚούμεΝα   : vengeances
- ΚαΙν   : Cain
- εὑρἰσΚοΝτα   : finding
- ΚαΙν   : Cain
- ΚατέναΝτι   : opposite [Eden]

From this point in scripture's narrative Cain will go 'hidden' from your face. Many, because they do not know this *'sign'*, will fail to recognise him. These readers are tantamount to blind.

Yet the disguise is far from impenetrable. Those who read in Greek and know the *'sign'* will benefit from something like X-ray vision. This will provide useful insights, particularly when we come to the four gospels.

Back in *Genesis*, no sooner has this *'sign'* been declared than it is extended and reinforced with a key passage about a character named Lamech, one of Cain's descendents.

From Enoch to Lamech

Gn.		
4:17	καὶ ἔγνω **ΚΑΙΝ** τὴν γυ**ναῖΚ**α αὐτοῦ καὶ συλλαβοῦσα ἔτεκεν τὸν ενωχ καὶ ἦν οἰκοδομῶν πόλιν καὶ ἐπωνόμασεν τὴν πόλιν ἐπὶ τῷ ὀνόματι τοῦ υἱοῦ αὐτοῦ ενωχ	And <u>Cain</u> *learned to know* his <u>woman</u> and she, conceiving, gave birth to Enoch. And he was building up a city and named the city after the name of his son, Enoch.
4:18	ἐγενήθη δὲ τῷ ενωχ γαιδαδ καὶ γαιδαδ ἐγέννησεν τὸν μαιηλ καὶ μαιηλ ἐγέννησεν τὸν μαθουσαλα καὶ μαθουσαλα ἐγέννησεν τὸν λαμεχ	But to Enoch was brought Gaidad, and Gaidad begat Maiel, and Maiel begat Methusala and Methusala begat Lamech.
4:19	καὶ ἔλαβεν ἑαυτῷ λαμεχ δύο γυ**ναῖΚ**ας ὄνομα τῇ μιᾷ αδα καὶ ὄνομα τῇ δευτέρᾳ σελλα	And Lamech took for himself two <u>women</u> : (the) name of the one (was) Ada and (the) name of the second (was) Sella.
4:20	καὶ ἔτεκεν αδα τὸν ιωβελ οὗτος ἦν ὁ πατὴρ οἰκούντων ἐν **σΚην**αῖς κτηνοτρόφων	And Ada gave birth to Jobel. This was the father of those who dwell in (the) <u>tents</u> of those who breed beasts [*possibly*: cattle]
4:21	καὶ ὄνομα τῷ ἀδελφῷ αὐτοῦ ιουβαλ οὗτος ἦν ὁ καταδείξας ψαλτήριον καὶ **ΚΙθάρΑν**	And (the) name of his brother (was) Jubal. This was the one who demonstrates harp and <u>lyre</u>.

4:22	σελλα δὲ ἔτεκεν καὶ αὐτὴ τὸν θοβελ καὶ ἦν σφυροκόπος χαλκεὺς χαλκοῦ καὶ σιδήρου ἀδελφὴ δὲ θοβελ νοεμα	But Sella gave birth by herself to Thobel and he was a hammer-wielding smith of bronze and iron. But (the) sister of Thobel (was) Noema.

Cain 'learns to know' his woman (presumably his own mother, for at this point in the narrative she is still the only woman). And she, conceiving, gives birth to Enoch.

By this means Cain was building up a city: the city too is named Enoch. Here we have the thematic basis for all of scripture's cities, which from their origin with Cain will now be deemed as evil (extending the *horticulturalist* stereotype identified in Chapter 2 of this book).

Using the genealogy listed, if Cain is the firstborn of all creation, and Abel the second, then Enoch is third, and Lamech the *seventh*. Now Lamech speaks to his women (wives):

Gn. 4:23	εἶπεν δὲ **λαμεχ** ταῖς ἑαυτοῦ γυναιξίν αδα καὶ σελλα ἀκούσατέ μου τῆς φωνῆς γυ**ναῖκ**ες λαμεχ ἐνωτίσασθέ μου τοὺς λόγους ὅτι ἄνδρα ἀπέ**κτ**ε**ιν**α εἰς τραῦμα ἐμοὶ καὶ νε**αν**ί**σκ**ον εἰς μώλωπα ἐμοί	And **Lamech** said to his women, Ada and Sella "Listen to my voice, you <u>women</u> of Lamech. HEAR my sayings: For <u>I killed</u> a man for wounding me, and <u>a young man</u> for bruising me.
4:24	ὅτι ἑπτάκις ἐκδεδίκηται ἐκ **καιν** ἐκ δὲ λαμεχ ἐβδομηκο**ντάκι**ς ἑπτά	For seven times there shall be vengeance from <u>Cain</u>, but from **Lamech** <u>seventy times seven</u>".

Just as Lamech demands of his *two* women, we shall do well to pay attention to what he says:

> Listen to my voice, you <u>women</u> of **Lamech**. HEAR my sayings. For <u>I killed</u> a man for wounding me - and <u>a young man</u> for bruising me. For seven times there shall be vengeance from <u>Cain</u>, but from **Lamech** <u>seventy times</u> seven

His disconcerting speech includes (in Greek) the following words, each evoking the name of his murderous ancestor Cain:

- γυναῖκες : women
- ἀπέκτεινα : I killed
- νεανίσκον : a young man
- Καιν : Cain
- ἑβδομηκοντάκις : seventy times

So in this passage the name of **Cain** appears five times, and the name of **Lamech** twice.

$$5 + 2 = 7$$

We have once again a SEVENFOLD '*sign*'.

General Extension of the Sign for Cain

Anagrammatic concealment of Cain's name seems to be one sense in which he goes '*hidden from our face*', just as he threatens at Gn.4:14.

But the application of this '*sign*' is far from being concluded at this point in the narrative. The same thematic device appears to have been embraced by the authors and extended yet further. In the narrative Lamech asserts to his women that:

> ... seven times there shall be vengeance from Cain,
>   but from Lamech **seventy times seven**.

$$70 \times 7 = 490$$

Here are some statistics for the TLG (Rahlfs) text of LXX *Genesis*:

No. of chapters	:	50
No. of verses	:	1531
No. of words	:	32566
No. of words as anagram source for καιν (Cain)	:	**488** [1.50%]

Character frequencies in the whole of LXX *Genesis*:

κ (kappa)	:	4.47 %
α (alpha)	:	12.44 %
ι (iota)	:	8.83 %
ν (nu)	:	8.13 %

The number of words in the Rahlfs edition of *Genesis* which have the power to 'spell' Cain's name turns out to be **488**. But the 'vengeance' derived through Lamech is to be ἑβδομηκοντάκις ἑπτά [*seventy times seven*], ie. **490**.

We notice that:

$$488 + 2 = 490$$

Could it be that Lamech's count of **70 x 7** serves to declare in advance the total number of words which the authors will introduce into the Greek text of *Genesis* as they write ... and that these words will function throughout as the '*sign*' for Cain?

If so, why is the fit not exact?

There is a discrepancy of two words, a shortfall amounting to 0.006% of all the words in *Genesis*.

In the limited passage at Gn.4:23-24 we obtained a total of seven by incrementing the five instances of Cain's name with two instances of

Lamech's name. But when we take the text of *Genesis* as a whole this rule will not work because the name of Lamech is mentioned ten times in all.

$$488 + 10 \neq 490$$

Could there be another word in LXX *Genesis*, occuring with just two instances, which is somehow associated with Cain and which we ought to be counting up, along with words able to spell out Cain's name?

The word **λίαν** [*exceedingly*] is used twice in LXX *Genesis*. It first appears at Gn.1:31 in making the observation that what was brought into being on **DAY 6** was '*exceedingly good*' (remember, this was the day when the **lord god** was brought into being). It is used for a second time at Gn.4:5 in relation to Cain, who was '*grieved exceedingly*' when ignored by **God**.

So perhaps we have the answer here. The word **λίαν** [*exceedingly*] is spelled closely alike to the name of **κάϊν** [*Cain*] and by its contextual use is associated with Cain. Perhaps it should be counted in as if it too were a '*sign*' for Cain? If this is the explanation it probably carries with it didactic significance in relation to the use of the word **λίαν** in scripture more generally, including in the gospels.

But there is another possibility. The word **κανᾶ** [*bread baskets made from reeds*] appears twice in LXX *Genesis* in connection with the riddle told to Joseph in the prison (Gn.40:16, 40:18). This passage appears to provide the basis for the narrative in the fourth gospel about the wedding feast which Jesus attends at **κανά** [*Cana*] in Galilee (Jn.2:1 *seq*). The word itself is strongly evocative of the name **κάϊν** [*Cain*]. Perhaps it is this which should be counted as equivalent?

Once the LXX authors (the eponymous '*seventy*') had devised their '*sign*' for Cain, it would be natural for them to be aware of which words, in their subsequent text, served this now critical function. We know too that it was quite normal for copyists in the ancient world to perform counting checks on copies as they were produced. For example we know that stichometric reckoning[5] was adopted as one means to guard against inadvertent omission or duplication.

It therefore seems reasonable to suppose that the authors of *Genesis* may have declared (in the narrative about Lamech) the number of times the 'sign' for Cain was to appear, then kept a running tally and completed their book in such a way as to match the total declared. By this means they might hope to ensure that the 'sign' would be accurately preserved in any future copies: it would always be possible for those with appropriate knowledge to verify[6] the total. If this is what the authors intended, it appears that over more than two millennia their foresight has served its purpose admirably well.

Now here are comparable statistics for the Fourth Gospel (*John*):

No. of chapters	:	21
No. of verses	:	879
No. of words	:	15640
No. of words as anagram source for ΚαΙΝ (Cain)	:	**149** [0.95%]

Character frequencies in the Fourth Gospel (*John*):

Κ (kappa)	:	3.27 %
α (alpha)	:	10.47 %
Ι (iota)	:	9.78 %
Ν (nu)	:	8.25 %

The word Κανά [*Cana*] appears precisely **4** times in this gospel (Jn.2:1, 2:11, 4:46, 21:2) but nowhere else in the NT canon. Adding these instances to the words which can make the name Καϊν [*Cain*], we have:

149 + 4 = 153

This is the number actually cited in the final chapter of the same gospel:

Jn. 21:3	λέγει αὐτοῖς σίμων πέτρος, ὑπάγω ἁλιεύειν. λέγουσιν αὐτῷ, ἐρχόμεθα καὶ ἡμεῖς σὺν σοί. ἐξῆλθον καὶ ἐνέβησαν εἰς τὸ πλοῖον, καὶ ἐν ἐκείνῃ τῇ νυκτὶ ἐπίασαν οὐδέν.	Simon Peter said to them "I'm off to fish". They said to him "We also are coming with you". They went off and boarded the boat, and on that night they concentrated nothing.
21:4	πρωΐας δὲ ἤδη γενομένης ἔστη ἰησοῦς εἰς τὸν αἰγιαλόν: οὐ μέντοι ᾔδεισαν οἱ μαθηταὶ ὅτι ἰησοῦς ἐστιν.	But already, with early morning happening, Jesus stood on the beach. Yet in truth the students did not know that it was Jesus.
21:5	λέγει οὖν αὐτοῖς [ὁ] ἰησοῦς, παιδία, μή τι προσφάγιοV ἔχετε; ἀπεΚρίθησαV αὐτῷ, οὔ.	Jesus therefore said to them "Little children, Do you not have any snack?" They replied to him "No".
21:6	ὁ δὲ εἶπεν αὐτοῖς, βάλετε εἰς τὰ δεξιὰ μέρη τοῦ πλοίου τὸ δίκτυον, καὶ εὑρήσετε. ἔβαλον οὖν, καὶ οὐκέτι αὐτὸ ἑλκύσαι ἴσχυον ἀπὸ τοῦ πλήθους τῶν ἰχθύων.	But he said to them "Cast the net on the right *side* of the boat and you will find (something). So they did cast - and from the abundance of fishes they no longer had the strength to draw it (in).

21:7	λέγει οὖν ὁ μαθητὴς ἐκεῖνος ὃν ἠγάπα ὁ ἰησοῦς τῷ πέτρῳ, ὁ κύριός ἐστιν. σίμων οὖν πέτρος, ἀκούσας ὅτι ὁ κύριός ἐστιν, τὸν ἐπενδύτην διεζώσατο, ἦν γὰρ γυμνός, καὶ ἔβαλεν ἑαυτὸν εἰς τὴν θάλασσαν:	That student whom Jesus loved then said to Peter "It is the lord". Then Simon Peter, hearing that 'It is the lord', wrapped the cloak around (for he was naked) and threw himself into the sea.
21:8	οἱ δὲ ἄλλοι μαθηταὶ τῷ πλοιαρίῳ ἦλθον, οὐ γὰρ ἦσαν μακρὰν ἀπὸ τῆς γῆς ἀλλὰ ὡς ἀπὸ πηχῶν δΙαΚοσίων, σύροντες τὸ δίκτυον τῶν ἰχθύων.	But the other students came in the little boat (for they were not far from the land but around <u>two hundred</u> cubits), dragging the net of the fishes.
21:9	ὡς οὖν ἀπέβησαν εἰς τὴν γῆν βλέπουσιν ἀνθραΚΙὰν κειμένην καὶ ὀψάριον ἐπικείμενον καὶ ἄρτον.	Then, as they got out onto the land, they saw <u>a burning coal</u> laid, and fish laid upon (it), and bread.
21:10	λέγει αὐτοῖς ὁ ἰησοῦς, ἐνέγκατε ἀπὸ τῶν ὀψαρίων ὧν ἐπιάσατε νῦν.	Jesus said to them "Bring some of the fish which now you (have) concentrated"
21:11	ἀνέβη οὖν σίμων πέτρος καὶ εἵλκυσεν τὸ δίκτυον εἰς τὴν γῆν μεστὸν ἰχθύων μεγάλων ἑκατὸν πεντήκοντα τριῶν:	Then Simon Peter went up and drew the net onto the earth full of ***a hundred and fifty three*** big fishes.
	καὶ τοσούτων ὄντων οὐκ ἐσχίσθη τὸ δίκτυον.	And (despite) there being so many, the net was not torn.

If we look at 21:5 we can see both ὄφιν [*serpent*] and κάϊν [*Cain*] concealed beneath the surface of the text and ready to be harvested ... or 'caught in our net'. There is a dreadful irony in the fact that without help from the (unrecognised) figure of Jesus, the 'students' in the story can catch nothing whatever.

What we should also recognise is that at 21:6 the word μέρη [*side*] itself has the number value **153**. So it is true that all we have to do is 'look on the right *side*' and we *will* find something of great interest. Moreover **153** is the number value for the following phrases:

- ῥεβέκκα   : Rebecca
- ἡ μαγδαληνὴ   : the Magdalene
- μαλακίαν   : sickness

It now appears that the '**153 big fishes**', concealed in this gospel and waiting to be 'found', is simply an allusion to the subset of words in the gospel which function as the '*sign*' for Cain. As readers we are 'fishermen' too ... and charged with locating these particular fish!

This evidence from the Fourth gospel tends to confirm our earlier hypothesis that Lamech's prediction of vengeance '*seventy times seven*' might play the same rôle in *Genesis*. So we conclude that in his speech Lamech discloses the checksum for the '*sign*' for Cain ... which consists in all those words with the power to spell out Cain's name, taken together with the evocative word κανά [*Cana*]. This clever scheme seems to have been implemented first in LXX *Genesis* ~250BCE then copied around 350 years later by whoever finalised the Fourth gospel (presumably by adding the passage inserted at Jn.7:53-8:11 along with Chapter 21).

If we have not now explained the matter correctly we are certainly looking at some remarkable arithmetic coincidences. For if we turn to Luke's *Acts of the Apostles* we obtain what appears to be yet further confirmation of this matter, although a little harder to elucidate.

The number of words in *Acts* which serve as anagram sources for the name **Κάϊν** [*Cain*] is **368**, whereas we find in the text itself this declaration:

Ac.	ἤμεθα δὲ αἱ πᾶσαι ψυχαὶ ἐν	But we were, all the souls in
27:37	τῷ πλοίῳ **διακόσιαι**	the ship, ***two hundred and***
	ἑβδομήκοντα ἕξ.	***seventy six***.

We notice that:

$$368 \times \tfrac{3}{4} = 276$$

The exact fractional relationship seems puzzling until we realise that precisely ¾ of the words in *Acts* which serve as anagram sources for the name of **Cain** are to be found in that part of the book which follows the death of Stephen. Essentially, this is the portion of *Acts* which relates to the activities of Saul/Paul (Ac.8:1 to Ac.28:31). It is within this portion that the number of Greek words yielding the name of **Cain** is found to be **276**.

It seems that the scriptural authors have implemented with great precision their scheme to set in place a '*sign*' for Cain. This '*sign*' assumes pivotal importance throughout Greek scripture (yet many will fail to recognise it). Where they see fit, the authors have set in place arithmetic checksums. Using these, readers who think they can follow what the authors have done can duly confirm their working hypothesis.

Now if persons are to penetrate successfully the 'mystery' enshrined within scripture it will be vital not only that they should read in Greek but that they should learn to scan-read for the '*sign*' for Cain ... that is, for all those words which contain the letters **Κ α ι ν**. Those not doing so will suffer (as readers) from 'vision' which is seriously impaired.

With this exegesis we appear to have confirmed the significant rôle assigned quite generally by the authors of Greek scripture to any word they write which conveys the name of **Cain**. The importance which this matter may hold for liturgical expression and for doctrine will emerge in the later chapters of this book.

Seth and Enos

4:25	ἔγνω δὲ αδαμ ευαν τὴν <u>γυ**ναῖκ**α</u> αὐτοῦ καὶ συλλαβοῦσα ἔτεκεν υἱὸν καὶ ἐπωνόμασεν τὸ ὄνομα αὐτοῦ σηθ λέγουσα ἐξανέστησεν γάρ μοι ὁ θεὸς σπέρμα ἕτερον ἀντὶ αβελ ὃν <u>ἀ**πέκτειν**εν **καιν**</u>	But Adam *learned to know* Eve, his <u>woman</u>, and she, conceiving, gave birth to a son and named his name Seth, saying "For God has resurrected for me another seed in exchange for Abel, whom <u>Cain</u> <u>killed</u>".
4:26	καὶ τῷ σηθ ἐγένετο υἱός ἐπωνόμασεν δὲ τὸ ὄνομα αὐτοῦ ενως οὗτος ἤλπισεν ἐπικαλεῖσθαι τὸ ὄνομα **κυρίου** τοῦ **θεοῦ**	And to Seth came a son but he named his name Enos. This one expected to call upon the name of **the lord god**.
=>		*Here ends the 'Book of Genesis of Heaven and Earth'.*

Expression of the '*sign*' for Cain continues with these words:

- γυ**ναῖκ**α : woman
- ἀ**πέκτειν**εν : he killed
- **κάϊν** : Cain

As for the narrative, at this juncture things look pretty bleak for the human race to come. They began well enough when **God** made Adam from the dust, so providing for him to 'know' **God** (as his maker). And, from the nature of the gifts he brings at Gn.4:4, it appears that Abel too 'knows' **God**. Yet Cain has killed Abel before he could father any children. In this way Cain has extinguished the race of those who know **God**.

Is humankind to be descended entirely from Cain, the *firstborn of all creation* (Gn.4:1; 4:17)? Will the earth be peopled with the offspring of a murderer? Will it be filled with those whose sacrifices are taken *from the fruits of the earth*, with those who know as their god only the impostor **lord god**?

It seems so. But all perhaps is not lost. For now we are told:

> Adam learned to know Eve, his woman, and she, conceiving, gave birth to a son, and named his name Seth, saying "For God has resurrected for me another seed in exchange for Abel, whom Cain killed".

It is plainly a Gnostic statement because we are told (as at Gn.4:1) that Adam *learned to know* Eve [*Gk*: ἔγνω]. And our hopes may be raised, for it appears that Adam is father to Seth.

Will Seth himself become father to a fresh line of those who *do* know **God**? We may suppose it was such a hope that in the early centuries CE inspired those Gnostics known as *Sethians*. Yet in the next verse we learn of Seth's son Enos that:

> This one expected to call upon the name of the **lord god**

The god known to Enos is the **lord god**: it is clearly asserted in the narrative. Then Enos takes after Cain: he does not know **God**. We can hardly escape this conclusion.

But what about Seth himself? The woman is not a reliable witness. But perhaps she is correct when she says of Seth that he is:

> ... another seed in exchange for Abel, whom Cain killed.

Perhaps Seth himself *does* know **God**, like Abel and Adam before him.

There may be more to the matter of transmitting the knowledge of **God** than physical progeny. This knowledge may not be inherited at all, but transmitted through *what one learns to know*. Could it be writing, and the learning which books can transmit, which are needed for this to happen?

Chapter 6

The Book of Genesis of 'Persons'

We now encounter an alternate version of the narrative, beginning from where we left off at Gn.2:3 (the end of the creation sequence). It is titled: *The Book of Genesis of 'Persons'*. It appears that the story is now reformulated to align with the deluded perspective demanded by the lord god, the so-called 'Persons' of Gn.1:27.

Gn.	αὕτη ἡ βίβλος γενέσεως	This (is) the Book of Genesis
5:1	ἀνθρώπων ᾗ ἡμέρᾳ ἐποίησεν ὁ **θεὸς** τὸν αδαμ κατ' ε<u>ἰ</u>Κό**Vα** θεοῦ ἐποίησεν αὐτόν	of Persons. On the day **God** made Adam, he made him according to (the) <u>image</u> of a god.
5:2	ἄρσεν καὶ θῆλυ ἐποίησεν αὐτοὺς καὶ εὐλόγησεν αὐτούς καὶ ἐπωνόμασεν τὸ ὄνομα αὐτῶν αδαμ ᾗ ἡμέρᾳ ἐποίησεν αὐτούς	Male and female he made them, and he blessed them and named their name Adam the day he made them.
5:3	ἔζησεν δὲ αδαμ διακόσια καὶ τρ<u>ι</u>ά**Κο**V**τα** ἔτη καὶ ἐγέννησεν κατὰ τὴν ἰδέαν αὐτοῦ καὶ κατὰ τὴν ε<u>ἰ</u>Κό**Vα** αὐτοῦ καὶ ἐπωνόμασεν τὸ ὄνομα αὐτοῦ σηθ	But Adam lived two hundred and <u>thirty</u> years. And he begat (one) according to his idea and according to his <u>image</u>, and he named his name Seth.
=>		*The intentionally deceitful narrative of this 'Book of Genesis of Persons' continues throughout the remainder of Genesis.*

We recall the tradition that the **lord god** thinks of himself as the only god. In this *blind man's version* of scripture a monotheist view is asserted and the prime **God** of Gn.1:1 is airbrushed out of the picture. Instead:

- The **lord god** is the only 'god'

- Adam and Seth are made in his image

Here is the mistaken perspective of Eve and of Cain ... and of all who embrace the serpent as their god.

We recognise too the doctrinal perspective long since adopted by the Christian church ... the claim that all mankind is descended from Adam who was made in the image of **God**.

This *volte face* in the narrative turns all subsequent scripture into dangerous territory for any reader who lacks a solid grounding of the kind set forth in the previous chapter of this book. From now on it is only by solving the riddles, by watching for designated 'signs', by watching for the 'works' (*ie.* actions) of the characters in the plot, and by looking out for personal traits such as diet, that we can tell who is good and who is evil. Readers inspired by the strong pull of their own enthusiasm but who lack the knowledge to do these things are almost certain to be led far along the broad and easy road which the gospels tell us leads to perdition (*qv.* Mt.7:13).

But we are not blind. Look! What do we have here in the Greek text at Gn.5:1? The assertion that on the day God made Adam, he made him:

> ... κατ' εἰκόνα θεοῦ
> ... according to (the) image of a god

It is the '*sign*' for Cain. What further warning should we need?

It seems that this *Book of Genesis of Persons* extends to include all the remaining chapters of LXX *Genesis*. Indeed such is the scope of scripture's plot that one might say it sets the presentational pattern for all that remains of the canon of Greek scripture.

In the narrative, Abraham, Isaac and Jacob will contend with the wiles of the **lord god**.

Moses will take on the rôle of prophet for **the lord** … with the result that the Israelites (who in the narrative are supposed to be finding the promised land) will be led astray for forty years in the desert.

Isaiah will become in turn the deluded prophet of the **lord Sabaoth**: it is a matter we shall address in the next chapter of this book.

Then from the first century CE, with the release of the four gospels into the public domain, the Hellenist world will encounter a fresh display of tricks. Once again it will be brought face to face with **Cain** … yet readers (for the most part) will fail to recognise him (*qv.* Gn.4:14).

We shall then be compelled to grapple with Paul, another prophet of **the lord**.

To contend with such challenges we shall need to remember all that we have learned so far. We have an important advantage: for already we hold the 'key' to the kingdom of the heavens.

This is the 'key of knowledge' which has the power to unlock the hidden portion of scripture's message.

Chapter 7

From *Genesis* to the Gospels

Having explored in some detail the first four chapters of *Genesis*, we are ready to address the texts which follow. Greek scripture is tightly packed with riddles and develops, in a recursive manner, the core theme we have now exposed. There are two gods. The first is good, the second evil. Inclined to deceit, the second seeks to play the rôle of the first. To deal with this we must keep our wits about us ... and solve the riddles.

The source material is abundant. We shall limit our consideration to a selection of passages chosen to illustrate worthwhile points.

Things Written Backwards and Forwards

The following excerpt from *Genesis* is important for what it has to teach us about how to read. Noah has three sons, Shem, Ham and Japheth. At this point in the story the flood has abated and all have emerged from the ark. Noah becomes, like Cain before him, ἄνθρωπος γεωργὸς [*an earthworker person*]. Immediately he plants a vineyard:

LXX Gn. 9:21	καὶ ἔπιεν ἐκ τοῦ οἴνου καὶ ἐμεθύσθη	And he drank from the wine and became drunken [*alt*: intoxicated].
	καὶ ἐγυμνώθη ἐν τῷ οἴκῳ αὐτοῦ	And he was made naked within his household.
9:22	καὶ εἶδεν χαμ ὁ πατὴρ χανααν τὴν γύμν<u>ΩΣΙΝ</u> τοῦ πατρὸς αὐτοῦ	And Ham, the father of Canaan, *saw* the <u>nakedness</u> of his father.
	καὶ ἐξελθὼν ἀνήγγειλεν τοῖς δυσὶν ἀδελ<u>φοῖς</u> αὐτοῦ ἔξω	And going out, he announced (it) <u>to</u> his two <u>brothers</u> outside.

Nakedness is an attribute of the serpent. Ham identifies this trait in his drunken father (afterwards Noah responds with a curse on account of Ham's insight, *qv*. Gn.9:24-25). Yet the behaviour of Shem and Japheth (who will not look) results in their *failing* to see what Ham sees:

LXX Gn. 9:23	καὶ λαβόντες σημ καὶ ιαφεθ τὸ ἱμάτιον ἐπέθεντο ἐπὶ τὰ δύο νῶτα αὐτῶν καὶ ἐπορεύθησαν ὀπ**ΙΣθΟΦ**ανῶς	And Shem and Japheth, taking the garment, placed (it) upon their two backs and were made to go <u>backwardly-appearing</u>.
	καὶ συνεκάλυψαν τὴν γύμν**ΩΣΙΝ** τοῦ πατρὸς αὐτῶν	And they concealed the <u>nakedness</u> of their father (Noah).
	καὶ τὸ πρόσωπον αὐτῶν ὀπ**ΙΣθΟΦ**ανές καὶ τὴν γύμν**ΩΣΙΝ** τοῦ πατρὸς αὐτῶν οὐκ εἶδον	And their face was (was) <u>backwards-appearing</u> and they did not see the <u>nakedness</u> of their father.

The two brothers conceal themselves beneath the garment. In this way they are '*made to go backwardly-appearing*'.

In the word ὀπ**ΙΣθΟΦ**ανῶς [*backwardly-appearing*] we find that we can <u>see</u> the serpent **ὄφΙΣ**[1], his name appearing partly backwards.

And when the two sons try to conceal τὴν γύμν**ΩΣΙΝ** [*the nakedness*] of their father, it is now that we <u>hear</u> the name of the serpent.

For the reader in Greek this works because:

- The **sight** we may *see* when we read the Greek word ὀπ**ΙΣθΟΦ**ανῶς [*backwardly-appearing*] embodies the word

 ὄφΙΣ [*a serpent; nominative case singular*]

- The **sound** we may *hear* when we pronounce the Greek word ωσιν [*with ears*] resembles that for the word ὄφιν [*a serpent; accusative case singular*]

And just in case we should miss such a neat illustration[2] of the serpent's ability to hide amidst the texts of scripture, the trick is repeated in the very same verse.

The passage illustrates nicely the didactic method of the scriptural authors. First there is the literal meaning, for all to see. This points to a further component concealed in some way in the text. The latter may be recognised by persons determined to read with particular care, or by those who know from experience what kind of thing to expect.

Our next passage is from the book of *Revelation*:

Rv. 5:1	καὶ εἶδον ἐπὶ τὴν δεξιὰν τοῦ καθημένου ἐπὶ τοῦ θρόνου βιβλίον γεγραμμένον ἔσωθεν καὶ ὄπισθεν, Κατεσφραγισμέvον σφραγῖσιν ἑπτά.	And I saw upon the right hand side of the one sitting upon the throne a book written within and backwards, <u>sealed down with</u> seven seals.
5:2	καὶ εἶδον ἄγγελον ἰσχυρὸν κηρύσσοντα ἐν φωνῇ μεγάλῃ, τίς ἄξιος ἀνοῖξαι τὸ βιβλίον καὶ λῦσαι τὰς σφραγῖδας αὐτοῦ;	And I saw a strong angel proclaiming in a loud voice "Who (is) <u>deserving</u> <u>to open</u> the book and to undo its seals?"
5:3	καὶ οὐδεὶς ἐδύνατο ἐν τῷ οὐρανῷ οὐδὲ ἐπὶ τῆς γῆς οὐδὲ ὑποκάτω τῆς γῆς ἀνοῖξαι τὸ βιβλίον οὔτε βλέπειν αὐτό.	And no one was able in Heaven, nor upon the earth nor beneath the earth, <u>to open</u> the book nor even to see it.

5:4	καὶ ἔΚΛΑΙοV πολὺ ὅτι οὐδεὶς ἄξΙΟς εὑρέθη ἀνΟῖξαι τὸ βιβλίον οὔτε βλέπειν αὐτό.	And <u>I wept</u> much because no one was found <u>deserving to open</u> the book nor even to see it.

The book in question has been written '*within and backwards*'. As an example of what is meant by '*writing within*', we can see twice *within* this passage the name of **ΚάϊV** [*Cain*]. It is fairly easy to spot because the letters are in the right order. Yet they are:

- **ΚΑ**τεσφραγΙσμέVον σφραγῖσιν ἑπτά   : **sealed down with seven seals**

Remember the sevenfold '*sign*' for Cain? And precisely because "*no one was found deserving to open the book nor even to see it*", the author of *Revelation* repeats the trick. He says:

- **ἔΚΛΑΙοV** πολὺ   : **I wept** much

At 5:2 we see an example of what is meant by '*writing backwards*':

τίς ἄξΙΟς ἀνΟῖξαι τὸ βιβλίον καὶ λῦσαι τὰς σφραγῖδας αὐτοῦ;
Who (is) **deserving to open** the book and to undo its seals?

This demonstration of mirror-reversal is repeated at Rv.5:4 (and again at Rv.5:9). Even so, few have understood. But perhaps from this explanation you will appreciate that there *is* more to scripture than most people know, a key portion of meaning lying concealed by such means.

Before moving on, it may be worth pointing out the ability of a word such as **κατεσφραγισμένον** [*sealed down with*] to yield a wide range of other words. Here are *seven* possibilities:

- **ὄφις**   : a serpent
- **κάϊν**   : Cain

- σαταν   : Satan
- ἅγιος   : holy
- σφραγίς   : a seal (7 characters)
- μάννα   : manna
- ἄρτος   : bread

And **κατεσφραγισμένον** is one of only *seven* words in the New Testament canon which include the letters required to spell out the first three names in the list above (the others are at Mt.6:24; Mk.13:35; Lk.16:13; Ac.7:19; Rm.2:4; 1 Tm.6:2).

Perhaps you will now understand this riddle:

Rv. 2:17	ὁ ἔχων οὖς ἀκουσάτω τί τὸ πνεῦμα λέγει ταῖς ἐκκλησίαις. τῷ νικῶντι δώσω αὐτῷ τοῦ μάννα τοῦ κεκρυμμένου,	The one having an ear, let him hear what the spirit says to the churches: "To the one who overcomes, I shall give of the hidden manna.
	καὶ δώσω αὐτῷ ψῆφον λευ**ΚῊ**ν καὶ ἐπὶ τὴν ψῆφον ὄνομα **ΚΑΙΝ**ὸν γεγραμμένον ὃ οὐδεὶς οἶδεν	And I shall give to him a *__white__* cipher [*alt*: pebble], and upon the cipher a *__new__* name written which no one knows ...
	εἰ μὴ ὁ λαμβάνων.	except the one 'getting' (it).

It is extremely easy to *see* the name of Cain here, for it forms the first portion of the Greek word **ΚΑΙΝ**ὸν [*new*]. In addition you can *hear* the name of Cain in the word λευ**ΚῊ**ν [*white*]. But what about the hidden **μάννα** [*manna*]?

The first answer is that it's right there, written '*backwards and within*' in the final word λ**αμβάν**ων [*getting*].

Yet there is more. In the book of *Exodus* the Greek word for manna is not **μαννα** but simply **μαν**. So if we look for words which can 'make' **μαν**, we find *five* in this particular verse:

Rv. 2:17	ὁ ἔχων οὖς ἀκουσάτω τί τὸ π**Ν**εῦ**μα** λέγει ταῖς ἐκκλησίαις. τῷ νικῶντι δώσω αὐτῷ τοῦ **μάν**να τοῦ κεκρυμμένου,	The one having an ear, let him hear what the <u>spirit</u> says to the churches: "To the one who overcomes, I shall give of the hidden <u>manna</u>.
	καὶ δώσω αὐτῷ ψῆφον λευκὴν καὶ ἐπὶ τὴν ψῆφον ὄ**Νο**μ**α** καινὸν γεγρ**αμ**μέ**Νον** ὃ οὐδεὶς οἶδεν	And I shall give to him a white cipher [*alt*: pebble], and upon the cipher a new <u>name</u> <u>written</u> which no one knows ...
	εἰ μὴ ὁ λα**μβάν**ων.	except the one <u>getting</u> (it).

There are only eight verses in the Greek NT canon which exhibit five [or more] instances of *manna* in this way. The others are Mt.7:22[8]; Lk.8:22[5]; Jn.3:11[8]; Jn.13:20[7]; Ac.21:7[5]; Rm.8:26[5]; Heb.1:3[5].

This passage from the book of *Revelation* is more broadly instructive:

Rv. 22:8	κἀγὼ **ἰωάννης** ὁ ἀκούων καὶ βλέπων ταῦτα. καὶ ὅτε ἤκουσα καὶ ἔβλεψα, ἔπεσα προσκυνῆσαι ἔμπροσθεν τῶν ποδῶν τοῦ ἀγγέλου τοῦ δεικνύοντός μοι ταῦτα.	And I, ***John***, (am) the one hearing and seeing these things. And when I heard and saw, I fell to worship before the feet of the angel who showed me these things.

22:9	καὶ λέγει μοι, ὅρα μή: σύνδουλός σού εἰμι καὶ τῶν ἀδελφῶν σου τῶν προφητῶν καὶ τῶν τηρούντων τοὺς λόγους τοῦ βιβλίου τούτου: **τῷ θεῷ** προσκύνησον.	And he said to me "*See that you don't*. I am a fellow slave of yours, and of your brothers the prophets, and of those keeping the sayings of this book. Worship to **God**".
22:10	καὶ λέγει μοι, μὴ σφραγίσῃς τοὺς λόγους τῆς προφητείας τοῦ βιβλίου τούτου, ὁ καιρὸς γὰρ ἐγγύς ἐστιν.	And he said to me "Do not seal these sayings of the prophecy of this book, for the time is near".

The angel's advice seems to reflect the Gnostic conviction that both humans and angels may be kept in a state of bondage to the evil second god. Indeed the book of *Revelation* begins with the words:

ἀποκάλυψις ἰησοῦ χριστοῦ, ἣν ἔδωκεν αὐτῷ ὁ θεός,
δεῖξαι τοῖς δούλοις αὐτοῦ ἃ δεῖ γενέσθαι ἐν τάχει ...

A revelation of Jesus Christ, which God gave to him,
to show *to his slaves* which things must come about in haste ...

For many, the condition of servitude is promoted and sustained by what little they understand from the message of scripture itself. But those who break through, those who can solve the riddles, those who can see what the 'catch' is, such persons may be freed from the yoke.

John is warned *against* falling to worship at the feet of the angel. Falling down to worship is amongst the traits assigned to the deluded figure of Cain (*qv.* Gn.4:5).

Instead the direction is 'Worship to God'.

The Theme of the Tainted Meal

Here is the first 'meal' we encounter in the narrative of scripture:

LXX Gn. 3:6	καὶ εἶδεν ἡ γυνὴ ὅτι καλὸν τὸ ξύλον εἰς βρῶσιν καὶ ὅτι ἀρεστὸν τοῖς ὀφθαλμοῖς ἰδεῖν καὶ ὡραῖόν ἐστιν τοῦ κατανοῆσαι καὶ λαβοῦσα τοῦ καρποῦ αὐτοῦ ἔφαγεν καὶ ἔδωκεν καὶ τῷ ἀνδρὶ αὐτῆς μετ' αὐτῆς καὶ ἔφαγον	And the woman saw the tree as good for <u>eating</u> and as agreeable <u>with the eyes</u> to see, and (that) it is beautiful for understanding fully. And taking (some) of its fruit, she ate. And she gave (some) also to her man with her, and they ate.
3:7	καὶ διηνοίχθησαν οἱ ὀφθαλμοὶ τῶν δύο καὶ ἔγνωσαν ὅτι γυμνοὶ ἦσαν καὶ ἔρραψαν φύλλα συκῆς καὶ ἐποίησαν ἑαυτοῖς περιζώματα	And the eyes of the two *were* opened up and ... *they learned to know* that they were naked. And they stitched leaves of a fig, and made for themselves aprons.

The woman sees the tree placed in the charge of ὁ ὄφις [*the serpent*] as:

καλὸν ... εἰς βρῶσιν [good for <u>eating</u>]

and as:

ἀρεστὸν τοῖς ὀφθαλμοῖς ἰδεῖν [agreeable <u>with the eyes</u> to see]

Notice how this meal embodies the word ὠσὶν [*with ears*] and the word ὀφθαλμοῖς [*with eyes*]. Any reader who fails *to hear* and *to see* ὁ ὄφ......ις [*the serpent*] risks being classed amongst 'the deaf and the blind'. But this combination is so far central to the method of these writers that we shall see it echoed in the gospels and *Acts*.

Then consider:

- That in the story Eve was deceived (*qv.* Gn.3:13). She saw the tree as attractive, but presumably *did not notice* what it concealed.

- That throughout all of scripture's narrative, and particularly in the gospels, *so many* are portrayed to have dysfunctional hearing or sight (presented as deaf or blind).

- That this may be the problem shared equally by many readers … that they are deceived precisely because *they do not know* how to 'hear', nor indeed how to 'see'.

Readers may be deaf and blind to the very παρουσία [*presence*] in the text of the ubiquitous *serpent*, himself the manifestation of the oppressive and deceitful **lord god**. Perhaps you recall the theme quoted in the opening pages of this book?

Jn.	τετύφλωκεν αὐτῶν τοὺς	He has blinded their eyes
12:40	ὀφθαλμοὺς καὶ ἐπώρωσεν	and petrified their <u>heart</u>,
	αὐτῶν τὴν **καρδίαν**	
	ἵνα μὴ ἴδωσιν τοῖς	that they may not see <u>with</u>
	ὀφθαλμοῖς	<u>the eyes</u>
	καὶ νοήσωσιν τῇ καρδίᾳ	and perceive with the heart.
	καὶ στραφῶσιν,	And they may be turned,
	καὶ ἰάσομαι αὐτούς.	and I may heal them.

And yet we have:

LXX	τότε ἀνοιχθήσονται	Then **eyes** of (the) blind <u>shall</u>
Is.	ὀφθαλμοὶ τυφλῶν	<u>be opened up</u>
35:5	καὶ ὦτα κωφῶν	and **ears** of (the) deaf <u>shall</u>
	ἀκούσονται	<u>hear</u>.

In the fifty chapters of LXX *Genesis* there are twelve instances of the word ὀφθαλμοῖς [*with eyes*]. Here is a list of the persons whose 'eyes' are mentioned:

	Verse	Person	Circumstance
1.	Gn.3:6	Eve	: seeing the serpent
2.	Gn.13:14	Abram	: seeing all the land granted
3.	Gn.18:2	Abraham	: seeing three men
4.	Gn.22:4	Abraham	: seeing the place far off
5.	Gn.22:13	Abraham	: seeing the ram
6.	Gn.24:63	Isaac	: seeing camels coming
7.	Gn.24:64	Rebecca	: when she sees Isaac
8.	Gn.31:10	Jacob	: seeing the goats and rams
9.	Gn.31:12	Jacob	: seeing the goats and rams
10.	Gn.37:25	Joseph's brothers	: seeing Ishmaelites & camels
11.	Gn.43:29	Joseph	: seeing Benjamin
12.	Gn.45:20	Joseph	: seeing his equipment

See how many famous names from the narrative of *Genesis* are cast contending with the serpent.

But we shall not investigate these incidents now. Instead we shall explore the theme of scripture as *'food for the mind'*, watching for further instances where the writers have used the phrase ὠσὶν [*with ears*] in conjunction with a disguised expression of the word ὄφις [*serpent*].

It is only natural that the combination should evoke the circumstances of its first use (Gn.3:6; the deceit of Eve). But from now on it will not be the woman who risks being deluded through failing to see who and what is placed before her. At risk will be every person bold enough to embark upon the challenge of reading the Bible.

The Bible is fiction, but cleverly written on the basis that the serpent is Satan, the one with a grand and effective plan for deceiving *the whole world* [*qv.* Rv.12:9]. Then for us the danger with meals is this. The

Bible itself may serve as the means by which *we* are tricked … tricked into making Cain's mistake, into embracing Satan as if he were God.

Let us turn now to a passage from the *Book of Proverbs*:

LXX Pr. 23:1	ἐὰν καθίσῃς δειπνεῖν ἐπὶ τραπέζης δυναστῶν νοητῶς νόει τὰ παρατιθέμενά σοι	If you sit down to dine at the table of those with power[3], consider carefully what is placed before you.
23:2	καὶ ἐπίβαλλε τὴν χεῖρά σου εἰδὼς ὅτι τοιαῦτά σε δεῖ παρασκευάσαι	And put down your hand, seeing that these things ought to prepare you.
23:3	εἰ δὲ ἀπληστότερος εἶ μὴ ἐπιθύμει τῶν ἐδεσμάτων αὐτοῦ ταῦτα γὰρ ἔχεται ζωῆς ψευδοῦς	Even if you are rather famished, do not desire his dishes, for these have a false nature.
23:4	μὴ <u>π**α**ρε**κ**τε**ί**ν**ο**υ</u> πένης ὢν πλουσίῳ τῇ δὲ σῇ ἐννοίᾳ ἀπόσχου	Let the poor man not <u>queue up</u> with the wealthy, but desist from your intention.
23:5	ἐὰν ἐπιστήσῃς τὸ σὸν ὄμμα πρὸς αὐτόν οὐδαμοῦ φανεῖται κατεσκεύασται γὰρ αὐτῷ πτέρυγες ὥσπερ ἀετοῦ καὶ ὑποστρέφει εἰς τὸν οἶκον τοῦ προεστηκότος αὐτοῦ	If you should set your eye[4] upon him, nothing will it bring to light. For he has been equipped with wings like those of an eagle, and you are turned back to the 'household' set before him.
23:6	μὴ συνδείπνει ἀνδρὶ βασκάνῳ μηδὲ ἐπιθύμει τῶν βρωμάτων αὐτοῦ	Do not dine together with a man who bewitches (people), nor desire his food

23:7	ὃν τρόπον γὰρ εἴ τις καταπίοι τρίχα οὕτως ἐσθίει καὶ πίνει	For in whatever manner someone may gulp down hair, so he eats and drinks.
23:8	μηδὲ πρὸς σὲ εἰσαγάγῃς αὐτὸν καὶ φάγῃς τὸν ψωμόν σου μετ' αὐτοῦ ἐξεμέσει γὰρ αὐτὸν καὶ λυμανεῖται τοὺς λόγους σου τοὺς καλούς	You may not have introduced him to your (home), and yet you 'eat your morsel' with him. Then you will vomit it up, and he will ill-treat your sayings which are good.
23:9	εἰς ὦτα ἄφρονος μηδὲν λέγε μήποτε μυκτηρίσῃ τοὺς συνετοὺς λόγους σου	Into a foolish ear say nothing, lest he may mock your sensible sayings.

The majority of scripture's texts pose a gnostic challenge. It is vital that we treat with circumspection the first impression we receive. But the Wisdom literature may provide an exception to this rule. The *Book of Wisdom* and *Book of Proverbs* can present to the reader straightforward advice on what to watch out for in the other books.

In the passage above we are warned about the quality of *the meal* offered at the table of those with power. What is served up may not be entirely wholesome. Indeed we are told that the dishes on offer have *a false nature*, and that we risk being *bewitched*. And we are warned that if we do decide to join in the feast we shall in due course *vomit up* what we consume.

It is a strong warning. So what is signified by this meal? It is plainly a metaphor for something. In the writings attributed to the prophet *Ezekiel* we find amongst his visions much the same theme:

LXX Ezk. 2:9	καὶ εἶδον καὶ ἰδοὺ χεὶρ ἐκτεταμένη πρός με καὶ ἐν αὐτῇ κεφαλὶς βιβλίου	And I saw. And look! A hand stretched out to me, and in it (the) scroll of a book

2:10	καὶ ἀνείλησεν αὐτὴν ἐνώπιον ἐμοῦ καὶ ἐν αὐτῇ γεγραμμένα ἦν τὰ ὄπισθεν καὶ τὰ ἔμπροσθεν καὶ ἐγέγραπτο εἰς αὐτήν θρῆνος καὶ μέλος καὶ οὐαί	And he unrolled it before me. And within it were things written, things backwards and things forwards. And there had been written into it lamentation, melody and woe.
3:1	καὶ εἶπεν πρός με υἱὲ ἀνθρώπου κατάφαγε τὴν κεφαλίδα ταύτην καὶ πορεύθητι καὶ λάλησον τοῖς υἱοῖς ισραηλ	And He said to me "Son of a person, eat down this scroll and go and speak to the sons of Israel".
3:2	καὶ διήνοιξα τὸ στόμα μου καὶ ἐψώμισέν με τὴν κεφαλίδα	And I opened my mouth and he fed me the scroll.
3:3	καὶ εἶπεν πρός με υἱὲ ἀνθρώπου τὸ στόμα σου φάγεται καὶ ἡ κοιλία σου πλησθήσεται τῆς κεφαλίδος ταύτης τῆς δεδομένης εἰς σέ καὶ ἔφαγον αὐτὴν καὶ ἐγένετο ἐν τῷ στόματί μου ὡς μέλι γλυκάζον	And he said to me "Son of a person, your mouth eats and your belly shall be filled with this scroll which has been given to you". And I ate it and it became in my mouth like sweetened honey.
3:4	καὶ εἶπεν πρός με υἱὲ ἀνθρώπου βάδιζε εἴσελθε πρὸς τὸν οἶκον τοῦ ισραηλ καὶ λάλησον τοὺς λόγους μου πρὸς αὐτούς	And he said to me "Son of a person, get along. Go in to the house of Israel and speak these sayings of mine to them.

3:5	διότι οὐ πρὸς λαὸν βαθύχειλον καὶ βαρύγλωσσον σὺ ἐξαποστέλλῃ πρὸς τὸν οἶκον τοῦ ισραηλ	Because you are not sent out to a people thick-lipped and heavy-tongued (but) to the house of Israel
3:6	οὐδὲ πρὸς λαοὺς πολλοὺς ἀλλοφώνους ἢ ἀλλογλώσσους οὐδὲ στιβαροὺς τῇ γλώσσῃ ὄντας ὧν οὐκ ἀκούσῃ τοὺς λόγους αὐτῶν καὶ εἰ πρὸς τοιούτους ἐξαπέστειλά σε οὗτοι ἂν εἰσήΚουσάν σου	Nor to many peoples with another voice or another tongue, nor being strong with the tongue, of whom you may not hear their sayings. Yet if I sent you to them, these (people) *might* even <u>listen</u> to you.
3:7	ὁ δὲ οἶκος τοῦ ισραηλ οὐ μὴ θελήσωσιν εἰσακοῦσαί σου διότι οὐ βούλονται εἰσαΚούεΙΝ μου ὅτι πᾶς ὁ οἶκος ισραηλ φιλόνεικοί εἰσιν καὶ σκληροκάρδιοι	But the House of Israel might *not* be willing to hear you. Because they do not wish <u>to</u> <u>listen</u> to me, for all the house of Israel are quarrelsome and hard of heart."

Surely Ezekiel's meal provides what we may think of as '*food for the mind*': for what he eats is the scroll *of a book*. In his mouth the book was like sweetened honey. As before, within it were '*things written backwards and things written forwards*'. It seems more and more probable that the book in question is scripture itself; and it may be a tainted meal.

In the passage above we see twice the name for Κάϊν [*Cain*]. It is written partly backwards and partly forwards. In each case it is concealed within Greek words meaning '*listen*'.

But the House of Israel does not wish to listen to the message of its own scriptures. Here may lie the crux of what could develop into a very considerable problem. For if they will not listen, how will they ever understand?

The theme from *Ezekiel* is reproduced in the NT book of *Revelation*:

Rv. 10:8	καὶ ἡ φωνὴ ἣν ἤκουσα ἐκ τοῦ οὐρανοῦ, πάλιν λαλοῦσαν μετ' ἐμοῦ καὶ λέγουσαν, ὕπαγε λάβε τὸ βιβλίον τὸ ἠνεῳγμένον ἐν τῇ χειρὶ τοῦ ἀγγέλου τοῦ ἑστῶτος ἐπὶ τῆς θαλάσσης καὶ ἐπὶ τῆς γῆς.	And the voice which I heard from Heaven, again speaking with me and saying "Go! Take the book opened up in the hand of the angel who stands upon the sea and upon the earth".
10:9	καὶ ἀπῆλθα πρὸς τὸν ἄγγελον λέγων αὐτῷ δοῦναί μοι τὸ βιβλαρίδιον. καὶ λέγει μοι, λάβε καὶ κατάφαγε αὐτό, καὶ π<ins>ΙΚρ</ins>α<ins>Ν</ins>εῖ σου τὴν Κοιλ<ins>ία</ins>ν, ἀλλ' ἐν τῷ στόματί σου ἔσται γλυκὺ ὡς μέλι.	And I went away to the angel, saying to him "Give me the booklet". And he said to me "Take and eat it down: and <ins>it will make bitter</ins> your <ins>belly</ins>, but in your mouth it will be sweet like honey".
10:10	καὶ ἔλαβον τὸ βιβλαρίδιον ἐκ τῆς χειρὸς τοῦ ἀγγέλου καὶ κατέφαγον αὐτό, καὶ ἦν ἐν τῷ στόματί μου ὡς μέλι γλυκύ: καὶ ὅτε ἔφαγον αὐτό, ἐπ<ins>ΙΚρ</ins>ά<ins>Ν</ins>θη ἡ κοιλία μου.	And I took the booklet from the hand of the angel and I ate it down. And it was in my mouth like sweet honey: yet when I ate it, my belly <ins>was made bitter</ins>.

There again we have the suggestion that the meal is not entirely wholesome. For although the first impression was sweetness, once digestion was under way the belly was made bitter.

We saw in Chapter 5 how the '*sign*' for Cain was configured and first set forth. In the passage above we find the name of Cain embedded as follows:

- πιΚρανεῖ   : it will make bitter
- Κοιλίαν   : belly
- ἐπιΚράνθη   : it was made bitter

Remember, Cain's works were evil (1 Jn.3:12), and so is Cain himself. When his name crops up in the text it is not too difficult to see what might be meant by the theme that:

> It was in my mouth like sweet honey:
> Yet when I ate it, my belly was made bitter

This is the way scripture works. There is the literal meaning, the first impression we form. It is '*like sweet honey in our mouth*'. Then there is the coded meaning, accessible to those readers able to solve the riddles.

The coded meaning serves eventually *to invert* our first impression. This explains its delayed action in '*making the belly bitter*'. Yet it has a most important rôle. It provides for the reader to distinguish reliably what is set forth to be good from what is set forth to be evil. Our next 'meal' comes in a passage already considered in Chapter 1 of this book:

LXX Gn. 22:13	καὶ ἀναβλέψας αβρααμ τοῖς ὀφθαλμοῖς αὐτοῦ εἶδεν	And, looking up, Abraham saw with his eyes.
	καὶ ἰδοὺ κριὸς εἷς κατεχόμενος ἐν φυτῷ σαβεκ τῶν κεράτων	And look! A single ram held down in a Sabek plant by the horns.
	καὶ ἐπορεύθη αβρααμ καὶ ἔλαβεν τὸν κριὸν καὶ ἀνήνεγκεν αὐτὸν εἰς ὁλοκάρπωσιν ἀντὶ ισαακ τοῦ υἱοῦ αὐτοῦ	And Abraham went and took the ram and brought it as a whole-fruit (offering) in exchange for Isaac, his son.

It is in the verse which follows (22:14) that Abraham makes his remark identifying κριὸς [*the ram*] as κύριος [*a lord*].

It was in Chapter 2 that we learned about the Egyptian god Amun:

Amun (*or* Amun-Re) was held to be king of the gods. His huge temple at Karnak on the Upper Nile was maintained for over 2000 years. His name means:

'The Hidden One',

his true nature held to be secret.

Amun

Statue in Sudan National Museum, Khartoum

Photo reproduced (head & shoulders only) courtesy of Sudan Archaeological Research Society, London

The god Amun was depicted as a ram-headed figure wearing a head-dress which incorporated a pair of tall feathers, a sun disk, and a Uraeus. The name for the latter is derived from Egyptian οὐραῖος [*basilisk; cobra*] but suggests also Greek ὡραῖος [*beautiful*]. The basilisk was a serpent renowned for its ability to spit venom in the eyes of its victim (so rendering the victim blind).

It is this cultural background which connects κριὸς [*the ram*] with ὄφις [*the serpent*], so making sense of the passage at Gn.22:13.

A Feast for the Senses ... and a Scheme to Deceive

The book of *Isaiah* functions in part as a prescriptive agenda for the later narrative of the gospels. First set down in Hebrew, and in three sections from different periods, *Isaiah* develops the original plot from *Genesis* and rehearses it in the form which one day the gospel writers will follow. In this way it plays the part of a thematic 'stepping stone'.

The passage at Chapter 6, known as '*The Call of Isaiah*', is of central importance:

LXX Is. 6:1	καὶ ἐγένετο τοῦ ἐνιαυτοῦ οὗ ἀπέθανεν οζιας ὁ βασιλεύς εἶδον τὸν κύριον καθήμενον ἐπὶ θρόνου ὑψηλοῦ καὶ ἐπηρμένου καὶ πλήρης ὁ οἶκος τῆς δόξης αὐτοῦ	And it happened in the year when Oziah the king died. I saw **the lord** sitting upon a throne, lofty and exalted - and the household filled with his glory.
6:2	καὶ σεραφιν εἰστήΚεισαν κύκλῳ αὐτοῦ ἓξ πτέρυγες τῷ ἑνὶ καὶ ἓξ πτέρυγες τῷ ἑνὶ καὶ ταῖς μὲν δυσὶν κατεκάλυπτον τὸ πρόσωπον καὶ ταῖς δυσὶν κατεκάλυπτον τοὺς πόδας καὶ ταῖς δυσὶν ἐπέταντο	And seraphim <u>were stood</u> around him, six wings for the one, six wings for the one. And with two they were concealing the face, and with two concealing the feet, and with two they were flying.
6:3	καὶ ἐκέκραγον ἕτερος πρὸς τὸν ἕτερον καὶ ἔλεγον ἅγιος ἅγιος ἅγιος κύριος σαβαωθ πλήρης πᾶσα ἡ γῆ τῆς δόξης αὐτοῦ	And they cried out one to another and said "Holy, holy, holy, **lord Sabaoth**, all the earth is filled with your glory".

6:4	καὶ ἐπήρθη τὸ ὑπέρθυρον	And the lintel was lifted from
	ἀπὸ τῆς φωνῆς ἧς ἐκέκραγον	the voice with which they
	καὶ ὁ οἶκος ἐπλήσθη καπνοῦ	cried out, and the household
		was filled with smoke.

The narrator (ostensibly the prophet Isaiah himself) describes a vision of the **lord Sabaoth**. We recall from Chapter 2 how:

> Severus, an associate of Marcion, said that this Yaldabaoth was not only the son of the Good God, but was also the devil whose other name was **Sabaoth**.

This identity of **Sabaoth** with the devil, duly manifested as ὁ ὄφις [*the serpent*], would account well for the features of this deity being '*concealed*', his abode being '*filled with smoke*'.

The prophet continues:

LXX	καὶ εἶπα ὦ τάλας ἐγὼ ὅτι	And I said "Oh, wretched
Is.	ΚατανέVυγμαι ὅτι ἄνθρωπος	(am) I, because <u>I have been</u>
6:5	ὢν καὶ ἀκάθαρτα χείλη ἔχων	<u>stupefied</u> ... because of
	ἐν μέσῳ λαοῦ ἀκάθαρτα	being a person and having
	χείλη ἔχοντος	unclean lips, in the midst of a
		people having unclean lips".
	ἐγὼ οἰκῶ καὶ τὸν βασιλέα	I was there, and the king,
	κύριον σαβαωθ εἶδον τοῖς	**lord Sabaoth**, I saw <u>with</u> my
	<u>ὀφθαλμοῖς</u> μου	(own) <u>eyes</u>.
6:6	καὶ ἀπεστάλη πρός με ἓν τῶν	And one of the seraphim was
	σεραφιν καὶ ἐν τῇ χειρὶ εἶχεν	sent off to me, and in his
	ἄνθρακα ὃν τῇ λαβίδι ἔλαβεν	hand he was holding a (live)
	ἀπὸ τοῦ θυσιαστηρίου	coal which he took with tongs
		from the altar.

6:7	καὶ ἥψατο τοῦ στόματός μου	And he touched my mouth
	καὶ εἶπεν ἰδοὺ ἥψατο τοῦτο	and he said "Look! This
	τῶν χειλέων σου καὶ ἀφελεῖ	touches your lips: and it will
	τὰς ἀνομίας σου καὶ τὰς	take away your lawlessness
	ἁμαρτίας σου περικαθαριεῖ	and clean away your
		mistakes [*alt*: your sins]".

In the story Isaiah becomes '*stupefied*'. The implication is that his rational faculties are rendered disfunctional. Yet he reports:

I was there, and the king, lord Sabaoth, *I saw* …
"τοῖς ὀφθαλμοῖς μου" [*with my own eyes*]

However disfunctional the state of Isaiah's mind, *you* may well have noticed there the **lord Sabaoth**. His name is not difficult to see. And could the live coals at the altar be further tokens of Satan's abode?

The wretched prophet continues:

LXX	καὶ ἤκουσα τῆς φωνῆς κυρίου	And I heard the voice of **a**
Is.	λέγοντος τίνα ἀποστείλω καὶ	**lord** saying "Whom shall I
6:8	τίς πορεύσεται πρὸς τὸν λαὸν	send and who will go to this
	τοῦτον	people?".
	καὶ εἶπα ἰδοὺ **εἰμι ἐγώ**	And I said "Look! **AM I**,
	ἀπόστειλόν με	send me".

The Greek word **προφήτης** [*prophet*] has a meaning similar to what we understand by the term *spokesman*, even *spin doctor*. In the story here, Isaiah volunteers to become the *prophet* of the one he has seen, the **lord Sabaoth**. But the features of this **Person** are concealed by the seraphim and Isaiah fails to recognise who it really is.

The narrative continues when **the lord** speaks again to Isaiah. Here is a passage of key didactic significance which later will reverberate through the NT texts:

LXX Is. 6:9	καὶ εἶπεν πορεύθητι καὶ εἰπὸν τῷ λαῷ τούτῳ	And he said "Go and say to this people:
	ἀκοῇ ἀκούσετε καὶ οὐ μὴ συνῆτε	With hearing, you will hear, but **NOT** understand.
	καὶ βλέποντες βλέψετε καὶ οὐ μὴ ἴδητε	And seeing, you will see, but **NOT** perceive.
6:10	ἐπαχύνθη γὰρ ἡ καρδία τοῦ λαοῦ τούτου	For the heart of this people has grown fat.
	καὶ τοῖς ὡσὶν αὐτῶν βαρέως ἤκουσαν καὶ τοὺς ὀφθαλμοὺς αὐτῶν ἐκάμμυσαν	And <u>with</u> their <u>ears</u> they heard heavily and they half-closed their eyes ...
	μήποτε ἴδωσιν τοῖς ὀφθαλμοῖς	lest <u>they should perceive with the eyes</u>,
	καὶ τοῖς ὡσὶν ἀκούσωσιν	and <u>hear with the ears</u>,
	καὶ τῇ καρδίᾳ συνῶσιν	and <u>understand</u> with the heart,
	καὶ ἐπιστρέψωσιν	and <u>they should turn back</u>,
	καὶ ἰάσομαι αὐτούς	and I may heal them".

The rôle which Isaiah will play as prophet is to go to the people and express himself in such a way that:

> With hearing, they will hear, but **NOT** understand.
> And seeing, they will see, but **NOT** perceive.

What a remarkable statement. A dreadful spell is to be cast anew upon the people. They will respond like the deaf and the blind to the text of scripture itself, which will lead them far astray. Failing to recognise the serpent, they will repeat Cain's mistake by adopting **Samael** [5] as their god. And scripture's coded warning is lost upon them … for they are not able to *hear*, nor to *see*, what lies concealed in the text.

If we are not to share in their fate we should notice what follows at 6:10. The phrase ωσιν appears <u>*six times*</u> in a single verse, twice having the literal meaning [*with ears*] and four times as the subjunctive verb ending [*they should …*].

And again we have the word ὀφθαλμοῖς [*with eyes*].

The combination of the two words ωσιν and ὀφθαλμοῖς evokes the points in the narrative of *Genesis* where the same combination arises, the encounter of Eve with the serpent (Gn.3:6) and that of Abram with the ram (Gn.22:13).

Later the NT authors will reproduce this passage in *Isaiah*, first at Mt.13:14-15, then at Ac.28:26-27 and again in paraphrase at Jn.12:39-41. Now we see why it held such significance for them. For here lie concealed the original '*mysteries of the kingdom of the Heavens*' (as anticipated at Mt.13:11).

The prophet inquires how long this deceit will endure:

| LXX Is. 6:11 | καὶ εἶπα ἕως πότε κύριε καὶ εἶπεν ἕως ἂν ἐρημωθ**ῶΣΙΝ** πόλεις παρὰ τὸ μὴ κατοικεῖσθαι καὶ οἶκοι παρὰ τὸ μὴ εἶναι ἀνθρώπους καὶ ἡ γῆ καταλειφθήσεται ἔρημος | And I said "Until when, **lord**?". And he said "Until cities are laid waste, with no-one settling down there and dwellings with no persons around, and the land shall be left deserted". |

6:12	καὶ μετὰ ταῦτα μαΚρυΝεῖ ὁ θεὸς τοὺς ἀνθρώπους καὶ οἱ ΚαταλειφθέΝτες πληθυνθήσονται ἐπὶ τῆς γῆς	And after these things **God** drives away **the Persons** and those left behind shall prevail upon the earth.
6:13	καὶ ἔτι ἐπ' αὐτῆς ἔστιν τὸ ἐπιδέΚατοΝ καὶ πάλιν ἔσται εἰς προνομὴν ὡς τερέβινθος καὶ ὡς βάλανος ὅταν ἐκπέσῃ ἀπὸ τῆς θήκης αὐτῆς	And yet from it there is the tenth part, and again it will be like a nucleus, like a terebinth, and like an acorn when it breaks out from its shell.

The consequence of failing to understand scripture's message is that cities will be laid waste, etc. Yet:

> ... after these things **God** drives away **the Persons**
> and those left behind shall prevail upon the earth

God drives away **the Persons** (*ie.* the **lord god**). It is now that good may prevail.

But that is not the end. It is from the remnant, '*the tenth part*' (and there we see Cain's name again), that the people may turn again to their former deluded condition. Presumably the lure is too strong for them, the serpent's promise of eternal life.

Something like 2,200 years have passed since this passage from Hebrew *Isaiah* was reformulated in Greek. Hindsight extends to us a great advantage. We see that what is predicted is precisely what has happened. The hidden meaning of scripture has remained just that, *hidden* ... for century after century. Yet, provided the Greek text was preserved, it was always likely that what was hidden so long ago *one day would be found*.

Indeed the gospels assert that *it will be found* (*qv.* Mt.10:26; Mk.4:22; Lk.8:17, 12:2). And perhaps, with this book, it has been.

The Risk of Mistaking Evil for Good

In *Isaiah* Chapter 5 we find this significant warning:

LXX	οὐαὶ οἱ λέγοντες τὸ πονηρὸν	Woe to those saying Evil is
Is.	καλὸν καὶ τὸ καλὸν πονηρόν	good and Good is evil,
5:20		
	οἱ τιθέντες τὸ σκότος φῶς καὶ	those putting Darkness for
	τὸ φῶς σκότος	light and Light for darkness,
	οἱ τιθέντες τὸ πικρὸν γλυκὺ	those putting Bitter for sweet
	καὶ τὸ γλυκὺ πικρόν	and Sweet for bitter.

At the outset *darkness* was the attribute of **God** (Gn.1:2). Then God said 'Let light happen' (Gn.1:3). And '*with the days*' (*ie.* with the light; Gn.1:5) Cain was able to produce (Gn.4:3) foods suited to the diet specified (Gn.1:29) for the **lord god**.

Yet the warning issued here suggests the possibility that some readers may make a serious mistake. It implies that some may misconstrue the position entirely, mistaking *at every turn* what is evil for what is good.

A related theme emerges in the NT letter of *James*:

Jm.	τὴν δὲ γλῶσσαν οὐδεὶς	But the tongue of Persons no
	δαμάσαι δύναται ἀνθρώπων:	one is able to tame : (it is) a
3:8	ἀκατάστατον κακόν, μεστὴ	disordered evil, ripe with
	ἰοῦ θανατηφόρου.	death-dealing poison.
3:9	ἐν αὐτῇ εὐλογοῦμεν τὸν	Within it we bless **the lord**
	κύριον καὶ πατέρα, καὶ ἐν	**and father**, and within it we
	αὐτῇ καταρώμεθα τοὺς	curse **the Persons** *who have*
	ἀνθρώπους τοὺς καθ'	*come into being according to*
	ὁμοίωσιν θεοῦ γεγονότας:	*likenesses of a god.*

3:10	ἐκ τοῦ αὐτοῦ στόματος ἐξέρχεται εὐλογία καὶ κατάρα. οὐ χρή, ἀδελφοί μου, ταῦτα οὕτως γίνεσθαι.	Out of the same mouth comes out blessing and cursing. *My brothers, these things ought not to happen thus.*
3:11	μήτι ἡ πηγὴ ἐκ τῆς αὐτῆς ὀπῆς βρύει τὸ γλυκὺ καὶ τὸ πικρόν;	Surely the spring does not gush from the same opening the sweet and the bitter?
3:12	μὴ δύναται, ἀδελφοί μου, συκῆ ἐλαίας ποιῆσαι ἢ ἄμπελος σῦκα; οὔτε ἁλυκὸν γλυκὺ ποιῆσαι ὕδωρ.	My brothers, can a fig-tree make olives, or a vine figs? Neither (can) a brackish (source) make sweet water.
3:13	τίς σοφὸς καὶ ἐπιστήμων ἐν ὑμῖν; δειξάτω ἐκ τῆς καλῆς ἀναστροφῆς τὰ ἔργα αὐτοῦ ἐν πραΰτητι σοφίας.	Who is wise and understanding amongst you? Let him show, from the good inversion, his works in gentleness of wisdom.

The tongue of Persons is a disordered evil. We notice too that the words ἀκατάστατον [*disordered*] and ἀναστροφῆς [*inversion*] both conceal the name of σαταν [*Satan*].

But the real significance of this passage is that it challenges those who bless '*the lord and father* ' whilst at the same time they curse '*the Persons who have come into being according to likenesses of a god* '.

The writer says "*My brothers, these things ought not to happen thus*", asserting that sweet and bitter cannot both flow from the same opening. In this way he makes it clear that, far from the one being good and the other evil, *these two parties share the same status.*

Then does he mean that both are good, or that both are evil? An answer is finally suggested at 3:12 when the common source is identified as '*brackish*' (*ie.* as *bitter*) ... which means that both must be evil.

In summary, the author of *James* implies that '*the **Persons** who have come into being according to likenesses of a god*' (a term which seems to refer to the '**Persons**' of Gn.1:27) are concomitant with '**the lord and father**' ... and that *both* of these are evil.

In this connection we may recall advice which features nearer to the beginning of *James* :

Jm.	ἀδελφοί μου, **μὴ** ἐν	My brothers, do **_NOT_** hold at
	προσωπολημψίαις ἔχετε τὴν	face value the faith of our
2:1	πίστιν τοῦ κυρίου ἡμῶν ἰησοῦ	lord Jesus Christ of glory.
	χριστοῦ τῆς δόξης.	

If you find all this surprising, please read on: we shall consider these matters further in the later chapters of this book.

The Pattern of Children in Pairs

We shall now examine the striking pattern which arises in the narrative of scripture in connection with the birth of children in pairs.

In Chapter 5 we noted that:

> Scripture is about good and evil. On this account it is robustly dualistic. Again and again we find in the narrative related pairs ... spouses, brothers, cousins, even twins. The pattern begins in *Genesis* with Adam and Eve. It is reinforced with Abel and Cain, with Isaac and Rebecca, with Esau and Jacob. Later it extends into the gospels, now with John the Baptist and Jesus.

> Which of these narrative characters the authors deem to be good, and which they deem to be evil, is usually plain from the '*works*' assigned to them; that is, from their activities, their behaviour, the things that they say and do. Certain traits, for example a preference in foods, can give away in a trice the true nature of a person. In this connection the diet prescribed for the **lord god** at Gn.1:29 has a key role to play. This alone can unlock for us the entire '*mystery*' of scripture.

We recall that Cain, the older brother, turned out to be evil; Abel, the younger brother, was good.

The first two children of Abraham are Ishmael and Isaac. Both the person of the mother and the age of the father at the time each child is born seem to indicate which child is good and which is not (*see also*: Ga.4:22-26). Abram is aged *eighty six* (*number value* for **γαλιλαία**; **ζιζάνια**; a token of what is evil?) when the servant Hagar gives birth to Ishmael (Gn.16:16). Yet by the time Sarah gives birth to Isaac, Abram's name has changed to Abraham and his age is now *one hundred* (Gn.21:5; a token of what is good?).

Ishmael will give birth to twelve nations (Gn.17:20); here is the parallel with Jacob and with Jesus. But it is surely significant that Abraham gives all his possessions to Isaac (Gn.25:5), the son he really loves (Gn.22:2).

Recalling the attributes of Abel and Cain, we can tell that Isaac is good. His preferred diet gives this away on its own (*qv*. Gn.25:28). Isaac comes close to being killed by his father, Abraham (Gn.22:10). But the plan is amended at the last minute and Abraham sacrifices a ram (or was it '**a lord**'?) in place of his own son Isaac (Gn.22:13-14).

In this way Isaac survives to marry **ρεβεκκα** [*Rebecca*] who turns out to be evil (Gn.27:5-17). Her *number value* is **153**. Once again two children are born:

LXX	ἦν δὲ ισαακ ἐτῶν	But Isaac was <u>forty</u> years
Gn.	τεσ**σα**ράκο**ντα** ὅτε ἔλαβεν	(old) when he took Rebecca,
25:20	τὴν ρεβεκκαν θυγατέρα	daughter of Bethuel the
	βαθουηλ τοῦ σύρου ἐκ τῆς	Syrian from Mesopotamia,
	μεσοποταμίας ἀδελφὴν	sister of Laban the Syrian, to
	λαβαν τοῦ σύρου ἑαυτῷ	himself as <u>woman</u>.
	γυ**ναῖκ**α	

25:21	ἐδεῖτο δὲ ισαακ **κυρίου** περὶ ρεβεκκας τῆς γυ**ναικ**ὸς αὐτοῦ ὅτι στεῖρα ἦν ἐπήκουσεν δὲ αὐτοῦ **ὁ θεός** καὶ ἔλαβεν ἐν γαστρὶ ρεβεκκα ἡ γυνὴ αὐτοῦ	But Isaac entreated (the) **lord** concerning Rebecca, his <u>woman</u>, for she was barren. But **God** heard him and Rebecca, his woman, conceived in (the) belly.
25:22	ἐσκίρτων δὲ τὰ παιδία ἐν αὐτῇ εἶπεν δέ εἰ οὕτως μοι μέλλει γίνεσθαι ἵνα τί μοι τοῦτο ἐπορεύθη δὲ πυθέσθαι παρὰ **κυρίου**	But the children were bouncing within her. And she said "If (it is) so with me, what is going to happen to me?". And she went to find out from (the) **lord**.
25:23	καὶ εἶπεν **κύριος** αὐτῇ δύο ἔθνη ἐν τῇ γαστρί σού εἰσιν καὶ δύο λαοὶ ἐκ τῆς κοιλίας σου διασταλήσονται καὶ λαὸς λαοῦ ὑπερέξει καὶ ὁ μείζων δουλεύσει τῷ ἐλάσσονι	And (the) **lord** said to her "Two nations are in your abdomen and two peoples shall be separated from your belly. And a people shall overcome a people, and the greater shall serve the lesser".
25:24	καὶ ἐπληρώθησαν αἱ ἡμέραι τοῦ τεκεῖν αὐτήν καὶ τῇδε ἦν δίδυμα ἐν τῇ κοιλίᾳ αὐτῆς	And the days were fulfilled for her to give birth, and so it was twins in her belly.
25:25	ἐξῆλθεν δὲ ὁ υἱὸς ὁ πρωτότοκος πυρράκης ὅλος ὡσεὶ δορὰ δασύς ἐπωνόμασεν δὲ τὸ ὄνομα αὐτοῦ ησαυ	And the firstborn son emerged reddish all over, like a hairy skin: and she named his name Esau.

25:26	καὶ μετὰ τοῦτο ἐξῆλθεν ὁ ἀδελφὸς αὐτοῦ καὶ ἡ χεὶρ αὐτοῦ ἐπειλημμένη τῆς πτέρνης ησαυ καὶ ἐκάλεσεν τὸ ὄνομα αὐτοῦ ιακωβ ισαακ δὲ ἦν ἐτῶν ἑξήκοντα ὅτε ἔτεκεν αὐτοὺς ρεβεκκα	And after that his brother emerged, and his hand grasping the heel of Esau. And she called his name Jacob. And Isaac was sixty years when Rebecca gave birth to them.
25:27	ηὐξήθησαν δὲ οἱ νεανίσκοι καὶ ἦν ησαυ ἄνθρωπος εἰδὼς κυνηγεῖν ἄγροικος ιακωβ δὲ ἦν ἄνθρωπος ἄπλαστος οἰκῶν οἰκίαν	But the <u>children</u> grew up. And Esau (was) a person knowing how to hunt, a countryman. But Jacob was an untrained person, dwelling in <u>a house</u>.

Jacob dwells in: οἰ**κίαν** [*a house*]. Here is the '*sign*' for Cain.

How interesting that we see the same device in the gospel at Mk.7:24, framed into a strong 'auto-didactic' context and referring now to Jesus:

Mk. 7:24	ἐκεῖθεν δὲ ἀναστὰς ἀπῆλθεν εἰς τὰ ὅρια τύρου. καὶ εἰσελθὼν εἰς οἰκίαν οὐδένα ἤθελεν γνῶναι, καὶ οὐκ ἠδυνήθη λαθεῖν:	But from there, <u>rising up</u>, he went away into the edges of Tyre. And entering into <u>a house</u>, he wished no one to know. ***Yet he was not able to escape detection!***

Jacob later schemes with his mother Rebecca to deceive his father Isaac whose vision, previously acute, is blunted now by age (Gn.27:1). Then it should come as no surprise that Jacob says of himself:

> ἐγὼ δὲ ἀνὴρ λεῖος   (Gn.27:11)
> But I'm a smooth man

To further the deceit, Rebecca places goat skins upon Jacob's arms and:

ἐπὶ τὰ γυμνὰ τοῦ τραχήλου αὐτοῦ   (Gn.27:16)
upon the nakedness of his neck

We should not need reminding that smoothness, like nakedness, is the attribute of the serpent. Everything to do with Jacob is deeply sinister.

But Esau and Jacob are children just grown up:

LXX Gn. 25:28	ἠγάπησεν δὲ ισαακ τὸν ησαυ ὅτι ἡ θήρα αὐτοῦ βρῶσις αὐτῷ ρεβεκκα δὲ ἠγάπα τὸν ιακωβ	And Isaac loved Esau because his wild beast was food for him. But Rebecca loved Jacob.
25:29	ἥψησεν δὲ ιακωβ ἕψεμα ἦλθεν δὲ ησαυ ἐκ τοῦ πεδίου ἐκλείπων	But Jacob boiled up soup. And Esau came from the plain, giving up (the hunt).
25:30	καὶ εἶπεν ησαυ τῷ ιακωβ γεῦσόν με ἀπὸ τοῦ ἐψέματος τοῦ πυρροῦ τούτου ὅτι ἐκλείπω διὰ τοῦτο ἐκλήθη τὸ ὄνομα αὐτοῦ εδωμ	And Esau said to Jacob "Let me taste some of this reddish soup because I am giving up. On account of this his name was called Edom.
25:31	εἶπεν δὲ ιακωβ τῷ ησαυ ἀπόδου μοι σήμερον τὰ πρωτοτόκιά σου ἐμοί	And Jacob said to Esau "Give away your birthrights (*lit*: your first births) to me today".
25:32	εἶπεν δὲ ησαυ ἰδοὺ ἐγὼ πορεύομαι τελευτᾶν καὶ ἵνα τί μοι ταῦτα τὰ πρωτοτόκια	But Esau said "I shall proceed to an end. And what are they to me, these birthrights?"

25:33	καὶ εἶπεν αὐτῷ ιακωβ ὄμοσόν μοι σήμερον καὶ ὤμοσεν αὐτῷ ἀπέδοτο δὲ ησαυ τὰ πρωτοτόκια τῷ ιακωβ	And Jacob said to him "Swear to me today". And he swore to him. And Esau gave away the birthrights to Jacob.
25:34	ιακωβ δὲ ἔδωκεν τῷ ησαυ ἄρτον καὶ ἔψεμα φακοῦ καὶ ἔφαγεν καὶ ἔπιεν καὶ **ἀναστὰς** ᾤχετο καὶ ἐφαύλισεν ησαυ τὰ πρωτοτόκια	And Jacob gave to Esau bread and lentil soup. And he ate and drank. And <u>rising up</u>, he departed. And Esau disparaged the birthrights.

Here is another meal which proves unsuited to the one consuming it.

Isaac and his son Esau are hunters of wild creatures, meat eaters in the style of the pastor, or hunter-gatherer. Theirs is the 'type' of Abel. By this the authors of scripture identify both as good.

But Jacob takes after his mother. His diet is bread, and a soup made not from meat but from another cereal crop, lentils. These foods identify Jacob as the 'type' of Cain; it is a consideration reinforced by his being '*smooth*' and by '*the nakedness of his neck*'.

Jacob's lentils are *red* lentils, providing for Esau to mistake the soup for one made from meat (and the colour may remind us of the blood of Abel, which at Gn.4:11 the earth 'opened its mouth' to receive from the hand of Cain).

For one reason or another Esau has failed in the hunt[6] for wild beasts. He is hungry. He eats the bread and he drinks the lentil soup.

These foods are suited to Jacob. If Esau is 'good' he should be avoiding them. But Esau has given up the hunt, and ends up consuming the wrong kind of food. His mistake seems to be a token of his own failure to understand that *he is supposed to be good*.

In the prior narrative Cain was firstborn over Abel but offended **God** by killing his brother. Perhaps you remember Cain's threat at Gn.4:14:

> If you throw me out today from a face of the earth,
> I shall be *hidden* also from your face.

Is Jacob presented as Cain reborn, but now going in disguise? If so he has been demoted, for as it happens Esau is now the firstborn.

At the least we can say that the authors of *Genesis* have cast Esau in a rôle analogous to that of Abel, whilst Jacob seeks the dominant rôle once played by evil Cain. To achieve priority, Jacob must displace his brother. This is why the two are struggling in the womb. In this connection we are warned of the risk that evil will overcome good: for '*a people shall overcome a people, and the greater shall serve the lesser*' (Gn.25:23). And now we see why Jacob emerges from the womb clutching at Esau's *heel*. Is it not plain that the narrative has been configured to fulfil the condition set by the curse imposed at Gn.3:15?

αὐτός σου τηρήσει κεφαλήν καὶ σὺ τηρήσεις αὐτοῦ <u>πτέρναν</u>
He shall watch you for a head and you shall watch him for a *heel*

The *heel* of the one who is good is always poised to crush the *head* of the one descended from the serpent. In normal childbirth infants are delivered head first. Here the two children are born in quick succession, with Jacob clutching at Esau's heel. By this means Esau is depicted with his heel 'over' Jacob's emerging head. Are we not expected to realise, in accordance with the curse, that in this way the writer identifies Jacob as 'seed of the serpent', the description also suited to Cain? How neatly the pieces of this puzzle have been fitted together.

But here is the irony. Esau *fails* to understand his favoured status. He *fails* in the hunt for 'wild beasts'. Disparaging his own birthright, he finishes up consuming Jacob's kind of food. By this Esau is utterly undone. He is '*the greater*': but he abandons his place and now will serve '*the lesser*'. Thus evil Jacob (*aka*. Israel) succeeds in recovering his lost priority. In the gospels we shall find the same scenario rehearsed yet again. But we shall not fail in the hunt for 'wild beasts'; we shall not fail to distinguish the tokens for what is deemed to be evil.

Isaiah Foresees Two Children

The view is widely held that *Isaiah* Chapter 7 refers prescriptively to the birth of Jesus, whose name shall be εμμανουηλ [*Emmanuel*; **Hebr**: *god with us*]. But this tradition must be wrong. In the gospels it is not Jesus who is Emmanuel, it is John the Baptist.

A probable cause for the misunderstanding is the passage at Mt.1:22-23. From this some readers may infer that Emmanuel is Jesus. But if you read the passage for yourself you will see that this is not what it says. Any writer may use innuendo to throw his reader off balance. Scripture is replete with tricks and riddles; we must keep our wits about us.

The child foretold at Is.7:14 aligns with the part in the gospels played by John. This we can easily tell from what is stated about his diet, which here is explicitly good:

LXX Is. 7:14	διὰ τοῦτο δώσει κύριος αὐτὸς ὑμῖν **σημεῖον** ἰδοὺ ἡ παρθένος ἐν γαστρὶ ἕξει καὶ τέξεται υἱόν καὶ καλέσεις τὸ ὄνομα αὐτοῦ εμμανουηλ	On this account (the) lord himself shall give you **a sign**. Look! The virgin[7] shall have in (her) belly, and give birth to, a son. And you shall call his name *Emmanuel* [8].
7:15	βούτυρον καὶ μέλι φάγεται πρὶν ἢ γνῶναι αὐτὸν ἢ προελέσθαι πονηρὰ **ἐκλέξεται** τὸ ἀγαθόν	**Butter and honey he shall eat**. Before either he knows or chooses evil things, **he shall choose the good**.
7:16	διότι πρὶν ἢ γνῶναι τὸ παιδίον ἀγαθὸν ἢ κακὸν ἀπειθεῖ πονηρίᾳ τοῦ ἐκλέξασθαι τὸ ἀγαθόν ...	Because before either the child knows good or evil, he disobeys cunning to choose the good ...

Butter and honey are foods of the 'type' brought by Abel (Gn.4:4).

It is in *Mark* that we are told:

Mk.	καὶ ἦν ὁ ἰωάννης ἐνδεδυμένος τρίχας καμήλου καὶ ζώνην δερματίνην περὶ τὴν ὀσφὺν αὐτοῦ,	And John was clothed in camel hair and a skin belt around his loins,
1:6	καὶ ἐσθίων ἀκρίδας καὶ **μέλι ἄγριον**.	and eating locusts and ***wild honey***.
1:7	καὶ ἐκήρυσσεν λέγων, ἔρχεται ὁ **ἰσχυρότερός** μου ὀπίσω μου, οὗ οὐκ εἰμὶ **ἱκανὸς** κύψας λῦσαι τὸν **ἱμάντα** τῶν ὑποδημάτων αὐτοῦ:	And he proclaimed, saying "Behind me comes the one stronger than me, for whom **I AM not** competent, bending down, to untie the thong of his sandals".

John seems to have encountered *a camel*. Perhaps he has left it shorn *naked*. But what really matters here is that we can tell from the diet that it must be John the Baptist of whom it is foretold in *Isaiah*:

> ... he disobeys cunning to choose the good   (Is.7:16)

When Adam was forbidden by the cunning **lord god** to eat from the '*tree for knowing good and evil*' (LXX Gn.2:17), the challenge he faced was to *disobey* cunning to choose the good. Then we see that John takes after the figure of Adam as well as that of Abel.

Incidentally, were you competent to see the name of **καϊν** concealed (above) in the word **ἱκανὸς** [*competent*]? Perhaps you noticed too that **χριστός** [*Christ*] lies concealed within the word **ἰσχυρότερός** [*stronger*]? The gospel begins by presenting us with these omens of what is to come.

It is when we reach *Isaiah* Chapter 8 that we find foretold *a second child*:

LXX	καὶ εἶπεν **κύριος** πρός με	And (the) **lord** said to me
Is.	λαβὲ σεαυτῷ τόμον **ΚΑΙΝ**οῦ	"Take for yourself a volume
8:1	μεγάλου καὶ γράψον εἰς	for a great **new** one and
	αὐτὸν γραφίδι ἀνθρώπου τοῦ	with a pen write in it of a
	ὀξέως προνομὴν ποιῆσαι	person swiftly making a
	σκύλων πάρεστιν γάρ	plunder of spoils: for he is present".
8:2	καὶ μάρτυράς μοι ποίησον	And make for me (as)
	πιστοὺς ἀνθρώπους τὸν	witnesses faithful persons,
	ουριαν καὶ τὸν ζαχαριαν υἱὸν	Urias and Zacharias, son of
	βαραχιου	Barachias.
8:3	καὶ προσῆλθον πρὸς τὴν	And I went to the
	πρ**Οφ**ῆτ**ΙΝ** καὶ ἐν γαστρὶ	**prophetess**[9] and she
	ἔλαβεν καὶ ἔτεκεν υἱόν καὶ	conceived in (her) belly and
	εἶπεν **κύριός** μοι κάλεσον τὸ	gave birth to a son. And (the)
	ὄνομα αὐτοῦ **ταχέως**	**lord** said to me "Call his
	σκύλευσον ὀξέως	name: **Spoil quickly,**
	προνόμευσον	**plunder swiftly.**
8:4	διότι πρὶν ἢ γνῶναι τὸ	Because before the child
	παιδίον **ΚΑλεῖΝ** πατέρα ἢ	learns to know (how) **to call**
	μητέρα λήμψεται δύναμιν	father or mother, he shall
	δαμασκοῦ καὶ τὰ σκῦλα	take the power of Damascus
	σαμαρείας ἔναντι βασιλέως	and the spoils of Samaria, in
	ἀσσυρίων	the presence of a king of Assyria".

Here is the passage prescriptive of Jesus. The '*new*' volume which is to be written seems to anticipate the books of the '*new*' testament.

Significantly, the Greek word for '*new*' embodies within it the name of
Cain (*qv.* Is.8:1 above). Then at Lk.2:16 the infant Jesus is found by the
shepherds ἐν τῇ φάτνῃ [*in the* **animal feed** *trough*]. This is the first
indication we get that the diet of Jesus will be of the 'type' preferred by
Cain.

What is said here about this second child is ominous indeed:

> Call his name: *Spoil quickly, plunder swiftly.*

> Because before the child learns to know (how) to call father or
> mother, he shall take the power of Damascus and the spoils of
> Samaria, in the presence of a king of Assyria.

Isaiah warns us further:

LXX Is. 8:13	κύριον <u>αὐτὸν</u> ἁγιάσατε καὶ <u>αὐτὸς</u> ἔσται σου φόβος	**A lord** [*in Hebr. MT:* **YHWH Sabaoth**], make *him* holy, then *he* shall be your fear
8:14	καὶ ἐὰν ἐπ' αὐτῷ πεποιθὼς ᾖς ἔσται σοι εἰς ἁγίασμα καὶ οὐχ ὡς λίθου προσκόμματι συναντήσεσθε αὐτῷ οὐδὲ ὡς πέτρας πτώματι ὁ δὲ οἶκος ιακωβ ἐν παγίδι καὶ ἐν κοιλάσματι <u>ἐγ**Κα**θή**μεΝοΙ**</u> ἐν ιερουσαλημ	And, *if you should have been persuaded about him,* he shall be to you for a holiness, and (then) you will not encounter him as a stone for stumbling, nor as a rock for falling. But the house (of) Jacob (is) in a snare, and those <u>seated</u> in Jerusalem (stuck) in a groove.

8:15	διὰ τοῦτο ἀδυνατήσουσιν ἐν αὐτοῖς <u>πολλοὶ</u> καὶ πεσοῦνται	Through this, <u>many</u> shall become weak in themselves, and they shall fall.
	καὶ συντριβήσονται καὶ ἐγγιοῦσιν καὶ ἁλώσονται ἄνθρωποι ἐν ἀσφαλείᾳ ὄντες	And they shall be crushed together and they shall get close and they shall be captured, persons existing in safety!
8:16	τότε φανεροὶ ἔσονται οἱ σφραγιζόμενοι τὸν νόμον τοῦ **μὴ** μαθεῖν	Then they shall be evident, those sealing the law for it **_NOT_** to be understood
8:17	καὶ ἐρεῖ μενῶ **τὸν θεὸν** τὸν ἀποστρέψαντα τὸ πρόσωπον αὐτοῦ ἀπὸ τοῦ οἴκου ιακωβ καὶ πεποιθὼς ἔσομαι ἐπ' αὐτῷ	And you shall say "I remain for **God**, who turns away his face from the house of Jacob, and I shall be persuaded about *him*".

Here is the prescription for the people to be deceived *en masse*.

Israel (the house of Jacob) is to adopt **the lord Sabaoth** as its god. Having adopted him, they will no longer recognise him as *a stone for stumbling*, nor as *a rock for falling*. In consequence they will be caught unwitting in a snare, stuck in a groove, captive to those who have '*sealed up*' the Law (ie. the *Torah*) so as to provide that it may **NOT** be understood!

Israel will adopt the impostor for its god, unaware of his true identity!

This shocking scenario will develop into what we know today as:

ἡ **ΚΑΙΝὴ** διαθήκη
the <u>New</u> Testament

Far from being confined to the house of Israel, this deceit will later be thrust upon the world through the medium of the gospels and their shallow interpretation by the Catholic Church.

That the second child at Is.8:3-4 is intended to be Jesus becomes plain from the obvious parallel between this continuation in *Isaiah*:

LXX Is. 8:23	καὶ οὐκ ἀπορηθήσεται ὁ ἐν στενοχωρίᾳ ὢν ἕως καιροῦ τοῦτο πρῶτον ποίει ταχὺ ποίει χώρα ζαβουλων ἡ γῆ νεφθαλιμ ὁδὸν θαλάσσης καὶ οἱ λοιποὶ οἱ τὴν παραλίαν **ΚΑτοικοῦΝτες** καὶ πέραν τοῦ ιορδάνου γαλιλαία τῶν ἐθνῶν τὰ μέρη τῆς ιουδαίας	And he is not at a loss, the one being for a while in straitened circumstances. This first thing he makes quickly: he makes (the) region of Zaboulon, the land of Nephthalim, way of (the) sea. And the rest (are) those <u>settling down</u> on the sea shore and beyond the Jordan, Galilee of the nations, the parts of Judaea.
9:1	ὁ λαὸς ὁ πορευόμενος ἐν σκότει ἴδετε φῶς μέγα οἱ **ΚΑτοικοῦΝτες** ἐν χώρᾳ καὶ σκιᾷ θανάτου φῶς λάμψει ἐφ' ὑμᾶς	The people coming in darkness saw a great light. Those <u>settling down</u> in (the) region and shadow of death, a light will shine upon them.

... and this passage in the gospel attributed to *Matthew*:

Mt. 4:13	καὶ **ΚΑταλιπὼΝ** τὴν ναζαρὰ ἐλθὼν κατῴκησεν εἰς καφαρναοὺμ τὴν παραθαλασσίαν ἐν ὁρίοις ζαβουλὼν καὶ νεφθαλίμ:	And <u>leaving</u> Nazareth, arriving he settled down in Capharnaum, the seaside within (the) boundaries of Zaboulon and Nephthalim

4:14	ἵνα πληρωθῇ τὸ ῥηθὲν διὰ ἠσαΐου τοῦ προφήτου λέγοντος,	So that it might be fulfilled, what was spoken through the prophet Isaiah saying:
4:15	γῆ ζαβουλὼν καὶ γῆ νεφθαλίμ, ὁδὸν θαλάσσης, πέραν τοῦ ἰορδάνου, γαλιλαία τῶν ἐθνῶν,	'Land of Zaboulon and land of Nephthalim, way of (the) sea, beyond the Jordan, Galilee of the nations'.
4:16	ὁ λαὸς ὁ καθήμενος ἐν σκότει φῶς εἶδεν μέγα, καὶ τοῖς **καθημένοις** ἐν χώρᾳ καὶ σκιᾷ θανάτου φῶς ἀνέτειλεν αὐτοῖς.	The people sitting in darkness saw a great light, and to those <u>sitting</u> in (the) region and shadow of death a light dawned for them.

Notice how the word **κατοικοῦντες** [*settling down*] used at Is.9:1 is replaced in the gospel with the word **καθημένοις** [*sitting*]; yet the '*sign*' for Cain is preserved.

The great '*light*' which, in the person of Jesus the Nazarene, dawns upon these people seems to be rather closely connected with the '*glory*' amidst which Isaiah first beheld the **lord Sabaoth**. Accordingly this great '*light*', once you recognise it, turns out to be '*a stone for stumbling and a rock for falling*'. Yet there is hope that the truth may survive to be told because further on within *1ˢᵗ Isaiah* we have this:

| LXX Is. 35:4 | παρακαλέσατε οἱ ὀλιγόψυχοι τῇ διανοίᾳ ἰσχύσατε μὴ φοβεῖσθε ἰδοὺ **ὁ θεὸς** ἡμῶν κρίσιν <u>ἀνταποδίδωσιν</u> καὶ ἀνταποδώσει αὐτὸς ἥξει καὶ σώσει ἡμᾶς | Let the faint-hearted take comfort! Be strong with the intellect! Do not fear! Look! Our **<u>God</u>** <u>may give in return</u> (his) judgement, and he *shall* give (it). He will come and save us. |

35:5	τότε ἀνοιχθήσονται ὀφθαλμοὶ τυφλῶν καὶ ὦτα κωφῶν ἀκούσονται	***Then eyes of (the) blind shall be opened up and ears of (the) deaf shall hear.***
35:6	τότε ἁλεῖται ὡς ἔλαφος ὁ χωλός καὶ τρανὴ ἔσται γλῶσσα μογιλάλων ὅτι ἐρράγη ἐν τῇ ἐρήμῳ ὕδωρ καὶ φάραγξ ἐν γῇ διψώσῃ	Then shall the lame leap like a deer and (the) stammering tongue be clear, for water has burst forth in the desert and a gully in a thirsty land.
35:7	καὶ ἡ ἄνυδρος ἔσται εἰς ἕλη καὶ εἰς τὴν διψῶσαν γῆν πηγὴ ὕδατος ἔσται ἐκεῖ εὐφροσύνη ὀρνέων ἔπαυλις καλάμου καὶ ἕλη	And the dry (land) shall turn into pools, and in the thirsting earth a spring of water. There shall be rejoicing of birds, a dwelling of reed(s) and pools.
35:8	ἐκεῖ ἔσται ὁδὸς καθαρὰ καὶ ὁδὸς ἁγία κληθήσεται καὶ οὐ μὴ παρέλθῃ ἐκεῖ ἀκάθαρτος οὐδὲ ἔσται ἐκεῖ ὁδὸς ἀκάθαρτος οἱ δὲ διεσπαρμένοι πορεύσονται ἐπ' αὐτῆς καὶ οὐ μὴ πλανηθῶσιν	There shall be a clean way and it shall be called a holy way. And there shall certainly not pass there anyone unclean, neither shall there be there an unclean way. But those who have been dispersed shall go upon it, and they should certainly not go astray.

35:9	καὶ οὐκ ἔσται ἐκεῖ λέων οὐδὲ τῶν θηρίων τῶν πονηρῶν οὐ μὴ ἀναβῇ ἐπ' αὐτὴν οὐδὲ μὴ εὑρεθῇ ἐκεῖ	And there shall be no lion there, nor might any of the evil beasts go up upon it, nor even be found there.
	ἀλλὰ πορεύσονται ἐν αὐτῇ λελυτρωμένοι	But *those who have been ransomed shall proceed within it.*
35:10	καὶ συνηγμένοι διὰ **κύριον** ἀποστραφήσονται	*And those gathered on account of* **a lord** *shall be turned away.*
	καὶ ἥξουσιν εἰς σιων μετ' εὐφροσύνης καὶ εὐφροσύνη αἰώνιος <u>ὑπὲρ κεφαλῆς αὐτῶν</u>	And they shall come into Sion with rejoicing, and eternal rejoicing <u>*above their head*</u> [10].
	<u>ἐπὶ γὰρ κεφαλῆς αὐτῶν</u> αἴνεσις καὶ ἀγαλλίαμα καὶ εὐφροσύνη καταλήμψεται αὐτούς	<u>*For upon their head*</u> [10] shall praise and exultation and rejoicing take them down.
	ἀπέδρα ὀδύνη καὶ λύπη καὶ στεναγμός	Grief has fled, and sorrow and sighing.

We are assured that those previously dispersed shall go upon the *clean way* of **God**. It is from this term **οἱ καθαροὶ** [*the clean ones*] that we have the name in English for the group known to historians as the *Cathars*[11]. These are the ones who have 'escaped' from the snare, *those who have been ransomed* for **God**. In *Matthew* (the Sermon on the Mount) we have:

| Mt. 5:8 | μακάριοι οἱ <u>καθαροὶ</u> τῇ καρδίᾳ, ὅτι αὐτοὶ **τὸν θεὸν** ὄψονται. | Fortunate (are) those <u>*clean*</u> with the heart ... for they shall see <u>**God**</u>. |

198 From *Genesis* to the Gospels

In contrast it is important to notice that *those gathered on account of* **a lord** *will be turned away*. The gospels repeat this theme of ultimate rejection for those unwise enough to embrace the **lord god** as their god:

Lk. 13:25	ἀφ' οὗ ἂν ἐγερθῇ ὁ οἰκοδεσπότης καὶ ἀποκλείσῃ τὴν θύραν, καὶ ἄρξησθε ἔξω ἑστάναι καὶ κρούειν τὴν θύραν λέγοντες, **κύριε**, ἄνοιξον ἡμῖν: καὶ ἀποκριθεὶς ἐρεῖ ὑμῖν, **οὐκ** οἶδα ὑμᾶς πόθεν ἐστέ.	From whenever the ruler of the house may rise up, and may close the door, and you shall begin to stand outside and knock at the door, saying, '**Lord**, open to us!': then answering he will say to you 'I do **not** know you, where you are from'.
13:26	τότε ἄρξεσθε λέγειν, ἐφάγομεν ἐνώπιόν σου καὶ ἐπίομεν, καὶ ἐν ταῖς πλατείαις ἡμῶν ἐδίδαξας:	Then you shall start to say 'We ate in your presence and we drank, and you taught in our streets'.
13:27	καὶ ἐρεῖ λέγων ὑμῖν, οὐκ οἶδα [ὑμᾶσ] πόθεν ἐστέ: ἀπόστητε ἀπ' ἐμοῦ, πάντες ἐργάται ἀδικίας.	And he will say, speaking to you: 'I do not know [you] where you are from; get away from me, all *workers of iniquity*'.
13:28	ἐκεῖ ἔσται ὁ κλαυθμὸς καὶ ὁ βρυγμὸς τῶν ὀδόντων, ὅταν ὄψησθε ἀβραὰμ καὶ ἰσαὰκ καὶ ἰακὼβ καὶ πάντας τοὺς προφήτας ἐν τῇ βασιλείᾳ τοῦ θεοῦ, ὑμᾶς δὲ ἐκβαλλομένους ἔξω.	There will be the whimpering and the grinding of the teeth, when you see Abraham and Isaac and Jacob, and all the prophets, in the kingdom of God ... *but yourselves thrown out outside*.

PART 2

~

CurtAINs
FOR
CAIN

~

Attributed to Galileo Galilei (1564-1642):

"It is very pious to say and prudent to affirm that the holy Bible can never speak untruth -- whenever its true meaning is understood. But I believe nobody will deny that it is often very abstruse, and may say things which are quite different from what its bare words signify."

"All truths are easy to understand once they are discovered. The point is to discover them".

Chapter 8

John and Jesus

The author of the gospel according to *Luke* extends his narrative by adding a second book. It is the one we know as *Acts of the Apostles*. He begins in this way:

Ac.	τὸν μὲν πρῶτον λόγον	The first explanation
1:1	ἐποιησάμην περὶ πάντων,	I made concerning everything,
	ὦ **θεόφιλε**, ὧν ἤρξατο ὁ	O ***Theophilus***, which Jesus
	ἰησοῦς ποιεῖν τε καὶ	began to do and also
	<u>διδάσκειν</u>	***<u>to teach</u>*** ...

He addresses his reader as **θεόφιλε** [*Theophilus*; *God-friend*]. It is the same word he has used at the beginning of his gospel (Lk.1:3).

Here, in the vocative case, the word develops an ending in -ε. But imagine that the sentence had been constructed to use instead the nominative case: θεόφιλος or the accusative: θεόφιλον. We should be addressed using a word which serves to conceal ὄφις or ὄφιν [*a serpent*]. How different then would the import be!

If you are puzzled by the point made here, or if you do not see why it should be cause for concern that Jesus had begun ***to teach***, then before reading further you may find it helpful to master the ground covered in Part 1 of this book.

Otherwise let us continue with this from the NT letter *2 Timothy*:

2 Tm. 3:16	πᾶσα γραφὴ θεόπνευστος καὶ ὠφέλιμος πρὸς διδασκαλίαν, πρὸς ἐλεγμόν, πρὸς ἐπανόρθωσιν, πρὸς παιδείαν τὴν ἐν δικαιοσύνη,	Every scripture god-inspired and helpful for teaching, for refutation, for correction, for training in righteousness
3:17	ἵνα ἄρτιος ἦ ὁ τοῦ θεοῦ ἄνθρωπος, πρὸς πᾶν ἔργον ἀγαθὸν ἐξηρτισμένος.	So that the person of **God** may be perfected, fully completed for every good work.

The passage has much to teach, and goes on to explain the benefit which should accrue to students who are willing to learn. The person of **God** '*may be perfected, fully completed for every good work*'.

We saw in Chapter 5 that the practice of anagrammatic dispersion is robustly established in scripture, with the '*sign*' for Cain first defined and exemplified at LXX Gn.4:15-16.

To recapitulate, the *fact* of Cain's name being hidden is consistent with LXX Gn.4:14 where Cain says:

> If you throw me out today from a face of the earth,
> I shall be *hidden* also from your face.

The *method* employed is dispersion. The use of this technique is consistent with Cain's identity as a '*worker of the earth*' (Gn.4:2). As such he is '*a sower*', and has scattered his '*seed*' in the text. Our task as readers is to take in the resulting '*harvest*' (*qv*. Mt.13:30, 13:39).

In the passage above, the words διδασΚαλίαV [*teaching; instruction*] and διΚαΙοσύVη [*rigtheousness*] convey the '*sign*' for Cain. It is not difficult to spot because in both cases the letters are arranged in the required order.

Then the words ωΦέλΙμΟς [*helpful*] and έπανόρθωσΙV [*correction*] provide in addition for us to see and to hear the name of the serpent (following the pattern explained in Chapter 7).

But has έλεγμόν [*refutation*] been included to refute any suggestion that *every* word of scripture should be regarded as conveying more than literal significance? It is reasonable that this should be amongst the points taught. For if the authors of scripture demand that our method of reading be extended beyond what is customary in other books, then it is up to them to define the limits for what features are to be found significant, and what are not.

For the authors to establish such limits, and for their readers to grasp what these are, is plainly essential. Without an established convention, readers would soon be mired in confusion. This must not (and will not) be our fate.

The Gospels as Recursive Sequels to *Genesis*

We noted in Chapter 1 of this book that a trend which developed in the fourth century CE was:

> to assign to scripture a historicity it did not deserve, as Constantine's biographer Eusebius of Caesarea sought to do with his inventive Εκκλησίαστικη Ίστορία [*Church History*].

Since the fourth century this false historicity has helped to lead many astray by distracting attention from those features of scripture which in reality were of most importance. For the gospels are fiction. They are packed with riddles which readers must solve before they can access the meaning in full and they sustain a narrative which plainly functions as a recursive sequel to events set forth in the early chapters of *Genesis*.

But this kind of fiction is clever. For the skill of these authors is such that down the generations they have induced large numbers of people to make, in real life, precisely the same mistake as that made by the fictional characters in the narrative. And it is typical that many readers should make this enduring mistake without becoming aware that for doing so they are condemned by the very texts upon which they pin all their hopes.

We are left to reflect upon the extraordinary quality of human nature, that it should be so easy to lead millions astray but so hard to assert the truth.

In the long span of scripture's narrative, the first successful deceit takes place at Gn.3:4-6. It is through what (and who) *she fails to recognise* that Eve is instantly undone. Yet scripture is structured in such a way that those readers who fail to grasp what really happens in the story about Paradise go on to miss the significant allegory which pervades all of the subsequent narrative. And because they miss it, they fall victim *themselves* to the same deceit.

In the letter of *James* we find an intriguing passage:

Jm.	καὶ ἡ γλῶσσα πῦρ, ὁ κόσμος	And the tongue (is) a fire.
3:6	τῆς ἀδικίας, ἡ γλῶσσα	The microcosm of iniquity,
	καθίσταται ἐν τοῖς μέλεσιν	the tongue is placed within
	ἡμῶν, ἡ σπιλοῦσα ὅλον τὸ	our members which, staining
	σῶμα καὶ φλογίζουσα τὸν	the whole body and having
	τροχὸν τῆς γενέσεως	set on fire *the wheel* [1] *of*
	καὶ φλογιζομένη ὑπὸ τῆς	*Genesis*, is also set on fire by
	γεέννης.	*Gehenna*.

Gehenna, for the Jews who lived in Jerusalem, was a token for hell. Does this passage suggest that the deception related in *Genesis* is given to recur in a cyclical fashion?

We have only to examine the record of our history to realise that, where Eve's deception does recur, so often scripture itself has served as the vehicle for the '*many*' to be deceived. For the authors of scripture, by writing all that they did, have provided for this result ... that those who do not penetrate the '*mystery*' are instead led astray by what they *think* they understand.

As suggested here, scripture functions like a double-edged sword:

Heb. 4:12	ζῶν γὰρ ὁ λόγος τοῦ θεοῦ καὶ ἐνεργὴς καὶ τομώτερος ὑπὲρ πᾶσαν μάχαιραν δίστομον	For the 'Logos' of God (is) alive and active, and sharper than every two-mouthed dagger
	καὶ διϊκνούμενος ἄχρι μερισμοῦ **ψυχῆς** καὶ **πνεύματος**, ἁρμῶν τε καὶ μυελῶν,	and penetrating even to the dividing of **Soul** and of **Spirit**, both of joints and marrow,
	καὶ κριτικὸς ἐνθυμήσεων καὶ ἐννοιῶν καρδίας:	and able to discern (the) considerations and notions of a heart.
4:13	καὶ οὐκ ἔστιν κτίσις ἀφανὴς ἐνώπιον αὐτοῦ, πάντα δὲ γυμνὰ καὶ τετραχηλισμένα τοῖς ὀφθαλμοῖς αὐτοῦ, πρὸς ὃν ἡμῖν ὁ λόγος.	And it is not a creature invisible in its countenance, but all things (are) naked and have had (their) neck twisted (round) <u>to the **eyes**</u> of that which (is) for us the Logos.

Perhaps you remember from Chapter 2 the distinction drawn by the authors of scripture between a *Soulish* (or psychic) person, to whom the things of the 'Spirit of God' are mere foolishness, and the *Spiritual* person who investigates all things, ***even the deep things of God*** (1 Cor.2:6-15). It is a distinction fundamental to Gnostic thinking.

In the passage above, the 'Logos' is alive and active … and penetrates to the dividing of *Soul* and of *Spirit*. It is able to discern the considerations and notions of a heart … and is not a creaure invisible in its 'countenance'. And at that point the 'Logos' becomes suddenly 'visible' before our very **eyes** [Ὀφθαλμοῖς]. It is that wily and deceitful creature with the 'naked neck', Ὄφις [the *serpent*].

Here we have a declaration, all but explicit, that with scripture a sharp and simultaneous divide will be drawn between:

- Those who can penetrate the 'mystery' and understand what it's really all about. These are the '*Spiritual*' ones, able to 'see' the serpent (the Logos) and to follow his tricks with equanimity.

- The '*many*' who cannot do this. These are the '*Soulish*' ones. They do not 'see' the serpent and end up being badly caught out.

How few down the centuries have suspected that scripture played such a rôle as this, actively leading astray those who failed to understand it?

We noted in Chapter 2 that Augustine of Hippo, in his *De Doctrina Christiana*, makes the general assertion that much is concealed behind the obscurity of scripture - which as a result can lead many astray.

There is little indication that even Augustine understood for himself anything much of how the riddles were solved. But whether Augustine knew it or not, these Gnostic authors *have* provided the means for their readers to learn much of what they knew themselves … surmounting the serpent's heady challenge and passing with flying colours the 'test' which they, as the writers, have set. All you have to do is read in Greek, follow the directions they give, and solve the 'mystery' for yourself.

And perhaps it is now clear that explaining how *that* may be done is the central purpose of this book.

Solving the 'Mystery'

The vital task of solving scripture's 'mystery' may be likened to the process of completing a large jigsaw puzzle. For a successful outcome, the puzzle must be received in good condition, with no pieces damaged or missing. To recover the original picture, it must then be assembled with meticulous care. It is usual to start with the four corners:

Mt.	λέγει αὐτοῖς ὁ ἰησοῦς,	Jesus said to them:
21:42	οὐδέποτε ἀνέγνωτε ἐν ταῖς	"Did you never read in the
	γραφαῖς, λίθον ὃν	scriptures 'A stone which the
	ἀπεδοΚίμασαν οἱ	builders <u>rejected</u>, this
	οἰκοδομοῦντες οὗτος ἐγενήθη	became a head of a corner'?
	εἰς κεφαλὴν γωνίας:	
	παρὰ κυρίου ἐγένετο αὕτη,	This came about from a lord,
	καὶ ἔστιν θαυμαστὴ ἐν	and is wondrous within our
	Όφθαλμοῖς ἡμῶν;	<u>eyes</u>".

Once we have Cain and the serpent in place, the method is then to examine the remaining pieces and find the right place for each one to fit.

Yet many neglect to begin with the corners. Instead they start with the first piece which comes to hand. And in the subsequent rush to make progress there is a risk that further pieces may be slightly forced, and so be fitted wrongly. The inclusion of any false step of this kind has two consequences, both of them adverse.

First, the puzzle cannot be completed: the 'picture' appears visibly defective and may well include several gaps. Second, some pieces remain unused, with no place found where they can be fitted in consistently. From the gospels two examples follow of 'pieces' which down the centuries so many have found could not be fitted in unless they were first distorted (*eg.* by erroneous translation).

In *Matthew* Jesus says:

Mt. 10:34	μὴ νομίσητε ὅτι ἦλθον βαλεῖν εἰρήνην ἐπὶ τὴν γῆν· οὐκ ἦλθον βαλεῖν εἰρήνην ἀλλὰ μάχαιραν.	Do not suppose that I came to confer peace upon the world: I did not come to confer peace but a dagger.
10:35	ἦλθον γὰρ διχάσαι ἄνθρωπον κατὰ τοῦ πατρὸς αὐτοῦ καὶ θυγατέρα κατὰ τῆς μητρὸς αὐτῆς καὶ νύμφην κατὰ τῆς πενθερᾶς αὐτῆς,	For I came to divide a person against his father, and a daughter against her mother, and a bride against her mother-in-law.

And in *Luke* Jesus says:

Lk. 14:26	εἴ τις ἔρχεται πρός με καὶ οὐ μισεῖ τὸν πατέρα ἑαυτοῦ καὶ τὴν μητέρα καὶ τὴν γυναῖκα καὶ τὰ τέκνα καὶ τοὺς ἀδελφοὺς καὶ τὰς ἀδελφάς, ἔτι τε καὶ τὴν ψυχὴν ἑαυτοῦ, οὐ δύναται εἶναί μου μαθητής.	If anyone comes to me and does not hate his own father and mother and <u>wife</u> and children and brothers and sisters, and even also his own soul, he is not able to be my student.

Where an early mistake has been made in the course of assembling the jigsaw (*ie.* the initial foundation work is defective), we later find that we cannot complete the puzzle. For this reason many readers have set aside these two gospel passages, unable to find any place where they could be fitted consistently into the interpretational framework (or *doctrine*) which from the outset these readers have chosen to prefer.

It is precisely this situation which is addressed by the author of *Luke* when (immediately following the second passage cited above) he has Jesus say:

Lk. 14:28	τίς γὰρ ἐξ ὑμῶν θέλων πύργον οἰκοδομῆσαι οὐχὶ πρῶτον καθίσας ψηφίζει τὴν δαπάνην, εἰ ἔχει εἰς ἀπαρτισμόν;	For which of you, wishing to build a tower, does not first sit down to reckon the cost, if he is to reach completion.
14:29	ἵνα μήποτε θέντος αὐτοῦ θεμέλιον καὶ <u>μὴ ἰσχύοντος ἐκτελέσαι</u> πάντες οἱ θεωροῦντες ἄρξωνται αὐτῷ ἐμπαίζειν	Lest perhaps, with his laying a foundation and <u>*not having strength to complete*</u>, all those watching begin to mock him
14:30	λέγοντες ὅτι οὗτος ὁ ἄνθρωπος ἤρξατο οἰκοδομεῖν καὶ οὐκ ἴσχυσεν ἐκτελέσαι.	Saying that this person began to build … and did not have the strength to complete!

Is it not plain that the two passages on the previous page have been included as deliberate *spoilers* to ensure that the 'tower' attempted by those who seek to interpet the gospels cannot be completed by anyone who starts from the wrong foundation?

Those who begin by assuming that Jesus is good are brought up short at this point. They have not first reckoned the cost of their assumption; nor do they have the strength to complete their fragile doctrine. For is it not clear that neither statement made by Jesus (see previous page) could possibly be made by anyone good?

When we assemble wrongly the first few pieces of a puzzle, we have set down a faulty foundation. It is only a matter of time before we find ourselves completely stuck. Try what we may, we cannot get the puzzle to come right.

As with the tower, there is only one way to resolve the impasse. It is to undo the puzzle and start again from scratch, this time taking greater care.

It is what the authors of scripture expect their readers to do. It is what we shall attempt in this book. Yet how reluctant some can be to see the need for this, and to do it.

A puzzle completed correctly may be recognised from the fact that all the pieces are used up, all are found to fit, none are left over when the task is complete. And the coherent picture, now freshly emerged, provides final confirmation that the solution we have is that intended by the person who designed the puzzle in the first place.

Two Children
... this time in the Gospels
... and this time *both* are 'Firstborn'

Long tradition holds that the four canonical gospels appeared between 65 CE and 100 CE. This was the era which saw the regional dispersal of Jews following the catastrophic destruction of Jerusalem by the Romans in 70 CE. It must be possible that a version of the gospels was compiled in an earlier period but not released until the moment was felt to be opportune. So did the destruction of Jerusalem serve as the trigger for the gospels to be released in their final form? It is hard to be sure.

The names conventional for the gospels were assigned long after the texts themselves appeared. About the real authors we know almost nothing except what we can infer, that they were Hellenist Jews and exceptionally well versed in Greek scripture. So when in this chapter we say *Matthew*, we refer not to the unknown writer himself but to the gospel which by long use has come to be known by that name.

Matthew begins with the phrase:

βίβλος γενέσεως ἰησοῦ χριστοῦ ...   (Mt.1:1)
A book of *of Genesis* of Jesus Christ ...

There is the same word used to denote the book of *Genesis*. Indeed the narrative commences by suggesting a genealogy for Jesus, tracing his ancestry from Abraham and Isaac, and then through Jacob, the sinister figure held to have deprived Esau of his birthright. It goes on to address the circumstances of Jesus' birth (although it may be preferable to speak of his rebirth, as will become clear shortly).

In this gospel we find Jesus living in Nazareth[2] before John the Baptist is even mentioned. It is not until the third chapter that John appears, and for him no infancy narrative is given.

In *Mark* no infancy narrative is given for either child. But in this gospel it is John the Baptist who comes first. When the two meet it is for John to baptise Jesus in the River Jordan.

Luke elaborates the story, giving far more detail. Elizabeth is from a priestly family and married to a Jewish priest. She is without child. But with the years there comes to Elizabeth and Zacharias a firstborn son. This child is to be called Zacharias, after the name of his father. But things turn out unexpectedly and his given name is John (this is John the Baptist).

Then we have a second child, a firstborn son for Mary. The intended husband of Mary is Joseph, but the narrative makes clear that Joseph is not the father of Jesus. Instead we are told:

Lk. 1:26	ἐν δὲ τῷ μηνὶ τῷ ἕκτῳ ἀπεστάλη ὁ ἄγγελος γαβριὴλ ἀπὸ τοῦ θεοῦ εἰς πόλιν τῆς γαλιλαίας ᾗ ὄνομα ναζαρὲθ	But in the sixth month the angel Gabriel was sent from God to a city of Galilee for which a name (was) Nazareth
1:27	πρὸς παρθένον ἐμνηστευμένην ἀνδρὶ ᾧ ὄνομα ἰωσὴφ ἐξ οἴκου δαυίδ, καὶ τὸ ὄνομα τῆς παρθένου μαριάμ.	To a virgin betrothed to a man for whom a name (was) Joseph from the house of David, and the name of the virgin (was) Mary.

| 1:28 | καὶ εἰσελθὼν πρὸς αὐτὴν εἶπεν, χαῖρε, ΚεχΑριτωμέVη, ὁ κύριος μετὰ σοῦ. | And coming in to her, he said: 'Rejoice, <u>who has been shown grace</u>: the **lord** (is) with you'. |
| 1:29 | ἡ δὲ ἐπὶ τῷ λόγῳ διεταράχΘη καὶ διελογίζετο ποταπὸς εἴη ὁ ἀσπασμὸς οὗτος. | But she was troubled over the saying and was considering from what origin this greeting might be. |

It is made clear that the 'conception' of **Jesus** takes place **six** months after that of John, so John is the older child.

Moreover it is disclosed to Mary that Elizabeth is:

ἡ συγγενίς σου   (Lk.1:36)
The one congenital with you

Then the writer would have us understand that Elizabeth and Mary are related by birth; the mothers could even be twins. And now we are told:

| Lk. 1:41 | καὶ ἐγένετο ὡς ἤκουσεν τὸν ἀσπασμὸν τῆς μαρίας ἡ ἐλισάβετ, ἐσκίρτησεν τὸ βρέφος ἐν τῇ κοιλίᾳ αὐτῆς, καὶ ἐπλήσθη πνεύματος ἁγίου ἡ ἐλισάβετ, | And it happened as Elizabeth heard the greeting of Mary (that) the foetus bounced in her belly, and Elizabeth was filled by a holy spirit. |

As with Esau and Jacob before them, John and Jesus are blood relations. This time round there are two separate mothers. Yet the Greek verb **σκίρταω** [*I bounce; I leap*], used here of Elizabeth's child in the womb, is the same word used at Gn.25:22 just before we are told of Rebecca:

LXX	καὶ εἶπεν **κύριος** αὐτῇ δύο	And (the) **lord** said to her
Gn.	ἔθνη ἐν τῇ γαστρί σού εἰσιν	*"Two nations are in your*
25:23	καὶ δύο λαοὶ ἐκ τῆς κοιλίας	*abdomen and two peoples*
	σου διασταλήσονται καὶ λαὸς	*shall be separated from*
	λαοῦ ὑπερέξει καὶ ὁ μείζων	*your belly. And a people*
	δουλεύσει τῷ ἐλάσσονι	*shall overcome a people -*
		and the greater shall serve
		the lesser".

In real life the birth of children is often unplanned. But there is nothing unplanned about the message set forth in the gospels. What we are looking at here is plainly recursive allegory[3].

His parents were astonished by Jesus' behaviour
... but *still* they did not understand

Chapters 7 & 8 of *Isaiah* foretell the birth of two children.

The first is to be born to a virgin/maid. He shall be called Emmanuel (*Hebr*: **God**-*with-us*). He shall eat butter and honey (these are foods of the same type as Abel's '*fats/dairy products*' at LXX Gn.4:4) ... and he shall disobey cunning to choose the good (LXX Is.7:16). As we have shown, this must be John the Baptist.

A second child shall be born, this time to a prophetess. As we have shown, this must be Jesus. Of this second child, Isaiah says:

| LXX Is. 8:3 | καὶ προσῆλθον πρὸς τὴν προΟφῆτιν καὶ ἐν γαστρὶ ἔλαβεν καὶ ἔτεκεν υἱόν καὶ εἶπεν κύριός μοι κάλεσον τὸ ὄνομα αὐτοῦ ταχέως σκύλευσον ὀξέως προνόμευσον | And I went to the **prophetess** and she conceived in (her) belly and gave birth to a son. And (the) **lord** said to me "Call his name: **Spoil quickly, plunder swiftly.** |
| 8:4 | διότι πρὶν ἢ γνῶναι τὸ παιδίον Καλεῖν πατέρα ἢ μητέρα λήμψεται δύναμιν δαμασκοῦ καὶ τὰ σκῦλα σαμαρείας ἔναντι βασιλέως ἀσσυρίων | Because before the child learns to know (how) **to call** father or mother, he shall take the power of Damascus and the spoils of Samaria in the presence of a king of Assyria". |

The use of the word προΟφῆτιν [*a prophetess*] is sinister because it serves as a rather thin disguise for Ὄφιν [*a serpent*].

Then the prescription made at 8:4 seems to account for the following passage in *Luke*:

| Lk. 2:41 | καὶ ἐπορεύοντο οἱ γονεῖς αὐτοῦ κατ' ἔτος εἰς ἱερουσαλὴμ τῇ ἑορτῇ τοῦ πάσχα. | And his parents went each year to Jerusalem for the Feast of the Passover. |
| 2:42 | καὶ ὅτε ἐγένετο ἐτῶν δώδεκα, ἀναβαινόντων αὐτῶν κατὰ τὸ ἔθος τῆς ἑορτῆς | And when he was twelve years (old) they were going up according to the custom of the Feast |

2:43	καὶ τελειωσάντων τὰς ἡμέρας, ἐν τῷ ὑποστρέφειν αὐτοὺς ὑπέμεινεν ἰησοῦς ὁ παῖς ἐν ἰερουσαλήμ, καὶ οὐκ ἔγνωσαν οἱ γονεῖς αὐτοῦ.	And with the completion of the days, with their returning, the child Jesus remained in Jerusalem, and his parents did not get to know.
2:44	νομίσαντες δὲ αὐτὸν εἶναι ἐν τῇ συνοδίᾳ ἦλθον ἡμέρας ὁδὸν καὶ ἀνεζήτουν αὐτὸν ἐν τοῖς συγγενεῦσιν καὶ τοῖς γνωστοῖς,	But supposing him to be in the party they went a day's journey and were searching for him amongst their relatives and experts.
2:45	καὶ μὴ εὑρόντες ὑπέστρεψαν εἰς ἰερουσαλὴμ ἀναζητοῦντες αὐτόν.	And not finding (him), they returned to Jerusalem, searching for him.
2:46	καὶ ἐγένετο μετὰ ἡμέρας τρεῖς **εὗρον αὐτὸν** ἐν τῷ ἱερῷ καθεζόμενον ἐν μέσῳ <u>τῶν διδασΚάλωΝ</u> καὶ ἀκούοντα αὐτῶν καὶ ἐπερωτῶντα αὐτούς:	And it happened after three days (that) **they found him** in the temple sitting in the midst <u>of the teachers</u> and listening to them and questioning them.
2:47	ἐξίσταντο δὲ πάντες οἱ ἀκούοντες αὐτοῦ ἐπὶ τῇ συνέσει καὶ ταῖς <u>ἀποΚρίσεσιΝ</u> αὐτοῦ.	But all those hearing him were astounded at (his) understanding and his <u>distinctions</u>.
2:48	καὶ **ἰδόντες αὐτὸν** ἐξεπλάγησαν, καὶ εἶπεν πρὸς αὐτὸν ἡ μήτηρ αὐτοῦ, τέκνον, τί ἐποίησας ἡμῖν οὕτως; ἰδοὺ ὁ πατήρ σου κἀγὼ ὀδυνώμενοι ἐζητοῦμέν σε.	And **seeing him** they were astonished, and his mother said to him "Child, why did you do this to us? Look, your father and I were seeking you, distressed".

2:49	καὶ εἶπεν πρὸς αὐτούς, τί ὅτι ἐζητεῖτέ με; οὐκ ᾔδειτε ὅτι ἐν τοῖς τοῦ **πατρός** μου δεῖ εἶναί με;	And he said to them "Why were you seeking me? Did you not know that I must be within the things of my _father_?"
2:50	καὶ αὐτοὶ οὐ συνῆκαν τὸ ῥῆμα ὃ ἐλάλησεν αὐτοῖς.	And they did not understand the word which he spoke to them.

Surely this passage has been composed to demonstrate the '*speedy plunder*' prescribed in *Isaiah*. For according to the narrative Jesus is twelve years old. And here he is already in the temple. Yes, _here_ he is:

... καθεζόμενον ἐν μέσῳ τῶν δἰδασΚἁλωΝ   (Lk.2:46)

... sitting *in the midst* of the teachers

We are told that it takes his parents three whole days to find him. Even so they do not appear to recognise who their child 'is'. But if you remember the lessons of Chapter 5 then you should have recognised Jesus. For at Lk.2:46 he is prominently concealed in the midst _of the teachers_, just as the narrator suggests.

If you read *Luke* from the beginning you will discover that the first occasion when we hear Jesus speak is here at 2:49. He has been teaching in the temple at the tender age of twelve and in this way he has '*taken the power of Damascus, etc*'. And now, in addressing his nominal 'parents', we hear him utter for the first time the word '*father*' when he says:

τί ὅτι ἐζητεῖτέ με;
Why were you seeking me?

οὐκ ᾔδειτε ὅτι ἐν τοῖς τοῦ **πατρός** μου δεῖ εἶναί με;
Did you not know that I must be within the things of my _father_?

Does this not complete the prescription imposed at Is.8:4?

> ... before the child learns to know (how) to call '*father*' or 'mother',
> he shall take the power of Damascus and the spoils of Samaria in
> the presence of a king of Assyria.

And yet we are told of his 'parents':

> καὶ αὐτοὶ οὐ συνῆκαν τὸ ῥῆμα ὃ ἐλάλησεν αὐτοῖς.
> And they did not understand *the word* which he spoke to them.

Quite apart from this clever piece of composition in *Luke*, the passage
at Is.8:4 presents to every reader a most serious and explicit warning.
For it confirms that this second child will do just as his name suggests
... *spoil quickly and plunder swiftly*. And because of the further link
which exists between the texts of Is.8:23-9:1 and Mt.4:13-16 (see
Chapter 7), we are unable to escape the conclusion that *the child who
will do this is Jesus himself*.

Then what is it with Jesus, that he should be given to spoil and plunder?

What John says about Jesus

In the fourth gospel John speaks of Jesus in riddles. But what is he
trying to explain?

Jn.	ἰωάννης μαρτυρεῖ περὶ αὐτοῦ	John testified about him and
1:15	καὶ κέκραγεν λέγων, οὗτος ἦν	has cried out, saying "This
	ὃν εἶπον, ὁ ὀπίσω μου	was (he) of whom I said: 'The
	ἐρχόμενος ἔμπροσθέν μου	one coming behind me has
	γέγονεν, ὅτι πρῶτός μου ἦν.	happened before me, for he
		was my first' ".

His theme is clearly important, for soon he repeats it:

Jn.	οὗτός ἐστιν ὑπὲρ οὗ ἐγὼ	This is he of whom I said:
1:30	εἶπον, ὀπίσω μου ἔρχεται	'Behind me comes a man
	ἀνὴρ ὃς ἔμπροσθέν μου	who has happened before
	γέγονεν, ὅτι πρῶτός μου ἦν.	me, for he was my first'.

From *Luke* we have it that Jesus appeared in the womb six months *after* John. Yet John says here of Jesus that he '*has happened before me*'. John seems to be hinting at some previous existence for Jesus. But if Jesus has been 'born again', then who was he in his previous life? And what does John mean when he says of Jesus: '*For he was my first*'?

In Chapter 7 we asked:

> Is Jacob presented as Cain reborn, but now going in disguise? If so he has been demoted, for as it happens Esau is the firstborn.

> At the least we can say that the authors of *Genesis* have cast Esau in a rôle analogous to that of Abel, whilst Jacob seeks the dominant rôle once played by evil Cain.

If Esau and Jacob were portrayed in this way, are we looking at an equivalent construction here in the gospels with John and Jesus?

The writer of the fourth gospel says of Jesus:

> **ὁ λόγος σὰρξ ἐγένετο** ...   (Jn.1:14)
> The Logos happened (as) flesh ...

To understand what he means we need to go back to the beginning:

Jn.	ἐν ἀρχῇ ἦν ὁ λόγος,	In origin was the Logos and
1:1	καὶ ὁ λόγος ἦν **πρὸς τὸν**	the Logos was ***with God***
	θεόν,	
	καὶ θεὸς ἦν ὁ λόγος.	and the Logos was **a** god.

1:2	οὗτος ἦν ἐν ἀρχῇ **πρὸς τὸν** **θεόν**.	This one was in origin **_with_** **God**.
1:3	πάντα δι' αὐτοῦ ἐγένετο, καὶ χωρὶς αὐτοῦ ἐγένετο οὐδὲ ἕν. ὃ γέγονεν	Everything happened through it, and without it there happened not one thing which has happened.
1:4	ἐν αὐτῷ ζωὴ ἦν, καὶ ἡ ζωὴ ἦν τὸ φῶς **τῶν ἀνθρώπων**:	In it was life, and the life was the Light **_of the_ Persons**.
1:5	καὶ τὸ φῶς ἐν τῇ σκοτίᾳ φαίνει, καὶ ἡ σκοτία αὐτὸ οὐ κατέλαβεν.	And the Light is revealed within the Darkness, but the Darkness did not comprehend it.

Like the book of *Genesis*, this gospel begins with the words ἐν ἀρχῇ [*in origin*]. It goes on to tell us (and lest there should be any mistake, it tells us twice) that the Logos was *with* **God**. Nowhere does it suggest that the Logos *was* **God**. On the contrary, it is apparent that the Logos is not **God,** but rather is 'another god'.

In line with Jn.1:14 (*qv.* previous page, also p.383), Christian doctrine asserts that Jesus is the Logos in carnal form. Thus far this makes sense. But such doctrine goes on to assert that the fourth gospel makes the Logos *identical* with **God**. It is an impression which seems to have gathered strength following translation of the gospels to Latin[4]. Yet it cannot be correct. What the original Greek says is clear:

> In origin was the Logos   (Jn.1:1)
> and the Logos was **_with_ God**
> and the Logos was **a** god.
> This one was in origin **_with_ God**.   (Jn.1:2)

The preposition **πρὸς** [**_with_**] implies dependent proximity, not identity. The gospel tells distinctly of *two gods*, one in the company of the other.

And recalling what we learned in Chapter 4, this makes perfect sense. At Gn.1:27 a 'second god' was introduced, the **Person(s)** made 'in the image of a god' (*aka.* the **lord god**). Here then is the Logos. And Jesus is the Logos in material form; but the Logos is <u>*not*</u> **God**.

In the narrative of *Genesis*, darkness is associated from the outset (1:2) with the uncreated **God** who is good. Then **God** said '*Let Light happen*' and Light happened (1:3). And we are told that '**God** *saw the Light as good*' (1:4).

Here in the fourth gospel it is John who testifies about 'the Light'.

Jn.	ἐγένετο ἄνθρωπος	A person happened: sent
1:6	ἀπεσταλμένος παρὰ θεοῦ,	from a god, his name (was)
	ὄνομα αὐτῷ ἰωάννης:	John.
1:7	οὗτος ἦλθεν εἰς μαρτυρίαν,	This one came as a witness
	ἵνα μαρτυρήσῃ περὶ τοῦ	that he might testify about
	φωτός, ἵνα πάντες	the Light, that all might
	πιστεύσωσιν δι' αὐτοῦ.	believe through him.
1:8	<u>οὐκ</u> ἦν ἐκεῖνος τὸ φῶς, ἀλλ'	That one was <u>not</u> the Light,
	ἵνα μαρτυρήσῃ περὶ τοῦ	but (he came) so that he
	φωτός.	might testify about the Light.

Yet we are told:

> And the Light is revealed within the Darkness   (Jn.1:5)
> but the Darkness did <u>not</u> comprehend it

The use of the verb **καταλαμβάνω** [*I comprehend; I grasp*] implies either that the Darkness did not *understand* the Light and/or that the Darkness did not successfully *contend* with the Light. Darkness and light are opposites: so if the primeval darkness is seen as good we are left to consider that the upstart 'Light' may be evil.

The suggestion that the Darkness did not *understand* the Light is shortly extended with the assertion that the entire cosmos, the ordered and structured world of light and of life in which we live, is in some way ignorant of its own origin. For we are told of the Light that:

Jn. 1:9	ἦν τὸ φῶς τὸ ἀληθινόν, ὃ φωτίζει πάντα ἄνθρωπον, ἐρχόμενον εἰς τὸν κόσμον.	The Light was the genuine (one) which lights up each person coming into the world.
1:10	ἐν τῷ κόσμῳ ἦν, καὶ ὁ κόσμος δι' αὐτοῦ ἐγένετο, καὶ ὁ κόσμος αὐτὸν οὐκ ἔγνω.	He was in the world and the world happened through him, and the world did not learn to know him.
1:11	εἰς τὰ ἴδια ἦλθεν, καὶ οἱ ἴδιοι αὐτὸν οὐ παρέλαβον.	He came to his own, and his own did not thoroughly receive him.

This is developed further into the theme of an ignorant populace, unable to recognise who's who. For:

Jn. 1:26	ἀπεκρίθη αὐτοῖς ὁ ἰωάννης λέγων, ἐγὼ βαπτίζω ἐν ὕδατι· μέσος ὑμῶν ἔστηκεν ὃν ὑμεῖς οὐκ οἴδατε,	John answered them, saying "I baptise in water. In your midst was standing (one) whom you do not know
1:27	ὁ ὀπίσω μου ἐρχόμενος, οὗ **οὐκ εἰμὶ [ἐγὼ]** ἄξιος ἵνα λύσω αὐτοῦ τὸν ἱμάντα τοῦ ὑποδήματος.	The one coming behind me, of whom ***not AM I*** deserving that I should untie the thong of his sandal."

Now the first person in scripture's narrative to use the phrase **εἰμι ἐγώ** [**AM I**] is Cain when he says:

οὐ γινώσκω μὴ φύλαξ τοῦ ἀδελφοῦ μού **εἰμι ἐγώ**   (LXX Gn.4:9)
I do not know. **AM I** my brother's guardian?

Notice that when John uses the same words he takes care to say:

οὐκ εἰμὶ [ἐγὼ]
***not* AM I** ...

At Jn.3:28 we hear John repeat this (and at Ac.13:25 attention is drawn to the matter again).

Yet we find the **εἰμὶ ἐγὼ** phrase ***is*** used by Jesus himself, five times in the fourth gospel alone (Jn.7:34, 7:36, 12:26, 14:3, 17:24). What should we conclude from the fact that Jesus freely repeats this phrase first spoken by Cain (also the reversed phrase, **ἐγὼ εἰμι**) ... but that John will ***not*** do so? Again we see the theme of opposites.

Then we have in the fourth gospel:

Jn. 8:54	ἀπεκρίθη ἰησοῦς, ἐὰν ἐγὼ δοξάσω ἐμαυτόν, ἡ δόξα μου οὐδέν ἐστιν: ἔστιν <u>ὁ πατήρ μου</u> ὁ δοξάζων με, ὃν <u>ὑμεῖς</u> λέγετε ὅτι θεὸς ἡμῶν ἐστιν:	Jesus replied "If I glorify myself, my glory is nothing. The one glorifying me is <u>my father</u>, (of) whom ***you*** <u>say that he is our god.</u>
8:55	καὶ οὐκ ἐγνώκατε αὐτόν, ἐγὼ δὲ οἶδα αὐτόν. κἂν εἴπω ὅτι οὐκ οἶδα αὐτόν, ἔσομαι ὅμοιος ὑμῖν ψεύστης: ἀλλὰ οἶδα αὐτὸν καὶ τὸν λόγον αὐτοῦ τηρῶ.	And you have not learned to know him, but I know him. And if I said that I do not know him, I should be like you a liar. But I know him, and I keep his message.
8:56	ἀβραὰμ ὁ πατὴρ ὑμῶν ἠγαλλιάσατο ἵνα ἴδῃ τὴν ἡμέραν τὴν ἐμήν, καὶ εἶδεν καὶ ἐχάρη.	Your father Abraham rejoiced in order that he might see mine day. And he saw and was glad."

8:57	εἶπον οὖν οἱ ἰουδαῖοι πρὸς αὐτόν, πεντήκοντα ἔτη οὔπω ἔχεις καὶ ἀβραὰμ ἑώρακασ;	Therefore the Judaeans said to him "You do not yet have fifty years, and you have seen Abraham?".
8:58	εἶπεν αὐτοῖς **ἰησοῦς**, ἀμὴν ἀμὴν λέγω ὑμῖν, πρὶν ἀβραὰμ γενέσθαι **ἐγὼ εἰμί**.	**Jesus** said to them "Truly, truly I say to you, before Abraham came into being **I AM**".
8:59	ἦραν οὖν λίθους ἵνα βάλ**ωσιν** ἐπ' αὐτόν· ἰησοῦς δὲ ἐκρύβη καὶ ἐξῆλθεν ἐκ τοῦ ἱεροῦ.	Therefore they took up stones that <u>they might throw</u> at him. But Jesus was hidden and went out from the temple.
9:1	καὶ παράγων εἶδεν ἄνθρωπον τυφλὸν ἐκ γενετῆς	And passing by he saw a person *blind from birth*.

So who is Jesus? He has come into being *before* John, even *before* Abraham. If we turn to the narrative of *Genesis*, we find Abraham first mentioned at Gn.11:26. Before this point:

- The phrase ἐγὼ εἰμι does not appear in the text at all.
- The reversed phrase εἰμι ἐγὼ appears just once … and the one who utters it is Cain (Gn.4:9).

Now in the gospel the author has Jesus say:

> Truly, truly I say to you, before Abraham came into being **I AM**.

Resembling the cryptic clue for a crossword puzzle, this seems to be a typical Gnostic riddle. The meaning is available only to those with a certain level of prior knowledge. We are left to appreciate that by putting the words '**I AM**' into the mouth of Jesus, then excluding all occasions but for their first use, *the writer associates Jesus with Cain.*

Cool Baptism of John ... extended to Jesus himself

John baptises with water[5] for repentance (Mt.3:11). In the three synoptic gospels John baptises even Jesus in the River Jordan:

Mk. 1:9	καὶ ἐγένετο ἐν ἐ**Κεί**ν**α**ις ταῖς ἡμέραις ἦλθεν ἰησοῦς ἀπὸ ναζαρὲτ τῆς γαλιλαίας καὶ ἐβαπτίσθη εἰς τὸν ἰορδάνην ὑπὸ ἰωάννου.	And it happened in <u>those</u> days (that) Jesus came from Nazareth of Galilee and was baptised in the Jordan under John.
1:10	καὶ εὐθὺς ἀναβαίνων ἐκ τοῦ ὕδατος εἶδεν σχιζομένους τοὺς οὐρανοὺς καὶ τὸ πνεῦμα ὡς **ΠΕΡΙσ**τερ**ὰ**ν **Κα**ταβ**αῖν**ον εἰς αὐτόν:	And immediately coming up from the water he saw the heavens parted and the spirit like <u>a pigeon</u> <u>coming down</u> into him.

It was in Chapter 5 that we considered how the 'face' of the **lord god** might be hidden in the midst of the tree **παραδείσο**υ [*of paradise*]. There we may have glimpsed (in part at least) **ὀ σπείρας** [*the one sowing*]. Adam and his woman then hear the voice of the lord god **ΠΕΡΙΠα**τοῦντ**Ος** [*walking about*] in Paradise.

Here at the baptism of Jesus the heavens are parted and Jesus sees the spirit ... ὡς **ΠΕΡΙσ**τερ**ὰ**ν [*<u>like</u> a pigeon*] and **Κα**ταβ**αῖν**ον [*coming down*] into him. The mention of a *pigeon* as the waters abate may remind us of Noah[6]. Yet this 'spirit' is not said to be a pigeon, but something *like* a pigeon.

Apart from suggesting **σπείρας** [*one sowing*], the word **ΠΕΡΙσ**τερ**ὰ**ν [*pigeon*] provides for the Greek word **σπείρα** [*a coil*], *eg.* that of a serpent.

The narrative in *Mark* continues:

Mk. 1:11	καὶ φωνὴ ἐγένετο ἐκ τῶν οὐρανῶν, σὺ εἶ ὁ υἱός μου ὁ ἀγαπητός, ἐν σοὶ εὐδόκησα.	And a voice happened from the heavens, 'You are my son, the beloved: in you I was well pleased'.
1:12	καὶ εὐθὺς τὸ πνεῦμα αὐτὸν ἐκβάλλει εἰς τὴν ἔρημον.	And immediately the spirit casts him out into the desert.
1:13	καὶ ἦν ἐν τῇ ἐρήμῳ τεσ**σ**ερ**ά**κο**ντα** ἡμέρας πειραζόμενος ὑπὸ τοῦ **σατανᾶ**, καὶ ἦν μετὰ τῶν θηρίων, καὶ οἱ ἄγγελοι διηκόνουν αὐτῷ.	And he was in the desert <u>forty</u> days, being tested under <u>Satan</u>: and he was with the wild beasts and the angels were ministering to him.
1:14	μετὰ δὲ τὸ παραδοθῆναι τὸν ἰωάννην ἦλθεν ὁ ἰησοῦς εἰς τὴν γαλιλαίαν κηρύσσων τὸ εὐαγγέλιον τοῦ θεοῦ	But with John being handed over, Jesus came into Galilee preaching the good news of God.

The voice of a father is heard from the heavens. Immediately Jesus commences forty days with **σαταν** [*Satan*] in the desert. The scene may remind us of forty years spent by the Israelites with Moses in the desert. The corresponding passages at Mt.4:1 and Lk.4:2 suggest that the devil was training Jesus and/or proving his competence. And with the advent of Satan on the scene we are left to consider whose voice it was addressing Jesus as '*my son*'.

It is now that we learn of John being handed over. In short, no sooner has he baptised Jesus than John is thrown into prison and there beheaded (Mt.14:3, 14:10). '*Spoil quickly, plunder swiftly* '?

And surely it must be significant (Mt.14:11; Mk.6:28) that the head of John is brought for inspection ἐπὶ πί**νακι** [*upon a platter*], for there we see the name of evil **καϊν** [*Cain*]. Could this be a hint that Cain is

the one ultimately responsible for the slaughter of John the Baptist …
thus silencing the one who seeks, with his riddles, to tell the truth and
so might blow Cain's cover?

Here is the recursive scenario etched so deeply in scripture's theme.
The key of knowledge has been taken away, and much blood spilled:

Lk.	διὰ τοῦτο καὶ ἡ σοφία τοῦ	On this account the wisdom
11:49	θεοῦ εἶπεν, ἀποστελῶ εἰς	of God also said "I shall send
	αὐτοὺς προφήτας καὶ	to you prophets and
	ἀποστόλους, καὶ ἐξ αὐτῶν	apostles: and some of them
	ἀποΚτενοῦσιΝ καὶ	they will kill and they will
	διώξουσιν,	persecute
11:50	ἵνα ἐκζητηθῇ τὸ αἷμα πάντων	So that the blood of all the
	τῶν προφητῶν τὸ	prophets, shed from laying
	ἐκκεχυμένον ἀπὸ καταβολῆς	down of world, may be
	κόσμου ἀπὸ τῆς γενεᾶς	demanded from this
	ταύτης,	generation."
11:51	ἀπὸ αἵματος ἄβελ ἕως	From (the) blood of **Abel** to
	αἵματος ζαχαρίου τοῦ	the blood of Zacharias, slain
	ἀπολομένου μεταξὺ τοῦ	between the altar and the
	θυσιαστηρίου καὶ τοῦ οἴκου:	dwelling. Yes I say to you, it
	ναί, λέγω ὑμῖν, ἐκζητηθήσεται	will be demanded from this
	ἀπὸ τῆς γενεᾶς ταύτης.	generation.
11:52	οὐαὶ ὑμῖν τοῖς νομικοῖς,	"Woe to you, the lawyers!
	ὅτι ἤρατε τὴν κλεῖδα τῆς	Because **you took away the**
	γνώσεως:	**key of Gnosis** (knowledge).
	αὐτοὶ οὐκ εἰσήλθατε καὶ τοὺς	You did not enter in
	εἰσερχομένους ἐκωλύσατε.	yourselves, and those
		entering in, you hindered."

11:53	Κἀκεῖθεν ἐξελθόντος αὐτοῦ ἤρξαντο οἱ γραμματεῖς καὶ οἱ φαρισαῖοι δεινῶς ἐνέχειν καὶ ἀποστοματίζειν αὐτὸν περὶ πλειόνων,	<u>And with that</u> emerging from him, the scribes and Pharisees began to take strongly against (him) and to interrogate him concerning more things
11:54	ἐνεδρεύοντες αὐτὸν θηρεῦσαί τι ἐκ τοῦ στόματος αὐτοῦ.	Lying in wait for him, to hunt down something from his mouth
12:1	ἐν οἷς ἐπισυναχθεισῶν τῶν μυριάδων τοῦ ὄχλου, ὥστε Καταπατεῖν ἀλλήλους, ἤρξατο λέγειν πρὸς τοὺς μαθητὰς αὐτοῦ πρῶτον, προσέχετε ἑαυτοῖς ἀπὸ τῆς ζύμης, ἥτις ἐστὶν ὑπόκρισις, τῶν φαρισαίων.	Within which, by the coming together of the myriads of the crowd so as <u>to tread down</u> one another, he began to say to his students first "Keep yourselves from the yeast of the Pharisees, which is hypocrisy.
12:2	οὐδὲν δὲ συγκεκαλυμμένον ἐστὶν ὃ οὐκ ἀποκαλυφθήσεται καὶ κρυπτὸν ὃ οὐ γνωσθήσεται.	But nothing is concealed which will not be revealed, and hidden which will not become known."

The statement at 11:51 connects the slaughter of Abel with that of John the Baptist. It does so because *John himself was first named Zacharias*:

Lk. 1:59	καὶ ἐγένετο ἐν τῇ ἡμέρᾳ τῇ ὀγδόῃ ἦλθον περιτεμεῖν τὸ παιδίον, καὶ ἐκάλουν αὐτὸ ἐπὶ τῷ ὀνόματι τοῦ πατρὸς αὐτοῦ ζαχαρίαν.	And it happened on the eighth day (that) they came to circumcise the child. And they were calling him Zacharias, after the name of his father.

1:60	καὶ ἀποκριθεῖσα ἡ μήτηρ αὐτοῦ εἶπεν, οὐχί, ἀλλὰ κληθήσεται ἰωάννης.	And answering, his mother said "No, but he shall be called John".
1:61	καὶ εἶπαν πρὸς αὐτὴν ὅτι οὐδείς ἐστιν ἐκ τῆς συγγενείας σου ὃς καλεῖται τῷ ὀνόματι τούτῳ.	And they said to her that there is no one from your relations who is called by this name.
1:62	ἐνένευον δὲ τῷ πατρὶ αὐτοῦ τὸ τί ἂν θέλοι καλεῖσθαι αὐτό.	But they beckoned to his father as to what he might wish to call him.
1:63	καὶ αἰτήσας πινακίδιον ἔγραψεν λέγων, ἰωάννης ἐστὶν ὄνομα αὐτοῦ. καὶ ἐθαύμασαν πάντες.	And asking for <u>a writing tablet</u>, he wrote saying "John is a name for him". And all wondered.

There once again we see that word πινακι, and within it the name of Κάϊν [*Cain*]. It is surely no accident.

- With the slaughter of Abel, Cain takes pride of place.

- With the elimination of Esau, Jacob takes pride of place.

- Now, with the slaughter of John the Baptist, Jesus takes to the stage … to begin what is known as his 'public life'.

Then who is left to explain the 'mystery' and uphold what is good … if not the readers of scripture themselves?

Fiery Baptism of Jesus ... extended now to the many

It is now that Jesus substitutes his own form of baptism. This is not achieved with *'water and repentance'* but instead with *'a holy spirit and fire'* (Mt.3:11; Lk.3:16). The experience is recorded here in *Acts*:

Ac. 2:1	καὶ ἐν τῷ συμπληροῦσθαι τὴν ἡμέραν τῆς πεντηκοστῆς ἦσαν πάντες ὁμοῦ ἐπὶ τὸ αὐτό.	And with the day of Pentecost being completed, they were all together with one another.
2:2	καὶ ἐγένετο ἄφνω ἐκ τοῦ οὐρανοῦ ἦχος ὥσπερ φερομένης πνοῆς βιαίας καὶ ἐπλήρωσεν ὅλον τὸν οἶκον οὗ ἦσαν καθήμενοι:	And all of a sudden there came from Heaven a sound like (the) drawing of a violent breath, and it filled the whole household in which they were sitting.
2:3	καὶ ὤφθησαν αὐτοῖς διαμεριζόμεναι γλῶσσαι ὡσεὶ πυρός, καὶ ἐ**ΚάθΙσε**Ν ἐφ' ἕνα ἕκαστον αὐτῶν,	And divided tongues were seen by them, as if of fire, and it took its seat upon each one of them.
2:4	καὶ ἐπλήσθησαν πάντες πνεύματος ἁγίου, καὶ ἤρξαντο λαλεῖν ἑτέραις γλώσσαις καθὼς τὸ πνεῦμα ἐδίδου ἀποφθέγγεσθαι αὐτοῖς.	And all were filled by **a** holy spirit, and they began to speak with other tongues, just as the spirit was giving them to deliver an opinion.

Such fiery and divided tongues may prove to be ἄσβεσται [*unquenchable*] (Mt.3:12; Mk.9:43; Lk.3:17). They are characteristic of any group amongst whom *not one person knows the truth* of the matter being debated. These tongues deliver innumerable opinions, each one at variance with every other. Notice that this form of baptism is achieved by being filled with **a** holy spirit, not **the** Holy Spirit.

This is the baptism which Jesus has to offer. And this, in *Romans*, is roughly the result it yields:

Rm.		
3:10	καθὼς γέγραπται ὅτι οὐκ ἔστιν δίκαιος οὐδὲ εἷς,	Just as it has been written that there is no one just, not even one.
3:11	οὐκ ἔστιν ὁ συνίων, οὐκ ἔστιν ὁ ἐκζητῶν **τὸν θεόν**.	There is no one understanding, no one seeking **God** .
3:12	πάντες ἐξέ**ΚΛΙΝΑ**ν, ἅμα ἠχρεώθησαν: οὐκ ἔστιν ὁ ποιῶν χρηστότητα, [οὐκ ἔστιν] ἕως ἑνός.	All <u>stepped out of line</u> as soon as they were corrupted. There is no one making goodness: [there is not] as much as one.
3:13	τάφος ἀνεῳγμένος ὁ λάρυγξ αὐτῶν, ταῖς γλώσσαις αὐτῶν ἐδολιοῦσαν, ἰὸς ἀσπίδων ὑπὸ τὰ χείλη αὐτῶν,	Their larynx (is) an opened up tomb. With their tongues they have used deceit, (the) poison of asps (is) under their lips!
3:14	ὧν τὸ στόμα ἀρᾶς καὶ πικρίας γέμει:	Whose mouth is filled with prayer and with bitterness,
3:15	ὀξεῖς οἱ πόδες αὐτῶν ἐκχέαι αἷμα,	Their feet swift to shed blood
3:16	σύντριμμα καὶ ταλαιπωρία ἐν ταῖς ὁδοῖς αὐτῶν,	Destruction and hardship in their ways
3:17	καὶ ὁδὸν εἰρήνης οὐκ ἔγνωσαν.	And the way of peace they did not learn to know.
3:18	οὐκ ἔστιν φόβος θεοῦ ἀπέναντι τῶν ὀφθαλμῶν αὐτῶν.	Opposite their eyes there is no fear of a god.

Their larynx is an opened up tomb. This must be a reference to the credulous claims made by those who find the tomb of Jesus 'opened up', the stone rolled away (*qv.* Mt.28:1-3). The above passage from the Pauline letter to the *Romans* combines a selection of verses taken from the Psalms. These comprise a part of the wisdom literature, writings which seek to warn readers of what is evil, and so to protect them from being led astray.

Notice how the stream of cool water which John uses for *his* kind of baptism is entirely opposite in character to the divided and conflicting tongues which scorch each person upon whom they may settle.

The sharp distinction between the two styles of baptism is drawn at Ac.1:5 and again in the passage at Ac.19:1-7. Yet so often the two are confused and conflated.

Notice too how repentance is alien to the Lawyers and the Pharisees, those teachers or priests in the Jewish community who seek to assert in a literal manner the law of Moses and to embrace the serpent's promise of eternal life. They reject the baptism of John:

Lk. 7:29	καὶ πᾶς ὁ λαὸς ἀκούσας καὶ οἱ τελῶναι ἐδικαίωσαν τὸν θεόν, βαπτισθέντες τὸ βάπτισμα ἰωάννου:	And all the people hearing and the tax collectors justified **God**, being baptised (with) the baptism of John.
7:30	οἱ δὲ Φαρισαῖοι καὶ οἱ νομικοὶ τὴν βουλὴν τοῦ θεοῦ ἠθέτησαν εἰς ἑαυτούς, μὴ βαπτισθέντες ὑπ' αὐτοῦ.	But the Pharisees and the Lawyers rejected the counsel of **God** for themselves, not being baptised under him.

Identity of John the Baptist

Mk. 1:6	καὶ ἦν ὁ ἰωάννης ἐνδεδυμένος τρίχας καμήλου καὶ ζώνην δερματίνην περὶ τὴν ὀσφὺν αὐτοῦ, καὶ ἐσθίων ἀκρίδας καὶ μέλι ἄγριον.	And John was clothed in camel hair and a skin belt around his loins, and eating locusts and wild honey.
1:7	καὶ ἐκήρυσσεν λέγων, ἔρχεται ὁ **ἰσχυρότερός** μου ὀπίσω μου, οὗ οὐκ εἰμὶ **ἱκανὸς** κύψας λῦσαι τὸν **ἱμάντα** τῶν ὑποδημάτων αὐτοῦ:	And he proclaimed, saying "Behind me comes the one <u>stronger</u> than me, for whom **I AM NOT** <u>competent</u>, bending down, to untie the <u>thong</u> of his sandals".

John comes eating locusts and wild honey. This makes him the 'type' of Abel and of Esau, the 'good' type of the genuine herdsman or pastor. Then we recall from Chapter 3, the place where **God** confirms that Adam _does_ know Good from Evil:

LXX Gn. 3:21	καὶ ἐποίησεν **κύριος ὁ θεὸς** τῷ αδαμ καὶ τῇ γυναικὶ αὐτοῦ **χιτῶνας** δερμ**ατίνους** καὶ ἐνέδυσεν αὐτούς	And **the lord god** made for Adam and for his woman <u>skin</u> <u>tunics</u> (under-garments), and put them on.
3:22	καὶ εἶπεν **ὁ θεός** ἰδοὺ αδαμ γέγονεν ὡς εἷς ἐξ ἡμῶν τοῦ γινώσκειν καλὸν καὶ πονηρόν καὶ νῦν μήποτε ἐκτείνῃ τὴν χεῖρα καὶ λάβῃ τοῦ ξύλου τῆς ζωῆς καὶ φάγῃ καὶ ζήσεται εἰς τὸν αἰῶνα	And **God** said "Look, Adam _has_ become alike to one of us ... for knowing good and evil. And now, lest perhaps he should put forth the hand, and take of the tree of life and eat, and live in the Aiona ...".

In Adam's case, clothing made from skins seems to be understood as an indicator that he knows good from evil (although for the woman it may indicate the opposite). Thus John's use of a skin belt likens him to Adam ... Adam who was sensible enough to eat from the *'Tree of Knowing the Knowledge of Good and Evil'* (see Chapter 5).

Then John consumes honey and locusts. His is a diet of 'secondary' foods (the distinction relied upon here is explained in Chapter 2). Such a diet matches John with the one named Emmanuel, the first child mentioned in Isaiah, the one of whom it is said that:

> ... ἀπειθεῖ πονηρίᾳ τοῦ ἐκλέξασθαι τὸ ἀγαθόν   (Is.7:16)
> ... he disobeys cunning to choose the good

Again this likens John to Adam for, as we noted in Chapter 7, Adam is the first one in scripture's narrative who finds it expedient to 'disobey cunning to choose the good'.

And now we realise that it takes only a modest adjustment to John's competent assertion that:

> οὐκ εἰμὶ **ἱκανὸς** ...   (Mk.1:7)
> I AM not **competent** ...

before we see that what he might prefer to say is:

> οὐκ εἰμὶ **Κάϊν**
> I AM not **Cain**

Like Abel before him, and like Esau, John the Baptist is set forth as good. Like them, he is speedily displaced from the narrative. This time round it is to make way for Jesus.

And we recall what John himself has said of Jesus:

Jn.	οὗτός ἐστιν ὑπὲρ οὗ ἐγὼ	This is he of whom I said
1:30	εἶπον, ὀπίσω μου ἔρχεται	`Behind me comes a man
	ἀνὴρ ὃς ἔμπροσθέν μου	who has happened before
	γέγονεν, ὅτι πρῶτός μου ἦν.	me, for he was my first`.

According to the gospel narrative, John is executed at the hands of King Herod. But is Herod to be held accountable for the elimination of John? Or does ultimate responsibility for the slaughter of John rest with Jesus himself, the one who according to scripture's underlying theme must be responsible for *all* the affairs of the world, the one portrayed as 'king of kings' (*qv.* 1 Tm.6:14-15; Rv.17:14)?

It is an intriguing question. By the time we get to the end of this chapter we should have an answer.

Identity of Jesus

Jesus consumes bread and wine, behaviour 'opposite' to that of John. The contrast is emphasised here (also Mt.11:18-19):

Lk. 7:33	ἐλήλυθεν γὰρ ἰωάννης ὁ βαπτιστὴς μὴ ἐσθίων ἄρτον μήτε πίνων οἶνον, καὶ λέγετε, δαιμόνιον ἔχει:	For John the Baptist came not eating bread and not drinking wine, and you say he has a demon!
7:34	ἐλήλυθεν ὁ υἱὸς τοῦ ἀνθρώπου ἐσθίων καὶ πίνων, καὶ λέγετε, ἰδοὺ ἄνθρωπος φάγος καὶ οἰνοπότης, φίλος τελωνῶν καὶ ἁμαρτωλῶν.	The son of the Person came eating and drinking (bread and wine) and you say: "Look, a gluttonous person and a wine-bibber, a friend of tax collectors and of those making a mistake [alt: of sinners]."

Many times in the gospels we find Jesus referring to himself by the cryptic title:

ὁ υἱὸς τοῦ ἀνθρώπου
the son of the Person

It will not be long before we realise why this title is appropriate. But how unfortunate, and how misleading, that so often it gets translated as 'the son of man'.

The scriptural prototype for the tax collector is the priest/king Melchizedek [μελχισέδεκ]. He brings forth *breads and wine* [ἄρτους καὶ οἶνον] before extracting from Abram *a tithe* [δεκάτην ἀπὸ πάντων]; and in the verse which follows he appears to be *a king of Sodom* [βασιλεὺς σοδομων] (LXX Gn.14:18-21).

Now   μελχισέδεκ = **919** (a prime number).
Whereas   κάϊν = **81** (the 4th power of 3).

These two add to **1000**,
Thus[7]: (μελχισέδεκ + κάϊν) = **1000** ≈ (310 + 8) * π
where: π ≈ **3.14**   and: ἥλιος [*sun*] = **318**

This mathematical equation appears to associate Melchizedek with Cain as *a complementary pair* which taken together represent the circumference of a sun with diameter **318**.

Then the two exhibit a common trait: both bring 'bread and wine' before seeking to 'overcome' someone else (Abram or Abel as the case may be).

In the letter to *Hebrews* it is five times said or implied that Jesus is:

... ἀρχιερεὺς κατὰ τὴν τάξιν **μελχισέδεκ**
... a chief priest according to the order of ***Melchizedek***

Consistent with this, Jesus too brings bread and wine. But we notice that this is a diet of the 'primary' foods first specified at Gn.1:29 for consumption by the **lord god** (see Chapter 4). And the 'sacrifice' brought by Jesus is 'from the fruits of the earth', matching in kind that brought by Cain ... who brought it not for **God**, but for the **lord** (LXX Gn.4:3).

We recall that this was the sacrifice to which **God** himself paid no attention (Gn.4:5). And we cannot help noticing that Jesus, following his own sacrificial meal, seems to share in Cain's disappointment:

Mt.	περὶ δὲ τὴν ἐνάτην ὥραν	But about the ninth hour
27:46	ἀνεβόησεν ὁ ἰησοῦς φωνῇ	Jesus cried up with a loud
	μεγάλῃ λέγων, ηλι ηλι λεμα	voice, saying "Eli, Eli, Lema
	σαβαχθανι; τοῦτ' ἔστιν, θεέ	Sabachthani?" ... that is "My
	μου θεέ μου, ἱνατί με	god, my god, for what did
	ἐγκατέλιπεσ;	you abandon me?"

Now in each of the three synoptic gospels Jesus is found asking who people think him TO BE. He appears concerned to discover how much others know. Indeed we are left with the solid impression that there is something about his identity which he would much prefer to keep secret.

The exchange on this topic follows a broadly similar course in each of the synoptic gospels. Let us investigate the narrative in *Luke*:

Lk.	καὶ **ἐγένετο ἐν τῷ εἶναι** αὐτὸν	And ***it happened in his***
9:18	προσευχόμενον κατὰ μόνας	***being*** praying alone, the
	συνῆσαν αὐτῷ οἱ μαθηταί, καὶ	students were with him. And
	ἐπηρώτησεν αὐτοὺς λέγων,	he asked them, saying "Who
	τίνα με λέγουσιν οἱ ὄχλοι	do the crowds say me to
	εἶναι;	be?"

A few verses further on we find the expression:

καὶ ἐγένετο ἐν τῷ προσεύχεσθαι αὐτὸν ...   (Lk.9:29)
And it happened in his praying ...

But here we have:

καὶ **ἐγένετο ἐν τῷ εἶναι** αὐτὸν προσευχόμενον ...   (Lk.9:18)
And it happened in his being praying ...

What is the reason for the curiously elaborated expression?

The phrase **καὶ ἐγένετο ἐν τῷ εἶναι** appears only three times in the NT canon, always in *Luke*, always referring to Jesus (Lk.5:12, 9:18, 11:1).

If we turn to the LXX Pentateuch we find the same phrase used only once. We have seen already in Chapter 5 where it was used:

LXX	καὶ εἶπεν καιν πρὸς αβελ τὸν	And Cain said to Abel, his
Gn.	ἀδελφὸν αὐτοῦ διέλθωμεν εἰς	brother "*Let us go into the*
4:8	τὸ πεδίον **καὶ ἐγένετο ἐν τῷ**	*plain*". ***And it happened in***
	εἶναι αὐτοὺς ἐν τῷ πεδίῳ καὶ	***their being*** in the plain, and
	ἀνέστη καιν ἐπὶ αβελ τὸν	Cain ***was resurrected*** upon
	ἀδελφὸν αὐτοῦ καὶ	Abel, his brother, and he
	ἀπέκτεινεν αὐτόν	killed him.

Then could its use at Lk.9:18 be intended as a hint to help with answering the question about the identity of Jesus?

Let us see what is said in reply:

Lk.	οἱ δὲ ἀποΚρΙθέΝτες εἶπαν,	But answering, they said
9:19	ἰωάννην τὸν βαπτιστήν, ἄλλοι	"John the Baptist, but others
	δὲ ἡλίαν,	Elijah,
	ἄλλοι δὲ ὅτι προφήτης τις τῶν	but others that *a certain*
	ἀρχαίων **ἀνέστη**.	*prophet from the beginnings*
		was resurrected".

We may notice the name of Cain concealed within the word ἀποΚρΙθέΝτες [*answering*].

There too is the suggestion, quite explicit, that Jesus may be '*a certain prophet from the beginnings*' ... and that: ἀνέστη [*he was resurrected*].

It is precisely the same word used of Cain at Gn.4:8 where:

... **ἀνέστη** καιν ἐπὶ αβελ τὸν ἀδελφὸν αὐτοῦ καὶ ἀπέκτεινεν αὐτόν

... Cain ***was resurrected*** upon his brother and he killed him.

Could this be all coincidence? Or is *Luke* written in this way to hint deliberately at the answer to the question Jesus has just posed about his own identity when he asks:

> ... τίνα με λέγουσιν οἱ ὄχλοι εἶναι;   (Lk.9:18)
> ... who do the crowds say me TO BE?

The narrative develops as follows:

Lk.	εἶπεν δὲ αὐτοῖς, ὑμεῖς δὲ τίνα με λέγετε εἶναι;	And he said to them "But you, who do you say me TO BE?".
9:20		
	πέτρος δὲ ἀποκριθεὶς εἶπεν, τὸν **χριστὸν** τοῦ θεοῦ.	And Peter, answering, said "***The Christ*** [alt: the annointed one] of God".
9:21	ὁ δὲ ἐπιτιμήσας αὐτοῖς παρήγγειλεν **μηδενὶ λέγειν τοῦτο,**	But he, warning them, gave instruction **to say this to no one**
9:22	εἰπὼν ὅτι δεῖ **τὸν υἱὸν τοῦ ἀνθρώπου** πολλὰ παθεῖν καὶ ἀποδοΚιμασθῆΝΑΙ ἀπὸ τῶν πρεσβυτέρων καὶ ἀρχιερέων καὶ γραμματέων καὶ ἀποΚτανθῆΝΑΙ καὶ τῇ τρίτῃ ἡμέρᾳ ἐγερθῆναι.	Saying that **the son of the Person** must suffer many things and <u>be rejected</u> by the elders and high priests and scribes and <u>be killed</u>, and on the third day be roused up".

At Gn.4:13-15 we had:

LXX Gn. 4:13	καὶ εἶπεν καιν πρὸς τὸν κύριον μείζων ἡ αἰτία μου τοῦ ἀφεθῆναί με	And Cain said to the lord "*My accusation (is) greater than (will allow) my acquittal*
4:14	εἰ ἐκβάλλεις με σήμερον ἀπὸ προσώπου τῆς γῆς καὶ ἀπὸ τοῦ προσώπου σου κρυβήσομαι καὶ ἔσομαι στένων καὶ τρέμων ἐπὶ τῆς γῆς καὶ ἔσται πᾶς ὁ εὑρίσκων με ἀποκτενεῖ με	*If you throw me out today from a face of the earth, I SHALL BE HIDDEN ALSO FROM YOUR FACE. And I shall be sighing and trembling upon the earth, and it shall be that each one finding me shall kill me*".
4:15	καὶ εἶπεν αὐτῷ **κύριος ὁ θεὸς** οὐχ οὕτως πᾶς ὁ ἀπο**ΚτεῖνΑς ΚΑΙΝ** ἑπτὰ ἐκδΙΚούμε**ΝΑ** παραλύσει καὶ ἔθετο **κύριος ὁ θεὸς** σημεῖον τῷ **ΚΑΙΝ** τοῦ μὴ ἀνελεῖν αὐτόν πάντα τὸν εὑρ**Ι**σΚο**Ντα** αὐτόν	And the **lord god** said to him "Not just so, each one <u>killing Cain</u> shall set free SEVEN <u>vengeances</u>". And the **lord god** placed A SIGN FOR CAIN, so that everyone <u>finding</u> him should NOT raise him up [*alt*: not do away with him].
4:16	ἐξῆλθεν δὲ **ΚΑΙΝ** ἀπὸ προσώπου **τοῦ θεοῦ** καὶ ᾤκησεν ἐν γῇ ναιδ **ΚΑ**τένα**Ντ**Ι εδεμ	So <u>Cain</u> went out from a face of **God** and settled in (the) earth of Nod, <u>opposite</u> Eden.

So is Jesus really depicted to be Cain ... 'anointed' in ancient times with the blood of his brother Abel, then going in disguise, thus '*hidden from our face'*? And will he be killed by those who fail to recognise him? It is beginning to look very like it.

If so, then Jesus is **ὁ χριστός** [*the Christ; the anointed one*]
… but he is *not* **ὁ χρηστός** [*the good one*].

Now we have seen what happened at Lk.9:20-21:

> εἶπεν δὲ αὐτοῖς, ὑμεῖς δὲ τίνα με λέγετε εἶναι;
> And he said to them "But you, who do you say me TO BE?".

> πέτρος δὲ ἀποκριθεὶς εἶπεν, τὸν χριστὸν τοῦ θεοῦ.
> And Peter, answering, said "The Christ of God".

> ὁ δὲ ἐπιτιμήσας αὐτοῖς παρήγγειλεν μηδενὶ λέγειν τοῦτο,
> But he, warning them, gave instruction to say this to no one

It is plain that Jesus wishes to keep his identity a secret. And at 9:22 he has once again referred to himself as:

> τὸν υἱὸν τοῦ ἀνθρώπου
> the son of the Person

At this point we may recall the parallel drawn by Jesus in the fourth gospel:

Jn.	καὶ καθὼς μωϋσῆς ὕψωσεν	And just as Moses raised up
3:14	τὸν **ὄφιν** ἐν τῇ ἐρήμῳ,	the ***serpent*** in the desert, so
	οὕτως ὑψωθῆναι δεῖ **τὸν υἱὸν**	must ***the son of the*** **Person**
	τοῦ ἀνθρώπου,	be raised up
3:15	ἵνα πᾶς ὁ πιστεύων ἐν αὐτῷ	So that each one believing in
	ἔχῃ ζωὴν αἰώνιον.	him may have eternal life.

The serpent is Satan. Here Jesus likens himself, soon to be raised up again on the cross, to the representation of the serpent in bronze which is raised up by Moses (Nb.21:8-9).

Jesus goes on to associate his own 'raising up' with the promise made by the serpent to the woman, the promise by which she is deceived (Gn.3:13), the promise of eternal life (Gn.3:4).

It is difficult to see how anyone could miss what is signified by all this.

But many do.

Chapter 9

The 'Father'

We encounter in *Luke* this instructive passage where Jesus says:

Lk. 10:15	καὶ σύ, καφαρναούμ, μὴ ἕως οὐρανοῦ ὑψωθήσῃ; **ἕως τοῦ ᾅδου καταβήσῃ.**	"And you, Capharnaum, you will not be raised up as far as Heaven, **you will go down as far as Hades** (aka. **Hell**).
10:16	ὁ ἀκούων ὑμῶν ἐμοῦ ἀκούει, καὶ ὁ ἀθετῶν ὑμᾶς ἐμὲ ἀθετεῖ· ὁ δὲ ἐμὲ ἀθετῶν ἀθετεῖ τὸν ἀποστείλαντά με.	The one hearing you hears me, and the one rejecting you rejects me. But the one rejecting me rejects the one who sent me."
10:17	ὑπέστρεψαν δὲ οἱ ἑβδομήκοντα [δύο] μετὰ χαρᾶς λέγοντες, κύριε, καὶ τὰ δαιμόνια ὑποτάσσεται ἡμῖν ἐν τῷ ὀνόματί σου.	But the seventy [two] turned back with joy saying: "Lord, even the demons is made subject to us in your name".
10:18	εἶπεν δὲ αὐτοῖς, ἐθεώρουν τὸν **σαταν**ᾶν ὡς **ἀστραπὴν** ἐκ τοῦ οὐρανοῦ πε**σόντα**.	But he said to them: "I beheld **Satan** like **lightning** falling from Heaven".

For the authors of scripture, cities are corrupt and evil: the notion has its origin at Gn.4:17. The fictional 'city' of Capharnaum (*qv.* Lk.4:31, 7:1) is where Jesus 'settles down' (Mt.4:13) and proceeds to manifest his miraculous powers in public. At 10:15 Capharnaum, far from being exalted to Heaven, will '*go down as far as Hell* ': it does not bode well.

Jesus, as 'son', has been sent by 'the Father'. At 10:16 Jesus claims that anyone hearing his followers in effect hears him, anyone rejecting his followers in effect rejects him. He goes on to claim that whoever rejects him rejects also the one who sent him (*ie*. the 'Father').

At 10:17 we hear of the seventy [two]: ostensibly this is a reference to those 'appointed' by Jesus and 'sent ahead' (Lk.10:1). But the mention of this number evokes the memory of the LXX translators (see Chapter 2). It may then call to mind the techniques they established, such as the '*sign*' for Cain achieved by dispersing within other Greek words the letters required to spell Cain's name.

At 10:18 we are confronted with the assertion Jesus makes about Satan:

ἐθεώρουν τὸν **σαταν**ᾶν ὡς **ἀστ**ρ**απὴν**
ἐκ τοῦ οὐρανοῦ πε**σ**όν**τα**.

I beheld **_Satan_** like **_lightning_**
falling from Heaven

The name for **_Satan_** is explicitly compared with the word for **_lightning_**. It is then easy to notice that all the letters for the name **σαταν** [*Satan*] are present in the second word **ἀστ**ρ**απὴν** [*lightning*]. Four of these letters appear again in the word πε**σ**όν**τα** [*falling*]. This looks very like another working example of anagrammatic dispersion.

In *Luke* there are five more verses (Lk.9:17, 11:32, 18:33, 20:11, 21:15) having non-repeated words of which two include the same five letters as here and one includes the same four letters. The final example is this:

| Lk. 21:15 | ἐγὼ γὰρ δώσω ὑμῖν στόμα καὶ σοφίαν ᾗ οὐ δυ**ν**ή**σ**ον**τα**ι **ἀντισ**τῆ**ν**αι ἢ ἀντειπεῖν ἅπ**αντ**ε**ς** οἱ **ἀν**τ**ικ**είμενοι ὑμῖν. | For I shall give to you a mouth and wisdom which <u>all</u> those <u>opposed</u> to you will not <u>be able</u> to <u>withstand</u> or to contradict. |

Already we have seen how often the names for **ΚΑϊν** [*Cain*] and for **ὄφιν** [*serpent*] are concealed by means of dispersion within other words, a trait characteristic of the 'sower'. Now in this passage at Lk.10:15-18 it appears to be taught by extension that the name **σαταν** [*Satan*] can be found concealed in just this same way.

And if we ask why the author should bother to cover such new ground at this point, the answer may not at first be obvious. Yet there must be a reason. Look again at the construction of the verse at 10:16:

ὁ δὲ ἐμὲ ἀθετῶν ἀθετεῖ τὸν **ἀποΣΤείλΑΝΤά** με

But the one rejecting me rejects ***the one who sent me***

In referring to the mysterious **Person** addressed by Jesus as 'Father', the writer has chosen to use the word **ἀποΣΤείλΑΝΤά** [*one who sent*].

Compare this with the word **ἀΣΤραπὴν** [*lightning*] which he uses just two verses further on. We have the *same* letters, in the *same* order: **ἀ.σ.τ.α.ν** . It is ***Satan***'s name dispersed.

A further link exists between Lk.10:16 and 10:18 in that the word **πεσόντα** [*falling*] is found wholly dispersed within the word ἀ**ΠΟΣ**τ**ε**ίλα**ΝΤά** [*one who sent*].

Then what should have caught our eye is this:

Lk.	ὁ ἀκούων ὑμῶν ἐμοῦ	"The one hearing you hears me,
10:16	ἀκούει, καὶ ὁ ἀθετῶν ὑμᾶς	and the one rejecting you rejects
	ἐμὲ ἀθετεῖ:	me.
	ὁ δὲ ἐμὲ ἀθετῶν ἀθετεῖ	But the one rejecting me rejects
	τὸν **ἀποΣΤείλΑΝΤά** με.	***the one who sent me***."

10:17	ὑπέστρεψαν δὲ οἱ	But the seventy [two] turned
	ἐβδομήκοντα [δύο] μετὰ	back with joy saying
	χαρᾶς λέγοντες,	
	κύριε, καὶ τὰ δαιμόνια	"Lord, even the demons is made
	ὑποτάσσεται ἡμῖν ἐν τῷ	subject to us in your name".
	ὀνόματί σου.	
10:18	εἶπεν δὲ αὐτοῖς,	But he said to them:
	ἐθεώρουν τὸν σαταν αν	"I beheld **_Satan_**
	ὡς ἀστραπὴν ἐκ τοῦ	like **_lightning_** falling from
	οὐρανοῦ πεσόντα.	Heaven".

Abruptly the core of scripture's mystery is laid bare. The author of *Luke* has composed his narrative in such a way that it is Jesus himself who makes this disclosure. *He has Jesus disclose the identity of the 'Father' ... but only to those who know the 'code'.*

We may term this technique 'Gnostic disclosure'. Now we see why it should be that:

> ... καὶ τὰ δαιμόνια ὑποτάσσεται ἡμῖν ἐν τῷ ὀνόματί σου.
> ... even the demons is made subject to us in your name.

It is only to be expcted that the demons should prove subject to those appointed by Jesus. For Jesus himself has been appointed by his 'Father' ... who we now realise is Satan, the one with ultimate control over *all* the evil demons. Moreover this explains:

| Lk.
11:15 | τινὲς δὲ ἐξ αὐτῶν εἶπον, ἐν
βεελζεβοὺλ τῷ ἄρχοντι
τῶν δαιμονίων ἐκβάλλει τὰ
δαιμόνια: | But some of them said "He casts
out the demons in Beelzebul,
the prince of the demons" |

The 'Father' to whom Jesus prays is now disclosed to be Satan, the **Person**(s) of Gn.1:27, the **'lord god'**, the one manifested as the serpent, the evil and cunning impostor who presents himself as if _he_ were the only god.

Already we have suspected that Jesus is Cain. This now explains why Jesus refers to himself as '*the son of the* **Person**' (*alt. trans*: **son of man**). For Cain is the offspring of the serpent (Gn.4:1; 1 Jn.3:12), and the serpent is a manifestation of Satan, *aka*: '**The Person**' at Gn.1:27. Jesus is correct to make cryptic reference to himself as '*the son of the* **Person**'.

And now we see why Jesus brings bread and wine, a sacrifice 'from the fruits of the earth'. In displaying this trait, Jesus is not emulating Cain, Jesus _is_ Cain. In Chapter 3 we saw how Cain was unable *to distinguish* rightly (LXX Gn.4:7). And Cain has learned nothing since. Here he is in the gospel narrative, still thinking of the **lord god** as if he were **God**.

It is by means of riddles such as the one we have just encountered at Lk.10:16-18 that a Gnostic author discloses to his reader what really matters most, the solution to the 'mystery' he has set forth. For dramatic effect such an approach can hardly be surpassed. And now at last the major pieces of our jigsaw puzzle are falling into place.

Are you surprised? Are you scandalised (Jn.16:1)? Well, we are not done yet. Shortly we shall derive the same conclusion from a different passage in the gospels, this time taken from *John*.

But before we do so there is one more thing to investigate in relation to the passage at Lk.10:16-18. Did you notice that at 10:17 the writer uses the 3rd person singular where he should have used 3rd person plural? He puts:

> ... καὶ τὰ δαιμόνια ὑποτάσσεται ἡμῖν ἐν τῷ ὀνόματί σου
> ... even the demons is made subject to us in your name

When it would have been correct to put:

> ... καὶ τὰ δαιμόνια ὑποτάσσονται ἡμῖν ἐν τῷ ὀνόματί σου
> ... even the demons are made subject to us in your name

The mistake is all the more striking because of the generally excellent quality of the Greek in *Luke*.

But look again at what the writer *would* have written if he had preserved the correct grammar.

He would have written this:

Lk.	ὁ ἀκούων ὑμῶν ἐμοῦ	"The one hearing you hears me,
10:16	ἀκούει, καὶ ὁ ἀθετῶν ὑμᾶς	and the one rejecting you rejects
	ἐμὲ ἀθετεῖ·	me.
	ὁ δὲ ἐμὲ ἀθετῶν ἀθετεῖ	But the one rejecting me rejects
	τὸν ἀποΣΤειλΑΝΤΑ με.	***the one who sent me***."
##.##	ὑπέΣΤρεψΑΝ δὲ οἱ	But the seventy [two] turned
	ἑβδομήκοντα [δύο] μετὰ	back with joy saying
	χαρᾶς λέγοντες,	
	κύριε, καὶ τὰ δαιμόνια	"Lord, even the demons ***are***
	ὑποτάΣΣονΤΑι ἡμῖν ἐν	***made subject*** to us in your
	τῷ ὀνόματί σου.	name".
10:18	εἶπεν δὲ αὐτοῖς,	But he said to them:
	ἐθεώρουν τὸν ΣΑΤΑΝᾶν	"I beheld ***Satan***
	ὡς ἀΣΤραπὴΝ ἐκ τοῦ	like ***lightning*** falling from
	οὐρανοῦ πεΣόνΤΑ.	Heaven".

He would have expressed *yet again* the name of ΣΑΤΑΝ [*Satan*] in its 'dispersed' form.

It seems probable that he has used the 3rd person singular at Lk.10:17 with the express purpose of calling attention to the important riddle he has configured in this passage. His deliberate error therefore serves a didactic purpose. It provides an additional trigger to compound the demonstration of a Gnostic device from which the more alert amongst his students (the readers) may learn all the better how to extract from the gospel the solution to its Gnostic 'mystery'.

The writer has Jesus continue as follows: but already we have cracked enough of the riddles to 'know' what 'no one (else) knows' …

Lk. 10:19	ἰδοὺ δέδωκα ὑμῖν τὴν ἐξουσίαν τοῦ πατεῖν ἐπάνω ὄφεων καὶ σκορπίων, καὶ ἐπὶ πᾶσαν τὴν δύναμιν τοῦ ἐχθροῦ, καὶ οὐδὲν ὑμᾶς οὐ μὴ ἀδικήσῃ.	"Look, I have given you the authority to tread over serpents and scorpions, and upon all the power of the enemy, and not one might injure you.
10:20	πλὴν ἐν τούτῳ μὴ χαίρετε ὅτι τὰ πνεύματα ὑμῖν ὑποτάσσεται, χαίρετε δὲ ὅτι τὰ ὀνόματα ὑμῶν ἐγγέγραπται ἐν τοῖς οὐρανοῖς.	But do not rejoice in this, that the spirits **is** made subject to you, but rejoice that your names **has** been inscribed in the heavens."
10:21	ἐν αὐτῇ τῇ ὥρᾳ ἠγαλλιάσατο [ἐν] τῷ πνεύματι τῷ ἁγίῳ καὶ εἶπεν, ἐξομολογοῦμαί σοι, πάτερ, κύριε τοῦ οὐρανοῦ καὶ τῆς γῆς, ὅτι ἀπέκρυψας ταῦτα ἀπὸ σοφῶν καὶ συνετῶν, καὶ ἀπεκάλυψας αὐτὰ νηπίοις: ναί, ὁ πατήρ, ὅτι οὕτως εὐδοκία ἐγένετο ἔμπροσθέν σου.	In that hour he rejoiced in the spirit, the holy one, and said "I acknowledge you, father, lord of Heaven and Earth, because you hid these things from (the) wise and intelligent and revealed them to infants. Yes, father, for so it happened (to be) approved before you.

10:22	πάντα μοι παρεδόθη ὑπὸ τοῦ πατρός μου, καὶ **οὐδεὶς γινώσκει τίς ἐστιν ὁ υἱὸς** εἰ μὴ ὁ πατήρ, καὶ **τίς ἐστιν ὁ πατὴρ** εἰ μὴ ὁ υἱὸς **καὶ ᾧ ἐὰν** βούληται ὁ υἱὸς ἀποκαλύψαι.	Everything has been given away to me under my father. And ***no one knows who the son is***, except the father - and ***who the father is***, except the son ***and he to whom, if he should wish, the son may reveal (him)***".
10:23	καὶ στραφεὶς πρὸς τοὺς μαθητὰς **κατ' ἰδίαν** εἶπεν, μακάριοι οἱ ὀφθαλμοὶ οἱ βλέποντες ἃ βλέπετε.	And turning to the students ***privately***, he said "Fortunate (are) the eyes which see what you see.
10:24	λέγω γὰρ ὑμῖν ὅτι πολλοὶ προφῆται καὶ βασιλεῖς ἠθέλησαν ἰδεῖν ἃ ὑμεῖς βλέπετε <u>καὶ οὐκ εἶδαν</u>, καὶ ἀκοῦσαι ἃ ἀκούετε <u>καὶ οὐκ ἤκουσαν</u>.	For I say to you that many prophets and kings wished to see what you see, ***and did not see*** ... and to hear what you hear, ***and did not hear***."
10:25	καὶ ἰδοὺ νομικός τις **ἀνέστη** <u>ἐΚπειρΆζωΝ</u> αὐτὸν λέγων, διδάσκαλε, τί ποιήσας ζωὴν αἰώνιον κληρονομήσω;	And look! A certain lawyer ***was resurrected***, <u>testing</u> him out, saying "Teacher, what shall I do (that) I shall inherit eternal life?"

Again and again in the gospel narrative we find that Jesus (who is Cain) makes the promise of eternal life. In doing this he is merely repeating the promise first made by the serpent (his father) when he said to Eve (Gn.3:4-5):

οὐ θανάτῳ ἀποθανεῖσθε. ᾔδει γὰρ ὁ θεὸς ὅτι ἐν ᾗ ἂν ἡμέρᾳ
φάγητε ἀπ' αὐτοῦ διανοιχθήσονται ὑμῶν οἱ ὀφθαλμοί
καὶ ἔσεσθε ὡς θεοὶ γινώσκοντες καλὸν καὶ πονηρόν.

By death you shall not die. For God knows that in the day
you may eat from it, your eyes shall be opened up,
and you shall be like gods, knowing good and evil.

The things which were hidden have been revealed 'to infants' (*qv. also* Mt.18:3). Yes, it is in the infant class that children learn to read. In this case it is *we* who must become again like infants, learning to read anew. When we have done this, we can teach prophets and kings.

Identifying both Father and Son

Let us examine now a passage from the fourth gospel which turns out to serve the same function of forthright Gnostic disclosure. The author has Jesus say:

Jn.		
15:21	ἀλλὰ ταῦτα πάντα ποιήσουσιν εἰς ὑμᾶς διὰ τὸ ὄνομά μου, ὅτι οὐκ οἴδασιν τὸν πέμψαντά με.	"But all these things they will do to you on account of my name ... *because they do not know 'the one who sent me'*.
15:22	εἰ μὴ ἦλθον καὶ ἐλάλησα αὐτοῖς, ἁμαρτίαν οὐκ εἴχοσαν· νῦν δὲ πρΌΦασΙΝ οὐκ ἔχουσιν περὶ τῆς ἁμαρτίας αὐτῶν.	If I had not come and spoken to them, they were not having a mistake [*alt*: sin]. But now they do not have any **_excuse_** concerning their mistake.
15:23	ὁ ἐμὲ μισῶν καὶ τὸν πατέρα μου μισεῖ.	The one hating me hates my father also.
15:24	εἰ τὰ ἔργα μὴ ἐποίησα ἐν αὐτοῖς ἃ οὐδεὶς ἄλλος ἐποίησεν, ἁμαρτίαν οὐκ εἴχοσαν· νῦν δὲ καὶ ἑωράΚΑσΙΝ καὶ μεμισήΚΑσΙΝ καὶ ἐμὲ καὶ τὸν πατέρα μου.	If I had not done the works amongst them which not one other did, they were not having a mistake [*alt*: sin]. But now both **_they have seen_** and **_they have hated_** *both me and my father.*"

In this last verse the author has Jesus make the claim:

νῦν δὲ καὶ ἑωράκασιν καὶ μεμισήκασιν
καὶ ἐμὲ καὶ τὸν πατέρα μου

But <u>now</u> both <u>they have seen</u> and they have hated
<u>both me and my father</u>.

Here is an explicit declaration that 'they' (in effect this means every reader of this passage) '*have* seen ... both me and my father'. The use of the perfect tense gives a strong impression that whatever it was we should have 'seen', we have seen it already: it is by now 'water under the bridge'. And the suggestion of this perception (or disclosure) having been quite recent is sustained by the use of the word **νῦν** [*now*]. But when did we (or indeed anyone else) 'see' both Jesus and his father? To the informed and careful reader the answer is not long in coming.

For look what the writer has done! In the very same verse which makes this claim we have both the word ἑωρά**ΚΑσΙΝ** [*they have seen*] and the word μεμισή**ΚΑσΙΝ** [*they have hated*] ... words which without difficulty we perceive to conceal the name of **ΚάϊΝ** [*Cain*]. As we have deduced already, Jesus *is* Cain ... so it is true that we have 'seen' Jesus already.

Incidentally, there are only thirteen verses in the whole of the Greek NT which include a word in the form **ΚΑ#ΙΝ**, where # stands for any single character (a wildcard). This verse at Jn.15:24 is the only verse with two such instances. The twelve others are as follows:

Mt.2:20	τεθνή**ΚΑσΙΝ**	they have died
Mt.12:47	ἑστή**ΚΑσΙΝ**	they have stood
Mt.13:42	**Κά**μ**ΙΝ**ον	furnace
Mt.13:50	**Κά**μ**ΙΝ**ον	furnace
Mk.8:3	ἥ**ΚΑσΙΝ**	they have come
Mk.8:20	ἑστή**ΚΑσΙΝ**	they have stood

Lk.17:6	συ**ΚαμΙ̇Ν**ῳ	mulberry tree (*it 'complies' with what you say to it, ending up in the sea; this forms one part of a compound anagram riddle, variants of which span more than one gospel*)
Jn.4:38	κεκοπιά**ΚασΙΝ**	they have grown weary
Jn.17:28	εἰρή**ΚασΙΝ**	they have said
Rv.1:15	**Κά**μ**ΙΝ**ῳ	furnace
Rv.8:2	ἑστή**ΚασΙΝ**	they have stood
Rv.9:2	**Κα**μ**Ι̇Ν**ου	furnace

But what of the person Jesus refers to as 'Father'? Here is the answer. All we have to do is look at 15:22:

νῦν δὲ πρ**Ό**φ**ασΙΝ** οὐκ ἔχουσιν περὶ τῆς ἁμαρτίας αὐτῶν.
But now they do not have an **_excuse_** concerning their mistake.

Again the word **νῦν** [*now*] serves as a pointer to what may be seen. It points to the word πρ**Ό**φ**ασΙΝ** [*excuse*] … and there we see the name for the 'Father'. It is **Ό**φ**ΙΝ** [*serpent*]. We have no **_excuse_** if we fail to 'see' him! And in case you are in any doubt about the significance of this:

| Rv. 12:9 | καὶ ἐβλήθη ὁ δράκων ὁ μέγας, ὁ **Ό**φ**Ις** ὁ ἀρχαῖος, ὁ καλούμενος διάβολος καὶ ὁ **σαταΝ**ᾶς, ὁ πλανῶν τὴν οἰκουμένην ὅλην _ ἐβλήθη εἰς τὴν γῆν, καὶ οἱ ἄγγελοι αὐτοῦ μετ' αὐτοῦ ἐβλήθησαν. | And he was thrown down, the great dragon, the ancient **_serpent_**, the one called a devil and **_Satan_**, the deceiver of the whole world. He was thrown down onto the earth, and his angels were thrown down with him. |

The identity has now been disclosed *both* for Jesus *and* for the one he refers to as 'Father'. Our earlier conclusion from *Luke* is confirmed here in *John*. Jesus *is* Cain, whilst the 'Father' who has sent him *is* the serpent, who is Satan. It is easy now to understand why both should be 'hated', just as Jesus states at Jn.15:24 (above). And now we understand the passage at Jn.9:39-41. The Pharisees may claim that they see. But they cannot see, so their sin remains.

Incidentally there are only five verses in the whole of the Greek NT which include a word in the form Οϕ##ΙϚ or Οϕ##ΙΝ (where # stands for any single character). This verse at Jn.15:22 provides one instance. The remaining four are:

Lk.2:36	προϕῆτιϚ	prophetess (*Anna*)
Ac.9:17	ὁ ὀϕθείϚ σοι	the one who appeared to you (*to Paul on the way to Damascus*)
Rv.2:20	προϕῆτιΝ	prophetess (*Jezebel*)
Rv.9:19	ὄϕεσιΝ	to serpents

So much now makes sense, so much we never understood before:

> But all these things they will do to you on account of my name - *because they do not know 'the one who sent me'*.

> If I had not come and spoken to them, they were not having a mistake. But now they do not have any **excuse** concerning their mistake.

> The one hating me hates my father also.

> If I had not done the works amongst them which not one other did, they were not having a mistake. But now both ***they have seen*** and ***they have hated*** both me and my father.

It is with this passage that the author of the fourth gospel makes Jesus himself explain to those readers better informed:

- That many will do 'all these things' for the simple reason that 'they do not know the one who sent me'.

- That it is he, Jesus, who has caused these persons to make a mistake (ie. to sin).

- That those embracing what he has to offer have ***no excuse*** for their mistake. They have no excuse because he has disclosed his own identity as well as that of the 'Father' ... ***but they have failed to see.***

- That those who 'hate' him will also 'hate' the father ... which is fair enough, for both father and son are portrayed to be evil.

With all this understood, we should not now be surprised by what emerges in an earlier sequence from the same gospel:

Jn. 8:19	ἔλεγον οὖν αὐτῷ, ποῦ ἐστιν ὁ πατήρ σου; ἀπεκρίθη ἰησοῦς, οὔτε ἐμὲ οἴδατε οὔτε τὸν πατέρα μου· εἰ ἐμὲ ᾔδειτε, καὶ τὸν πατέρα μου ἂν ᾔδειτε.	Therefore they said to him "Where is your father?". Jesus answered "You know neither me nor my father. If you knew me then you would also know my father."
8:20	ταῦτα τὰ ῥήματα ἐλάλησεν ἐν τῷ γαζοφυλακίῳ δɪδάσKωV ἐν τῷ ἱερῷ· καὶ οὐδεὶς ἐπίασεν αὐτόν, ὅτι οὔπω ἐληλύθει ἡ ὥρα αὐτοῦ.	He spoke these words in the treasury, <u>teaching</u> in the temple. And no one caught him because his hour had not yet come.

Here again Jesus implies to the Pharisees that they 'know' neither his identity nor that of his 'Father'. And immediately we are (almost) given a double clue, for Jesus is to be found *teaching* (again we see the name of **Cain**) in the *treasury*.

Within the four gospels and *Acts* there are eighteen instances of words which provide the letters both to form the word ὄφιν [*serpent*] and to form the word Κάϊν [*Cain*].

Of these, the word γαζοφυλάκιον [*treasury*] has the highest incidence (Mk.12:41, 12:43; Lk.21:1).

In the verse above (Jn.8:20) the author of the fourth gospel puts this word into the dative case, by saying that Jesus was teaching:

> ... <u>ἐν</u> τῷ γαζοφυλακίῳ
> ... <u>in</u> the treasury

If he had chosen to write instead that Jesus was teaching:

> ... <u>παρὰ</u> τὸ γαζοφυλάκιον
> ... <u>by</u> the <u>treasury</u>

then he would have produced a word which served to present the attributes of Cain and the serpent 'combined into one'. In this way the writer would have followed up cleverly upon the easy assertion which Jesus makes in the previous verse:

> You know neither me nor my father.
> If you knew me then you would also know my father.

Yet by using the dative case the writer has stopped short of achieving this. Why? Presumably because, for Jesus:

> ... his hour had not yet come

To write in this way would have given too much away too early in the gospel. But later, in Chapter 15 of the same gospel, the identity of both father and son <u>is</u> disclosed ... as we have seen already.

Identity of the Father Confirmed Yet Again

Working from a different passsage in the fourth gospel, we have:

Jn.		
Jn. 8:31	ἔλεγεν οὖν ὁ ἰησοῦς πρὸς τοὺς πεπιστευκότας αὐτῷ ἰουδαίους, ἐὰν ὑμεῖς μείνητε ἐν τῷ λόγῳ τῷ ἐμῷ, ἀληθῶς μαθηταί μού ἐστε,	Therefore Jesus said to those Judaeans who had believed in him "If you remain in mine word, truly you are my students.
8:32	καὶ γνώσεσθε τὴν ἀλήθειαν, καὶ ἡ ἀλήθεια ἐλευθερώσει ὑμᾶς.	And you will know the truth, and the truth will make you free."

Here Jesus addresses *those Judaeans who have believed in him* ... to tell them that: 'You *will* know the truth'. Notice too that Jesus asserts: 'the truth will make you free'.

He proceeds to tell them the truth ... but they do not believe him:

Jn.		
Jn. 8:37	οἶδα ὅτι σπέρμα ἀβραάμ ἐστε: ἀλλὰ ζητεῖτέ με ἀποΚτεῖΝαι, ὅτι ὁ λόγος ὁ ἐμὸς οὐ χωρεῖ ἐν ὑμῖν.	"I know that you are seed of Abraham: but you seek to kill me because mine message [alt: mine 'Logos'] does not find a place in you.
8:38	ἃ ἐγὼ ἑώρακα παρὰ τῷ πατρὶ λαλῶ: καὶ ὑμεῖς οὖν ἃ ἠκούσατε παρὰ τοῦ πατρὸς ποιεῖτε.	I speak the things I have seen with the father; and you then make the things which you heard from the father."

8:39	ἀπεΚρίθησαν καὶ εἶπαν αὐτῷ, ὁ πατὴρ ἡμῶν ἀβραάμ ἐστιν. λέγει αὐτοῖς ὁ ἰησοῦς, εἰ τέκνα τοῦ ἀβραάμ ἐστε, τὰ ἔργα τοῦ ἀβραὰμ ἐποιεῖτε:	They replied and said to him "Our father is Abraham". Jesus said to them "If you are children of Abraham, you were making the works of Abraham.
8:40	νῦν δὲ ζητεῖτέ με ἀποΚτεῖναι, ἄνθρωπον ὃς τὴν ἀλήθειαν ὑμῖν λελάληκα ἣν ἤκουσα παρὰ τοῦ θεοῦ: τοῦτο ἀβραὰμ οὐκ ἐποίησεν.	But now you seek to kill me, a person who has has spoken the truth to you, which I heard from God. This Abraham did not do.
8:41	ὑμεῖς ποιεῖτε τὰ ἔργα τοῦ πατρὸς ὑμῶν. εἶπαν [οὖν] αὐτῷ, ἡμεῖς ἐκ πορνείας οὐ γεγεννήμεθα: ἕνα πατέρα ἔχομεν τὸν θεόν.	You make the works of your father." They [then] said to him "We were not born of sexual immorality. We have one father, God."
8:42	εἶπεν αὐτοῖς ὁ ἰησοῦς, εἰ ὁ θεὸς πατὴρ ὑμῶν ἦν, ἠγαπᾶτε ἂν ἐμέ, ἐγὼ γὰρ ἐκ τοῦ θεοῦ ἐξῆλθον καὶ ἥκω: οὐδὲ γὰρ ἀπ' ἐμαυτοῦ ἐλήλυθα, ἀλλ' ἐκεῖνός με ἀπέστειλεν.	Jesus said to them "If God was your Father, you would keep loving me. For I came forth from God and have come. For neither have I come of myself, but that one sent me.
8:43	διὰ τί τὴν λαλιὰν τὴν ἐμὴν οὐ γινώσκετε; ὅτι οὐ δύνασθε ἀΚούειν τὸν λόγον τὸν ἐμόν.	Why do you not know mine speech? Because you are not able to hear mine message [alt: mine 'Logos'].

8:44	ὑμεῖς ἐκ τοῦ πατρὸς τοῦ διαβόλου ἐστὲ καὶ τὰς ἐπιθυμίας τοῦ πατρὸς ὑμῶν θέλετε ποιεῖν.	*You are from the father, the devil, and you wish to make the desires of your father.*
	ἐκεῖνος ἀνθρωποκτόνος ἦν ἀπ' ἀρχῆς, καὶ ἐν τῇ ἀληθείᾳ οὐκ ἔστηκεν, ὅτι οὐκ ἔστιν ἀλήθεια ἐν αὐτῷ.	*'That one' was a mankiller from (the) beginning and has not stood in the truth because truth is not within him.*
	ὅταν λαλῇ τὸ ψεῦδος, ἐκ τῶν ἰδίων λαλεῖ, ὅτι ψεύστης ἐστὶν καὶ ὁ πατὴρ αὐτοῦ.	*When he speaks the lie, he speaks from (what are) his own. For he is a liar, and his father.*
8:45	ἐγὼ δὲ ὅτι τὴν ἀλήθειαν λέγω, οὐ πιστεύετέ μοι.	But I, because I speak the truth, you do not believe me.
8:46	τίς ἐξ ὑμῶν ἐλέγχει με περὶ ἁμαρτίας; εἰ ἀλήθειαν λέγω, διὰ τί ὑμεῖς οὐ πιστεύετέ μοι;	Which of you convicts me of a mistake [*alt*: of sin]? If I tell the truth, why do you not believe me?
8:47	ὁ ὢν ἐκ **τοῦ θεοῦ** τὰ ῥήματα **τοῦ θεοῦ** ἀκούει· διὰ τοῦτο ὑμεῖς οὐκ ἀκούετε, ὅτι ἐκ **τοῦ θεοῦ** οὐκ ἐστέ.	The one (being) from **God** hears the words of **God**. On this account you do not hear, because you are not from **God**."

Jesus accuses '*those who <u>have</u> believed in him*' of seeking to kill him … and then explains their behaviour by telling them that their 'father' is the devil (*aka*. Satan). But surely the one he has assigned to be *their* father is in fact *his own* 'Father'?

Then he is disclosing to them that the 'Father' is the devil.

This passage may prove puzzling to many. But in the light of what we have learned already, it should come to us as no surprise.

Yet what dreadful irony is here: for Jesus actually *tells* his followers that the 'Father' is Satan. And they do not believe him!

Why do they not believe him?

> διὰ τοῦτο ὑμεῖς οὐκ ἀκούετε, ὅτι ἐκ **τοῦ θεοῦ** οὐκ ἐστέ.
> On this account you do not hear, because you are not from **God**.

They are 'not from **God**', so cannot hear the words of **God**.

We shall end the chapter with two related passages from *Mark*:

Mk.	καὶ ἐθεράπευσεν πολλοὺς	And he healed many (of
1:34	κακῶς ἔχοντας ποικίλαις	those) badly having various
	νόσοις, καὶ δαιμόνια πολλὰ	diseases, and cast out many
	ἐξέβαλεν, καὶ οὐκ ἤφιεν	demons. And he did not
	λαλεῖν τὰ δαιμόνια, ὅτι	allow the demons to speak
	ᾔδεισαν αὐτόν.	because *they knew him*.
.....	(*verses omitted here*)	
3:11	καὶ τὰ πνεύματα τὰ	And the spirits (the unclean
	ἀκάθαρτα, ὅταν αὐτὸν	ones), when they saw him,
	ἐθεώρουν, προσέπιπτον	fell down to him and cried
	αὐτῷ καὶ ἔκραζον λέγοντες	out, saying that "*You are the*
	ὅτι σὺ εἶ ὁ υἱὸς τοῦ θεοῦ.	*son of God* !"
3:12	καὶ πολλὰ ἐπετίμα αὐτοῖς ἵνα	And repeatedly he
	μὴ αὐτὸν φανερὸν	reprimanded them so that
	ποιήσ**ωσιν**.	*they should* not *make* him
		known

Jesus is Cain. As such, he is _not_ the son of **God**.

Instead (as he himself says correctly) he is 'the son of the **Person'**, *ie.* son of the **lord god** (*aka.* Satan).

Cain, and his mother Eve, embrace the **lord god** as their god. The 'unclean spirits' do the same. All exist under a curse, or spell.

The curse is incurred by the fact that they do not know **God**. Instead they think of the **lord god** as their god. From this it follows that they think of Jesus as 'son of god'.

It is their *mistaken perception* which explains why the 'unclean spirits' say to Jesus:

> σὺ εἶ ὁ υἱὸς τοῦ θεοῦ
> *You are the son of God !*

And they are forbidden by Jesus to disclose his real identity (Mk.3:12).

Chapter 10

Cain and the Serpent
at the Core of Scripture's Plot

It is at Gn.4:14 that Cain issues the threat :

> εἰ ἐκβάλλεις με σήμερον ἀπὸ προσώπου τῆς γῆς
> καὶ ἀπὸ τοῦ προσώπου σου κρυβήσομαι

> If you throw me out today from a face of the earth,
> I shall be hidden also from your face.

Cain does indeed go '*hidden from your face*'. All subsequent scripture is written in such a way that his threat should be fulfilled.

The authors provide for this by two means simultaneously. First they conceal Cain's own name within other words in the text (the '*sign*' for Cain). Second, they write to exploit the technique of impersonation within the narrative itself; so in the NT texts they present to us Cain under the *persona* of Jesus.

Perhaps you remember the popular children's story about *Little Red Riding Hood*. The child walks one day through the forest to visit her grandmother's house. On the way she meets with the wolf. She notices his **eyes**, his **ears** and his **teeth** - which are striking and handsomely large. Now the cunning wolf, having ascertained from Red Riding Hood her destination, takes a short cut and arrives at the house before her. He gulps down the grandmother, dresses himself in her night gown, then settles himself down in her bed to wait. Any suspicions Red Riding Hood may have will be allayed because she is fully accustomed to find her grandmother dressed in this way and sitting up in bed.

The wolf is implementing an impersonational deception. He is delighted when the little girl arrives at the house, addressing him as

'*Grandmama*'. And it is not until he answers the little girl's remark about the size of his teeth with the riposte: '*All the better to eat you with, my dear!*' that suddenly it becomes clear to the child what a bad mistake she has made.

Of course such tales are the stuff of narrative fiction. How many of us would make such a mistake in real life?

The appropriate word in Greek is:

αἰφνίδιος [*sudden*]   (*qv.* Lk.21:34; 1 Tm.5:3).

For there we see ὄφις [*a serpent*]. This is the way scripture works.

An explicit warning not to be deceived

It is against just this scenario that we are warned in the NT letter *2 Thesssalonians*:

2 Th. 2:1	ἐρωτῶμεν δὲ ὑμᾶς, ἀδελφοί, ὑπὲρ τῆς παρουσίας τοῦ κυρίου ἡμῶν ἰησοῦ χριστοῦ καὶ ἡμῶν ἐπισυναγωγῆς ἐπ' αὐτόν,	But we ask you, brothers, concerning the presence of our lord Jesus Christ and our gathering together against him
2:2	εἰς τὸ μὴ ταχέως σαλευθῆναι ὑμᾶς ἀπὸ τοῦ νοὸς μηδὲ θροεῖσθαι μήτε διὰ πνεύματος μήτε διὰ λόγου μήτε δι' ἐπιστολῆς ὡς δι' ἡμῶν, ὡς ὅτι ἐνέστηκεν ἡ ἡμέρα τοῦ κυρίου.	That you be not quickly shaken from your mind, nor disturbed, neither through spirit nor through message nor through a letter such as through us, such that the day of the lord has begun.

2:3	μή τις ὑμᾶς ἐξαπατήσῃ κατὰ μηδένα τρόπον: ὅτι ἐὰν μὴ ἔλθῃ ἡ ἀποστασία πρῶτον καὶ ἀποκαλυφθῇ ὁ **ἄνθρωπος** τῆς ἀνομίας, ὁ υἱὸς τῆς ἀπωλείας,	<u>Do not let anyone deceive you in any way</u>. Because unless the apostasy comes first, and **the Person** of Lawlessness is revealed, the son of Perdition
2:4	ὁ **ἀ**ν**τικ**είμενος καὶ ὑπεραιρόμενος ἐπὶ πάντα λεγόμενον θεὸν ἢ σέβασμα, ὥστε αὐτὸν εἰς τὸν ναὸν τοῦ θεοῦ καθίσαι, ἀποδε**ικν**ύντ**α** ἑαυτὸν ὅτι ἔστιν θεός.	The one <u>opposing</u> and exalting himself over all that is called 'god' or worshipped, seated just like him in the temple of God, <u>demonstrating</u> that he himself is a god.
2:5	οὐ μνημονεύετε ὅτι ἔτι ὢν πρὸς ὑμᾶς ταῦτα ἔλεγον ὑμῖν;	Do you not remember that when I was still with you I said these things to you?
2:6	καὶ νῦν τὸ κατέχον οἴδατε, εἰς τὸ ἀπ**οκα**λυ**φ**θῆ**ναι** αὐτὸν ἐν τῷ ἑαυτοῦ καιρῷ.	And now you know the incumbent, for him <u>to be revealed</u> in his own season.
2:7	τὸ γὰρ μυστήριον ἤδη ἐνεργεῖται τῆς ἀνομίας: μόνον ὁ κατέχων ἄρτι ἕως ἐκ μέσου γένηται.	For the mystery of lawlessness is already working itself out: (he is) only the incumbent for now, until he comes into being from the midst …

2:8	καὶ τότε ἀπΟκαλυφθήσεται ὁ ἄνομος, ὃν ὁ κύριος [ἰησοῦσ] ἀνελεῖ τῷ πνεύματι τοῦ στόματος αὐτοῦ καὶ καταργήσει τῇ ἐπιφανείᾳ τῆς παρουσίας αὐτοῦ,	And then <u>he will be revealed</u>, the lawless one whom the lord [Jesus] will raise up [*alt*: adopt] through the breath [*alt*: the spirit] of his mouth, and will make redundant through the manifestation of his (own) presence
2:9	οὗ ἐστιν ἡ παρουσία κατ' ἐνέργειαν τοῦ **σατανᾶ** ἐν πάσῃ δυνάμει καὶ σημείοις καὶ τέρασιν ψεύδους	Of whom the presence is according to the activity of <u>Satan</u> in all power and signs and freak phenomena of falsehood
2:10	καὶ ἐν πάσῃ ἀπάτῃ ἀδικίας τοῖς ἀπολλυμένοις, ἀνθ' ὧν τὴν ἀγάπην τῆς ἀληθείας οὐκ ἐδέξαντο εἰς τὸ σωθῆναι αὐτούς.	And in all deception of wickedness for those being lost, instead of which they did not receive the love of truth for them to be saved.
2:11	καὶ διὰ τοῦτο πέμπει αὐτοῖς ὁ θεὸς ἐνέργειαν πλάνης εἰς τὸ πιστεῦσαι αὐτοὺς τῷ ψεύδει,	And on this account **God** sends to them an activity of error, that they should believe the lie
2:12	ἵνα κριθῶσιν πάντες οἱ μὴ πιστεύσαντες τῇ ἀληθείᾳ ἀλλὰ εὐδοκήσαντες τῇ ἀδικίᾳ.	That they all <u>may be judged</u>, those not believing the truth but being satisfied with iniquity.

The allusion at 2:4 may call to mind the activities of Jesus in the temple at Jerusalem, as recorded in the gospels (Mt.21:12, 21:23; Mk.11:15, 12:35; Lk.2:46, 19:45 seq.; Jn.8:2, 8:20).

The warning is focused first upon Cain, *the Person of Lawlessness, the son of Perdition*, whose name appears twice at 2:4. At 2:6 it is then focused upon Cain and the serpent together, both now '*revealed in their own season*'. For the word ἀπΟΚΑλυΦθῆVαι [*to be revealed*] is another like γαζΟΦυλΑΚIοV [*treasury*]: it serves to conceal both ὄΦIV [*serpent*] and ΚΑϊV [*Cain*].

Then at 2:8-9 we learn that:

> … the lawless one will be revealed, whom the lord [Jesus] will raise up through the breath of his mouth and will make redundant through the manifestation of his (own) presence … of whom the presence is according to the activity of Satan in all power and signs, and freak phenomena of falsehood.

The *lawless one* is now the serpent, *revealed* at 2:8. And then we are told that the lord Jesus, *through the manifestation of his own presence*, will make the serpent redundant. Yet this presence remains what it always was, a presence '*according to the activity of Satan in all power and signs and freak phenomena of falsehood*'.

'*Those being lost*' are those deceived by the serpent and by Cain. They are the readers of scripture who have *believed the lie*, those who *did not receive the love of truth for them to be saved*, those *satisfied with iniquity*.

The entire passage serves only to confirm what we have learned already from the gospels. It is a useful confirmation nonetheless.

Christ a Curse upon Us

This passage from the Pauline letter *Galatians* is frequently mistranslated, perhaps by those who cannot believe what it says:

Ga. 3:13	χριστὸς ἡμᾶς ἐξηγόρασεν ἐκ τῆς κατάρας τοῦ νόμου γενόμενος ὑπὲρ ἡμῶν κατάρα,	Christ bought us off from the curse of the Law, <u>he becoming a curse upon us.</u>
	ὅτι γέγραπται, ἐπικατάρατος πᾶς ὁ κρεμάμενος ἐπὶ ξύλου,	Because it is written, "Cursed is everyone who hangs upon a tree" (Dt.21:23)

The Mosaic Law embodied '*a curse*' because it presented the **lord god** (the **Person** of Gn.1:27) as the god of Israel, in substitution for **God** himself.

With the advent of the NT texts the '*curse*' of the Law is deemed to be set aside (in part at least).

But the curse is merely transferred. Instead of being mediated through the **Person**, it is now Christ himself (that is, Cain, the <u>son</u> of the **Person**) who becomes '*a curse upon us*'.

And there we see the association drawn between the Tree of (Eternal) Life upon which the serpent 'hangs' (Gn.3:4-6) … and the NT 'tree', the cross upon which the Christ will be exposed to view.

The promise is the same: the tree is really the same. And with it comes a curse.

Do not Hold at Face Value the lord Jesus Christ

These verses from the letter of *James* are important, but once again they pose a challenge to the translator:

Jm. 2:1	ἀδελφοί μου, **μὴ** ἐν προσωπολημψίαις ἔχετε τὴν πίστιν τοῦ κυρίου ἡμῶν ἰησοῦ χριστοῦ τῆς δόξης.	My brothers, do **not** hold <u>at face value</u> the faith of our lord Jesus Christ of glory.
.....	(*verses omitted here*)	
2:9	εἰ δὲ προσωπολημπτεῖτε, ἁμαρτίαν ἐργάζεσθε, ἐλεγχόμενοι ὑπὸ τοῦ νόμου ὡς παραβάται.	But if <u>you do take at face value</u> you are practising a mistake [*alt*: practising sin], censured under the Law as transgressors.

The word **προσωπο-λημψία** is a compound made up from two words. First we have the noun:

> **πρόσωπόν** :   *a face*; look; countenance; *mask*; *persona*; a character (in a book or play)

and then from the future tense **λήμψομαι** of the verb:

> **λαμβάνω** :   I take; receive; I apprehend (with the mind)

we have the noun:

> **λῆμψις** :   a taking; receiving; *an assumption* (in logic)

The literal meaning seems to be *face-assumption* or *received-persona*. Whatever vernacular idiom we prefer, these verses surely convey a warning *against* any simplistic 'faith' in the figure of the *lord Jesus Christ*, as depicted throughout NT scripture.

The warning is understandable since we know already that the character of the 'lord Jesus Christ' is merely a *mask* or *persona* for Cain.

Firstborn of All Creation

This passage from the Pauline letter to *Colossians* is most instructive:

Col.		
1:9	διὰ τοῦτο καὶ ἡμεῖς, ἀφ' ἧς ἡμέρας ἠκούσαμεν, οὐ παυόμεθα ὑπὲρ ὑμῶν προσευχόμενοι καὶ αἰτούμενοι ἵνα πληρωθῆτε τὴν ἐπίγνωΣΙΝ τοῦ θελήματος αὐτοῦ ἐν πάσῃ σοφίᾳ καὶ συνέσει πΝευμΑτΙΚῇ,	On this account we also, from the day we heard, do not cease praying on your behalf and asking that you may be filled with the <u>recognition</u> of his wish in all wisdom and <u>spiritual</u> knowledge.
1:10	περιπατῆσαι ἀξίως **τοῦ κυρίου** εἰς πᾶσαν <u>ἀρεσΚεΙαν</u>, ἐν παντὶ ἔργῳ ἀγαθῷ καρποφοροῦντες καὶ αὐξανόμενοι τῇ ἐπιγνώσει **τοῦ θεοῦ,**	To walk around worthy of **the lord** in every <u>compliance</u>, bearing fruit in every good work and increasing the recognition of **God.**
1:11	ἐν πάσῃ δυνάμει δυναμούμενοι κατὰ τὸ κράτος τῆς δόξης αὐτοῦ εἰς πᾶσαν ὑπομονὴν καὶ μαΚροθυμΙαν, μετὰ χαρᾶς	Made mighty in every mighty work according to the strength of his glory, with joy in every endurance and <u>patience</u>
1:12	εὐΧαρΙΣΤΟῦντεΣ τῷ πατρὶ τῷ ἱΚανώΣαντι ὑμᾶς εἰς τὴν μερίδα τοῦ κλήρου τῶν ἁγίων ἐν τῷ φωτί:	<u>Giving thanks</u> to the father, the one <u>qualifying</u> us into the share of the inheritance of the holy ones in the light

1:13	ὃς ἐρρύσατο ἡμᾶς ἐκ τῆς ἐξουσίας τοῦ σκότους καὶ μετέστησεν εἰς τὴν βασιλείαν τοῦ υἱοῦ τῆς ἀγάπης αὐτοῦ,	Who delivered us from the authority of darkness and removed (us) into the kingdom of the son of his love,
1:14	ἐν ᾧ ἔχομεν τὴν ἀπολύτρ<u>ωσιν</u>, τὴν ἄφεσιν τῶν ἁμαρτιῶν:	In whom we have the <u>ransoming</u>, the forgiveness of mistakes [alt: of sins],
1:15	ὅς ἐστιν εἰκὼν τοῦ θεοῦ τοῦ ἀοράτου, <u>πρωτότοκος πάσης κτίσεως</u>,	Who is an image of the invisible God, ***firstborn of all creation***.

The superficial impression of pastoral concern is typical of the Pauline letters. Yet surely this passage has been constructed to lead far astray those who do not know the identity of **the lord**, meanwhile issuing familiar '*signs*' to those who know rather better.

At 1:9 ἐπίγν<u>ωσιν</u> [*recognition*] and πν<u>ευματικ</u>ῇ [*spiritual*] evoke respectively the serpent and Cain. Then ἀρεσ<u>κείαν</u> [*compliance*] and μα<u>κροθυμίαν</u> [*patience*] continue to evoke Cain.

Meanwhile a better option is kept open with the mention of:

> bearing fruit in every good work
> and increasing the recognition of **God** (*sic*)

At 1:12 the word εὐ<u>χαριστο</u>ῦντες [*giving thanks*] evokes <u>χριστός</u> [*Christ*] … but it is essential to notice that this is the one ἱ<u>καν</u>ώσαντι [*qualifying*] us into the share of the inheritance, etc … for here we see both σα<u>ταν</u> [*Satan*] and <u>κάϊν</u> [*Cain*] combined in one word.

The authority of darkness is surely a token of the good God of Gn.1:1 from which those who are truly wise may prefer *not* to be removed into the so-called '*kingdom of the son of his love*'.

Yet to those who understand the deeper theme of scripture it should be clear that the one offering *'forgiveness for sins'* and *'a ransom'* from any expected punishment is Jesus Christ. And there at 1:15 his identity is given away again in a single straightforward assertion. For we learn that he is:

> ... εἰκὼν τοῦ θεοῦ τοῦ ἀοράτου, πρωτότοκος πάσης κτίσεως
> ... an image of the invisible God, firstborn of all creation

The description here is certainly that of Cain. For Cain *is* the first one 'born' in the whole of scripture's creation sequence. Adam was made by **God** from the earth and the woman from Adam's rib. Then at Gn.4:1 Cain was *born* to the woman, Eve.

It also makes sense that Cain should be described as *'an image of the invisible God'* because at Gn.1:27 the **lord god** was made *in the image of a god*. We may expect Cain to inherit this attribute from his 'father'.

The passage above (from *Colossians*) provides us with a straightforward assertion confirming the identity of Jesus as Cain. It is direct and easy to understand. See now what we have in *2 Corinthians*:

2 Cor. 4:3	εἰ δὲ καὶ ἔστιν κεκαλυμμένον τὸ εὐαγγέλιον ἡμῶν, ἐν τοῖς ἀπολλυμένοις ἐστὶν κεκαλυμμένον,	But if also our good news is concealed, it is concealed within those being lost.
4:4	ἐν οἷς ὁ θεὸς τοῦ αἰῶνος τούτου ἐτύφλωσεν τὰ νοήματα τῶν ἀπίστων εἰς τὸ μὴ αὐγάσαι τὸν φωτισμὸν τοῦ εὐαγγελίου τῆς δόξης τοῦ χριστοῦ, ὅς ἐστιν εἰκὼν τοῦ θεοῦ.	Within whom the god of this age blinded the minds of the unbelieving so that the illumination of the gospel of the glory of Christ, who is an image **of God**, should *not* be clearly seen.

The 'god of this age' *has blinded their minds* so that the gospel should *not* be clearly seen! As before, the Christ is *'an image of* **God**'.

Can anything Good come from Nazareth?

We have in *Luke*:

Lk.	καὶ ἐπηρώτησέν τις αὐτὸν	And a certain ruler asked
18:18	ἄρχων λέγων, διδάσκαλε	him, saying "Good teacher,
	ἀγαθέ, τί ποιήσας ζωὴν	(by) doing what shall I inherit
	αἰώνιον κληρονομήσω;	eternal life?"
18:19	εἶπεν δὲ αὐτῷ ὁ ἰησοῦς, τί με	But Jesus said to him "Why
	λέγεις ἀγαθόν; οὐδεὶς ἀγαθὸς	do you call me good? No one
	εἰ μὴ εἷς **ὁ θεός**.	(is) good except one … **God**"

The ruler addresses Jesus as 'good'. But we hear Jesus himself
challenge the assumption. Why should he challenge it? Of course we
know the answer already. Jesus is Cain: he is busy asserting the
promise first made by his father, the serpent … the promise of eternal
life. It is a deceitful promise. No kind of deceit can be good. But the
reply which Jesus gives *is* plausible. He implies that only **God** [ὁ θεός]
is good.

The passages at Mt.19:17 and Mk.10:18 are almost equivalent to this.
But in the fourth gospel *(John)* we have instead:

Jn.	εὑρίσκει **φίλιππος** τὸν	Philip finds Nathanael and
1:45	ναθαναὴλ καὶ λέγει αὐτῷ, ὃν	says to him "We have found
	ἔγραψεν μωϋσῆς ἐν τῷ νόμῳ	him (of) whom Moses in the
	καὶ οἱ προφῆται εὑρήκαμεν,	Law and the prophets wrote,
	ἰησοῦν υἱὸν τοῦ ἰωσὴφ τὸν	Jesus, the son of Joseph, the
	ἀπὸ ναζαρέτ.	one from Nazareth".

1:46	καὶ εἶπεν αὐτῷ ναθαναὴλ, ἐκ ναζαρὲτ δύναταί τι ἀγαθὸν εἶναι; λέγει αὐτῷ [ὁ] **φίλιππ**ος, ἔρχου καὶ ἴδε.	And Nathanael said to him "Is it possible for anything good to come from Nazareth?". <u>Philip</u> says to him "Come and see".
1:47	εἶδεν ὁ ἰησοῦς τὸν ναθαναὴλ ἐρχόμενον πρὸς αὐτὸν καὶ λέγει περὶ αὐτοῦ, ἴδε ἀληθῶς ἰσραηλίτης ἐν ᾧ δόλος οὐκ ἔστιν.	Jesus saw Nathanael coming towards him and says concerning him "Look, truly an Israelite in whom there is no deceit"
1:48	λέγει αὐτῷ ναθαναήλ, πόθεν με γινώσκεισ;	Nathanael says to him "Do you know me from somewhere?".
	ἀπεκρίθη ἰησοῦς καὶ εἶπεν αὐτῷ, πρὸ τοῦ σε **φίλιππ**ον φωνῆσαι ὄντα ὑπὸ τὴν συκῆν εἶδόν σε.	Jesus answered and said to him "Before calling you <u>Philip</u> I saw you existing under the fig tree".

It is transparently easy to see the name for the serpent embodied within the name Philip. Yet Nathanael, not Philip, is identified by Jesus as *an Israelite in whom there is no deceit.*

The name Nathanael suggests in Hebrew '*god given*'. But in Greek it tends to evoke ἀθάνατος [*immortal*]. At 1:48 Jesus addresses Nathanael in terms which suggest that although his current name is Philip, he is (as it were) an old friend … previously seen *under the fig tree*. Then in this very curious riddle it seems that Nathanael and Philip may both be aliases for the serpent himself, the one who under the fig tree first gave the promise of immortality to the woman (*qv.* Gn.3:4-6).

So *can* anything good come from Nazareth?

Mt.	οὐαὶ ὑμῖν, γραμματεῖς καὶ	Woe to you, scribes and
23:27	φαρΙΣαῖΟι ὑποκριταί,	Pharisee hypocrites.
	ὅτι παρομοιάζετε τάφΟΙς	For you resemble plastered
	κεΚοΝΙΑμένοις, οἵτινες	tombs which outwardly
	ἔξωθεν μὲν φαίΝΟνται	appear **beautiful** but
	ὡραῖοι ἔσωθεν δὲ γέμουσιν	inwardly are filled with bones
	ὀστέων νεκρῶν καὶ πάσης	of (the) dead, and of all
	ἀκαθαρσίας.	uncleanness.

Here we see the serpent's name three times, that of Cain once. What outwardly appears as **ὡραῖος** [*beautiful*] is inwardly unclean.

And we may recall from Genesis:

LXX	καὶ εἶδεν ἡ γυνὴ ὅτι καλὸν τὸ	And the woman saw the tree
Gn.	ξύλον εἰς βρῶΣΙΝ καὶ ὅτι	as good for eating and as
3:6	ἀρεστὸν τοῖς ὀφθαλμοῖς	agreeable with the eyes to
	ἰδεῖν καὶ ὡραῖόν ἐστιν τοῦ	see, and (that) it is **beautiful**
	κατανοῆσαι καὶ λαβοῦσα τοῦ	for understanding fully. And
	καρποῦ αὐτοῦ ἔφαγεν καὶ	taking (some) of its fruit, she
	ἔδωκεν καὶ τῷ ἀνδρὶ αὐτῆς	ate. And she gave (some)
	μετ' αὐτῆς καὶ ἔφαγον	also to her man with her, and
		they ate.

Here the woman sees the fruit as **ὡραῖόν** [*beautiful*] for understanding fully. Jesus is brought up in fictional Nazareth so he can be described as **ὁ ναζωραῖος** [*the Nazarene*] (Lk.18:37; Jn.19:19; Ac.6:14, 22:8). The first syllable **ναζ** may suggest (from Hebrew) נָחָשׁ [*nachash = serpent*]. Then from Greek we have **ὡραῖος** [*beautiful*]. So the name **ὁ ναζ-ωραῖος** seems to suggest '*the serpent-beautiful*'. This makes good sense if Jesus inherits from his 'father' the attributes of the serpent.

The Baptism of Jesus

We have seen how the baptism of Jesus culminates in his vision of '*the heavens parted and the spirit like a pigeon comimg down into him*'. In *Mark* the voice of the 'father' is heard to say '*You are my son, the beloved: in you I was well pleased*' (Mk.1:10-11).

We know by now that the authors portray the father of Jesus to be the serpent. So it is this relationship between father and son which provides for Jesus to receive forty days of testing '*under Satan*' (Mk.1:13). It appears that Cain is receiving an intellectual checkup which will prepare him to take on the world.

In *Luke* the story of his baptism begins in much the same way:

Lk.	ἐγένετο δὲ ἐν τῷ βαπτισθῆναι	But it happened with the
3:21	ἄπαντα τὸν λαὸν καὶ ἰησοῦ	entire people being baptised,
	βαπτισθέντος καὶ	and from Jesus being
	προσευχομένου ἀνεῳχθῆναι	baptised and praying (for)
	τὸν οὐρανὸν	Heaven to be opened up
3:22	καὶ Καταβῆναι τὸ πνεῦμα τὸ	And (for) the spirit, the holy
	ἅγιον σωματικῷ εἴδει ὡς	one, to come down in bodily
	περιστερὰν ἐπ' αὐτόν, καὶ	form as a pigeon, upon him.
	φωνὴν ἐξ οὐρανοῦ γενέσθαι,	And there came a voice from
	σὺ εἶ ὁ υἱός μου ὁ ἀγαπητός,	heaven "You are my son, the
	ἐν σοὶ εὐδόκησα.	beloved. In you I was well
		pleased."

The narrative is interrupted by Luke's genealogy for Jesus. It resumes at Lk.4:1, with riddles shared between Jesus and his father. These are framed to conclude the 'tests' which Satan sets for his 'beloved son'.

The riddles presented here are of pivotal importance to the impact made by the gospels. But scripture is written in such a way that its readers are actually drawn into the plot themselves; so in reality these riddles constitute a test set by the authors and aimed at every single reader. In the next section we shall see if we can solve them. Before we can do that, there is one key topic we shall need to learn about. It is the special significance assigned in scripture to the digram ασ (or ας as it appears at the end of a word) and to the digram χθ (alternatively the letter ψ).

Riddles about 'Bread' and 'Fish'

Bruce Metzger[1] lists what Ludwig Trauber termed the *Nomina Sacra*, standard abbreviations widely employed in the early manuscripts of Greek scripture.

The first five abbreviations given by Metzger are digrams. Thus:

θς	stood for	θεός [*god*]
κς	stood for	κύριος [*lord*]
ις	stood for	ἰησοῦς [*Jesus*]
χς	stood for	χριστός [*Christ*]
υς	stood for	υἰὸς [*son*]

The letters chosen for these abbreviations are the first and the last of the word concerned. We might imagine that a logical extension to such a scheme would be:

ας	to stand for	ἄρτος [*bread*]

But it was never open to the copyist to use this particular digram as a form of shorthand notation. Instead ας (or ασ in the middle of a word) was effectively reserved for use by the original author. He alone decided how and where to include this letter pair, controlling with care the selection and use of those words within which it appears. Here then is a further 'dispersion' format, another important form of 'code' ... a means to conceal '*bread*' within the texts of Greek scripture.

A digram of comparable importance is χθ. This encapsulates not the first and last letters, but the consonantal pair from the word ἰχθύς [*fish*]. An alternative token appears to be Ψ, taken from the word ὀψάριον [*small fish*].

The origin of the convention outlined here can be traced to the first chapter of LXX *Genesis* (for a straightforward derivation by the rigorous analysis of the *Genesis* text, see Appendix 1). It is one of several devices used in Greek scripture to configure counting riddles. For example, the reader may be expected to 'see', within a particular passage, five pieces of '*bread*' or, in another passage, seven. Its use is ubiquitous in the gospels. In this way an abundance of what the writer knows as '*bread*' lies hidden, entirely concealed from the eyes of 'the blind' (*ie.* those readers in Greek who do not know what to look for, together with all who read in translation to another language).

A convention like this would be tricky to implement in English. But Greek favours such a scheme because it declines nouns, adjectives and participles in such a way that connected word endings tend to rhyme.

The practice is best explained using the didactic examples given in the gospels. Here in *Mark* the 'students' (the disciples with Jesus) go hungry because there is only one piece of '*bread*' with them in the boat. And surely you can see it there for yourself:

Mk. 8:13	καὶ ἀφεὶς αὐτοὺς πάλιν ἐμβὰς ἀπῆλθεν εἰς τὸ πέραν.	And dismissing them again, <u>embarking</u> he went off to the other side
8:14	καὶ ἐπελάθοντο λαβεῖν ἄρτους, καὶ εἰ μὴ ἕνα ἄρτον οὐκ εἶχον μεθ' ἑαυτῶν ἐν τῷ πλοίῳ.	And they forgot to take breads, and except for one bread they did not have (any) with them in the boat.

Then in *Mark* we have the feeding of the crowd of five thousand. Jesus begins by addressing a question to his 'students':

Mk. 6:38	ὁ δὲ λέγει αὐτοῖς, πόσους ἄρτους ἔχετε; ὑπάγετε ἴδετε. καὶ γνόντες λέγουσιν,	But he said to them "How many breads do you have? Go and see." And, knowing, they said
	πέντε, καὶ δύο ἰχθύας.	"*Five*, and *two* <u>fishes</u>".
6:39	καὶ ἐπέταξεν αὐτοῖς ἀνακλῖναι πάντας συμπόσια συμπόσια ἐπὶ τῷ χλωρῷ χόρτῳ.	And he commanded them <u>all</u> to lie, party by party, upon the green grass.
6:40	καὶ ἀνέπεσαν πρασιαὶ πρασιαὶ κατὰ ἑκατὸν καὶ κατὰ πεντήκοντα.	They sat down, <u>bed</u> by <u>bed</u>, by a hundred and by fifty.
6:41	καὶ λαβὼν τοὺς πέντε ἄρτους καὶ τοὺς δύο ἰχθύας ἀναβλέψας εἰς τὸν οὐρανὸν εὐλόγησεν καὶ κατέκλασεν τοὺς ἄρτους καὶ ἐδίδου τοῖς μαθηταῖς [αὐτοῦ] ἵνα παρατιθῶσιν αὐτοῖς, καὶ τοὺς δύο ἰχθύας ἐμέρισεν πᾶσιν.	And taking the *five* breads and the *two* <u>fishes</u>, <u>looking up</u> into Heaven, he blessed and <u>he broke</u> the breads. And he gave to [his] students so that they would set before them and the two <u>fishes</u> he divided amongst <u>all</u>.

Concentrated in that last verse, you will indeed see five pieces of '*bread*' and two '*fish*.' Notice that the students with Jesus 'know' in advance what the answer is going to be (6:38). Clearly the author has constructed the whole passage to match the answer given. Without going into all the details here, that is how the miracle is 'done'.

The process we have learned to undertake here is what the authors know either as '*harvesting*' or as '*fishing*' within the texts of scripture. This is why we have the direction at Lk.5:4:

Lk. 5:4	ὡς δὲ ἐπαύσατο λαλῶν, εἶπεν πρὸς τὸν σίμωνα, ἐπανάγαγε εἰς τὸ βάθος καὶ χαλάσατε τὰ δίκτυα ὑμῶν εἰς ἄγραν.	But as he finished speaking he said to Simon "Go back to the deep and let out your nets for a catch".

It is a process which *feeds the crowd* because it yields *food for the mind*. In *Mark* the riddle is shortly repeated, this time for the crowd of four thousand. On this occasion the format is more extended:

Mk. 8:5	καὶ ἠρώτα αὐτούς, πόσους ἔχετε ἄρτουσ; οἱ δὲ εἶπαν, **ἑπτά.**	And he asked them "How many breads do you have?". And they said "**Seven**".
8:6	καὶ παραγγέλλει τῷ ὄχλῳ ἀναπεσεῖν ἐπὶ τῆς γῆς: καὶ λαβὼν τοὺς **ἑπτὰ** ἄρτους εὐχαριστήσ**ας** ἔκλ**ασ**εν καὶ ἐδίδου τοῖς μαθηταῖς αὐτοῦ ἵνα παρατιθ**ῶσιν** καὶ παρέθηκαν τῷ ὄχλῳ.	And he gave orders to the crowd to recline upon the earth. And taking the **seven** breads, <u>giving thanks</u> <u>he</u> <u>broke</u> (them) and gave them to his students so that they might serve (them) up, and they served (them) to the crowd.
8:7	καὶ εἶχον ἰ<u>χθ</u>ύδια ὀλίγα: καὶ εὐλογήσ**ας** αὐτὰ εἶπεν καὶ ταῦτα παρατιθέναι.	And they had a few <u>small</u> <u>fish</u>, and, <u>blessing</u> them, he said to serve these also

8:8	καὶ ἔφαγον καὶ ἐχορτ**άσθ**ησαν, καὶ ἦραν περισσεύματα κλ**ασ**μάτων ἑπτὰ σπυρί**δας**.	And they ate and were foddered. And they took away a surplus <u>of fragments</u>, seven <u>hampers</u>
8:9	ἦσαν δὲ ὡς τετρακισχίλιοι. καὶ ἀπέλυσεν αὐτούς.	But there were (something) like four thousand. And he released them.
8:10	καὶ εὐθὺς ἐμβ**άς** εἰς τὸ πλοῖον μετὰ τῶν μαθητῶν αὐτοῦ ἦλθεν εἰς τὰ μέρη δαλ**μαν**ουθά.	And immediately, <u>embarking</u> in the boat with his students, he came into the parts (of) <u>Dalmanoutha</u>.

By the time Jesus is seen *embarking* in the boat, we do indeed have seven pieces of *bread* and one *fish* (or two if we count **ὦσιν** at 8:6). And with the task complete, there at 8:10 is the hidden *manna* [**μαν**]. It is embedded within the place name δαλ**μαν**ουθά (*contrast*: **μ**αγαδ**άν** in the parallel passage at Mt.15:39).

Now the author of *Mark* realises that amongst his readers will be those who have yet to fathom what is going on here. So he proceeds with a challenge, followed by a further demonstration of how things are done:

Mk. 8:20	ὅτε τοὺς **ἑπτὰ** εἰς τοὺς τετρακισχιλίους, πόσων σπυρίδων πληρώματα κλ**ασ**μάτων ἤρατε; καὶ λέγουσιν [αὐτῷ], ἑπτά.	"When the **seven** (were given) to the four thousand, how many hampers filled with <u>fragments</u> were taken up?". And they said [to him] "Seven".
8:21	καὶ ἔλεγεν αὐτοῖς, οὔπω συνίετε;	And he said to them "Do you not yet understand?"

And then we get:

Mk.	καὶ ἔρχονται εἰς βηθσαϊδάν.	And he came into Bethsaida.
8:22	καὶ φέρΟυσΙν αὐτῷ τυφλὸν	And <u>they brought</u> to him a
	καὶ παραΚΑλοῦσΙν αὐτὸν	blind man, and <u>they begged</u>
	ἵνα αὐτοῦ ἅΨηται.	him that <u>he might grasp</u> him.

The name Bethsaida means in Hebrew 'house of the hunt' or (by extension) 'house of fishing'. It is at this location that we see concentrated in the text an assortment of those hidden 'creatures' for which the disciples of Jesus (this really means us, the readers) are supposed to be 'hunting' (or 'fishing'). These creatures are of course invisible to the man who is 'blind'. He sees nothing beyond the literal.

Yet perhaps his sight can be restored? In the three verses which follow you will see yet again *seven pieces of bread and one fish*.

Mk.	καὶ ἐπιλαβόμενος τῆς χειρὸς	And taking the hand of the
8:23	τοῦ τυφλοῦ ἐξήνεγκεν αὐτὸν	blind man, he brought him
	ἔξω τῆς κώμης, καὶ πτύσΑς	outside the village; and
	εἰς τὰ ὄμματα αὐτοῦ, ἐπιθεὶς	<u>spitting</u> in his eyes, placing
	τΑς χεῖρΑς αὐτῷ, ἐπηρώτα	<u>the hands</u> on him, he asked
	αὐτόν, εἴ τι βλέπεις;	him if he saw anything.
8:24	καὶ ἀναβλέΨΑς ἔλεγεν,	And <u>looking up</u> he said "I
	βλέπω **τοὺς ἀνθρώπους**, ὅτι	perceive **the Persons**,
	ὡς δένδρα ὁρῶ	because I see (something)
	περιπατοῦντΑς.	like trees <u>walking about</u>".
8:25	εἶτα πάλιν ἐπέθηκεν τΑς	Next he placed <u>the hands</u>
	χεῖρΑς ἐπὶ τοὺς ὀφθαλμοὺς	*again* upon his eyes. And he
	αὐτοῦ, καὶ διέβλεψεν, καὶ	looked hard and reinstated
	ἀπεκατέστη, καὶ ἐνέβλεπεν	(what he saw) ... and he was
	τηλαυγῶς ἅπαντα.	seeing *everything* clearly!

8:26	καὶ ἀπέστειλεν αὐτὸν εἰς οἶκον αὐτοῦ λέγων, μηδὲ εἰς τὴν κώμην εἰσέλθῃς.	And he sent him away to his household saying "But do not go into the village".

The 'miracle' of healing is done. The blind man now sees clearly.

Incidentally, we have at 8:24 what looks like another deliberate error in grammar. To agree with neuter plural **δένδρα** [*trees*] we should have **περιπατοῦντα** [*walking about*]. But to make up the required total of seven pieces of '*bread*', what we actually have is **περιπατοῦντας** [*walking about*], agreeing now with **τοὺς ἀνθρώπους** [*the Persons*].

Here now is a *tour de force*, with ten pieces of '*bread*' in a single verse:

Mt. 9:35	καὶ περιῆγεν ὁ ἰησοῦς **τὰς** πόλεις **πάσας** καὶ **τὰς** κώμ**ας**, **διδάσκων** ἐν ταῖς συναγωγαῖς αὐτῶν καὶ κηρύσσων τὸ εὐαγγέλιον τῆς **βασιλείας** καὶ θεραπεύων **πᾶσαν** νόσον καὶ **πᾶσαν** μαλα**κίαν**.	And Jesus went about all the cities and the villages, <u>teaching</u> in their synagogues and preaching the good news of the kingdom and healing every sickness and every <u>moral weakness</u>.

This passage is heavily loaded with irony, for true healing is possible only for those who can recognise Cain (his name twice in that verse) along with everything else which has been 'hidden' in the gospels.

In the following example the '*bread*' is reclassed as '*evil spirits*' … and we have seven pieces (just as stated), as many as three pieces in a single word:

Lk.	τότε πορεύεται καὶ	Then he goes and takes
11:26	παραλαμβάνει ἕτερα	**seven** other spirits more
	πνεύματα πονηρότερα	wicked than himself, and
	ἑαυτοῦ **ἑπτά**, καὶ εἰσελθόντα	entering, they make their
	κατοικεῖ ἐκεῖ, καὶ γίνεται τὰ	home there. And the last
	ἔσχατα τοῦ ἀνθρώπου	(state) of that person
	ἐκείνου χείρονα τῶν πρώτων.	becomes worse than the first.
11:27	ἐγένετο δὲ ἐν τῷ λέγειν αὐτὸν	But it happened in his saying
	ταῦτα ἐπάρ**ασ**ά τις φωνὴν	these things: a woman from
	γυνὴ ἐκ τοῦ ὄχλου εἶπεν	the crowd, <u>raising</u> a certain
	αὐτῷ, μακαρία ἡ κοιλία ἡ	voice, said to him "Blessed
	β**ασ**τ**ασασ**ά σε καὶ	the womb which <u>bore</u> you,
	μ**ασ**τοὶ οὓς ἐθήλ**ασας**.	and the <u>breasts</u> which <u>you</u>
		<u>sucked</u>".

Here in the letter to *Ephesians* the origin of these particular '*spirits*' is indicated. They may cause trouble if they are not recognised:

Ep. 6:11	ἐνδύσασθε τὴν πανοπλίαν τοῦ θεοῦ πρὸς τὸ δύνασθαι ὑμᾶς στῆναι πρὸς τὰς μεθοδείας τοῦ διαβόλου:	Put on the full armour **of God** to make you strong (enough) to stand against the wiles of the devil.
6:12	ὅτι οὐκ ἔστιν ἡμῖν ἡ πάλη πρὸς αἷμα καὶ σάρκα, ἀλλὰ πρὸς τὰς ἀρχάς, πρὸς τὰς ἐξουσίας, πρὸς τοὺς κοσμοκράτορας τοῦ σκότους τούτου, πρὸς τὰ πνευματικὰ τῆς πονηρίας ἐν τοῖς ἐπουρανίοις.	Because for us the struggle is not against blood and flesh, but against the princes, against the authorities, against the cosmic rulers of this darkness, against the spiritual things of the wickedness in the heavenly places.

At this point we are far from having explained everything there is to know about the '*bread*' and '*fish*'. But this limited exegesis should be sufficient to meet our ongoing needs.

The Source for Jesus' Authority and Glory

We return now to Luke's version of the encounter between Jesus and his father in the desert. We shall watch out for the hidden '*bread*', and for some other things besides:

Lk.		
4:1	ἰησοῦς δὲ πλήρης πνεύματος ἁγίου ὑπέστρεψεν ἀπὸ τοῦ ἰορδάνου, καὶ ἤγετο ἐν τῷ πνεύματι ἐν τῇ ἐρήμῳ	But Jesus, full of a holy spirit, returned from the Jordan and was led in the spirit in the desert
4:2	ἡμέρας τεσσεράκοντα πειραζόμενος ὑπὸ τοῦ διαβόλου.	(for) <u>forty</u> days (of) testing under the devil.
	καὶ οὐκ ἔφαγεν οὐδὲν ἐν ταῖς ἡμέραις ἐκείναις, καὶ συντελεσθεισῶν αὐτῶν ἐπείνασεν.	And he did not eat anything within <u>those</u> days, And from their <u>completion</u> he was hungry.
4:3	εἶπεν δὲ αὐτῷ ὁ διάβολος, εἰ υἱὸς εἶ τοῦ θεοῦ, εἰπὲ τῷ λίθῳ τούτῳ ἵνα γένηται ἄρτος.	But the devil said to him "If you are a son **of God**, say to this <u>stone</u> that it may become bread"
4:4	καὶ ἀπεκρίθη πρὸς αὐτὸν ὁ ἰησοῦς, γέγραπται ὅτι οὐκ ἐπ' ἄρτῳ μόνῳ ζήσεται ὁ ἄνθρωπος.	And Jesus answered him "It has been written that 'Not on bread alone shall **the Person** live' " (Dt.8:3)
4:5	καὶ ἀναγαγὼν αὐτὸν ἔδειξεν αὐτῷ πάσας τὰς βασιλείας τῆς οἰκουμένης ἐν στιγμῇ χρόνου:	And, taking him up, he showed him all the kingdoms of the world within a moment of time

As 4:2 begins we have a single instance of ας (*bread*) present within the word ἡμέρας [*days*]. The riddle proceeds by allowing that within

forty (the word τεσΟερἀκοΝΤα conceals the name *Satan*) days Jesus did not eat anything:

> ... ἐν ταῖς ἡμέραις ἐκείναις
> ... within those days
>
> (the final word here conceals *Cain*)

Do you see what has been done? By putting a whole phrase with feminine endings into the dative case (-αις) instead of the accusative case (-ας), the author has provided that *no bread* is available: accordingly Jesus goes hungry *'within those days'*.

It is with the *completion* [συντελεσθεισῶν] of those days that we can see the letters we shall need in the very next verse to make up the word λίθῳ [*to a stone*] (significantly in the *dative* case as well).

And it is following their *completion* that it is now possible for Jesus to eat again, because just one piece of *bread* may be found within the word ἐπείναΣεν [*he was hungry*]. Do you follow how the riddle works?

The devil now says to Jesus:

> εἰ υἱὸς εἶ τοῦ θεοῦ, εἰπὲ τῷ λίθῳ τούτῳ ἵνα γένηται ἄρτος
> If you are a son of God, say to this stone that it may become bread

Well, we have seen already how it may be done. The word for the *stone* was dispersed within the word for *completion*: and it was when he reached this *completion* that Jesus found the *bread* and was at last able to 'eat'. In the narrative it is the devil who puts Jesus to the test. But the devil is a fictional character in a fictional narrative. What we have here in reality is a didactic riddle set by the author of the gospel for us, the readers, to solve if we can.

The reply which Jesus gives at 4:4 serves to remind us that at Gn.1:29 it was foodstuffs inclusive of bread which were specified for the diet of the **Person** created at Gn.1:27. Indeed bread forms a part of the diet appropriate both to this **Person** (who we now know as the serpent, as Satan, or as the devil) and to Jesus (who we now know as Cain).

This first section of the riddles is brought to a conclusion with:

καὶ ἀναγαγὼν αὐτὸν ἔδειξεν αὐτῷ
And, taking him up, he showed him

πάσας τὰς βασιλείας τῆς οἰκουμένης ἐν στιγμῇ χρόνου:
all the kingdoms of the world within a moment of time

And there, *'in a moment of time'* (*ie.* all bunched together), we have *five* more pieces of *bread*.

The examination continues as follows:

Lk. 4:6	καὶ εἶπεν αὐτῷ ὁ διάβολος, σοὶ δώσω τὴν ἐξουσίαν ταύτην ἅπ<u>ασ</u>αν καὶ τὴν δόξαν αὐτῶν, ὅτι ἐμοὶ παραδέδοται καὶ ᾧ ἐὰν θέλω δίδωμι αὐτήν:	And the devil said to him "To you I shall give this authority <u>in its entirety</u>, and the glory of them. For it has been given away to me, and to whomsoever I wish, I give it.
4:7	σὺ οὖν ἐὰν προσκυνήσῃς ἐνώπιον ἐμοῦ, ἔσται σοῦ π<u>ᾶσ</u>α.	Then if you will worship in my presence, it shall <u>all</u> be yours".
4:8	καὶ ἀποκριθεὶς ὁ ἰησοῦς εἶπεν αὐτῷ, γέγραπται, **κύριον τὸν θεόν** σου προσκυνήσεις καὶ αὐτῷ μόνῳ λατρεύσεις.	And Jesus, answering, said to him "It has been written **'The lord** your **god** you shall worship and him alone shall you serve' " (Dt.6:13)

With these verses we see another *two* pieces of *bread* appear. That makes *seven* pieces in just three verses (Lk.4:5-4:7).

Yet we are far from being finished. There are further things to notice. The first is the devil's claim at 4:6 that *authority* and *glory* have been given away to him and are now his to give away once more. The original gift to him must refer to the verse at Gn.1:28 where we were told :

LXX	καὶ ηὐλόγησεν αὐτοὺς ὁ **θεὸς**	And **God** blessed them,
Gn.	λέγων αὐξάνεσθε καὶ	saying "Grow and multiply
1:28	πληθύνεσθε καὶ πληρώσατε	and fill the earth and **LORD**
	τὴν γῆν καὶ κατα**ΚΥΡΙ**εύσατε	over it. And rule (over) the
	αὐτῆς καὶ ἄρχετε τῶν ἰχθύων	fishes of the sea and (over)
	τῆς θαλάσσης καὶ τῶν	the birds of heaven, and
	πετεινῶν τοῦ οὐρανοῦ καὶ	(over) all the pastoral beasts
	πάντων τῶν κτηνῶν καὶ	and (over) all the earth, and
	πάσης τῆς γῆς καὶ πάντων	(over) all the creeping things
	τῶν ἑρπετῶν τῶν ἑρπόντων	which creep upon the earth"
	ἐπὶ τῆς γῆς	

Here is the origin for the devil's *authority*. It is an authority derived from **God**, but which **God** has long since 'given away' and cannot now retrieve.

The devil offers to transfer to Jesus this *authority*, and the *glory* which goes with his native deity. But the offer the devil makes is conditional upon Jesus 'worshipping in his presence' (*ie.* worshipping him).

The second important thing to notice is that Jesus (who is Cain) does actually meet this condition by quoting from *Deuteronom*y to confirm his conviction that:

κύριον τὸν θεόν σου προσκυνήσεις καὶ αὐτῷ μόνῳ λατρεύσεις
The lord your god you shall worship and him alone shall you serve

For the one with the title '**the lord your god**' _is_ the devil … the 'father' in whose company Jesus now is.

The testing continues as follows:

Lk. 4:9	ἤγαγεν δὲ αὐτὸν εἰς ἰερουσαλὴμ καὶ ἔστησεν ἐπὶ τὸ πτ**ερύγ**ι**ο**ν τοῦ **ἱερο**ῦ, καὶ εἶπεν αὐτῷ, εἰ υἱὸς εἶ **το**ῦ **θεο**ῦ, βάλε σεαυτὸν ἐντεῦθεν κάτω:	But he brought him into Jerusalem and he stood upon the <u>ridge of the temple</u> and said to him "If you are a son **of God**, throw yourself down from here
4:10	γέγραπται γὰρ ὅτι τοῖς ἀγγέλοις αὐτοῦ ἐντελεῖται περὶ σοῦ τοῦ διαφυλάξαι σε,	For it has been written that 'He will charge his angels concerning you, to guard you'
4:11	καὶ ὅτι ἐπὶ χειρῶν ἀροῦσίν σε μήποτε προσκόψῃς πρὸς λίθον τὸν πόδα σου.	And that 'Upon hands they will raise you, lest ever you should trip your foot upon a stone' " (Ps.91:11-12)
4:12	καὶ ἀποκριθεὶς εἶπεν αὐτῷ ὁ ἰησοῦς ὅτι εἴρηται, οὐκ ἐκ**πειρά**σ**ει**ς κύριον τὸν **θεό**ν σου.	And, answering, Jesus said to him that it has been said '<u>You shall</u> not <u>test out</u> **the lord** your **god**' (Dt.6:16)

We see some interesting word play at 4:9.

Then at 4:10-11 we come close to recognising Jesus himself as the _stone of stumbling_ identified at Is.8:14 (_qv._ Chapter 7). In the narrative Jesus turns down the option to jump. Yet in doing so he refers once again to his examiner as '**the lord your god**'. This is the one he knows as his 'father' … the one we know as the serpent, Satan, or the devil.

It will not be long before we see Jesus manifesting his newfound *authority* and *glory*, the attributes he has just been promised by the devil. The passage continues:

Lk. 4:13	καὶ συντελέσ**ας** πάντα πειρ**ασ**μὸν ὁ διάβολος ἀπέστη ἀπ' αὐτοῦ ἄχρι καιροῦ.	And <u>completing</u> every <u>test</u>, the devil departed from him … until (another) time
4:14	καὶ ὑπέστρε**ψ**εν ὁ ἰησοῦς ἐν τῇ δυνάμει τοῦ πνεύματος εἰς τὴν γαλιλαίαν. καὶ φήμη ἐξῆλθεν καθ' ὅλης τῆς περιχώρου περὶ αὐτοῦ.	And Jesus returned (below) in the power of the spirit into Galilee. And fame went out down the whole of the surrounding area concerning him
4:15	καὶ αὐτὸς ἐ**δίδασ**κ**ε**ν ἐν ταῖς συναγωγαῖς αὐτῶν, **δοξ**αζόμενος ὑπὸ πάντων.	And <u>he taught</u> in their synagogues, being ***glorified*** by all

It is in completing [συντελέσ**ας**] every test [πειρ**ασ**μὸν] that we see the final pieces of *bread* in this clever sequence. The 'Father' departs from him until another time.

Jesus returns (in the spirit) from Jerusalem to Galilee. The location seems appropriate, for Cain is *a sower*. And is not Galilee the *garden* of Israel?

We learn that Jesus ***taught*** [ἐ**δίδασ**κ**ε**ν] in their synagogues: immediately we see the name of ***Cain***.

And there at 4:15 is the ***glory*** [**δόξ**α] which the devil promised to Jesus (Lk.4:6-7). In the synagogues he is glorified by all.

The narrative continues:

Lk. 4:16	καὶ ἦλθεν εἰς ναζαρά, οὗ ἦν τεθραμμένος, καὶ εἰσῆλθεν κατὰ τὸ εἰωθὸς αὐτῷ ἐν τῇ ἡμέρᾳ τῶν σαββάτων εἰς τὴν συναγωγήν, καὶ **ἀνέστη** ἀναγνῶναι.	And he came to Nazareth where he had been brought up and, as was the custom with him on the day of the Sabbaths, entered into the synagogue, and <u>he was resurrected</u> to read
4:17	καὶ ἐπεδόθη αὐτῷ βιβλίον τοῦ προφήτου ἡσαΐου, καὶ ἀναπτύξας τὸ βιβλίον εὗρεν τὸν τόπον οὗ ἦν γεγραμμένον,	And the book of the prophet Isaiah was given to him, and opening up the book he found the place where it was written:
4:18	πνεῦμα κυρίου ἐπ' ἐμέ, οὗ εἵνεκεν ἔχρισέν με εὐαγγελίσασθαι πτωχοῖς, ἀπέσταλκέν με κηρύξαι αἰχμαλώτοις ἄφεσιν καὶ τυφλοῖς ἀνάβλεψιν, ἀποστεῖλαι τεθραυσμένους ἐν ἀφέσει,	"A spirit of a lord (is) upon me, which (is) because he anointed me to bring good news to (the) poor, he has sent me to proclaim release for captives and looking up for (the) blind, to send the broken into release
4:19	κηρύξαι ἐνιαυτὸν κυρίου δεκτόν.	To proclaim an acceptable year for a lord".
4:20	καὶ πτύξας τὸ βιβλίον ἀποδοὺς τῷ ὑπηρέτῃ **ἐκάθισεv**: καὶ πάντων οἱ ὀφθαλμοὶ ἐν τῇ συναγωγῇ ἦσαν ἀτενίζοντες αὐτῷ.	And closing the book, giving (it) to the attendant, <u>he sat down</u>. And the eyes of all in the synagogue were staring at him.

| 4:21 | ἤρξατο δὲ λέγειν πρὸς αὐτοὺς ὅτι σήμερον πεπλήρωται ἡ γραφὴ αὕτη ἐν τοῖς ὠσὶν ὑμῶν. | But he began to say to them that 'Today this scripture has been fulfilled within your ears'. |

Jesus was *resurrected* [ἀνέστη] to read. It is a word first used of Cain (Gn.4:8). He then quoted from the book of *Isaiah* ... which referred to him. But it was when *he sat down* [ἐκάθισεν] that the eyes of all in the synagogue were staring at him. And surely you can see for yourself what they were staring at?

ἐκάθισεν [*he/she/it sat down*]. There we have the sequence .Κά.ι..ν . This word occurs seventeen times in the NT canon. Later in the works ascribed to Luke the same word will explain the behaviour of the fiery tongues 'divided' when the baptism promised by Jesus arrives (Ac.2:3). It is just one amongst so many examples of the '*sign*' for Cain.

In this case the author of *Luke* writes that Jesus '*sat down*'. It is all he needs to say. And if he had preferred not to issue the '*sign*' at this particular point in the narrative there were plenty of alternatives open to him. He could easily have used what in Greek is termed the 'middle' voice of the verb, writing ἐκάθισατο [*he sat himself down*] instead of ἐκάθισεν [*he sat down*]. The literal sense would have been the same, but there would be no '*sign*' for Cain. Do you see how easy it was for the authors to implement this amazing scheme? Then it is with calculated intent that *Luke* identifies Jesus here as Cain.

But let us return to the narrative. Once the inhabitants of Nazareth begin to recognise who Jesus must be, they react accordingly:

| Lk. 4:28 | καὶ ἐπλήσθησαν πάντες θυμοῦ ἐν τῇ συναγωγῇ ἀκούοντες ταῦτα, | And all in the synagogue hearing him were filled with anger. |

4:29	καὶ ἀ**ναστά**ντες ἐξέβαλον	And <u>rising up</u>, they threw him
	αὐτὸν ἔξω τῆς πόλεως,	out from the city
	καὶ ἤγαγον αὐτὸν ἕως	and they took him as far as a
	Ὀφ**ρύος** τοῦ **ὄρους** ἐφ'	<u>brow</u> of the <u>hill</u> upon which
	οὗ ἡ πόλις ᾠκοδόμητο	their city was built
	αὐτῶν,	
	ὥστε **κατ**ακρημ**νῖσα**ι	so as <u>to throw</u> him <u>down a</u>
	αὐτόν:	<u>precipice</u>.
4:30	αὐτὸς δὲ διελθὼν διὰ μέσου	But he, passing through (the)
	αὐτῶν ἐπορεύετο.	midst of them, went away.

Within the word ἀ**ναστά**ντες [*rising up*] we see **σαταν** [*Satan*]. To sustain our attention, we then have some incidental but instructive wordplay with Ὀφ**ρύος** τοῦ **ὄρους** [*brow of the hill*].

And finally with **κατ**ακρημ**νῖσα**ι [*to throw down a precipice*] we see both **σαταν** [*Satan*] and **καϊν** [*Cain*] concealed within a single word.

It is thematic in scripture that Satan has been *thrown down* to the earth (*qv.* Rv.12:9). According to the gospels, Jesus has been brought up in Nazareth (*qv.* Mt.2:23). In this passage he too is *thrown down*, significantly by those who have come to know him well.

He has been expelled from what was his native 'city' (*qv.* Lk.2:39), so now we find:

| Lk. 4:31 | καὶ κατῆλθεν εἰς καφαρναοὺμ πόλιν τῆς γαλιλαίας. καὶ ἦν δι**δάσκω**ν αὐτοὺς ἐν τοῖς σάββασιν: | And he went down to Capharnaum, a city of Galilee. And he was <u>teaching</u> them on the Sabbaths |

| 4:32 | καὶ ἐξεπλήσσοντο ἐπὶ τῇ διδαχῇ αὐτοῦ, ὅτι ἐν ἐξουσίᾳ ἦν ὁ λόγος αὐτοῦ. | And they were astonished about his teaching, for his message [*alt:* his 'Logos'] was within **_authority_**. |

There you have it. Jesus has now acquired both **authority** and **glory**, just as the devil promised to him (*qv.* Lk.4:6-7 above).

But even this is not the end of the matter. Eventually these sinister attributes *will* be passed on to others. At Lk.4:13 we were told:

| Lk. 4:13 | καὶ συντελέσας πάντα πειρασμὸν ὁ διάβολος ἀπέστη ἀπ' αὐτοῦ ἄχρι καιροῦ. | And completing every test, the devil departed from him … until (another) time |

Later on in the same gospel we find Jesus speaking at the last meal he takes with those he has 'chosen':

Lk. 22:27	τίς γὰρ μείζων, ὁ ἀνακείμενος ἢ ὁ διακονῶν; οὐχὶ ὁ ἀνακείμενος; ἐγὼ δὲ ἐν μέσῳ ὑμῶν εἰμι ὡς ὁ διακονῶν.	For which (is) greater, the one reclining or the one serving? Is it not the one reclining? But I AM in the midst of you as the one serving.
22:28	ὑμεῖς δέ ἐστε οἱ διαμεμενηκότες μετ' ἐμοῦ ἐν τοῖς πειρασμοῖς μου:	But you are those who have remained with me in my testings.
22:29	κἀγὼ διατίθεμαι ὑμῖν καθὼς διέθετό μοι ὁ πατήρ μου βασιλείαν	And I appoint to you, **_just as my father appointed to me_**, a kingdom

The 'testing' has been sustained throughout the intervening verses of the gospel. You will know enough by now to meet without difficulty the modest challenge posed here, for who cannot see Κάϊν 'in the midst' of: ὁ διακονῶν [*the one serving*]?

At 22:29 the inheritance is formally passed on. It is here, in this passage at the Eucharistic meal, that the *authority* and *glory* first assigned to Jesus by the devil is transmitted once again, this time from Jesus to those he has 'appointed'.

The claim of apostolic authority for the Christian church finds its origin here. There are two points we should be sure to note:

- The gospel author derives this *authority* and *glory* from **God** via 'the devil' (LXX Gn.1:26-28), then via Jesus (Lk.4:6-7) and finally via those whom Jesus appoints (Lk.22:29). *Here is the chain of satanic inheritance.*

- The church's claim to *authority* is founded upon the gospel narrative. Yet however cleverly they are composed, *the gospels are essentially fiction*. The church's claim is therefore void.

How deep is the mire into which those persons fall who hanker after glory, authority and eternal life! It is fortunate for them that what they embrace with such enthusiasm is founded only in fictive writing. For how much worse would things be for them if the gospel's theme was really true?

Or have they, by the very act of embracing what they never properly understood, made it all come true anyway? It is an intriguing question.

Jesus continues speaking to those he has now appointed:

Lk. 22:30	ἵνα ἔσθητε καὶ πίνητε ἐπὶ τῆς τραπέζης μου ἐν τῇ βασιλείᾳ μου, καὶ καθήσεσθε ἐπὶ θρόνων τὰς δώδεκα φυλὰς κρίνοντες τοῦ ἰσραήλ.	That you may eat and drink at my table in my <u>kingdom</u>. And you shall sit upon thrones, judging <u>the</u> twelve <u>tribes</u> of Israel.
22:31	σίμων σίμων, ἰδοὺ ὁ σατανᾶς ἐξητήσατο ὑμᾶς τοῦ σινιάσαι ὡς τὸν σῖτον:	Simon, Simon, look! <u>Satan</u> demanded <u>you</u> for <u>sifting</u> like the wheat.
22:32	ἐγὼ δὲ ἐδεήθην περὶ σοῦ ἵνα μὴ ἐκλίπῃ ἡ πίστις σου: καὶ σύ ποτε ἐπιστρέψας στήρισον τοὺς ἀδελφούς σου.	But I pleaded about you that your faith might not vanish. And you, once <u>corrected</u>, support your brothers".

It is their last meal together. And look! Do we not have again **seven** pieces of bread (ασ; ας) … and one fish (Ψ) ?

Satan's kingdom has now been transferred from Jesus to those who will think of him as their god. This is the New Testament tradition.

How ironic that this *authority* and *glory* should be inherited by those who do not know its source … that these attributes should be transferred to those whose *blindness* to the message of scripture itself leaves them unable to see any '*bread*' there at all.

And the instruction to Simon Peter?

> You, once corrected, support your brothers.

The correction, it seems, must come first … before support is provided.

The Serpent in the 'Our Father' Prayer

Here is the narrative which develops when Jesus' students ask him how to pray (Lk.11:1). We know already that the 'Father', the one to whom Jesus prays himself, is the serpent (*aka.* Satan). Jesus replies to the question by advancing what many know as the '*Our Father*' prayer:

Lk.	εἶπεν δὲ αὐτοῖς, ὅταν	So he said to them "When
11:2	προσεύχησθε, λέγετε,	you pray, say:
	πάτερ, ἁγιασθήτω τὸ ὄνομά	Father, let your name <u>be</u>
	σου· ἐλθέτω ἡ βασιλεία σου·	<u>hallowed</u>, let your <u>kingdom</u>
		come
11:3	τὸν ἄρτον ἡμῶν τὸν	Give to us our sufficient
	ἐπιούσιον δίδου ἡμῖν τὸ καθ'	*bread* for the day
	ἡμέραν·	
11:4	καὶ ἄφες ἡμῖν τὰς ἁμαρτίας	And dismiss for us our <u>sins</u>
	ἡμῶν, καὶ γὰρ αὐτοὶ	[*alt*: our mistakes], for these
	ἀφίομεν παντὶ ὀφείλοντι	also <u>we may dismiss</u> for each
	ἡμῖν·	one <u>indebted</u> to us.
	καὶ μὴ εἰσενέγκῃς ἡμᾶς εἰς	And do not bring <u>us</u> into
	πειρασμόν.	<u>testing</u>."

Within this prayer we can easily find concealed six pieces of *bread* (ασ; ας) and two *serpents* [ὄφιν; ὄφις]. And if you look carefully you may be able to spot four pieces of *manna* [μαν] dispersed as well.

The word ἀφίομεν is mis-spelled; it should be ἀφιῶμεν (1st plural present subjunctive from the verb ἀφίημι, *qv.* Jn.14:27, 16:28). What is the significance of this mistake? Almost certainly it is made intentionally, for without it no second *serpent* would be found concealed within the text of the prayer. Then what we have here is yet another 'didactic' mistake.

But why two _serpents_ and not two _fish_? We shall discover the answer shortly.

Meanwhile the same basic theme is deployed again as the narrative continues:

Lk.	καὶ εἶπεν πρὸς αὐτούς, τίς ἐξ	And he said to them "Which
11:5	ὑμῶν ἕξει **φίλον** καὶ	of you will have <u>a friend</u> and
	πορεύσεται πρὸς αὐτὸν	might go to him at midnight
	μεσονυκτίου καὶ εἴπῃ αὐτῷ,	and might say to him:
	φίλε, χρῆσόν μοι **τρεῖς**	Friend, supply to me **three**
	ἄρτους,	**breads**
11:6	ἐπειδὴ **φίλος** μου	Because <u>a friend</u> of mine has
	παρεγένετο ἐξ ὁδοῦ πρός με	come to me from a journey
	καὶ οὐκ ἔχω ὃ παραθήσω	and I do not have what I shall
	αὐτῷ·	provide for him.
11:7	**Κἀκεῖνος** ἔσωθεν	<u>And that one</u> within, replying,
	ἀποκριθεὶς εἴπῃ, μή μοι	might say: Do not cause me
	κόπους πάρεχε· ἤδη ἡ θύρα	trouble. Already the door has
	κέκλεισται, καὶ τὰ παιδία μου	been closed, and my children
	μετ' ἐμοῦ εἰς τὴν κοίτην εἰσίν·	are with me in the bed.
	οὐ δύναμαι **ἀναστὰς** δοῦναί	I am not able, <u>rising up</u>, to
	σοι.	give to you.

Within the word ἀν**αστὰς** [_rising up_] we have two pieces of _bread_ (**ασ**; **ας**). And with the words **φίλον**; **φίλος** [_friend_] we can again make out **two** _serpents_ [**ὄφιν**; **ὄφις**].

The pieces of _bread_ arise within the word **ἀναστὰς** [_rising up_], itself an obvious anagram for the name **σατανᾶς** [_Satan_]. Then in the phrase: **Κἀκεῖνος** <u>ἔσωθεν</u> [_and that one <u>within</u>_] even the name for **κάϊν** [_Cain_] is found hidden 'within'.

But the lesson is not over yet. The passage continues:

Lk. 11:8	λέγω ὑμῖν, εἰ καὶ οὐ δώσει αὐτῷ ἀν<u>αστὰς</u> διὰ τὸ εἶναι <u>φίλον</u> αὐτοῦ, διά γε τὴν ἀναίδειαν αὐτοῦ ἐγερθεὶς δώσει αὐτῷ ὅσων χρῄζει.	I say to you, if also he will not give to him, <u>rising up</u> on account of being his <u>friend</u>, at least on account of his shamelessness, being roused up, he will give him from as much as he lacks.
11:9	κἀγὼ ὑμῖν λέγω, αἰτεῖτε, καὶ δοθήσεται ὑμῖν· ζητεῖτε, καὶ εὑρήσετε· κρούετε, καὶ <u>ἀνοιγήσεται</u> ὑμῖν.	And I say to you: Ask, and it *will* be given you. Seek, and you *will* find. Knock, and <u>it *will* be opened</u> to you.

In the two verses above we have again two pieces of *bread* (and now one *serpent*). Then we get:

Lk. 11:10	<u>πᾶς</u> γὰρ ὁ αἰτῶν λαμβάνει,	For <u>each one</u> asking *will* receive,
	καὶ ὁ ζητῶν εὑρίσκει,	and the one seeking *will* find,
	καὶ τῷ κρούοντι <u>ἀνοιγ[ήσ]εται</u>.	and to the one knocking <u>it is [*will* be] opened</u>.

We keep searching, we keep asking ... and there in the word πᾶς [*each one*] we find the third piece of *bread*.

We notice too the name of Satan within the phrase:

... <u>ἀνοιγήσεται</u> ὑμῖν
... it will be opened to you

These passages illustrate well the way in which the 'bread' riddles work. By this it has indeed been '*opened to us*'. And all that we have learned has been learned direct from the gospel itself - which functions as a fully *auto-didactic* instructional text.

One point still remains to be answered. In the 'Our Father' prayer why did we have two *serpents* concealed (ἀφίομεν; Ὀφείλοντι) to accompany the *bread*, and not two *fish* (χθ, ψ) as was the case with the feeding of the five thousand (Mk.6:41)?

We find that the two species are considered interchangeable. A serpent is considered an acceptable substitute for a fish, presumably because both are encompassed by the declaration made at LXX Gn.1:28. Precisely this point is addressed in the very next verse in *Luke*:

Lk.	τίνα δὲ ἐξ ὑμῶν τὸν πατέρα	But which of you (when) the
11:11	αἰτήσει ὁ υἱὸς ἰχθύν,	son asks the father for <u>a fish</u>,
	καὶ ἀντὶ ἰχθύος	*also* instead of <u>a fish</u>
	ὄφιν αὐτῷ ἐπιδώσει;	will give him <u>a serpent</u>?

Every concern of the careful reader is catered for by what has been written so long ago. The pieces of the jigsaw puzzle fit together neatly.

In this chapter we have seen much evidence that the four canonical gospels are deeply Gnostic. There is more to them than the 'face reading', more by far than many suppose. And it is characteristic of scripture that the additional component of knowledge conveyed by its inner (or hidden) message turns upon its head the first impression received by so many readers.

From the gospels we learn that Jesus is not good … for he is *Cain*, seed of the *serpent* (1 Jn.3:12). We learn too that the *serpent*, the 'Father' to whom Jesus would have his followers pray, is not **God** … but is **Satan**, the intending *deceiver* of the entire world (Rv.12:9).

So take care with the gospels. There is more to their message than most people know.

Chapter 11

Jesus further portrayed as Cain

Judas Gives Jesus Away

We shall trace out now an impressive segment of the parallel which exists between the narrative of LXX *Genesis* and that of the gospel. For this purpose we shall choose the gospel according to *Matthew*. The vital piece of exegesis which follows does not rely (or not initially) upon a knowledge of techniques for hiding words within other words, as with the '*sign*' for Cain. It relies instead upon the starkest of allegory.

We begin by recalling this from the narrative of *Genesis*:

LXX Gn. 4:3	καὶ ἐγένετο μεθ' ἡμέρας ἤνεγκεν καιν ἀπὸ τῶν καρπῶν τῆς γῆς θυσίαν **τῷ κυρίῳ**	And it happened with (the) days that Cain brought from the fruits of the earth a sacrifice **for the lord.**
4:4	καὶ αβελ ἤνεγκεν καὶ αὐτὸς ἀπὸ τῶν πρωτοτόκων τῶν προβάτων αὐτοῦ καὶ ἀπὸ τῶν στεάτων αὐτῶν καὶ ἐπεῖδεν **ὁ θεὸς** ἐπὶ αβελ καὶ ἐπὶ τοῖς δώροις αὐτοῦ	And Abel brought both he from the firstborn of his flock, and from their fats. And **God** looked upon Abel and upon his gifts
4:5	ἐπὶ δὲ καιν καὶ ἐπὶ ταῖς θυσίαις αὐτοῦ οὐ προσέσχεν καὶ ἐ<u>λύπη</u>σεν τὸν καιν λίαν καὶ συνέπεσεν τῷ προσώπῳ	But upon Cain and upon his 'sacrifices' he did not pay attention. And <u>it grieved</u> Cain exceedingly, and he fell to the face.

4:6	καὶ εἶπεν **κύριος ὁ θεὸς** τῷ καιν ἵνα τί **περίλυπος** ἐγένου καὶ ἵνα τί συνέπεσεν τὸ πρόσωπόν σου	And **the lord god** said to Cain "*Why* did you become <u>sorrowful</u>? And *why* did your face fall?
4:7	οὐκ ἐὰν ὀρθῶς προσενέγκῃς ὀρθῶς δὲ μὴ διέλῃς ἥμαρτες	Did you not make a mistake [*alt:* did you not sin] if you brought (your sacrifices) rightly but did not distinguish rightly?
	ἡσύχασον πρὸς σὲ ἡ ἀποστροφὴ αὐτοῦ καὶ σὺ ἄρξεις αὐτοῦ	Wait quietly for his recourse to you and (then) you shall take first place over him."

To ensure that we do not repeat Cain's mistake it is vital we should know what it was. With the days Cain brought *from the fruits of the earth* a sacrifice for the **lord**. But upon Cain, and upon his sacrifices, **God** paid no attention. Why?

In Chapter 5 of this book we saw that Cain does not know **God**. He thinks mistakenly of the **lord god** as his god. This is why he brings for a sacrifice foods suited for the **lord** but which are not appropriate for **God**. *Cain has failed to distinguish rightly* (LXX Gn.4:7).

Cain and his sacrifices are ignored by **God**. It is not surprising. But Cain is a monotheist: he is unable to grasp the nature of his mistake.

Cain's initial reaction is as follows:

- He is filled with grief [λύπη] and becomes sorrowful [περίλυπος]
- He falls to the face
- He schemes to take first place over Abel, his brother

Subsequently:

- Cain goes into the plain with his brother
- He is resurrected [ἀνέστη] upon his brother
  - *and he kills him* (Gn.4:8)

God now challenges Cain for what he has done. Cain's reply is directed not to **God**, but to the **lord**. What happens here sets the parameters which will direct and constrain the gospel narrative:

LXX Gn. 4:13	καὶ εἶπεν καιν πρὸς τὸν κύριον μείζων ἡ αἰτία μου τοῦ ἀφεθῆναί με	And Cain said to the lord "*My accusation (is) greater than (will allow) my acquittal*
4:14	εἰ ἐκβάλλεις με σήμερον ἀπὸ προσώπου τῆς γῆς καὶ ἀπὸ τοῦ προσώπου σου κρυβήσομαι καὶ ἔσομαι στένων καὶ τρέμων ἐπὶ τῆς γῆς καὶ ἔσται πᾶς ὁ εὑρίσκων με ἀποκτενεῖ με	If you throw me out today from a face of the earth, I SHALL BE HIDDEN ALSO FROM YOUR FACE. And I shall be sighing and trembling upon the earth, *and it shall be that each one finding me shall kill me*".
4:15	καὶ εἶπεν αὐτῷ **κύριος ὁ θεός** οὐχ οὕτως πᾶς ὁ ἀποκτείνας καιν ἑπτὰ ἐκδικούμενα παραλύσει καὶ ἔθετο **κύριος ὁ θεός** σημεῖον τῷ καιν τοῦ μὴ ἀνελεῖν αὐτὸν πάντα τὸν εὑρίσκοντα αὐτόν	And **the lord god** said to him "Not just so, each one killing Cain shall set free SEVEN vengeances". And **the lord god** placed A SIGN FOR CAIN, so that everyone finding him should not raise him up [*alt*: not do away with him].

4:16	ἐξῆλθεν δὲ καιν ἀπὸ προσώπου **τοῦ θεοῦ** καὶ ᾤκησεν ἐν γῇ ναιδ κατέναντι εδεμ	So Cain went out from a face **of God** and settled in (the) earth of Nod, opposite Eden.

The serpent has the attributes of a god. Cain has the serpent as father but a human mother. And Cain is *the firstborn of all creation* (Col.1:15). He is inherently evil, yet inherits divine properties from his 'father'. He is also the first murderer, for he has killed his brother Abel, the first purely human child, the son of Adam.

In the passage above:

- Cain asserts that the accusation he is charged with is greater than will permit him to be acquitted. In effect, he pleads guilty.
- He anticipates that he will be excluded, thrown out from the face of the earth.
- And he promises this outcome: *that he will be hidden also from your face*.
- He will appear *sighing and trembling* [στένων καὶ τρέμων] upon the face of the earth.
- He expects that every person 'finding him' (*ie.* encountering him) *will seek to kill him*. Here is the theme of retributive justice (an eye for an eye, etc).

This sets up an interesting scenario. For if Cain goes 'hidden' and in disguise, then how may he be recognised? It is Cain's own parent, the **lord god**, who makes a protective (but characteristically devious) contribution to the resolution of this dilemma. Each one killing his beloved son shall set free seven vengeances. Accordingly the **lord god** sets in place a sevenfold '*sign*' for Cain. It is a sign by which he may be recognised.

Those who encounter Cain unexpectedly, but succeed in recognising him by virtue of this '*sign*', are *not* to raise him up. In contrast, those who do not know the sign will fail to recognise him. Failing to recognise him, *they will go on to kill him.* They will kill him *without even realising who he is.*

We established in Chapter 5 of this book what the '*sign*' for Cain was. Since then we have relied upon it for its intended purpose, identifying Cain. *But now for a time we shall play the part of those who do not know this sign.* We shall ignore it, attending for a while only to the 'face reading' of scripture's recursive narrative.

Because Cain is configured as a demigod he may be dismissed from the face of the earth but he cannot be killed, or not with any degree of permanence. Evil he may be, but he exhibits the 'eternal life' of the gods. He cannot be disposed of. Any attempt made upon his life is pure folly. All such attempts will fail, for time after time *Cain will be resurrected.* His 'divine' nature ensures that this will be so.

Let us turn now to the gospel according to *Matthew*. The students (disciples) have done as Jesus arranged with them and prepared the Passover meal:

Mt. 26:20	ὀψίας δὲ γενομένης ἀνέκειτο μετὰ τῶν δώδεκα.	But with evening happening he was reclining with the twelve.
26:21	καὶ ἐσθιόντων αὐτῶν εἶπεν, ἀμὴν λέγω ὑμῖν ὅτι εἷς ἐξ ὑμῶν παραδώσει με.	And with their eating he said "Truly I say to you that one of you will give me away".
26:22	καὶ **ΛΥΠ**ούμενοι σφόδρα ἤρξαντο λέγειν αὐτῷ εἷς ἕκαστος, μήτι **ἐγώ εἰμι**, κύριε;	And they, exceedingly <u>grieved</u>, began to say to him one by one "Surely not **I AM**, lord?"

26:23	ὁ δὲ ἀποκριθεὶς εἶπεν, ὁ ἐμβάψας μετ' ἐμοῦ τὴν χεῖρα ἐν τῷ τρυβλίῳ οὗτός με παραδώσει.	But answering he said "The one dipping the hand into the cup with me, this one gives me away.
26:24	ὁ μὲν υἱὸς τοῦ ἀνθρώπου ὑπάγει καθὼς γέγραπται περὶ αὐτοῦ, οὐαὶ δὲ τῷ ἀνθρώπῳ ἐκείνῳ δι' οὗ ὁ υἱὸς τοῦ ἀνθρώπου παραδίδοται·	The son of the Person goes off just as it has been written about him: but woe to that person through whom the son of the Person is given away.
	καλὸν ἦν αὐτῷ εἰ οὐκ ἐγεννήθη ὁ ἄνθρωπος ἐκεῖνος.	It were good for him if that person was not born."
26:25	ἀποκριθεὶς δὲ ἰούδας ὁ παραδιδοὺς αὐτὸν εἶπεν, μήτι **ἐγώ εἰμι**, ῥαββί; λέγει αὐτῷ, σὺ εἶπας.	But replying, Judas, the one giving him away, said "Surely not **I AM**, Rabbi?". He said to him "You said (it)".
26:26	ἐσθιόντων δὲ αὐτῶν λαβὼν ὁ ἰησοῦς ἄρτον καὶ εὐλογήσας ἔκλασεν καὶ δοὺς τοῖς μαθηταῖς εἶπεν, λάβετε φάγετε, τοῦτό ἐστιν τὸ σῶμά μου.	But with their eating, Jesus, taking bread and blessing, broke (it) and giving to the students said: "Take, eat. This is my body".
26:27	καὶ λαβὼν ποτήριον καὶ εὐχαριστήσας ἔδωκεν αὐτοῖς λέγων, πίετε ἐξ αὐτοῦ πάντες,	And taking a cup and giving thanks he gave (it) to them, saying "All drink from this.

26:28	τοῦτο γάρ ἐστιν τὸ αἷμά μου τῆς διαθήκης τὸ περὶ πολλῶν ἐκχυννόμενον εἰς ἄφεσιν ἁμαρτιῶν.	For this is my blood of the testament, that poured out concerning many for the dismissal of mistakes [alt: of sins].
26:29	λέγω δὲ ὑμῖν, οὐ μὴ πίω ἀπ' ἄρτι ἐκ τούτου τοῦ γενήματος τῆς ἀμπέλου ἕως τῆς ἡμέρας ἐκείνης ὅταν αὐτὸ πίνω μεθ' ὑμῶν καινὸν ἐν τῇ βασιλείᾳ τοῦ πατρός μου.	But I say to you, from now on I may not drink from this, the produce of the vine, until that day when I drink it with you anew in the kingdom of my father."

If you remember:

Cain brought *from the fruits of the earth* a sacrifice **for the lord**.

Here Jesus has done the same. For *bread* and *wine* are derived from cereals and from fruit, the foods specified at Gn.1:29.

After the meal the party goes out to the Mount of *Olives*:

Mt. 26:36	τότε ἔρχεται μετ' αὐτῶν ὁ ἰησοῦς εἰς χωρίον λεγόμενον γεθσημανί, καὶ λέγει τοῖς μαθηταῖς, καθίσατε αὐτοῦ ἕως [οὗ] ἀπελθὼν ἐκεῖ προσεύξωμαι.	Then Jesus came with them to a place called Gethsemani[1] and he said to the students "Sit at it until going over there I might pray".
26:37	καὶ παραλαβὼν τὸν πέτρον καὶ τοὺς δύο υἱοὺς ζεβεδαίου ἤρξατο ΛΥΠεῖσθαι καὶ ἀδημονεῖν.	And taking Peter and the two sons of Zebedee he began <u>to be grieved</u> and in anguish.

26:38	τότε λέγει αὐτοῖς,	Then he says to them:
	περίλυπός ἐστιν ἡ ψυχή	"My soul is <u>sorrowful</u> until
	μου ἕως θανάτου· μείνατε	death. Stay here and watch
	ὧδε καὶ γρηγορεῖτε μετ' ἐμοῦ.	with me".
26:39	καὶ προελθὼν μικρὸν ἔπεσεν	And going on a little he fell
	ἐπὶ πρόσωπον αὐτοῦ	upon his face praying and
	προσευχόμενος καὶ λέγων,	saying:
	πάτερ μου, εἰ δυνατόν ἐστιν,	"My father, if it is possible let
	παρελθάτω ἀπ' ἐμοῦ τὸ	this cup pass on away from
	ποτήριον τοῦτο· πλὴν οὐχ ὡς	me. Yet not as I wish, but as
	ἐγὼ θέλω ἀλλ' ὡς σύ.	you (wish)".

Both Cain and his sacrifice were ignored by God. And if you remember:

> … <u>it grieved</u> Cain exceedingly, *and he fell to the face.*

We notice that:

- *The same* verb **λυπέω** [*I am grieved*] is used of Cain at Gn.4:5 and of Jesus at Mt.26:37.

- *The same* adjective **περίλυπός** [*sorrowful*] is used of Cain at Gn.4:6 and of Jesus at Mt.26:38.

- *The same* desription is made of Cain at Gn.4:5 and of Jesus at Mt.26:39: for each 'falls to the face' in prayer.

- More than that, Jesus pleads with his 'Father' to accept his 'sacrifice' (in this case the cup of wine; Mt.26:29, 26:39). The anxiety of Jesus, and his disappointment when the 'cup' is not accepted, surely mirrors the behaviour of Cain at Gn.4:5.

How could anyone miss the gospel's extended parallel?

| Mt. 26:40 | καὶ ἔρχεται πρὸς τοὺς μαθητὰς καὶ εὑρίσκει αὐτοὺς καθεύδοντας, καὶ λέγει τῷ πέτρῳ, οὕτως οὐκ ἰσχύσατε μίαν ὥραν γρηγορῆσαι μετ' ἐμοῦ; | And he comes to the students and finds them sleeping. And he says to Peter "So you do not have strength to watch for one hour with me. |
| 26:41 | γρηγορεῖτε καὶ προσεύχεσθε, ἵνα μὴ εἰσέλθητε εἰς πειρασμόν: τὸ μὲν πνεῦμα πρόθυμον ἡ δὲ σὰρξ ἀσθενής. | Watch and pray so that you may not enter into testing. The spirit (is) eager but the flesh is weak" |

The students with Jesus have slept through it all, even Peter. They have noticed nothing … and certainly not the actions of Jesus. This is why they fail to recognise him (the contrast between the spirit {good} and the flesh {evil} is of course a Gnostic theme).

The narrator continues:

| Mt. 26:42 | πάλιν ἐκ δευτέρου ἀπελθὼν προσηύξατο λέγων, πάτερ μου, εἰ οὐ δύναται τοῦτο παρελθεῖν ἐὰν μὴ αὐτὸ πίω, γενηθήτω τὸ θέλημά σου. | Again going off for a second time he prayed, saying "My father, if it is not possible for this to pass on unless I drink it, let your will come about". |
| 26:43 | καὶ ἐλθὼν πάλιν εὗρεν αὐτοὺς καθεύδοντας, ἦσαν γὰρ αὐτῶν οἱ ὀφθαλμοὶ βεβαρημένοι. | And coming again he found them sleeping, for their eyes were made heavy. |

Jesus pleads a second time for his 'sacrifice' to be accepted. Yet still those with him notice nothing untoward: their eyes are heavy with sleep!

Mt. 26:44	καὶ ἀφεὶς αὐτοὺς πάλιν ἀπελθὼν προσηύξατο ἐκ τρίτου τὸν αὐτὸν λόγον εἰπὼν πάλιν.	And sending them away again, going off he prayed for a third time, saying the same message again.
26:45	τότε ἔρχεται πρὸς τοὺς μαθητὰς καὶ λέγει αὐτοῖς, καθεύδετε [τὸ] λοιπὸν καὶ ἀναπαύεσθε; ἰδοὺ ἤγγικεν ἡ ὥρα καὶ **ὁ υἱὸς τοῦ ἀνθρώπου** παραδίδοται εἰς χεῖρας ἁμαρτωλῶν.	Then he comes to the students and says to them "Sleep on and take rest? Look, the hour has come near and **the son of the Person** is given away into the hands of those making a mistake [*alt*: of sinners].
26:46	ἐγείρεσθε, ἄγωμεν: ἰδοὺ ἤγγικεν ὁ παρ<u>αδιδούς</u> με.	Rouse yourselves, let us go. Look, <u>the one giving me away</u> has come near".

Now a third time ... and *still* they did not see what Jesus was doing.

Those who fail to recognise Cain are destined to be those who kill him (Gn.4:14-15). The plot of scripture is unfolding fast, and filled with a dreadful irony. The blindness of the students with Jesus in the garden is going to result in *their being held accountable* for his eventual death.

| Mt. 26:47 | καὶ ἔτι αὐτοῦ λαλοῦντος <u>ἰδοὺ</u> <u>ιούδας</u> εἷς τῶν δώδεκα ἦλθεν καὶ μετ' αὐτοῦ ὄχλος πολὺς μετὰ μαχαιρῶν καὶ ξύλων ἀπὸ τῶν ἀρχιερέων καὶ πρεσβυτέρων τοῦ λαοῦ. | And with him still speaking, <u>look</u>: <u>Judas</u>, one of the twelve, came, and with him a large crowd with daggers and woods from the chief priests and elders of the people. |

26:48	ὁ δὲ παραδιδοὺς αὐτὸν	But the one giving him away
	ἔδωκεν αὐτοῖς σημεῖον	gave them a sign, saying
	λέγων, ὃν ἂν φιλήσω αὐτός	"Whoever I may kiss, it is he:
	ἐστιν: κρατήσατε αὐτόν.	overpower him".
26:49	καὶ εὐθέως προσελθὼν τῷ	And immediately, going to
	ἰησοῦ εἶπεν, χαῖρε, ῥαββί: καὶ	Jesus, he said "Hail, Rabbi"
	κατεφίλησεν αὐτόν.	and he kissed him.

There: it is done. He has been betrayed by one of those he himself has chosen. But let us look at that sequence one more time:

Mt.	ὁ δὲ παραδιδοὺς αὐτὸν	But the one giving him away
26:48	ἔδωκεν αὐτοῖς **σημεῖον**	gave them **_a sign_**, saying
	λέγων, ὃν ἂν φιλήσω αὐτός	"Whoever I may kiss, it is he:
	ἐστιν: κρατήσατε αὐτόν.	overpower him".
26:49	καὶ εὐθέως προσελθὼν τῷ	And immediately going to
	ἰησοῦ εἶπεν, χαῖρε, ῥαββί: καὶ	Jesus he said "Hail, Rabbi"
	Κ̲α̲τ̲ε̲φ̲ί̲λ̲η̲σ̲ε̲ν̲ αὐτόν.	and **_he kissed_** him.

It is ἰούδας [*Judas*], whose name is found appropriately in the word παραδιδούς [*the one giving away*], who now will 'give away' Jesus. He is to greet him with a _sign_ agreed beforehand. The sign is to be a kiss. And look, Κ̲α̲τ̲ε̲φ̲ί̲λ̲η̲σ̲ε̲ν̲ [*he kissed*].   The sign which Judas gives **is** the '*sign*' for κ̲α̲.̲.̲.̲ι̲.̲.̲.̲.̲.̲.̲.̲ν̲ !

Because of the strong allegorical parallel developed in the narrative there has been no call for the writer to issue the '*sign*' for Cain as well. For the last fifteen verses this '*sign*' has been withheld. ***But it is finally called upon again as the means for Judas to identify Jesus as Cain.***

The '*sign*' for Cain can be seen only by those who read in Greek. But why do so many miss the allegorical parallel here? Just like the students in the narrative, the majority of readers 'sleep' through this whole episode in *Matthew*, failing entirely to see who Jesus is supposed to be.

Jesus Washes the Feet of his Students (Disciples)

We saw in Chapter 5 of this book the curse imposed upon the serpent:

LXX	καὶ εἶπεν κύριος ὁ θεὸς τῷ	And the lord god said to the
Gn.	ὄφει ὅτι ἐποίησας τοῦτο	serpent "Because you
3:14	ἐπικατάρατος σὺ ἀπὸ	made/did this, cursed (are)
	πάντων τῶν κτηνῶν καὶ ἀπὸ	you from all the pastoral
	πάντων τῶν θηρίων τῆς γῆς	beasts and from all the wild
	ἐπὶ τῷ στήθει σου καὶ τῇ	beasts of the earth. Upon
	κοιλίᾳ πορεύσῃ καὶ γῆν φάγῃ	your chest and belly shall
	πάσας τὰς ἡμέρας τῆς ζωῆς	you go - and eat earth all the
	σου	days of your life.
3:15	καὶ ἔχθραν θήσω ἀνὰ μέσον	And I shall put enmity amidst
	σου καὶ ἀνὰ μέσον τῆς	you and amidst the <u>woman</u>,
	γυναικὸς καὶ ἀνὰ μέσον τοῦ	and amidst your seed and
	σπέρματός σου καὶ ἀνὰ	amidst her seed.
	μέσον τοῦ σπέρματος αὐτῆς	
	αὐτός σου τηρήσει κεφαλήν	He shall watch you for a
	καὶ σὺ τηρήσεις αὐτοῦ	head, and you shall watch
	<u>πτέρναν</u>	him for ***a heel*** ".

The woman and *her* offspring are declared as the opponents of the serpent and *his* offspring. The former are to watch out for *a head* ... as a sign for the serpent before it can strike them. The offspring of the serpent are to watch out for *a heel* ... which may crush them at any time.

In the Hebrew Masoretic text the curse is much the same:

וְאֵיבָה אָשִׁית, בֵּינְךָ וּבֵין הָאִשָּׁה, וּבֵין זַרְעֲךָ, וּבֵין
זַרְעָהּ: הוּא יְשׁוּפְךָ רֹאשׁ, וְאַתָּה תְּשׁוּפֶנּוּ עָקֵב.

> And I shall put enmity between you and the woman, and between
> your seed and her seed. He shall lie in wait for a head, and you
> shall lie in wait for a heel.

The Hebrew word שׁוּף [*to lie in wait for*; **Strong's H7779**] seems to be
cognate with שׁוֹפֵט [a *judge*]. The use of the Greek word τηρέω
[*I watch for*] is therefore consistent with the Hebrew. It suggests a
period spent in waiting, watching for vital evidence to materialise.

Unfortunately many translations of this passage are found to be
misleading. Even the Vulgate Latin alters both <u>gender</u> and <u>the general
sense</u>:

> Inimicitias ponam inter te et mulierem et semen tuum et semen
> illius : <u>ipsa</u> <u>conteret</u> caput tuum et tu insidiaberis calcaneo eius

> I shall place hostility between you and the woman, and your seed
> and her seed. <u>She</u> <u>shall bruise</u> your head, and you shall be laid in
> wait for her heel"

With such alterations to meaning we are left to suspect the motive: but
we shall not go into that here.

From this passage at Gn.3:15 it follows that any use in subsequent
scripture of the word κεφαλή [*head*] may stand as a token for the
serpent, whilst any use of the word πτέρνα [*heel*] may stand as a token
for the one in whose power it lies to crush that head.

Unsurprisingly the writers remember this provision and rely for effect upon it. We find it engaged when we come to the story in *Genesis* about Rebecca giving birth to twins:

LXX Gn. 25:24	καὶ ἐπληρώθησαν αἱ ἡμέραι τοῦ τεκεῖν αὐτήν καὶ τῆδε ἦν δίδυμα ἐν τῇ κοιλίᾳ αὐτῆς	And the days were fulfilled for her to give birth, and so it was twins in her belly.
25:25	ἐξῆλθεν δὲ ὁ υἱὸς ὁ πρωτότοκος πυρράκης ὅλος ὡσεὶ δορὰ δασύς ἐπωνόμασεν δὲ τὸ ὄνομα αὐτοῦ ησαυ	And the firstborn son emerged reddish all over, like a hairy skin: and she named his name Esau.
25:26	καὶ μετὰ τοῦτο ἐξῆλθεν ὁ ἀδελφὸς αὐτοῦ καὶ ἡ χεὶρ αὐτοῦ ἐπειλημμένη τῆς <u>πτέρνης</u> ησαυ	And after that his brother emerged, and his hand grasping the <u>heel</u> of Esau.
	καὶ ἐκάλεσεν τὸ ὄνομα αὐτοῦ ιακωβ ισαακ δὲ ἦν ἐτῶν ἑξήκοντα ὅτε ἔτεκεν αὐτοὺς ρεβεκκα	And she called his name Jacob. And Isaac was sixty years when Rebecca gave birth to them.

The two children are opponents (Gn.25:22). Esau is the first to be born, presumably head first. Jacob then follows. His hand is still grasping the heel of Esau in the precocious struggle to take first place over him.

In this clever vignette it is Esau who has his heel over the head of Jacob. Relying upon the curse from Gn.3:14-15, we may surmise that Esau is cast by the writer as a descendent of the woman. But ambitious Jacob (who later takes the name Israel) is cast by the writer(s) as 'seed of the serpent'. Then it should come as no surprise that Jacob turns out to be a liar. He impersonates Esau for advantage, lying three times to Isaac, his father (twice about his own identity). The pattern indicated by the curse is taking its scriptural course. Before long Jacob (*alias* Cain) usurps the position of Esau entirely and Esau is eliminated from the scene. It is a scenario which will be repeated in the gospels with the displacement of John the Baptist by Jesus.

In the books of the *New Testament* the word for *a heel* is used only once. It is in Chapter 13 of the fourth gospel (*John*) that we find the ancient curse invoked yet again. We are told of Jesus:

Jn. 13:3	εἰδὼς ὅτι πάντα ἔδωκεν αὐτῷ ὁ πατὴρ εἰς τὰς χεῖρας καὶ ὅτι ἀπὸ θεοῦ ἐξῆλθεν καὶ πρὸς τὸν θεὸν ὑπάγει,	Knowing that the father gave all things into his hands and that he came from a god and is going to God
13:4	ἐγείρεται ἐκ τοῦ δείπνου καὶ τίθησιν τὰ ἱμάτια, καὶ λαβὼν λέντιον διέζωσεν ἑαυτόν.	He rose from the supper and laid aside his garments. And, taking a towel, he girded himself
13:5	εἶτα βάλλει ὕδωρ εἰς τὸν νιπτῆρα καὶ ἤρξατο νίπτειν τοὺς πόδας τῶν μαθητῶν καὶ ἐΚμάσσειΝ τῷ λεντίῳ ᾧ ἦν διεζωσμένος.	Next he threw water into the wash basin and began to wash the feet of the students, and <u>to wipe off</u> with the towel with which he was girded
13:6	ἔρχεται οὖν πρὸς σίμωνα πέτρον. λέγει αὐτῷ, κύριε, σύ μου νίπτεις τοὺς πόδασ;	Then he came to Simon Peter. He said to him "Lord, are you washing my feet?"
13:7	ἀπεκρίθη ἰησοῦς καὶ εἶπεν αὐτῷ, ὃ ἐγὼ ποιῶ σὺ οὐκ οἶδας ἄρτι, γνώσῃ δὲ μετὰ ταῦτα.	Jesus answered and said to him "What I am doing you do not now perceive, *but after these things you shall learn to know*"

| 13:8 | λέγει αὐτῷ πέτρος, οὐ μὴ νίψῃς μου τοὺς πόδας εἰς τὸν αἰῶνα. ἀπεκρίθη ἰησοῦς αὐτῷ, ἐὰν μὴ νίψω σε, οὐκ ἔχεις μέρος μετ' ἐμοῦ. | Peter said to him "You shall not wash my feet in eternity". Jesus replied to him "If I do not wash you, you do not have a part with me". |
| 13:9 | λέγει αὐτῷ σίμων πέτρος, κύριε, μὴ τοὺς πόδας μου μόνον ἀλλὰ καὶ τὰς χεῖρας καὶ τὴν κεφαλήν. | Simon Peter said to him "Lord, not my feet alone but also the hands and the head". |

A gnostic scenario … and a gnostic statement to go with it:

> What I am doing you do not now perceive …
> but after these things *you shall learn to know*.

Raymond Brown[2], in his book *The Gospel According to John*, notes that:

> … it was customary hospitality to provide water for a guest to wash his own feet. But as the Midrash Mekilta on Exodus xxi 2 tells us, the washing of a master's feet could not be required [even] of a Jewish slave.

Again Brown writes that:

> … there was nothing in the ritual of the Passover meal that can be compared to the footwashing. Footwashing was done when one entered the house, not during the course of the meal.

Taken at face value, the story seems thus incongruous. As a record of a social gathering, it is hardly realistic.

But this well known passage from the gospel has a substantial burden to carry. For just look what happens:

- Jesus first removes his clothes (the serpent is invariably smooth/naked: *qv*. Jacob at Gn.27:11, 27:16).

- Next Jesus stoops (upon your chest and belly shall you go: *qv*. Gn.3:14) to wash the feet of the students, even Peter.

To wash the foot in a basin the heel must be raised. This action brings the *heel* of Peter into proximity with the *head* of Jesus. The symbolism is hard to overlook. Is it not clear that by formulating this story line the author has invoked once again the '*heel over head*' curse, the curse configured at Gn.3:15?

And now, to confirm the mind of the Gnostic author beyond reasonable doubt, we hear the link to prior scripture established through the mouth of Jesus himself:

Jn.	εἰ ταῦτα οἴδατε, μακάριοί ἐστε ἐὰν ποιῆτε αὐτά.	If you perceive these things, you are fortunate if you 'make' them.
13:17		
13:18	οὐ περὶ πάντων ὑμῶν λέγω· ἐγὼ οἶδα τίνας ἐξελεξάμην· ἀλλ' ἵνα ἡ γραφὴ πληρωθῇ, ὁ τρώγων μου τὸν ἄρτον ἐπῆρεν ἐπ' ἐμὲ τὴν **πτέρναν** αὐτοῦ.	Not about all of you do I speak. I perceive who I picked out. But so that the scripture may be fulfilled: 'The one nibbling my bread raised up upon me his ***heel***'.
13:19	ἀπ' ἄρτι λέγω ὑμῖν πρὸ τοῦ γενέσθαι, ἵνα πιστεύσητε ὅταν γένηται ὅτι **ἐγώ εἰμι**.	From now on I (shall) tell you before the happening - that you may believe, when it happens, that ' **I AM** '.

This is the only place in the NT canon where a *heel* is mentioned. With it, the ancient curse is invoked again. The '*heel*' is the heel of Peter and the '*head*' is the head of Jesus.

By this means the author identifies Jesus as *seed of the serpent*. And this makes perfect sense, for we know already that Jesus is Cain, the offspring of the serpent (Gn.4:1; 1 Jn.3:12).

Yet the author portrays Peter as failing to understand. Peter misses the chance handed him by fate. He fails to realise who Jesus is.

Events in the narrative will now unfold to culminate in the crucifixion of wretched Cain … *precisely* as he himself has predicted:

LXX	εἰ ἐκβάλλεις με σήμερον ἀπὸ	If you throw me out today
Gn.	προσώπου τῆς γῆς καὶ ἀπὸ	from a face of the earth, I
4:14	τοῦ προσώπου σου	SHALL BE HIDDEN ALSO
	κρυβήσομαι καὶ ἔσομαι	FROM YOUR FACE. And I
	στένων καὶ τρέμων ἐπὶ τῆς	shall be sighing and
	γῆς	trembling upon the earth,
	καὶ ἔσται πᾶς ὁ εὑρίσκων με	***AND IT SHALL BE THAT***
	ἀποκτενεῖ με	***EACH ONE FINDING ME***
		WILL KILL ME.

Pilate knows ... and washes his Hands

In the gospel narrative the Roman governor Pontius Pilate is depicted to be amongst the few who discover the identity of Jesus He is portrayed as responding appropriately:

Mt. 27:19	καθημένου δὲ αὐτοῦ ἐπὶ τοῦ βήματος ἀπέστειλεν πρὸς αὐτὸν ἡ γυνὴ αὐτοῦ λέγουσα, μηδὲν σοὶ καὶ τῷ δικαίῳ ἐκείνῳ, πολλὰ γὰρ ἔπαθον σήμερον κατ' ὄναρ δι' αὐτόν.	But with his being seated upon the podium, his woman sent to him saying "Have nothing to do with that righteous one, for I suffered many things today in a dream on account of him".
27:20	οἱ δὲ ἀρχιερεῖς καὶ οἱ πρεσβύτεροι ἔπεισαν τοὺς ὄχλους ἵνα αἰτήσωνται τὸν βαραββᾶν τὸν δὲ ἰησοῦν ἀπολέσωσιν.	But the chief priests and the elders persuaded the crowds that they might ask for Barabbas but might destroy Jesus.

The name Barabbas is generic. It means simply *son of the father*. The description could fit any man (or even Jesus himself). Plainly the priests and the elders do not know who Jesus is; neither does the crowd:

Mt. 27:21	ἀποκριθεὶς δὲ ὁ ἡγεμὼν εἶπεν αὐτοῖς, τίνα θέλετε ἀπὸ τῶν δύο ἀπολύσω ὑμῖν; οἱ δὲ εἶπαν, τὸν βαραββᾶν.	But answering, the leader said to them "I shall free whichever you like of the two". And they said "Barabbas".
27:22	λέγει αὐτοῖς ὁ πιλᾶτος, τί οὖν ποιήσω ἰησοῦν τὸν λεγόμενον χριστόν; λέγουσιν πάντες, σταυρωθήτω.	Pilate said to to them "What then shall I do (with) Jesus, the one called Christ?". They all said "Let him be crucified".

27:23	ὁ δὲ ἔφη, τί γὰρ κακὸν ἐποίησεν; οἱ δὲ περισσῶς ἔκραζον λέγοντες, σταυρωθήτω.	But he said "Why, what evil has he done?". But they were clamouring exceedingly, saying "Let him be crucified".
27:24	ἰδὼν δὲ ὁ πιλᾶτος ὅτι οὐδὲν ὠφελεῖ ἀλλὰ μᾶλλον θόρυβος γίνεται, λαβὼν ὕδωρ ἀπενίψατο τὰς χεῖρας ἀπέναντι τοῦ ὄχλου, λέγων, ἀθῷός εἰμι ἀπὸ τοῦ αἵματος τούτου: ὑμεῖς ὄψεσθε.	But Pilate, seeing that nothing is any use but rather (that) an uproar was happening, taking water washed off his hands before the crowd, saying "I am free from guilt for the blood of this one: you shall see"
27:25	καὶ ἀποκριθεὶς πᾶς ὁ λαὸς εἶπεν, τὸ αἷμα αὐτοῦ ἐφ' ἡμᾶς καὶ ἐπὶ τὰ τέκνα ἡμῶν.	And answering, the whole crowd said "His blood (is) upon us and upon our children"
27:26	τότε ἀπέλυσεν αὐτοῖς τὸν βαραββᾶν, τὸν δὲ ἰησοῦν φραγελλώσας παρέδωκεν ἵνα σταυρωθῇ.	Then he freed Barabbas for them: but flogging Jesus, he gave (him) away so that he might be crucified.

Pilate knows to ignore Cain, and all his antics. In this way Pilate responds just like the prime **God**, of Gn.1:1. It is a key theme of scripture that this is the right way to deal with Cain ... simply to ignore him.

It is the crowd, considered as 'blind' because they do not understand the scriptures, which ensures Cain's own prediction about his death (Gn.4:14) is thoroughly fulfilled.

It is at their ignorant hands that Jesus will be lynched ... and will die upon the cross.

Of course Jesus will be resurrected too, for his character is divine. But many do not understand what must happen to Cain:

Mk.	καὶ ἤρξατο διδά̱σ̱Κε̱ι̱Ν̱	And he began <u>to teach</u> them
8:31	αὐτοὺς ὅτι δεῖ τὸν υἱὸν τοῦ ἀνθρώπου πολλὰ παθεῖν	that it must be for the son of the Person to suffer many things
	καὶ ἀποδοΚ̱ιμασθῆ̱Ν̱Α̱Ι̱ ὑπὸ τῶν πρεσβυτέρων καὶ τῶν ἀρχιερέων καὶ τῶν γραμματέων	and <u>to be rejected upon</u> <u>scrutiny</u> by the elders and the chief priests and the scribes,
	καὶ ἀποΚ̱τανθῆ̱Ν̱Α̱Ι̱ καὶ μετὰ τρεῖς ἡμέρας ἀ̱Ν̱Α̱Σ̱Τ̱ῆναι:	and <u>to be killed</u> and after three days <u>to be resurrected</u>.
8:32	καὶ παρρησίᾳ τὸν λόγον ἐλάλει. καὶ προσλαβόμενος ὁ πέτρος αὐτὸν ἤρξατο ἐπιτιμᾶν αὐτῷ.	And he spoke the message frankly. And Peter, taking him up, began to rebuke him.
8:33	ὁ δὲ ἐπιστραφεὶς καὶ ἰδὼν τοὺς μαθητὰς αὐτοῦ ἐπετίμησεν πέτρῳ καὶ λέγει, ὕπαγε ὀπίσω μου, Σ̱Α̱Τ̱Α̱Ν̱ᾶ, ὅτι οὐ φ̱ρΟ̱νε̱ῖ̱ς̱ τὰ τ̱ο̱ῦ̱ θ̱ε̱ο̱ῦ̱ ἀλλὰ τὰ τ̱ῶ̱ν̱ ἀ̱ν̱θ̱ρ̱ώ̱π̱ων.	But he, turning and seeing his students, rebuked Peter and said: "Get behind me, <u>Satan</u>. For <u>you do not know</u> the things of **God** but the things of **the Persons**".

At 8:31 we have the mention of **three** days. And look, we have the '*sign*' for Cain **three** times in that verse. Then, with the resurrection, we see the name for Satan too.

At 8:32-33 Peter does not understand. He can recognise nothing for what it is: yet there again is the serpent in the phrase 'o̱ὐ̱ φ̱ρΟ̱νε̱ῖ̱ς̱' [*you do <u>not</u> know*].

It is just as Jesus says. Peter does _not_ know the things of **God**, he only knows the things of **The Persons** (the **lord god** of Gn.1:27). And surely this must be why Jesus addresses Peter himself as '*Satan*'.

It is a just rebuke in every way. For Cain's own limited perspective is Peter's limited perspective too. And here is Cain telling Peter that 'he does not know the things of **God**'... ironic because Cain himself does not know **God**.

In the narrative which follows, it is at the hands of the ignorant, at the hands of *those who do not know the underlying plot of scripture*, that Cain does indeed die upon the cross. And upon the third day he is again *resurrected* (the first resurrection was at Gn.4:8 when Cain was '*resurrected upon Abel, his brother, and he killed him*').

This is what the gospel myth is all about ... that the death of Cain should happen, when it never should have happened ... that it should happen purely on account of human folly ... that it should happen thus through **IGNORANCE** of '*the things of God*'.

In contrast, here is the wisdom of those who have understood the scriptures. It is the wisdom of those accomplished, of those who *are* familiar with **τὰ βάθη τοῦ θεοῦ** [*the deep things of God*] (1 Cor.2:10):

1 Cor. 2:6	σοφίαν δὲ λαλοῦμεν ἐν τοῖς τελείοις, σοφίαν δὲ οὐ τοῦ αἰῶνος τούτου οὐδὲ τῶν ἀρχόντων τοῦ αἰῶνος τούτου τῶν καταργουμένων:	And we speak wisdom amongst those accomplished, yet a wisdom not of this age, nor of the rulers of this age, of those being made redundant.

2:7	ἀλλὰ λαλοῦμεν θεοῦ σοφίαν	But we speak a godly
	ἐν μυστηρίῳ, τὴν	wisdom within a mystery,
	ἀποκεκρυμμένην, ἣν	hidden away, which God
	προώρισεν ὁ θεὸς πρὸ τῶν	fore-ordained before the
	αἰώνων εἰς δόξαν ἡμῶν:	ages purposed for our glory,
2:8	ἣν οὐδεὶς τῶν ἀρχόντων τοῦ	Which not one of the rulers of
	αἰῶνος τούτου ἔγνωκεν, εἰ	this age has known. *For if*
	γὰρ ἔγνωσαν, οὐκ ἂν τὸν	*they knew, they would not*
	κύριον τῆς δόξης	*have crucified the 'lord of*
	ἐσταύρωσαν.	*glory'.*

How has this wisdom become lost in our age?

It is by embracing the death and resurrection of Cain, by relying upon these things, by exploiting them for all they are worth, that the Christian church demonstrates its overwhelming ignorance of scripture. It demonstrates too what is deemed by the authors of scripture themselves to be the evil which lies at the very _heart_ [Καρδίαν] of mankind.

Then is it not a shocking verdict upon the wits of so many that it should _still_ *be necessary, more than 1900 years after the gospels first appeared, to write a book to explain these things?*

Herod sees for himself the Sevenfold 'Sign'

Here in *Luke*, the elders of the people, the chief priests and the scribes, have taken charge of Jesus. They begin 'ΚΑτηγορεῖν αὐτοῦ' [*to accuse him*]. Yet still they do not recognise him:

Lk.		
Lk. 23:1	καὶ **ἀναστὰν** ἅπαν τὸ πλῆθος αὐτῶν ἤγαγον αὐτὸν ἐπὶ τὸν πιλᾶτον.	And ***rising up***, the whole mass of them took him to Pilate.
23:2	ἤρξαντο δὲ **ΚΑτηγορεῖν** αὐτοῦ λέγοντες, τοῦτον εὕραμεν διαστρέφοντα τὸ ἔθνος ἡμῶν καὶ κωλύοντα φόρους καίσαρι διδόναι καὶ λέγοντα ἑαυτὸν χριστὸν βασιλέα εἶναι.	And they began to accuse him, saying "We found this one perverting our nation, and hindering giving payments to Caesar, and saying himself to be Christ, a king".
23:3	ὁ δὲ πιλᾶτος ἠρώτησεν αὐτὸν λέγων, σὺ εἶ ὁ βασιλεὺς τῶν ἰουδαίων; ὁ δὲ ἀποκριθεὶς αὐτῷ ἔφη, σὺ λέγεις.	But Pilate questioned him, saying "Are you the king of the Judaeans?". But answering he said to him "You say (it)".
23:4	ὁ δὲ πιλᾶτος εἶπεν πρὸς τοὺς ἀρχιερεῖς καὶ τοὺς ὄχλους, οὐδὲν εὑρίσκω αἴτιον ἐν τῷ ἀνθρώπῳ τούτῳ.	And Pilate said to the chief priests and the crowds "I find not one fault in this Person".
23:5	οἱ δὲ ἐπίσχυον λέγοντες ὅτι ἀνασείει τὸν λαὸν **διδάσΚων** καθ' ὅλης τῆς ἰουδαίας, καὶ ἀρξάμενος ἀπὸ τῆς γαλιλαίας ἕως ὧδε.	But they insisted, saying that he stirs up the people teaching through the whole of Judaea, beginning from Galilee even as far as here.

23:6	πιλᾶτος δὲ ἀκούσας ἐπηρώτησεν εἰ ὁ ἄνθρωπος γαλιλαῖός ἐστιν:	But hearing, Pilate inquired whether the Person is a Galilean.
23:7	καὶ ἐπιγνοὺς ὅτι ἐκ τῆς ἐξουσίας ἡρῴδου ἐστὶν ἀνέπεμψεν αὐτὸν πρὸς ἡρῴδην, ὄντα καὶ αὐτὸν ἐν ἱεροσολύμοις ἐν ταύταις ταῖς ἡμέραις.	And recognising that he is from the authority of Herod, he sent him up to Herod, he being also in Jerusalem in those days.
23:8	ὁ δὲ ἡρῴδης ἰδὼν τὸν ἰησοῦν ἐχάρη λίαν, ἦν γὰρ ἐξ ἰ**καν**ῶν χρόνων θέλων ἰδεῖν αὐτὸν διὰ τὸ ἀ**Κ**ούε**ιν** περὶ αὐτοῦ, καὶ ἤλπιζέν τι σημεῖον ἰδεῖν ὑπ' αὐτοῦ γινόμενον.	But Herod, seeing Jesus, rejoiced exceedingly. For he was from <u>considerable</u> times wishing to see him on account of <u>hearing</u> about him, and **he expected to see some sign come about** through him.
23:9	ἐπηρώτα δὲ αὐτὸν ἐν λόγοις ἰ**καν**οῖς: αὐτὸς δὲ οὐδὲν ἀπε**Κρίνατο** αὐτῷ.	So he questioned him in <u>sufficient</u> words. But <u>he answered</u> to him nothing.
23:10	εἱστή**Κεισαν** δὲ οἱ ἀρχιερεῖς καὶ οἱ γραμματεῖς εὐτόνως κατηγοροῦντες αὐτοῦ.	Yet the chief priests and the scribes <u>stood</u> vigorously accusing him.

In this passage we see the '*sign*' for Cain asserted. From the point when they begin [sic] <u>*to accuse*</u> him (23:2) to the point where <u>*they stood*</u> vigorously accusing him (23:10), we have exactly **seven** words which constitute the '*sign*' for Cain.

In the narrative Pilate and Herod seem to realise who Jesus is. Indeed we are told that Herod **expected to see some sign come about** (23:8), even though (23:9) Jesus 'οὐδὲν ἀπεΚρίΝατο' [*answered nothing*] (what we have here is certainly clever composition).

What dreadful irony there is in the fact that the priests and the crowd do not know who Jesus is. It is the theme of the gospel that they seek his death precisely on account of their failure to recognise him.

In part this is down to their ignorance of scripture, in part to the deluded nature of their own hearts. Heaven forbid that any of us should make the same mistake.

Confronted by Cain, Herod and Pilate know what steps to take:

Lk. 23:11	ἐξουθενήσας δὲ αὐτὸν [καὶ] ὁ ἡρῴδης σὺν τοῖς στρατεύμασιν αὐτοῦ καὶ ἐμπαίξας περιβαλὼν ἐσθῆτα λαμπρὰν ἀνέπεμψεν αὐτὸν τῷ πιλάτῳ.	But [even] Herod held him in contempt with his campaign, and mocking (him), putting on bright clothing, he sent him up to Pilate.
23:12	ἐγένοντο δὲ φίλοι ὅ τε ἡρῴδης καὶ ὁ πιλᾶτος ἐν αὐτῇ τῇ ἡμέρᾳ μετ' ἀλλήλων· προϋπῆρχον γὰρ ἐν ἔχθρᾳ ὄντες πρὸς αὐτούς.	And both Herod and Pilate became friends on that day with one another: for they were first disposed to enmity being with them.
23:13	πιλᾶτος δὲ συγκαλεσάμενος τοὺς ἀρχιερεῖς καὶ τοὺς ἄρχοντας καὶ τὸν λαὸν	But Pilate, calling together the chief priests and the rulers and the people,

23:14	εἶπεν πρὸς αὐτούς,	Said to them:
	προσηνέγκατέ μοι τὸν	"You brought this Person to
	ἄνθρωπον τοῦτον ὡς	me as turning aside the
	ἀποστρέφοντα τὸν λαόν,	people.
	καὶ ἰδοὺ ἐγὼ ἐνώπιον ὑμῶν	And look ... I, <u>examining</u>
	ἀν**ακ**ρ**ίν**ας οὐθὲν εὗρον ἐν	before you, found no fault in
	τῷ ἀνθρώπῳ τούτῳ αἴτιον ὧν	this Person of those things
	κατηγορεῖτε κατ' αὐτοῦ,	which you accuse against
		him".
23:15	ἀλλ' οὐδὲ ἡρῴδης·	And neither (has) Herod.
	ἀνέπεμψεν γὰρ αὐτὸν πρὸς	For he sent him up to us.
	ἡμᾶς·	
	καὶ ἰδοὺ οὐδὲν ἄξιον θανάτου	And look, nothing deserving
	ἐστὶν πεπραγμένον αὐτῷ.	of death is accomplished by
		him.
23:16	παιδεύσας οὖν αὐτὸν	Then cautioning him, I shall
	ἀπολύσω.	set (him) free.

Pilate says:

Nothing deserving of death is accomplished by him.

Surely he recognises Jesus as Cain. Then he will appreciate that a demi-god like Cain can never die. It follows that whatever Cain does - and he *has* killed his brother Abel - it is nothing deserving of his *own* death.

Pilate washes his hands in public (Mt.27:24) and sets Jesus free. In doing this he seeks to ignore Cain, just as God has done himself (Gn.4:5). It is the theme of scripture that this is the right thing to do.

But the chief priests and the Judaean crowd, not knowing the '*sign*' for Cain and failing to recognise him, will take him and lynch him upon the cross. Cain has killed Abel and now the crowd will kill Cain. Events are taking precisely the course which Cain himself has foretold (Gn.4:14).

But the 'crowd' will be held accountable for their folly … and all of its dreadful consequences (in practice it has not been members of the Jewish race but the members of the various Christian churches all down the centuries who have sought vicarious benefit from the death of Jesus and are therefore guilty; see *The Sacrifice of the Mass explicitly Prohibited*, p.339).

The blood of Cain will be upon them, and upon their children (Mt.27:25).

For upon them the significance of Gn.4:15 is entirely lost:

Ac. 13:27	οἱ γὰρ **ΚΑτοΙ**κοῦ**Ντες** ἐν ἱερουσαλὴμ καὶ οἱ ἄρχοντες αὐτῶν	For those <u>settling down</u> in Jerusalem and their leaders,
	τοῦτον ἀ̓γνοή**ΣΑΝΤ**ες καὶ	<u>being ignorant</u> of this and of
	τὰς φωνὰς τῶν προφητῶν	the voices of the prophets
	τὰς κατὰ πᾶν σάββατον	<u>read out</u> at every sabbath,
	ἀν**ΑγΙΝ**ωσ**Κ**ομένας	
	Κρ**ΙΝ**αντες ἐπλήρωσαν,	<u>condemning</u> (him) fulfilled (them)
13:28	καὶ μηδεμίαν αἰτίαν θανάτου εὑρόντες	And finding not one accusation for death,
	ἠτήσαντο πιλᾶτον ἀναιρεθῆναι αὐτόν:	they asked Pilate for him to be raised up.

The Marriage Feast at Cana

At *Genesis* Chapter 40 we find an intriguing story set in Egypt. The chief winepourer [ὁ ἀρχιοινοχόος] and the chief miller/baker [ὁ ἀρχισιτοποιὸς] have offended their lord, the Pharaoh. The two are committed to prison and find themselves in the company of Joseph.

Each officer has a dream which Joseph then claims to interpret. The chief winepourer learns that he will be restored to his position in the household. But then we have this:

LXX Gn. 40:16	καὶ εἶδεν ὁ ἀρχισιτοποιὸς ὅτι ὀρθῶς συνέκρινεν καὶ εἶπεν τῷ ιωσηφ	And the chief miller/baker saw that he (Joseph) interpreted rightly and said to Joseph
	κἀγὼ εἶδον ἐνύπνιον καὶ ᾤμην τρία **κανᾶ** χονδριτῶν αἴρειν ἐπὶ τῆς κεφαλῆς μου	"I too saw a dream and I was thinking three <u>bread baskets</u> of oatbreads to lift up upon my head.
40:17	ἐν δὲ τῷ κανῷ τῷ ἐπάνω ἀπὸ πάντων τῶν γενῶν ὧν ὁ βασιλεὺς φαραω ἐσθίει ἔργον σιτοποιοῦ	And in the upper bread basket (was), from all the kinds of which Pharaoh the king eats, some work of a baker.
	καὶ τὰ πετεινὰ τοῦ οὐρανοῦ **Κα**τήσθιε**ν** αὐτὰ ἀπὸ τοῦ κανοῦ τοῦ ἐπάνω τῆς κεφαλῆς μου	And the birds of Heaven <u>was eating</u> them <u>down</u> from the bread basket uppermost of my head."

40:18	ἀποκριθεὶς δὲ ιωσηφ εἶπεν αὐτῷ αὕτη ἡ σύγκρισις αὐτοῦ τὰ τρία **κανᾶ** τρεῖς ἡμέραι εἰσίν	But answering, Joseph said to him "This (is) the interpretation of it. The three <u>bread baskets</u> are three days.
40:19	ἔτι τριῶν ἡμερῶν ἀφελεῖ φαραω τὴν κεφαλήν σου ἀπὸ σοῦ καὶ κρεμάσει σε ἐπὶ ξύλου καὶ φάγεται τὰ ὄρνεα τοῦ οὐρανοῦ τὰς σάρκας σου ἀπὸ σοῦ	With three days more Pharaoh will take your head from you and will hang you upon a tree. And the birds of Heaven will eat your flesh from you."

At 40:17 we have the word **Κατήσθιεν** [*it was eating down*] used in the singular form when it should be plural **Κατήσθιον** [*they were eating down*]. It appears to be yet another grammatical error introduced deliberately to draw attention to the '*sign*' for Cain. Furthermore it is anomalous that in *Genesis* Chapter 40 this is the *only* word with the letters **Κ.α.ι.ν** (all other chapters include multiple instances).

This too is the passage in *Genesis* where we find the two instances of the word **κανᾶ** [*bread baskets*]. We deduced in Chapter 5 of this book that to obtain the explicit checksum values of **490** (*Genesis*) and **153** (*fourth gospel*) we need to count all the words in each book which contain the letters **Κ.α.ι.ν** ... then to this total we must add the number of instances of the word **κανᾶ**. On this basis, the contribution made by the passage at Gn.40:16-19 to the *Genesis* total of **490** is *three* ... which presumably accounts for the riddle (otherwise somewhat obscure) about the *three* bread baskets.

The outcome predicted by Joseph for the chief miller/baker is opposite to that for the winepourer. Far from being restored to his position, with the passage of three days the head of the chief miller/baker is to be taken off and he is to be hanged upon a tree where the birds of Heaven will eat his flesh. Does this prefigure the death of Jesus in the gospel narrative, hanging upon the cross?

It is worth noting that what distinguishes the chief miller/baker [Ὁ ἀρχισιτοποιὸς] from the chief winepourer [ὁ ἀρχιοινοχόος] is that his name can re reformulated to yield Ὁ ΧΡΙΣΤὸς [*Christ*]. Perhaps it is this which explains his demise.

We are left to speculate upon how far Lewis Carroll (whose real name was Charles Dodgson) had penetrated the mystery of scripture when he wrote his nonsense poem *The Hunting of the Snark* [3], first published in 1876. Carroll was a teacher of mathematics and logic. He had an extensive knowledge of scripture and was an enthusiast for anagram riddles. At Oxford he was an associate of Henry Liddell, Dean of Christchurch, the man remembered for the Greek lexicon which still bears his name (the name of Liddell's daughter Alice is preserved in Carroll's other books *Alice's Adventures in Wonderland* and *Through The Looking Glass*).

The mysterious poem about the *Snark* is curiously evocative of scripture's underlying theme. It ends in this way:

> They hunted till darkness came on, but they found
> Not a button, or feather, or mark,
> By which they could tell that they stood on the ground
> Where the Baker had met with the Snark.
>
> In the midst of the word he was trying to say,
> In the midst of his laughter and glee,
> He had softly and suddenly vanished away -
> For the Snark <u>was</u> a Boojum, you see.

----- o -----

Let us now turn to Chapter 2 of the fourth gospel (*John*). The first thing we find in common with the story in *Genesis* is the use of the word κανὰ. It is given now as the name for the fictional Galilean settlement where Jesus attends a marriage feast, turning water into wine.

We recall that in the gospel narrative Jesus is born at Bethlehem [**Hebrew**: *house of bread*]. Now he turns water into *wine* at a location named κανᾶ [*bread baskets*]. Cited here are foods of the type specified for the **lord god** at Gn.1:29.

The story begins like this:

Jn.		
Jn. 2:1	καὶ τῇ ἡμέρᾳ τῇ τρίτῃ γάμος ἐγένετο ἐν **κανὰ** τῆς γαλιλαίας, καὶ ἦν ἡ μήτηρ τοῦ ἰησοῦ ἐκεῖ:	And with the third day a marriage happened in <u>Cana</u> of Galilee, and the mother of Jesus was there.
2:2	ἐκλήθη δὲ καὶ ὁ ἰησοῦς καὶ οἱ μαθηταὶ αὐτοῦ εἰς τὸν γάμον.	But Jesus also was summoned, and his students, to the marriage.
2:3	καὶ ὑστερήσαντος οἴνου λέγει ἡ μήτηρ τοῦ ἰησοῦ πρὸς αὐτόν, οἶνον οὐκ ἔχουσιν.	And with the wine wanting, the mother of Jesus said to him "They do not have (any) wine".
2:4	[καὶ] λέγει αὐτῇ ὁ ἰησοῦς, τί ἐμοὶ καὶ σοί, γύναι; οὔπω ἥκει ἡ ὥρα μου.	[And] Jesus said to her "What (is it) with me and you, woman? My hour has not yet come".

And it continues like this:

Jn. 2:5	λέγει ἡ μήτηρ αὐτοῦ τοῖς διακόνοις, ὅ τι ἂν λέγῃ ὑμῖν ποιήσατε.	His mother said to the servants "Whatever he says to you, do it".
2:6	ἦσαν δὲ ἐκεῖ λίθιναι ὑδρίαι ἓξ κατὰ τὸν καθαρισμὸν τῶν ἰουδαίων κείμεναι, χωροῦσαι ἀνὰ μετρητὰς δύο ἢ τρεῖς.	And there were there six stone water pots laid according to the purification rite of the Judaeans, having a capacity of two or three measures each.
2:7	λέγει αὐτοῖς ὁ ἰησοῦς, γεμίσατε τὰς ὑδρίας ὕδατος. καὶ ἐγέμισαν αὐτὰς ἕως ἄνω.	Jesus said to them "Fill up the water pots with water". And they filled them to the brim.
2:8	καὶ λέγει αὐτοῖς, ἀντλήσατε νῦν καὶ φέρετε τῷ ἀρχιτρικλίνῳ: οἱ δὲ ἤνεγκαν.	And he said to them "Draw (it) out now and take (it) to the president (of the banquet)". And they took it.
2:9	ὡς δὲ ἐγεύσατο ὁ ἀρχιτρίκλινος τὸ ὕδωρ οἶνον γεγενημένον, καὶ οὐκ ᾔδει πόθεν ἐστίν, οἱ δὲ διάκονοι ᾔδεισαν οἱ ἠντληκότες τὸ ὕδωρ, φωνεῖ τὸν νυμφίον ὁ ἀρχιτρίκλινος	But as the president tasted the water-become-wine, and he did not know where it is from but the servants who had drawn the water did know, the president called the bridegroom.

2:10	καὶ λέγει αὐτῷ, πᾶς	And he said to him "Each
	ἄνθρωπος πρῶτον τὸν καλὸν	person puts out the good
	οἶνον τίθησιν, καὶ ὅταν	wine first, and the lesser
	μεθυσθῶσιν τὸν ἐλάσσω· σὺ	once they have become
	τετήρηκας τὸν καλὸν οἶνον	drunk. You have kept the
	ἕως ἄρτι.	good wine until now".

In this story there is no 'chief winepourer', nor (as such) 'chief baker'.

Instead we have ὁ ἀρχιτρίΚΛΙΝος [*the president of the banquet*; *lit*: *chief of three couches*]. The title appears ***three*** times. Four further words are found which contain the letters Κ.α.Ι.Ν. So in the passage from Jn.2:5-10 we have once again ***seven*** words which constitute the '*sign*' for Cain.

We notice too that ἀρΧΙΤρίκλιΝος is one of only two words in the Greek New Testament which not only conceals the name of κάϊν [*Cain*] but also ΧΡΙΣΤόΝ [*Christ*]; the other example is ΚεΧΡηματΙΣμέΝον [*revelation*; *warning*] at Lk.2:26.

It is interesting too that at 2:9 it is the *servants* who are said 'to know' where the wine [οἶνος] has come from. The only word in this passage which provides the letters Ο.Ι.V.Ο.ς is in fact διακόΝΟΙς [*to servants*] at 2:5. Those who can spot this explanation may then stumble upon the fact that the word διακόνοις embodies also the '*sign*' for Cain. As we have seen before, this is typical of the way scripture works. The writer creates multiple entry points to the underlying riddles. In this way the reader is given many chances to gain access to the core of the mystery.

Finally we notice at 2:9 the name of the serpent [ὄφιν]. It is barely concealed within the word νυμφίον [*bridegroom*].

It is surely significant that Jesus begins with water, a token of cleanliness as used at the baptism of John, and promptly turns it into wine. For wine is a token of depravity, as exhibited by Noah (*qv.* Gn.9:21) and by all that pertains to the corrupted 'city' of Sodom (*qv.* Gn.14:18, 19:32). The city of Jerusalem itself is charged in these terms:

LXX	πλὴν τοῦτο τὸ ἀνόμημα	Full (was) this, the iniquity of
Ezk.	σοδομων τῆς ἀδελφῆς σου	your sister Sodom : pride in
16:49	ὑπερηφανία ἐν πλησμονῇ	sufficiency *of breads*, and in
	ἄρτων καὶ ἐν εὐθηνίᾳ **οἴνου**	her squandering an
	ἐσπατάλων αὐτὴ ...	abundance *of wine* ...

We noted in Chapter 5 of this book that at Gn.4:17 Cain seems to 'marry' his own mother Eve, for at that point in the narrative she is still the only woman. Here in the gospel Jesus is present, accompanied by his mother (2:1). But if Jesus is Cain then his mother is Eve. So are we to understand that this story of the marriage at Cana repeats in allegory the earlier marriage of Cain, with the bridegroom identified now as Jesus and the bride once again his mother? Then it seems that Jesus is not only ὁ νυμ**φίος** [*the bridegroom*] but also ἀ**ρχιτ**ρίκλι**νος** [*president*] at the ongoing celebrations.

One way or another, we are assured that this (on the **third** day) was the beginning of the *signs* which Jesus made ...

Jn.	ταύτην ἐποίησεν ἀρχὴν τῶν	Jesus made this beginning of
2:11	σημείων ὁ ἰησοῦς ἐν **κανὰ**	the 'signs' in ***Cana*** of Galilee
	τῆς γαλιλαίας	
	καὶ ἐφανέρωσεν τὴν δόξαν	and revealed his glory, and
	αὐτοῦ, καὶ ἐπίστευσαν εἰς	his students believed in him.
	αὐτὸν οἱ μαθηταὶ αὐτοῦ.	

And no sooner has Jesus left Cana than we are told:

Jn. 2:12	μετὰ τοῦτο κατέβη εἰς **καφαρναοὺμ** αὐτὸς καὶ ἡ μήτηρ αὐτοῦ καὶ οἱ ἀδελφοὶ [αὐτοῦ] καὶ οἱ μαθηταὶ αὐτοῦ, καὶ ἐκεῖ ἔμειναν οὐ πολλὰς ἡμέρας.	And after this he went down to Capharnaum, he and his mother and [his] brothers and his students. And there they stayed not many days.

Does not the spelling of the name **καφαρναοὺμ** [*Capharnaum*] evoke the suggestion of **φαρμακ**εία [*sorcery*]?

The following verse in *Revelation* seems to be connected with this idea:

Rv. 18:23	καὶ φῶς λύχνου οὐ μὴ φάνῃ ἐν σοὶ ἔτι,	And (the) light of a lamp should not be seen in you again.
	καὶ φωνὴ νυμφίου καὶ νύμφης οὐ μὴ ἀκουσθῇ ἐν σοὶ ἔτι·	And (the) sound of a bridegroom and a bride should not be heard in you again.
	ὅτι οἱ ἔμποροί σου ἦσαν οἱ μεγιστᾶνες τῆς γῆς,	Because your mechants were the grandees of the earth,
	ὅτι ἐν τῇ **φαρμ**ακ**ε**ί**α** σου ἐπλανήθησαν πάντα τὰ ἔθνη,	because all the nations were deceived in your sorcery.
18:24	καὶ ἐν αὐτῇ **αἷμα** προφητῶν καὶ ἁγίων εὑρέθη καὶ πάντων τῶν ἐσφαγμένων ἐπὶ τῆς γῆς.	And within it (the) blood of prophets and holy ones is found, and of all those slaughtered upon the earth.

The Sacrifice of the Mass explicitly Prohibited

Let us now examine this passage in the Pauline letter *1 Corinthians*:

1 Cor. 11:17	τοῦτο δὲ παραγγέλλων οὐκ ἐπαινῶ ὅτι <u>οὐκ</u> εἰς τὸ κρεῖσσον ἀλλὰ εἰς τὸ ἧσσον συνέρχεσθε.	But (in) passing this on, I do not commend (you) because you come together <u>not</u> for the better but for the worse.
11:18	πρῶτον μὲν γὰρ συνερχομένων ὑμῶν ἐν ἐκκλησίᾳ ἀκούω σχίσματα ἐν ὑμῖν ὑπάρχειν, καὶ μέρος τι πιστεύω.	For first of all, with your coming together in assembly [*alt*: in a church], I hear schisms exist amongst you, and in some part I believe (it).
11:19	δεῖ γὰρ καὶ αἱρέσεις ἐν ὑμῖν εἶναι, ἵνα [καὶ] οἱ δόκιμοι φανεροὶ γένωνται ἐν ὑμῖν.	For there must be also heresies [*alt*: choices] amongst you in order that [also] those of proven ability may become evident amongst you.
11:20	συνερχομένων οὖν ὑμῶν ἐπὶ τὸ αὐτὸ <u>οὐκ</u> ἔστιν Κυρι**α**κὸ**ν** δεῖπνον φαγεῖν,	Therefore, with your coming together at the same time, it is <u>not</u> to eat a <u>lordish</u> supper.
11:21	ἕκαστος γὰρ τὸ ἴδιον δεῖπνον προλαμβάνει ἐν τῷ φαγεῖν, καὶ ὃς μὲν πεινᾷ, ὃς δὲ μεθύει.	For each anticipates his own 'supper' in the eating. And one hungers but another is drunken!

| 11:22 | μὴ γὰρ οἰκίας οὐκ ἔχετε εἰς τὸ ἐσθίειν καὶ πίνειν; ἢ τῆς ἐκκλησίας τοῦ θεοῦ ΚΑταφροΝεῖτε, καὶ ΚΑταισχύΝετε τοὺς μὴ ἔχοντασ; τί εἴπω ὑμῖν; ἐπαινέσω ὑμᾶσ; ἐν τούτῳ οὐκ ἐπαινῶ. | For do you not have houses for eating and drinking? Or <u>do you disdain</u> the assembly of God and <u>put to shame</u> those not grasping what I say to you? Shall I commend you? In this I do <u>not</u> commend (you). |

The writer addresses those who come together *not* for the better but for the worse. When they come together it should be *not* to eat a lordish supper. For do they not have houses in which to eat and drink?

The '*sign*' for Cain is issued here three times as follows:

- ΚυρΙΑκὸV   : lordish
- ΚΑταφροΝεῖτε   : you disdain
- ΚΑταισχύΝετε   : you put to shame

As the address continues we hear of the 'New Covenant' (*alt*: New Testament). This passage is very important, but widely misconstrued:

| 1 Cor. 11:23 | ἐγὼ γὰρ παρέλαβον ἀπὸ **τοῦ** **κυρίου**, ὃ καὶ παρέδωκα ὑμῖν, ὅτι **ὁ κύριος** ἰησοῦς ἐν τῇ νυκτὶ ᾗ παρεδίδετο ἔλαβεν ἄρτον | For I received from **the lord** that which I also gave away to you, that **the lord** Jesus, in the night on which he was given away, took bread. |

11:24	καὶ εὐχαριστήσας ἔκλασεν καὶ εἶπεν, τοῦτό μού ἐστιν τὸ σῶμα τὸ ὑπὲρ ὑμῶν: τοῦτο ποιεῖτε εἰς τὴν ἐμὴν ἀνάμνησιν.	And giving thanks, he broke (it) and said "This is my body, on your behalf. Do this in my memory".
11:25	ὡσαύτως καὶ τὸ ποτήριον μετὰ τὸ δειπνῆσαι, λέγων, τοῦτο τὸ ποτήριον ἡ **ΚΑΙΝ**ὴ διαθήκη ἐστὶν ἐν τῷ ἐμῷ αἵματι: τοῦτο ποιεῖτε, ὁσάκις ἐὰν πίνητε, εἰς τὴν ἐμὴν ἀνάμνησιν.	Likewise also the cup, after making a meal of it, saying "This cup is the <u>new</u> covenant in my blood. Do this, whenever you drink, in my memory".
11:26	ὁσάκις γὰρ ἐὰν ἐσθίητε τὸν ἄρτον τοῦτον καὶ τὸ ποτήριον πίνητε, τὸν θάνατον **τοῦ κυρίου** καταγγέλλετε, ἄχρις οὗ ἔλθῃ.	For whenever you eat this bread and drink the cup, you declaim the death **of the lord**, until he may come from it.
11:27	ὥστε ὃς ἂν ἐσθίῃ τὸν ἄρτον ἢ πίνῃ τὸ ποτήριον **τοῦ κυρίου** ἀναξίως, ἔνοχος ἔσται τοῦ σώματος καὶ τοῦ αἵματος **τοῦ κυρίου**.	*And so whoever may eat the bread or drink the cup of the lord unworthily <u>will be liable</u> for the body and the blood of the lord.*
11:28	δοκιμαζέτω δὲ ἄνθρωπος ἑαυτόν, καὶ **οὕτως** ἐκ τοῦ ἄρτου ἐσθιέτω καὶ ἐκ τοῦ ποτηρίου πινέτω:	But let a person test himself, and *in this way* let him 'eat' from the bread and 'drink' from the cup.

11:29	ὁ γὰρ ἐσθίων καὶ πίνων κρίμα ἑαυτῷ ἐσθίει καὶ πίνει μὴ δια**κ**ρί**ν**ων τὸ σῶμα.	*For the one eating and drinking eats and drinks judgement to himself,* not <u>distinguishing</u> the body.
11:30	διὰ τοῦτο ἐν ὑμῖν πολλοὶ ἀσθενεῖς καὶ ἄρρωστοι καὶ **κ**οιμῶ**ν**ται ἱ**καν**οί.	On this account many within you (are) weak and sickly, and <u>plenty</u> <u>may be asleep</u>.
11:31	εἰ δὲ ἑαυτοὺς διεκρίνομεν, οὐκ ἂν ἐ**κ**ρι**ν**όμεθα:	But if we were distinguishing (for) ourselves, <u>we would</u> not <u>be judged</u>.
11:32	κρινόμενοι δὲ ὑπὸ [τοῦ] κυρίου παιδευόμεθα, ἵνα μὴ σὺν τῷ κόσμῳ **κ**α**τ**α**κ**ρι**θ**ῶμε**ν**.	But being judged, we are trained under [the] lord so that <u>we may</u> not <u>be condemned</u> with the world.
11:33	ὥστε, ἀδελφοί μου, συνερχόμενοι εἰς τὸ φαγεῖν ἀλλήλους ἐκδέχεσθε.	And so, my brothers, coming together to eat, take up (the argument) from one another.
11:34	εἴ τις πεινᾷ, ἐν οἴκῳ ἐσθιέτω, ἵνα μὴ εἰς κρίμα συνέρχησθε.	If anyone hungers, *let him eat at home so that you do not come together into judgement*.
	τὰ δὲ λοιπὰ ὡς ἂν ἔλθω διατάξομαι.	But the rest I shall make arrangements for, whenever I might come.

The '*sign*' for Cain is issued six more times in this passage as follows:

- καινή   : New (Testament)
- διακρίνων   : distinguishing
- ἱκανοί   : plenty
- κοιμῶνται   : may be asleep
- ἐκρινόμεθα   : we would be judged
- κατακριθῶμεν   : we may be condemned

The death of Jesus is inextricably tied up with eating the bread and drinking the cup:

> For whenever you eat this bread and drink the cup, you declaim
> the death of the lord, until he may come from it.

Moreover those who copy the actions of Jesus in the narrative, eating and drinking *without knowing what they do*, will be held liable for the killing of Cain:

> And so whoever may eat the bread or drink the cup of the lord
> unworthily will be liable for the body and the blood of the lord.

What the process of 'eating and drinking' *should* involve is the testing of your reading and interpretational skills. For as we saw in Chapter 7 of this book, the 'meal' involves 'eating' the scroll of the Bible itself ... which is 'food for the mind' (*qv.* Ezk.3:1; Rv.10:9):

> But let a person test himself, and ***in this way*** let him 'eat' from the
> bread and 'drink' from the cup.

Yet '*the many*' are '*weak*' and they are '*sickly*': and plenty of them may be '*asleep*'. They eat and drink *without knowing what they do*.

Unable to distinguish '*the body*' (which is Cain's body), it is in this way that they seek to derive vicarious benefit from what they think of as the suffering and death of Jesus upon the cross.

In doing so, they renew the sacrifice of Cain. As a direct result they '*eat and drink judgement to themselves*'. According to scripture they will be condemned ... held jointly liable for the suffering and death upon which they have sought to rely:

> For the one eating and drinking eats and drinks judgement to himself, not distinguishing the body.

Remember Cain's problem at Gn.4:7? His mistake was the same. He failed '*to distinguish rightly*'. And so we are told:

> But if we were distinguishing (for) ourselves, we would not be judged.

It is the substantial theme of this book that it is you, the reader, who must *distinguish rightly* ... and so make sense of scripture for yourself.

But to do this you must learn many things ... and of course you must learn the '*sign*' for Cain.

The Trip to Emmaus

Lk. 24:13	καὶ ἰδοὺ δύο ἐξ αὐτῶν ἐν αὐτῇ τῇ ἡμέρᾳ ἦσαν πορευόμενοι εἰς κώμην ἀπέχουσαν σταδίους ἑξήκοντα ἀπὸ ἰερουσαλήμ, ᾗ ὄνομα ἐμμαοῦς,	And look, two of them on that same day were going to a village sixty stadia away from Jerusalem, for which a name (was) Emmaus.
24:14	καὶ αὐτοὶ ὡμίλουν πρὸς ἀλλήλους περὶ πάντων τῶν συμβεβηκότων τούτων.	And they were conversing with one another about all these things which had come to pass.
24:15	καὶ ἐγένετο ἐν τῷ ὁμιλεῖν αὐτοὺς καὶ συζητεῖν καὶ αὐτὸς ἰησοῦς ἐγγίσας συνεπορεύετο αὐτοῖς,	And it happened in their conversing and disputing. And Jesus himself, coming near, was going with them.
24:16	οἱ δὲ ὀφθαλμοὶ αὐτῶν ἐκρατοῦντο τοῦ μὴ ἐπιγνῶναι αὐτόν.	But their eyes were kept from recognising him.
24:17	εἶπεν δὲ πρὸς αὐτούς, τίνες οἱ λόγοι οὗτοι οὓς ἀντιβάλλετε πρὸς ἀλλήλους περιπατοῦντεσ; καὶ ἐστάθησαν σκυθρωποί.	And he said to them "What are these sayings which you are putting to one another as you walk?". And they remained gloomy.

24:18	ἀποκριθεὶς δὲ εἷς ὀνόματι κλεοπᾶς εἶπεν πρὸς αὐτόν, σὺ μόνος παροικεῖς ἰερουσαλὴμ καὶ οὐκ ἔγνως τὰ γενόμενα ἐν αὐτῇ ἐν ταῖς ἡμέραις ταύταισ;	But one (of them) answering, Cleopas by name, said to him "Are you the only one living near Jerusalem and did not learn to know the things which have happened there in these days?"
24:19	καὶ εἶπεν αὐτοῖς, ποῖα; οἱ δὲ εἶπαν αὐτῷ, τὰ περὶ ἰησοῦ τοῦ ναζαρηνοῦ, ὃς ἐγένετο ἀνὴρ προφήτης δυνατὸς ἐν ἔργῳ καὶ λόγῳ ἐναντίον τοῦ θεοῦ καὶ παντὸς τοῦ λαοῦ,	And he said to them "What things?". And they said to him "The things concerning Jesus the Nazarene who became a man, a prophet mighty in work and saying before God and all the people.
24:20	ὅπως τε παρέδωκαν αὐτὸν οἱ ἀρχιερεῖς καὶ οἱ ἄρχοντες ἡμῶν εἰς κρίμα θανάτου καὶ ἐσταύρωσαν αὐτόν.	And how the chief priests and our rulers gave him away to a judgement of death and crucified him.
24:21	ἡμεῖς δὲ ἠλπίζομεν ὅτι αὐτός ἐστιν ὁ μέλλων λυτροῦσθαι τὸν ἰσραήλ: ἀλλά γε καὶ σὺν πᾶσιν τούτοις τρίτην ταύτην ἡμέραν ἄγει ἀφ' οὗ ταῦτα ἐγένετο.	And we hoped that he is the about to redeem Israel. Yes, and with all these things it is now the third day since this happened.
24:22	ἀλλὰ καὶ γυναῖκές τινες ἐξ ἡμῶν ἐξέστησαν ἡμᾶς: γενόμεναι ὀρθριναὶ ἐπὶ τὸ μνημεῖον	But then some of our women amazed us, happening at daybreak upon the tomb.

24:23	καὶ μὴ εὑροῦσαι τὸ σῶμα αὐτοῦ ἦλθον λέγουσαι καὶ ὀπτασίαν ἀγγέλων ἑωραΚέΝΑΙ, οἳ λέγουσιν αὐτὸν ζῆν.	And not finding his body they came claiming also <u>to have seen</u> a vision of angels who said he was alive.
24:24	καὶ ἀπῆλθόν τινες τῶν σὺν ἡμῖν ἐπὶ τὸ μνημεῖον, καὶ εὗρον οὕτως καθὼς καὶ αἱ γυΝΑῖΚές εἶπον, **αὐτὸν δὲ οὐκ εἶδον.**	And some of those with us went off to the tomb and found it just as the <u>women</u> said … ***but they did not see him.***"
24:25	καὶ αὐτὸς εἶπεν πρὸς αὐτούς, ὦ ἀνόητοι καὶ βραδεῖς τῇ καρδίᾳ τοῦ πιστεύειν ἐπὶ πᾶσιν οἷς ἐλάλησαν οἱ προφῆται:	And he said to them "Oh ignorant and slow with the heart for believing in all which the prophets said.
24:26	οὐχὶ ταῦτα ἔδει παθεῖν τὸν χριστὸν καὶ εἰσελθεῖν εἰς τὴν δόξαν αὐτοῦ;	Must not the Christ suffer these things and enter into his glory?"
24:27	καὶ ἀρξάμενος ἀπὸ μωϋσέως καὶ ἀπὸ πάντων τῶν προφητῶν διερμήνευσεν αὐτοῖς ἐν πάσαις ταῖς γραφαῖς τὰ περὶ ἑαυτοῦ.	And beginning from Moses and from all the prophets he interpreted to them in all the scriptures the things concerning himself.
24:28	καὶ ἤγγισαν εἰς τὴν κώμην οὗ ἐπορεύοντο, καὶ αὐτὸς προσεποιήσατο πορρώτερον πορεύεσθαι.	And they neared the village where they were going, and he made ready to go further.

24:29	καὶ παρεβιάσαντο αὐτὸν λέγοντες, μεῖνον μεθ' ἡμῶν, ὅτι πρὸς ἑσπέραν ἐστὶν καὶ κέκλικεν ἤδη ἡ ἡμέρα. καὶ εἰσῆλθεν τοῦ μεῖναι σὺν αὐτοῖς.	And they pressed him, saying "Stay with us because it is evening and the day has declined already". And he went in to stay with them.
24:30	καὶ ἐγένετο ἐν τῷ **Κα**τακλιθ**ῆ**Ναι αὐτὸν μετ' αὐτῶν λαβὼν τὸν ἄρτον εὐλόγησεν καὶ **κλάσας** ἐπεδίδου αὐτοῖς:	And it happened in his <u>being laid down</u> with them. Taking the bread he blessed (it) and <u>breaking</u> gave to them.
24:31	αὐτῶν δὲ διηνοίχθησαν οἱ ὀφθαλμοὶ καὶ ἐπέγνωσαν αὐτόν: καὶ αὐτὸς **ἄφαΝΤος** ἐγένετο ἀπ' αὐτῶν.	But their eyes were opened up and they did recognise him. And he became <u>invisible</u> from them.
24:32	καὶ εἶπαν πρὸς ἀλλήλους, οὐχὶ ἡ καρδία ἡμῶν **Κα**Ιομέ**Ν**η ἦν [ἐν ἡμῖν] ὡς ἐλάλει ἡμῖν ἐν τῇ ὁδῷ, ὡς διήνοιγεν ἡμῖν τὰς γραφάς;	And they said to one another "Was not our heart <u>burning</u> [within us] as he spoke to us on the way, as he opened up to us the scriptures?".

The *'sign'* for Cain is five times implemented in this well known passage. Moreover the word **κλάσας** [*breaking*] evokes **σάκλας** [*Saklas; in Aramaic = **fool**, an alternate name for Satan*].

The impression is given that the travellers in the story should have known the *'sign'*, for it is they who recognise Jesus in his being *laid down* [**Κα**τακλιθ**ῆ**Ναι] with them and in the *breaking* [**κλάσας**] of bread.

Yet Jesus becomes invisible [ἄφαντος] from them. This very word conceals the name for Satan [σαταν].

The travellers finish by deciding that their heart was burning [καιομένη] within them as Jesus spoke to them on the way. Once more we see there the name of Cain.

Some of the manuscript sources for this gospel adapt the final verse a little. What we mostly have is:

οὐχὶ ἡ καρδία ἡμῶν καιομένη ἦν

But some sources give:

οὐχὶ ἡ καρδία ἡμῶν καιομένη ἦν ἐν ἡμῖν

By adding the phrase: ἐν ἡμῖν [*within us*] attention is drawn to the spelling of the adjacent word καιομένη [*burning*].

In this way the reader is prompted to recognise in addition the name of Cain. As we have seen already, such a ploy seems typical of the method of the Gnostic author (or here perhaps of the informed redactor).

Chapter 12

Paul: A False Apostle

No exegesis of New Testament scripture can overlook the rôle which is cast for Paul. Yet we should distinguish two aspects.

First is the turbulent character portrayed in the narrative of *Acts of the Apostles*. As a Pharisee, Saul is devoted to the elimination of those who believe in Jesus. Pursuing his appointed task, he is on the way to Damascus when he suffers a vision which leaves him blinded. But with three days his sight is said to be restored, his convictions now inverted. He develops into a tyrannical promoter (Ac.19:9), advocating all that pertains to Jesus.

The plot deepens when σαῦλος [*Saul*] lands at σαλαμίς [*Salamis*] in Cyprus and his name mysteriously mutates at πάφος [*Paphos*] to παῦλος [*Paul*]. His subsequent Odyssey is recorded in *Acts* where we learn of journeys which span the Mediterranean from Jerusalem in the east to Rome in the west.

The second aspect of the rôle cast for Paul adds substantially to the risk that readers will be led astray. For a series of letters found written in Greek is structured to imply that the writer is Paul. With this tactic the Gnostic authors (whose real identity remains unknown) seek to create the illusion of Paul as a real person.

Indeed their ploy worked well. For in due course the Catholic church embraced these letters as if they were textual witnesses upon which it could rely to further its claim for the deity of Jesus and for what it now said was the doctrine of Paul.

Put another way, these letters were hallowed as historical records and with the status of scripture. But there is no reliable evidence for Jesus as a historical person, let alone for Paul.

The scope of this book precludes a full inquiry into these matters. But with this chapter we shall explore a little further the complex part which is played by Paul.

Reviewing what many have missed

The first thing to understand about *Acts* is that it forms a sequel to the gospel attributed to *Luke*, itself a sequel to *Genesis*. The second is that *Acts* is fiction.

But before we investigate Paul, let us review what so many readers miss in prior scripture. Importantly, we begin with the encounter in Paradise between the serpent and the woman:

LXX	καὶ εἶδεν ἡ γυνὴ ὅτι καλὸν τὸ	And the woman saw the tree
Gn.	ξύλον εἰς βρῶσιν καὶ ὅτι	as good for <u>eating</u> and as
3:6	ἀρεστὸν τοῖς ὀφθαλμοῖς	agreeable <u>with</u> the <u>eyes</u> to
	ἰδεῖν	see
	καὶ ὡραῖόν ἐστιν τοῦ	and (that) it is beautiful for
	καταΝοῆσαι	<u>understanding fully</u>.
	καὶ λαβοῦσα τοῦ καρποῦ	And taking (some) of its fruit,
	αὐτοῦ ἔφαγεν καὶ ἔδωκεν καὶ	she ate. And she gave
	τῷ ἀνδρὶ αὐτῆς μετ' αὐτῆς καὶ	(some) also to her man with
	ἔφαγον	her, and they ate.

The woman 'saw' the tree as:

καλὸν ... εἰς βρῶσιν [good for *eating*]

and as:

ἀρεστὸν τοῖς ὀφθαλμοῖς ἰδεῖν [agreeable *with the eyes* to see]

Manifested here in the text is ὁ ὄφις [*the serpent*]. It is a creature barely disguised from the hearing and sight of any reader in Greek.

In addition, the remarkable 'tree' was and still is:

ὡραῖον ... τοῦ ΚΑΤΑVοῆσαι [beautiful for *understanding fully*]

The word ΚΑΤΑVοῆσαι [*to understand fully*] scores on two counts. It conceals the name of σατΑV [*Satan*] as well as that of Κάïν [*Cain*]. In the earlier chapters of this book we have seen that hiding these names by dispersing them within other words is a technique:

- Implemented consistently from LXX *Genesis* through to the gospels and other NT texts

- Disclosed to the more attentive reader through the extensive use of didactic riddles, with an important contribution from counting schemes

- Evidently planned, controlled and fully intended by the writers

In the narrative of *Genesis* the woman is deceived by all that the serpent has to offer. She is deceived above all by the attractive suggestion that she can '*be like the gods*' and '*live for ever*' (Gn.3:4-5).

She '*eats*' without recognising the true nature of the meal which has been set before her. Once she has eaten, the consequences are irreversible. The offspring of her ill-fated union with the serpent is evil Cain (Gn.4:1; 1 Jn.3:12). No one now can dispose of Cain. His divine nature renders him immune to death. It is the theme of New Testament scripture (relying upon what is said at Gn.4:10-14) that Cain prevails as a curse over all his descendants.

Cain is the firstborn of all creation (Col.1:15), lord of lords and king of kings (Rv.17:14, 19:16). He is the Christ (the Messiah), anointed with the blood of his brother Abel:

| Rv. 19:13 | καὶ περιβεβλημένος ἱμάτιον βεβαμμένον αἵματι, καὶ κέκληται τὸ ὄνομα αὐτοῦ ὁ λόγος τοῦ θεοῦ. | And thrown around him a garment dipped in blood, and his name has been called the Logos of God |

Thus we have in *Galatians*:

| Ga. 3:13 | χριστὸς ἡμᾶς ἐξηγόρασεν ἐκ τῆς κατάρας τοῦ νόμου γενόμενος ὑπὲρ ἡμῶν κατάρα, ὅτι γέγραπται, ἐπικατάρατος πᾶς ὁ κρεμάμενος ἐπὶ ξύλου, | Christ bought us off from the curse of the Law, he becoming a curse upon us. Because it is written, "Cursed is everyone who hangs upon a tree" (Dt.21:23) |

The story in *Genesis* is fiction. Yet remarkably every reader of the Bible is exposed to the same temptation as the woman in the story; for it turns out that subsequent scripture has been written to present recursively to the reader just the same attractive suggestion as that first posed by the serpent to Eve. Then let *all* beware of this tainted meal which is scripture. Many have been led astray before you. The risk is real that if you do not understand what has been written then you may be next to succumb.

It is by using their eyes and ears that those who read in Greek should be able to spot what the writers have done. Then, _understanding fully_, they will recognise Jesus as Cain ... and the 'father' to whom Jesus prays as the serpent. It is by acquiring this *knowledge* that they may be saved from many further 'sins' (*ie.* mistakes).

But what of those who read in translation, and those who struggle to solve the riddles? These are the blind at the scriptural banquet. Vital *knowledge* lies hidden from their eyes. Thus deprived, they are vulnerable to all the compositional tricks which subsist in the pages of scripture, notionally put there to serve the serpent's purpose. These persons are at a serious disadvantage; and yet they do not know it. Failing to recognise what the authors have done, they generally go on to mistake what is set forth as attractive (but evil) for what is set forth as good.

Next, in our review of what many have missed, comes this from Isaiah:

LXX	καὶ εἶπα ὦ τάλας ἐγώ ὅτι	And I said "Oh, wretched
Is.	ΚατανέVυγμΟI ὅτι ἄνθρωπος	(am) I, because <u>I have been</u>
6:5	ὢν καὶ ἀκάθαρτα χείλη ἔχων	<u>stupefied</u> ... because of
	ἐν μέσῳ λαοῦ ἀκάθαρτα	being a person and having
	χείλη ἔχοντος	unclean lips, in the midst of a
		people having unclean lips".
	ἐγὼ οἰκῶ καὶ τὸν βασιλέα	I was there, and the king,
	κύριον σαβαωθ εἶδον τοῖς	**lord Sabaoth**, I saw <u>with</u> my
	ὀφθαλμοῖς μου	(own) <u>eyes</u>.

Isaiah declares how he sees *with his eyes* the lord **Sabaoth**, the dwelling filled with his glory. And when we turn *with our own eyes* to the text, it is without difficulty that once again we see the serpent [Οφ...Iϛ]. This is how Greek scripture works. To be properly informed we must learn to read in the right kind of way. This is the remedy for 'blindness'.

In the narrative, no sooner has Isaiah encountered the serpent than we find him volunteering to act as mouthpiece for this duplicate deity. Isaiah responds as if he himself were blind. Henceforth it is through the advocacy of this fictional 'prophet' that the people of Israel will be deceived into embracing the serpent as their 'god' ... the serpent who is cast by the authors as Satan, the impostor and opponent to **God** himself. To the extent that it goes unrecognised, this Gnostic theme of scripture engenders a cultural calamity. For it seems that no sooner do most people read scripture than promptly they embrace Satan as if he were God.

This passage in Isaiah is important precisely because it is recursive of scripture's original theme. If misunderstood, it has the potential to extend and to reinforce the calamity … but if understood, to resolve it.

It is to help his readers resolve it that the writer now presents them with the stimulus required to rouse them from their lethargy. Accordingly the narrative continues:

LXX Is. 6:9	καὶ εἶπεν πορεύθητι καὶ εἰπὸν τῷ λαῷ τούτῳ	And he said "Go and say to this people:
	ἀκοῇ ἀκούσετε καὶ οὐ μὴ συνῆτε	With hearing, you will hear, but **NOT** understand.
	καὶ βλέποντες βλέψετε καὶ οὐ μὴ ἴδητε	And seeing, you will see, but **NOT** perceive.
6:10	ἐπαχύνθη γὰρ ἡ καρδία τοῦ λαοῦ τούτου	For the heart of this people has grown fat.
	καὶ τοῖς ὠσὶν αὐτῶν βαρέως ἤκουσαν καὶ τοὺς ὀφθαλμοὺς αὐτῶν ἐκάμμυσαν	And with their ears they heard heavily and they half-closed their eyes …
	μήποτε ἴδωσιν τοῖς ὀφθαλμοῖς	lest they should perceive with the eyes,
	καὶ τοῖς ὠσὶν ἀκούσωσιν	and hear with the ears,
	καὶ τῇ καρδίᾳ συνῶσιν	and understand with the heart,
	καὶ ἐπιστρέψωσιν	and they should turn back,
	καὶ ἰάσομαι αὐτούς	and I may heal them".

The warning clues are all there, thickly studded in the text for those with attentive *eyes* and *ears*, and those blessed with hearts for *understanding*. It was in Chapter 7 of this book that we first saw how the name of the serpent may be seen and heard in this pivotal passage. Its importance to the NT authors may be judged from the fact that they repeat it verbatim, first at Mt.13:14 and then at Ac.28:26, the point in the narrative where we find Paul arriving in Rome and seeking (with mixed results) to persuade the Jews about Jesus.

Isaiah is plainly deluded. In the story he becomes possessed, the unwitting agent of the serpent he thinks of as God. His mistake is the same as that made by Cain. The rôle he will now play is that of ψευδοπροφήτης [*a false prophet*]. It is a status which should be familiar to us from the gospels:

Lk.	οὐαὶ ὅταν ὑμᾶς καλῶς	Woe when all the Persons
6:26	εἴπ**ωσιν** πάντες οἱ ἄνθρωποι,	<u>may speak</u> well of you,
	κατὰ τὰ αὐτὰ γὰρ ἐποίουν	for their fathers did the same
	τοῖς ψευδοπρ**οφ**ήτα**ις** οἱ πατέρες αὐτῶν.	to the <u>false prophets</u>.

The technique we have witnessed with Isaiah, the introduction of the 'deluded prophet' within the narrative of scripture, is a powerful tool in the hands of the writer. For is it not in human nature to follow unsuspectingly the one who claims access to the divine?

- The flock follows the pastor.

- The pastor *claims* to be well informed as to what is good.

- The flock will follow him anyway, whether he is right or not.

It is upon this axiom that the authors of scripture rely. The parallel between Isaiah and Paul is drawn at Ac.28:25. Surely amongst the greatest weaknesses of the human spirit is a reluctance to question the competence of those who promote themselves as leaders.

The Conversion of Saul

When in *Acts* we first encounter Saul, it is he who has made the arrangements for Stephen to be stoned to death (Ac.7:58, 8:1). He is busy persecuting all those who seek to follow Jesus.

The writer now qualifies Saul with the account of a sudden conversion to Christ. He proceeds to exploit his 'convert' in the ruthlesss quest to lead astray the more impressionable amongst his readers. For in his narrative the writer has developed a figure who will prove deeply compelling to many expressly on account of his remarkable *volte-face*. Yet it should not be difficult for us to recognise that here is one more 'deluded prophet'.

Let us see how the conversion of Saul comes about:

Ac.	ὁ δὲ σαῦλος, ἔτι ἐμπνέων	But Saul, still breathing
9:1	ἀπειλῆς καὶ φόνου εἰς τοὺς	threat(s) and murder at the
	μαθητὰς τοῦ κυρίου,	students of the lord, coming
	προσελθὼν τῷ ἀρχιερεῖ	to the chief priest
9:2	ᾐτήσατο παρ' αὐτοῦ	Asked for letters from him for
	ἐπιστολὰς εἰς δαμασκὸν	the synagogues at
	πρὸς τὰς συναγωγάς,	Damascus so that if he found
	ὅπως ἐάν τινας εὔρῃ τῆς	anyone being of the Way,
	ὁδοῦ ὄντας, ἄνδρας τε καὶ	both men and <u>women</u>, he
	γυναῖκας, δεδεμένους	might take them bound to
	ἀγάγῃ εἰς ἰερουσαλήμ.	Jerusalem.
9:3	ἐν δὲ τῷ πορεύεσθαι ἐγένετο	But in the going he happened
	αὐτὸν ἐγγίζειν τῇ δαμασκῷ,	to come near to Damascus.
	ἐξαίφνης τε αὐτὸν	And suddenly there flashed
	περιήστραψεν φῶς ἐκ τοῦ	around him a light from
	οὐρανοῦ,	Heaven.

9:4	καὶ πεσὼν ἐπὶ τὴν γῆν ἤκουσεν φωνὴν λέγουσαν αὐτῷ, σαοὺλ σαούλ, τί με διώκεισ;	And falling upon the earth, he heard a voice saying to him "Saul, Saul, why are you pursuing me?"
9:5	εἶπεν δέ, τίς εἶ, κύριε;	So he said "Who are you, lord"?
	ὁ δέ, **ἐγώ εἰμι** ἰησοῦς ὃν σὺ διώκεις:	But he (said) "**I AM** Jesus, whom you are pursuing.
9:6	ἀλλὰ ἀνάστηθι καὶ εἴσελθε εἰς τὴν πόλιν, καὶ λαληθήσεταί σοι ὅ τί σε δεῖ ποιεῖν.	But <u>rise up</u> and go into the city, and it will be told to you what you must do".
9:7	οἱ δὲ ἄνδρες οἱ συνοδεύοντες αὐτῷ εἱστήκεισαν ἐνεοί, ἀκούοντες μὲν τῆς φωνῆς μηδένα δὲ θεωροῦντες.	But the men on the way with him <u>stood</u> dumbfounded, hearing the voice but beholding nothing.
9:8	ἠγέρθη δὲ σαῦλος ἀπὸ τῆς γῆς, ἀνεῳγμένων δὲ τῶν ὀφθαλμῶν αὐτοῦ οὐδὲν ἔβλεπεν: χειραγωγοῦντες δὲ αὐτὸν εἰσήγαγον εἰς δαμασκόν.	And Saul was roused up from the ground, but with opening up his eyes he saw nothing. And <u>leading</u> him <u>by the hand</u>, they led on into Damascus.
9:9	καὶ ἦν ἡμέρας τρεῖς μὴ βλέπων, καὶ οὐκ ἔφαγεν οὐδὲ ἔπιεν.	And he was three days not seeing, and he did not eat nor drink.

Why does this event take place '*near to Damascus*'? It is surely recursive of the story at LXX Gn.14:14-24 where it is near Damascus that Abraham encounters Melchizedek, *King of Salem* and *King of Sodom*, the one who brings forth bread and wine (there are eight pieces of '*bread*' visible in the verse where Damascus is first mentioned at

Ac.9:2 above). But Saul, being 'blind', would not be able to see the vast quantities of '*bread*' (ασ, ας) dispersed in this passage ... which seems to explain why we are told that '*he did not eat nor drink*' (the writer's construction resembles that which he has developed already at Lk.4:2, see Chapter 10 of this book).

The impressionable Saul is *led by the hand*, assisted by those who '*saw nothing*'. Even with his eyes '*opened up*', Saul himself '*sees nothing*' (Ac.9:8). For ourselves however we may notice that concealed within this passage are the names for Satan (*rise up*), for Cain (*they stood dumbfounded*) and for Christ (*leading* him *by the hand*).

But we are not done yet. The narrative continues:

Ac.	ἦν δέ τις μαθητὴς ἐν	But there was a certain
9:10	δαμασκῷ ὀνόματι ἀνανίας,	student in Damascus, by
	καὶ εἶπεν πρὸς αὐτὸν ἐν	name Ananias. And the lord
	ὁράματι ὁ κύριος, ἀνανία. ὁ	said to him in a dream
	δὲ εἶπεν,	"Ananias". So he said:
	ἰδοὺ ἐγώ, κύριε.	"Look (it is) I, lord".
9:11	ὁ δὲ κύριος πρὸς αὐτόν,	But the lord (said) to him
	ἀναστὰς πορεύθητι ἐπὶ	"Rising up, go to the street
	τὴν ῥύμην τὴν καλουμένην	called straight and seek in a
	εὐθεῖαν καὶ ζήτησον ἐν οἰκίᾳ	house a Judaean (of) Tarsus,
	ἰούδα σαῦλον ὀνόματι	Saul by name.
	ταρσέα:	
	ἰδοὺ γὰρ προσεύχεται,	For look, he is praying."
9:12	καὶ εἶδεν ἄνδρα [ἐν ὁράματι]	And he saw [in a dream] a
	ἀνανίαν ὀνόματι εἰσελθόντα	man, Ananias by name,
	καὶ ἐπιθέντα αὐτῷ [τὰσ]	coming in and placing on him
	χεῖρας ὅπως ἀναβλέψῃ.	[the] hands in such a manner
		that he might see.

Presumably the street is 'straight' in conformity with 'the straight way of the lord' (Is.40:3, 42:16, etc). The general idea is that the path for those who are being deluded is made *to appear* straight and easy. And Ananias places upon Saul *the hands* [τὰσ χεῖρας] '*in such a manner that he might see*'. The scenario evokes that at Mk.8:23 (see Chapter 10 of this book).

Ac. 9:13	ἀπεκρίθη δὲ ἀνανίας, κύριε, ἤκουσα ἀπὸ πολλῶν περὶ τοῦ ἀνδρὸς τούτου, ὅσα κακὰ τοῖς ἁγίοις σου ἐποίησεν ἐν ἰερουσαλήμ:	But Ananias answered "Lord, I heard from many about this man, how much evil he did to your holy ones in Jerusalem.
9:14	καὶ ὧδε ἔχει ἐξουσίαν παρὰ τῶν ἀρχιερέων δῆσαι πάντας τοὺς ἐπικαλουμένους τὸ ὄνομά σου.	And in this he has authority from the chief priests to bind all those calling upon your name."
9:15	εἶπεν δὲ πρὸς αὐτὸν ὁ κύριος, πορεύου, ὅτι σκεῦος ἐκλογῆς ἐστίν μοι οὗτος τοῦ βαστάσαι τὸ ὄνομά μου ἐνώπιον ἐθνῶν τε καὶ βασιλέων υἱῶν τε ἰσραήλ:	But the lord said to him "Go, for this one is a chosen vessel for me, to bear my name before both nations and kings, and sons of Israel.
9:16	ἐγὼ γὰρ ὑποδείξω αὐτῷ ὅσα δεῖ αὐτὸν ὑπὲρ τοῦ ὀνόματός μου παθεῖν.	For I shall show him how much he must suffer on behalf of my name."

| 9:17 | ἀπῆλθεν δὲ ἀνανίας καὶ εἰσῆλθεν εἰς τὴν οἰκίαν, καὶ ἐπιθεὶς ἐπ' αὐτὸν τὰς χεῖρας εἶπεν, σαοὺλ ἀδελφέ, ὁ κύριος ἀπέσταλκέν με, ἰησοῦς ὁ ὀφθείς σοι ἐν τῇ ὁδῷ ᾗ ἤρχου, ὅπως ἀναβλέψῃς καὶ πλησθῇς πνεύματος ἁγίου. | So Ananias went off and entered into the **house**. And placing upon him the hands, he said "Brother Saul, the lord **has sent** me - Jesus, **the one seen** by you in the way by which you were coming - so you may look up and may be filled with a holy spirit". |

Saul is to be σκεῦος ἐκλογῆς [*a chosen vessel*] for the **lord**. The function of a vessel is to contain something … something which goes unseen within. But Ananias, in placing hands upon Saul, refers to Jesus with the phrase:

ὁ ὀφθείς σοι
the one seen by you

It is without difficulty that we realise the one supposed '*to be seen*' by us (as readers) is ὁ ὄφις [*the serpent*]. This phrase is not a new one. Its first use is at LXX Gn.31:13 where Jacob recounts a startling vision of his own. But its use here makes all the more sense if we recall the association claimed by Jesus:

ἐγὼ καὶ ὁ πατὴρ ἕν ἐσμεν   (Jn.10:30)
I and the father are one

Now who can fail to be struck by the similarity between this passage and the '*Call of Isaiah*'? In each case the serpent is manifested, in each case concealed in the text. And in each case we end up in the narrative with a 'prophet' who goes on to act as an advocate for all that pertains not to **God** … but to the impostor, the **lord god**.

The narrative continues:

Ac. 9:18	καὶ εὐθέως ἀπέπεσαν αὐτοῦ ἀπὸ τῶν ὀφθαλμῶν ὡς λεπίδες, ἀνέβλεψέν τε, καὶ **ἀναστὰς** ἐβαπτίσθη,	And immediately there fell away from his eyes (something) like scales. He both looked up and, <u>rising up</u>, was baptised.
9:19	καὶ λαβὼν τροφὴν ἐνίσχυσεν. ἐγένετο δὲ μετὰ τῶν ἐν δαμ**ασ**κῷ μαθητῶν ἡμέρ**ας** τιν**άς**,	And taking nourishment, he gained strength. But it happened <u>within the students in Damascus for some days</u>.

There fell away from his eyes something like scales. There is a strong element of suggestion here. Every species of serpent has the eyes covered over by scaly lids. And with Saul's '*rising up*' we see concealed the name of Satan.

Next we are told that Saul was taking nourishment. And there again we see the bread concealed (**ασ, ας**). Three pieces are to be found '<u>*within the students in Damascus for some days*</u>'.

Ac. 9:20	καὶ εὐθέως ἐν ταῖς συναγωγαῖς ἐκήρυσσεν τὸν ἰησοῦν ὅτι οὗτός ἐστιν ὁ υἱὸς τοῦ θεοῦ.	And immediately in the synagogues he preached Jesus, that *this one* is the son of God.

| 9:21 | ἐξίσταντο δὲ πάντες οἱ ἀκούοντες καὶ ἔλεγον, οὐχ οὗτός ἐστιν ὁ πορθήσ**ας** εἰς ἰερουσαλὴμ τοὺς ἐπ**ικα**λουμέ**ν**ους τὸ ὄνομα τοῦτο, καὶ ὦδε εἰς τοῦτο ἐληλύθει ἵνα δεδεμένους αὐτοὺς ἀγάγῃ ἐπὶ τοὺς ἀρχιερεῖσ; | But all those hearing were amazed and they said "Isn't it *this one* who in Jerusalem ravaged those <u>calling upon</u> this name, and had come here for this, that he might take them bound to the chief priests?". |

There is a play here upon which person may be intended by the use of the pronoun **οὗτός** [*this one*]. With its use by Saul at 9:20, Jesus is identified as 'son of god'. But with its use by 'those hearing' at 9:21, the phrase now refers to Saul.

| Ac. 9:22 | σαῦλος δὲ μᾶλλον ἐνεδυναμοῦτο καὶ συνέχυννεν [τοὺσ] ἰουδαίους τοὺς **κα**τοικοῦ**ντας** ἐν δαμ**ασ**κῷ, συμβιβάζων ὅτι οὗτός ἐστιν ὁ χριστός. | But Saul was being more empowered, and he confounded [the] Judaeans, those <u>settling down</u> in Damascus, inferring that *this one* is the Christ. |
| 9:23 | ὡς δὲ ἐπληροῦντο ἡμέραι **ἱκαν**αί, συνεβουλεύσαντο οἱ ἰουδαῖοι ἀνελεῖν αὐτόν: | But as <u>sufficient</u> days were fulfilled, the Judaeans agreed to raise him up [*alt*: to kill him]. |

At 9:22 Saul infers that '*this one*' is the Christ. Is he still speaking about Jesus? It seems clear that for the Judaeans '*this one*' still means Saul. On the strength of this confusion the Judaeans will now treat Saul in the same way they treated Jesus. They will try to kill him (9:23).

So much in scripture is recursive. Experienced readers will spot that:

- Those in Jerusalem ἐπικαλουμένους [*calling upon*] the name of Jesus are tagged with the name of Κάϊν [*Cain*].

- These Judaeans κατοικοῦντας [*settling down*] in Damascus are tagged with the names of both σαταν [*Satan*] and Κάϊν [*Cain*].

- It is with ἱκαναί [*sufficient*] days that the Judaeans plan to kill Saul, much as they sought to kill Jesus before him.

Paul's Accounts of his own Conversion

The details of Paul's conversion are later recounted by Paul himself. In the narrative of *Acts* he gives two accounts. Here is the first:

Ac. 22:6	ἐγένετο δέ μοι πορευομένῳ καὶ ἐγγίζοντι τῇ δαμασκῷ περὶ μεσημβρίαν ἐξαίφνης ἐκ τοῦ οὐρανοῦ περιαστράψαι φῶς ἱκανὸν περὶ ἐμέ,	But it happened, with my going and nearing Damascus around midday. Suddenly from Heaven there flashed around me a <u>sufficient</u> light.
22:7	ἔπεσά τε εἰς τὸ ἔδαφος καὶ ἤκουσα φωνῆς λεγούσης μοι, σαοὺλ σαούλ, τί με διώκεισ;	And I fell to the ground and heard a voice saying to me "Saul, Saul, why are you pursuing me?".
22:8	ἐγὼ δὲ ἀπεκρίθην, τίς εἶ, κύριε; εἶπέν τε πρός με, ἐγώ εἰμι ἰησοῦς ὁ ναζωραῖος ὃν σὺ διώκεις.	So <u>I replied</u> "Who are you, lord?". And he said to me "**I AM** Jesus the Nazarene whom you are pursuing".
22:9	οἱ δὲ σὺν ἐμοὶ ὄντες τὸ μὲν φῶς ἐθεάσαντο τὴν δὲ φωνὴν οὐκ ἤκουσαν τοῦ λαλοῦντός μοι.	But those being with me, <u>they did perceive</u> the light but did not hear the voice speaking to me".

The first thing to notice is Paul's claim that the 'light' seen by him was *sufficient* [ἱκανὸν][1] and that those with him *did perceive* it [ἐθεάσαντο][1]. Is it not clear what the writer intends by referring to the 'light' in a manner so suggestive?

The second thing important to notice is this: in Paul's report we have on our hands a direct contradiction.

Here again is the statement from the primary narrative:

Ac. 9:7	οἱ δὲ ἄνδρες οἱ συνοδεύοντες αὐτῷ εἰστήΚεισΑΝ ἐνεοί, ἀκούοντες μὲν τῆς φωνῆς μηδένα δὲ θεωροῦντες.	But the men on the way with him stood dumbfounded, hearing the voice but beholding nothing.

In that verse the writer informs us that Saul's fellow travellers *heard* the voice but *saw* nothing. Then at 22:9 (above) the writer has Paul himself make *the opposite claim* … that those with him *did* see the light but did *not* hear the voice.

This contradiction, displaying as it does all the freedom of construction available to a writer of narrative fiction, roundly invalidates the witness of Paul. If he cannot report correctly the circumstances of his own conversion then he cannot be relied upon at all.

Here is Paul's second account, given this time to King Agrippa:

Ac. 26:15	ἐγὼ δὲ εἶπα, τίς εἶ, κύριε; ὁ δὲ κύριος εἶπεν, ἐγώ εἰμι ἰησοῦς ὃν σὺ διώκεις.	But I said "Who are you, lord". So the lord said "I AM Jesus whom you are pursuing.
26:16	ἀλλὰ ἀνάστηθι καὶ στῆθι ἐπὶ τοὺς πόδας σου: εἰς τοῦτο γὰρ ὤφθην σοι, προχειρίσασθαί σε ὑπηρέτην καὶ μάρτυρα ὧν τε εἶδές [με] ὧν τε ὀφθήσομαί σοι,	But rise up and stand upon your feet. Because for this I was seen by you, to appoint you an assistant and witness, both from what things you saw [me] and from what things I shall be seen by you.
26:17	ἐξαιρούμενός σε ἐκ τοῦ λαοῦ καὶ ἐκ τῶν ἐθνῶν, εἰς οὓς ἐγὼ ἀποστέλλω σε	Delivering you from the people and from the nations to which I send you

26:18	ἀνοῖξαι ὀφθαλμοὺς αὐτῶν,	To open up their eyes for
	τοῦ ἐπιστρέψαι ἀπὸ σκότους	turning away from darkness
	εἰς φῶς	to light
	καὶ τῆς ἐξουσίας τοῦ	and (turning away) from the
	σατανᾶ ἐπὶ τὸν θεόν,	authority of <u>Satan</u> over God,
	τοῦ λαβεῖν αὐτοὺς ἄφεσιν	for taking them forgiveness
	ἁμαρτιῶν καὶ κλῆρον ἐν τοῖς	of sins [*alt*: of mistakes] and
	ἡγιασμένοις πίστει τῇ εἰς ἐμέ.	an inheritance amongst
		those hallowed by a faith
		which is in me.

ὀφθήσομαί σοι   (Ac.26:16)
I shall be seen by you

What may be 'seen' in that phrase is plainly ὄφις [*a serpent*]. Two verses later we have the explicit mention of Satan's authority. It is '*the authority of Satan over God*' which (if possible) they are not to notice when they '*open up their eyes*' and '*turn to light*'.

So Paul has been appointed by the serpent, sent to the people and nations in the rôle of deluded prophet. And this is his task:

- To open up their eyes for turning *away* from darkness to light (remember that at Gn.1:2 darkness was the attribute of **God**; the '*light*' does not intrude until Gn.1:3).

- To open up their eyes for turning *away* from the authority of Satan over God (but those who look away will miss the trick).

- To take them forgiveness of sins (it is Satan who seeks to discount the impact of sin and the consequence of fatal mistakes).

- To convey to them the promise of '*an inheritance amongst those hallowed by a faith which is in me*' (and by the time they discover who '*me*' is, and what this particular '*inheritance*' entails, it may well be too late).

Paul counts himself as a False Apostle

By the process of his conversion, Paul counts himself as thirteenth amongst the apostles (*eg.* 1 Cor.15:9). But here is confirmation that, just like the others, Paul is a *false* apostle. The letter *2 Corinthians* is presented as if written by Paul. But Paul, taking after Satan himself, is given to boasting. Here he lets his guard slip, disclosing his true rôle:

2 Cor. 11:10	ἔστιν ἀλήθεια χριστοῦ ἐν ἐμοὶ ὅτι ἡ καύχησις αὕτη οὐ φραγήσεται εἰς ἐμὲ ἐν τοῖς ΚλίμΟσΙΝ τῆς ἀχαΐας.	It is a truth of Christ within me that this boasting will not be fenced into me in the latitudes of Achaia
11:11	διὰ τί; ὅτι οὐκ ἀγαπῶ ὑμᾶσ; ὁ θεὸς οἶδεν.	On account of what? Because I do not love you? God knows.
11:12	ὃ δὲ ποιῶ καὶ ποιήσω, ἵνα ἐκκόψω τὴν ἀφορμὴν τῶν θελόντων ἀφορμήν, ἵνα ἐν ᾧ ΚαυχῶVΤΟΙ εὑρεθῶΣΙΝ καθὼς καὶ ἡμεῖς.	But the one I make also I shall make, so that I may cut out the starting point of those wishing for a starting point, so that in whom they boast *they may be found just as we (are) also*.
11:13	οἱ γὰρ τοιοῦτοι ψευδαπόστολοι, ἐργάται δόλιοι, μεΤΟΣχημΟτιζόμεΝοι εἰς ἀποστόλους χριστοῦ.	For such (are) false apostles, deceitful workers, transformed into apostles of Christ.
11:14	καὶ οὐ θαῦμα, αὐτὸς γὰρ ὁ ΣΟΤΟΝᾶς μετασχηματίζεται εἰς ἄγγελον φωτός:	And no wonder, for Satan himself is transformed into an angel of light.

11:15	οὐ μέγα οὖν εἰ καὶ	No great thing then if also
	οἱ διάκονοι αὐτοῦ	his <u>servants</u>
	μεTασχημaτίζοVται	<u>are transformed</u>
	ὡς διάκονοι δικαιοσύνης,	as <u>servants</u> <u>of righteousness</u>,
	ὧν τὸ τέλος ἔσται κατὰ τὰ	of whom the end will be
	ἔργα αὐτῶν.	according to their works.

Paul distinctly numbers himself with those who are:

- **ψευδαπόστολοι**   : false apostles

- **ἐργάται δόλιοι**   : deceitful workers

- **διάκονοι τοῦ σατανᾶ**   : servants of Satan

In this way Paul discloses his *own* status.

This status explains many things.

Saul's Mysterious Change of Name

To avoid being drawn into a spiral of confusion it is vital in scripture to know who's who. The challenge deepens with the passage in *Acts* in which Saul emerges with the identity of Paul. The name change comes about as follows. Saul and Barnabas have been sent from Antioch to Cyprus:

Ac. 13:6	διελθόντες δὲ ὅλην τὴν νῆσον ἄχρι πάφου εὗρον ἄνδρα τινὰ μάγον ψευδοπροφήτην ἰουδαῖον ᾧ ὄνομα βαριησοῦ,	But going through the whole island as far as Paphos, they found a certain man, a wizard, a Judaean false prophet by the name of Bar-Jesus
13:7	ὃς ἦν σὺν τῷ ἀνθυπάτῳ σεργίῳ παύλῳ, ἀνδρὶ συνετῷ. οὗτος προσκαλεσάμενος βαρναβᾶν καὶ σαῦλον ἐπεζήτησεν ἀκοῦσαι τὸν λόγον τοῦ θεοῦ:	Who was together with the proconsul Sergius Paul, an intelligent man. This one, <u>calling in</u> Barnabas and Saul, was seeking to hear the 'Logos' [*alt*: the message] of God.
13:8	ἀνθίστατο δὲ αὐτοῖς ἐλύμας ὁ μάγος, οὕτως γὰρ μεθερμηνεύεται τὸ ὄνομα αὐτοῦ, ζητῶν διαστρέψαι τὸν ἀνθύπατον ἀπὸ τῆς πίστεως.	And Elumas the wizard (for so his name is interpreted) <u>stood against</u> them, seeking to pervert the proconsul from the faith.
13:9	σαῦλος δέ, ὁ καὶ παῦλος, πλησθεὶς πνεύματος ἁγίου ἀτενίσας εἰς αὐτὸν	But Saul, who also (was) Paul, filled with a holy spirit, <u>staring</u> at him ...

There are several things to notice. First is that the wizard *stood against* [ἀνθίστατο] them, seeking to pervert the *proconsul* [ἀνθύπατον] from the faith. Our attention may be drawn to the fact that both words include the groups ἀνθ and ατο. Then we notice that with modest rearrangement they yield respectively θάνατος and θάνατον [*death*].

Next, in accordance with what we learned in Chapter 9 of this book, we see that when the wizard *stood against* [ἀνθίστατο] them there lies concealed the name of σαταν [*Satan*]. Indeed with Saul *staring* [ἀτενίσας] at the wizard it may be hard to miss the identity intended.

Barnabas (*aka.* Joseph; *qv.* Ac.4:36) is mentioned once in this passage. And at first there appear to be three more persons here:

- **Bar-Jesus** the wizard, *a Judaean false prophet*.

- **Sergius Paul** the proconsul, apparently a Roman governor in Cyprus. In Greek he is σεργίος παύλος.

- **Saul**, the Pharisee from Tarsus (in Greek he is σαούλ or σαῦλος).

The name for the wizard means '*son of Jesus*'. From the description given, this character could be an alter-ego for Saul himself. The possibility is reinforced when we are told that his name is 'interpreted' as ἐλύμας [*Elumas*]. It is close to being an anagram for σαμουήλ [*Samuel*; perhaps implying *blind*], within which we may find also the name of the recently blinded σαούλ [*Saul*]. Then both Samuel and Saul are mentioned explicitly a few verses further on at Ac.13:20-21 which could be intended to draw attention to the anagrams already presented.

Finally we have the assertion at 13:9 that σαῦλος [*Saul*] was 'also' παῦλος [*Paul*]. So are we to understand now that Saul has merged his identity with the 'intelligent' Roman proconsul Paul? It is hard to understand what has happened, but this would align with scripture's recursive theme of what is evil displacing what is good. Whatever the case, the story moves on with the activities of Paul … who shortly turns out to hold Roman citizenship, a status first apparent at Ac.16:37.

Ac. 13:10	εἶπεν, ὦ πλήρης παντὸς δόλου καὶ πάσης ῥᾳδιουργίας, υἱὲ διαβόλου, ἐχθρὲ πάσης δικαιοσύνης, οὐ παύση διαστρέφων τὰς ὁδοὺς [τοῦ] κυρίου τὰς εὐθείας;	He (Saul; now Paul) said "O full of all cunning and all trickery, son of a devil, enemy of all <u>righteousness</u>, will you not cease to pervert the ways of [the] lord which are straight?
13:11	καὶ νῦν ἰδοὺ χεὶρ κυρίου ἐπὶ σέ, καὶ ἔση τυφλὸς μὴ βλέπων τὸν ἥλιον ἄχρι καιροῦ. παραχρῆμά τε ἔπεσεν ἐπ' αὐτὸν ἀχλὺς καὶ σκότος, καὶ περιάγων ἐζήτει χειραγωγούς.	And now look! A hand of a lord upon you, and you shall be blind, not seeing the sun for a season." And instantly there fell upon him a mist and darkness, and going around he sought someone to lead him by the hand.

The newly named 'Paul' addresses the wizard in terms which here provide seven pieces of *bread* (ασ, ας) and one *fish* (χθ), accompanied by the name of Cain concealed within the word δικαιοσύνης [*righteousness*]. It is a manifestation which parallels the one we saw when Saul himself was first struck down in the vision at Ac.9:2. Again we have blindness, again the need to be '*led by the hand*'. Only this time the blindness strikes not Saul but, at his command, the magician. This 'blindness' may explain why at 13:11 (above) we see no more *bread* nor *fish*.

Ac. 13:12	τότε ἰδὼν ὁ ἀνθύπατος τὸ γεγονὸς ἐπίστευσεν ἐκπλησσόμενος ἐπὶ τῇ διδαχῇ τοῦ κυρίου.	Then the <u>proconsul</u>, seeing what was done, believed ... astounded at the teaching of the lord.

13:13	ἀναχθέντες δὲ ἀπὸ τῆς πάφου οἱ περὶ παῦλον ἦλθον εἰς πέργην τῆς παμφυλίας· ἰωάννης δὲ ἀποχωρήσας ἀπ' αὐτῶν ὑπέστρεψεν εἰς ἱεροσόλυμα.	So <u>putting to sea</u> from Paphos, those around Paul went to Perga of Pamphylia. But John, separating from them, returned to Jerusalem.
13:14	αὐτοὶ δὲ διελθόντες ἀπὸ τῆς πέργης παρεγένοντο εἰς ἀντιόχειαν τὴν πισιδίαν, καὶ [εἰσ]ελθόντες εἰς τὴν συναγωγὴν τῇ ἡμέρᾳ τῶν σαββάτων ἐκάθισαν.	And they, passing through from Perga, arrived at Antioch (of) Pisidia. And entering into the synagogue on the day of the <u>Sabbaths</u>, <u>they sat down</u>.

The proconsul was earlier identified as τὸν ἀνθύπατον (accusative case). But the next time he is mentioned it is in the nominative case. This gives us:

ὁ ἀνθύπατος   (Ac.13:12)

from which emerges not only: θάνατος [death]
but also: σαταν [Satan].

This implication may be extended by the word used of those with Paul:

ἀναχθέντες   (Ac.13:13)
putting to sea (lit: being led up)

Finally we learn of those with Paul that, entering into the synagogue:

... τῇ ἡμέρᾳ τῶν σαββάτων ἐκάθισαν
... on the day of the <u>Sabbaths</u>, <u>they sat down</u>

There once again is the '*sign*' for καϊν [*Cain*].

Chapter 13

The Pauline Letters

In his *Introduction to the New Testament Epistles*, Joseph Fiztmyer[1] says this:

> ### The Pauline Corpus
> In the NT 13 letters are attributed by name to Paul. This number appears too in the Muratorian Canon. Since the time of Cyril of Jerusalem, 14 letters have been ascribed to him {Paul}, including Hebrews. Modern scholars, however, following the lead of ancients like Origen, abandon the Pauline authorship of Hebrews. As for authenticity, Paul's letters fall into three categories:
>
> a) genuine writings:
> > 1 Thessalonians,Galatians, Philippians,
> > 1-2 Corinthians, Romans and Philemon
>
> b) doubtfully genuine writings (sometimes called "Deutero-Pauline", ie. written by a disciple of Paul):
> > 2 Thessalonians, Colossians and Ephesians
>
> c) pseudonymous writings:
> > 1-2 Timothy, Titus

The seven letters listed by Fitzmyer as 'genuine' are commonly dated to the period 50-60 CE. This is prior to the dates generally given for the four gospels and 20 to 30 years before the commonly accepted date for *Acts*, with its narrative about the conversion and travels of Saul/Paul.

Many others attribute the seven letters at a) to Paul. But all appear to overlook certain difficulties. For example:

- It is in one of these letters (*2 Corinthians*) that the supposed writer alludes to himself as '*a false apostle*'.

- Historians in the first century CE make no reference whatever to Paul. We are left to suppose that the person of Saul/Paul may be entirely fictional.

- There is no record of the Pauline letters themselves until around the middle of the second century CE. So if the seven letters were written in the period 50-60 CE then almost a century seems to have passed before they first came to light.

It seems likely that *all* the letters attributed to Paul are pseudepigraphic. This means they were not written by Paul (who is fictional) but composed in such a way that *they appear to have been written by Paul*. False authorship is a widely adopted technique, even today. For one example, author Sue Townsend took this approach when she wrote *The Secret Diary of Adrian Mole Aged 13¾*.

In *The Falsified Paul: Early Christianity in the Twilight*, Hermann Detering[2] takes this same view. Here is the summary given for his book:

In theology and church Paul is regarded as the most important and most reliable historial witness to Jesus and early Christianity. This book nevertheless contradicts the common conception and shows that all the Pauline letters are in fact skillful falsifications from the second century.

The author solves the numerous unresolved questions that surround the figure and the writings of Paul until today in convincing and scholarly original ways. At the same time, the reader accompanies him on his breath-taking trip through the mysterious world of Gnosticism and the early Christianities.

Numerous individual observations which have not been considered by theologians until now are brought together to produce an entirely new picture of early Christianity. At the end of the book the puzzle of Paul finds a solution that is as amazing as it is illuminating.

This exciting history of the spuriousness of all the Pauline writings allows the time of earliest Christianity to appear in an entirely new light and invites a critical consideration and new evaluation of presumably certain facts of Christian history.

Chapter 14

The Theme of Scripture Summarised

The scriptural authors have selected certain elements from Persian and Egyptian religious traditions and combined them to produce an amalgam which at the same time is Jewish and comprehensively Gnostic. They begin with **God**, uncreated and alone, but good. Next they disclose a second god, the androgynous **Person** (or **Persons**), brought into being on the sixth day of creation (Gn.1:27) and given charge over the world (Gn.1:28). This is the **lord god** whose dominant control leaves the world encumbered with evil. A diet is set for him, a diet derived from cereals and fruits (Gn.1:29). These are foods which grow in the Light. It is from this diet that both he and his subjects *may be recognised.*

This **lord god** is later equated with the **Logos** [ὁ λόγος; the *saying*; or *what was said*], for here we have the **Person** brought forth by the *saying* of **God** (Gn.1:26). In line with this, the fourth gospel (*John*) begins by confirming the existence of two gods:

Jn.	ἐν ἀρχῇ ἦν ὁ λόγος,	In origin was the **Logos**
1:1	καὶ ὁ λόγος ἦν πρὸς τὸν θεόν,	and the **Logos** was with **God**
	καὶ θεὸς ἦν ὁ λόγος.	and the **Logos** _was_ a god.
1:2	οὗτος ἦν ἐν ἀρχῇ πρὸς τὸν θεόν.	This one was in origin with **God**.
1:3	πάντα δι' αὐτοῦ ἐγένετο,	Everything happened through it.
	καὶ χωρὶς αὐτοῦ ἐγένετο οὐδὲ ἕν. ὃ γέγονεν	And without it there happened not one thing which has happened.

1:4	ἐν αὐτῷ ζωὴ ἦν, καὶ ἡ ζωὴ ἦν τὸ φῶς **τῶν ἀνθρώπων**:	In it was life, and the life was the Light of the **Persons**.
1:5	καὶ τὸ φῶς ἐν τῇ σκοτίᾳ φαίνει, καὶ ἡ σκοτία αὐτὸ <u>οὐ</u> κατέλαβεν.	And the Light is revealed within the Darkness, but the Darkness did _**not**_ comprehend it.

The prime **God** (who is good) is associated (Gn.1:2) with darkness and disorder (higher entropy). In contrast, the Light is the energetic attribute of the **Logos/Persons** which promotes order and structure in the world (lower entropy). And the gospel asserts that the Darkness did not _comprehend_ the Light.

It is a bipolar scenario. Darkness and light, what is good and what is evil: and the two deemed incompatible. There is no overlap between them, no accommodation. Nor can the one comprehend the other. It is part of the sinister theme that the 'Light' goes unrecognised by those who live in the world he dominates:

Jn. 1:10	ἐν τῷ κόσμῳ ἦν, καὶ ὁ κόσμος δι' αὐτοῦ ἐγένετο, καὶ ὁ κόσμος αὐτὸν <u>οὐκ</u> ἔγνω.	He was in the world and the world happened through him, and the world did _**not**_ learn to know him.
1:11	εἰς τὰ ἴδια ἦλθεν, καὶ οἱ ἴδιοι αὐτὸν <u>οὐ</u> παρέλαβον.	He came to his own, and his own did _**not**_ thoroughly receive him.

Few know the true identity of the **Logos**. Yet here is the warning:

Mt. 5:37	ἔστω δὲ **ὁ λόγος** ὑμῶν ναὶ ναί, οὒ οὔ: τὸ δὲ περισσὸν τούτων ἐκ τοῦ πονηροῦ ἐστιν.	So let _your_ **Logos** [_alt_: your saying] be 'Yes yes, no no'. _**But what is more than these is from the evil one**_.

The fourth gospel asserts that within this second god we have 'life' which is 'the Light of the Persons' (presumably a further reference to the '**Persons**' brought into being at Gn.1:27). And when we finally penetrate scripture's 'mystery' we find that this second god is disclosed to be **Satan**, the deceiver of the whole world:

2 Cor. 11:14	καὶ οὐ θαῦμα, αὐτὸς γὰρ ὁ σατανᾶς μετασχηματίζεται εἰς ἄγγελον φωτός:	And no wonder, for Satan himself is transformed into an angel of light.

The core of Satan's deceit resides in his own conviction that he is the only god, or in other words that he is God. In his blind and arrogant pride, he seeks to keep his subjects in a corresponding state of ignorance. Unaware of his identity, they are to think of him as God.

In the guise of the serpent, Satan deceives the first woman into believing that she can be like him and live for ever. From this union with Eve comes the offspring of the serpent, evil Cain.

Meanwhile *Adam is not deceived* [1 Tm.2:14]: and from his union with the woman comes Abel, who is good.

But Cain kills his brother, Abel. For this, Cain is cursed. Now he will go hidden from your face. The authors continue with the formulation of their extensive 'mystery', making elaborate provision for Cain to be 'hidden' within the very texts they now continue to write.

It is by this means that those who pay attention will be able to follow the allegory and to solve the riddles, *recognising Cain* ... just as we have done in this book. And once they recognise him they will treat him with entire disdain, just as God does himself (Gn.4:5).

But those who fail to recognise Cain (and his diet) are those who will take him and kill him. They are ignorant of what they do. Yet their ignorance will not excuse them. They will be held accountable, along with the 'many' who claim vicarious benefit through relying upon the death and resurrection of Cain to 'save them from their sins'. All those who make this claim bring upon themselves an ancient curse because:

| Ga. 3:13 | χριστὸς ἡμᾶς ἐξηγόρασεν ἐκ τῆς κατάρας τοῦ νόμου γενόμενος ὑπὲρ ἡμῶν κατάρα, | Christ bought us off from the curse of the Law, *he becoming a curse upon us*. |
| | ὅτι γέγραπται, ἐπικατάρατος πᾶς ὁ κρεμάμενος ἐπὶ ξύλου, | Because it is written, "Cursed is everyone who hangs upon a tree" (Dt.21:23) |

Attention is drawn again, in the passage which follows, to the mistake (or 'sin') which is made by so many:

1 Cor. 11:26	ὁσάκις γὰρ ἐὰν ἐσθίητε τὸν ἄρτον τοῦτον καὶ τὸ ποτήριον πίνητε, τὸν θάνατον τοῦ κυρίου καταγγέλλετε, ἄχρις οὗ ἔλθῃ.	For whenever you eat this bread and drink the cup, you declaim the death of the lord, until he may come from it.
11:27	ὥστε ὃς ἂν ἐσθίῃ τὸν ἄρτον ἢ πίνῃ τὸ ποτήριον τοῦ κυρίου ἀναξίως, ἔνοχος ἔσται τοῦ σώματος καὶ τοῦ αἵματος τοῦ κυρίου.	And so whoever may eat the bread or drink the cup of the lord unworthily will be liable for the body and the blood of the lord.
11:28	δοκιμαζέτω δὲ ἄνθρωπος ἑαυτόν, καὶ οὕτως ἐκ τοῦ ἄρτου ἐσθιέτω καὶ ἐκ τοῦ ποτηρίου πινέτω:	But let a person test himself, and in this way let him 'eat' from the bread and 'drink' from the cup.

11:29	ὁ γὰρ ἐσθίων καὶ πίνων **κρίμα**	For the one eating and
	ἑαυτῷ ἐσθίει καὶ πίνει	drinking **eats and drinks**
		judgement to himself,
	μὴ δια<ins>Κρί</ins>Νων τὸ σῶμα.	not <ins>distinguishing</ins> the body.

Now the authors of scripture write in such a way that the text of scripture itself comes to constitute a meal. This 'meal' is functionally equivalent to the one offered by the serpent to the woman Eve. It has the same properties. It is a tainted meal, and it can lead to your undoing.

This explains why we find Jesus repeating the promise first made by the serpent to Eve. From many examples, here is one:

Jn.	εἶπεν αὐτῇ ὁ ἰησοῦς, ἐγώ εἰμι	Jesus said to her (Martha) "I
11:25	ἡ **ἀνάστ**ασις καὶ ἡ ζωή: ὁ	AM the <ins>resurrection</ins> and the
	πιστεύων εἰς ἐμὲ κἂν	life: the one believing in me,
	ἀποθάνῃ ζήσεται,	even though he may die, will
		live.
11:26	καὶ πᾶς ὁ ζῶν καὶ πιστεύων	And each one living and
	εἰς ἐμὲ οὐ μὴ ἀποθάνῃ εἰς τὸν	believing in me may not die
	αἰῶνα:	in Eternity.
	πιστεύεις τοῦτο;	Do you believe this?"

No matter who repeats it, the promise of eternal life remains what it always was, the deceitful promise of the serpent (who is Satan). Adam (who is good) was formed by **God** from the dust of the earth. At death he will return to the earth (Gn.2:7, 3:19). Indeed **God** makes sure that Adam does *not* have access to eternal life (Gn.3:22-4).

The theme of the tainted meal accounts too for the passages at Ezk.3:1 and Rv.10:9-10 where it is the book itself (the Bible) which is to be '*eaten*'. It will be '*like honey in your mouth but bitter in your belly*'. Thus the first impression may be delightful; but upon digesting fully what has been written a *very* different response will be induced.

In a parallel metaphor, the text of scripture is presented to be the field for the harvest, or the lake to be fished. In either case *it is the Greek text itself* which must be 'gathered up', then sifted or sorted in order to separate 'the bad from the good'. Plainly this is the 'work' we are expected to do as *'workers at the harvest'* ... or as *'fishers putting out for the catch'*. It is a matter explained here:

Mt.	πάλιν ὁμοία ἐστὶν ἡ βασιλεία	Again, the kingdom of the
13:47	τῶν οὐρανῶν σαγήνῃ	heavens is like a drag net
	βληθείσῃ εἰς τὴν θάλασσαν	cast into the sea, and
	καὶ ἐκ παντὸς γένους	gathering together every kind
	συναγαγούσῃ:	
13:48	ἢν ὅτε ἐπληρώθη	Which when it was filled,
	ἀναβιβ<u>άσαντ</u>ες ἐπὶ τὸν	<u>making it go up</u> on the beach
	αἰγιαλὸν καὶ <u>καθίσαντ</u>ες	and <u>sitting down</u>, they
	συνέλεξαν τὰ καλὰ εἰς ἄγγη,	gathered the good into
	τὰ δὲ σαπρὰ ἔξω ἔβαλον.	buckets, but the rotten they
		threw out.
13:49	οὕτως ἔσται ἐν τῇ συντελείᾳ	So it shall be at the
	τοῦ αἰῶνος: ἐξελεύσονται οἱ	completion of the age: the
	ἄγγελοι καὶ <u>ἀφορ</u>ιοῦσ<u>ιν</u>	angels will come out and
	τοὺς πονηροὺς ἐκ μέσου τῶν	<u>they will distinguish</u> the evil in
	δι<u>καί</u>ων	the midst of the <u>righteous</u>
13:50	καὶ βαλοῦσιν αὐτοὺς εἰς τὴν	And they will throw them into
	<u>κάμιν</u>ον τοῦ πυρός:	the <u>furnace</u> of fire.
	ἐκεῖ ἔσται ὁ κλαυθμὸς καὶ ὁ	There will be the whimpering
	βρυγμὸς τῶν ὀδόντων.	and the grinding of the teeth.
13:51	συνήκατε ταῦτα πάντα;	Did you grasp these things?
	λέγουσιν αὐτῷ, ναί.	They say to him "Yes".

In that short passage we see the names of Cain, Satan and the serpent. It is Cain [Κάϊν] who ends up being extracted from the midst of 'the righteous' [τῶν δικαίων] and thrown into 'the furnace' [τὴν Κάμινον] of fire. This is how scripture works. Only 'the blind' fail to see these things.

A 'meal' of this kind must be consumed with circumspection. First we must sort the catch, being sure to identify and to reject what is recognisably unsavoury. In the process we find that Jesus himself is Cain, an unforgiven killer going in disguise, whilst the father who has sent him is Satan (*aka.* the devil), the intending deceiver of the whole world (Rv.12:9).

It is therefore no accident that in the gospels Jesus repeats the deceitful promise of the serpent: it is only to be expected.

As offspring of the serpent, Jesus is a manifestation of the sinister Logos, but now is the Logos 'made flesh':

| Jn. 1:14 | καὶ ὁ **λόγος** σὰρξ ἐγένετο καὶ ἐσκήνωσεν ἐν ἡμῖν, καὶ ἐθεασάμεθα τὴν δόξαν αὐτοῦ, δόξαν ὡς μονογενοῦς παρὰ πατρός, πλήρης χάριτος καὶ ἀληθείας. | And the **Logos** happened as flesh and tented amongst us. And we beheld his glory, a glory as of one unique beside a father, full of grace and truth |

In contrast we find that John the Baptist is good. The rôle he plays is analogous to that of Abel. It is made clear that John does *not* consume foods of the kind specified for the **lord god**:

| Lk. 7:33 | ἐλήλυθεν γὰρ ἰωάννης ὁ βαπτιστὴς <u>μὴ</u> ἐσθίων ἄρτον <u>μήτε</u> πίνων οἶνον, καὶ λέγετε, δαιμόνιον ἔχει: | For John the Baptist came <u>*not*</u> eating bread <u>*and not*</u> drinking wine, and you say *he* has a demon. |

With his riddles, John struggles to disclose the identity of Jesus. He gets as far as baptising Jesus with water. At that point he is violently eliminated.

In this way the theme of scripture is seen to be unremittingly recursive.

All that is good stems from **God**. It must struggle against what is evil, but does no evil itself.

All that is evil stems from the **lord god**. For it *anything* is possible: overt lies, artful deceit, public shows of religion, and the *pretence* to be good ... along with violence and coercion of every sort

Gnostic tradition holds that the world is dominated by the evil god. The worst of his tricks is his pretence to be **God**. The *knowledge* of how to distinguish good from evil is therefore vital if we are to escape from his overarching spell.

This *knowledge* is of the first importance to those who will read scripture. For how can you be confident that what you do is good until first you discover what good is?

To fathom the ancient 'mystery', one must read in Greek. All is not what at first it seems. What has been hidden in the text has been hidden there for *your* benefit ... and left there for *you* to find.

Chapter 15

In Conclusion

Rational behaviour presupposes rational concepts. Rational concepts are developed through the careful collation of evidence and strict logical interpretation. Yet the religious convictions of *Homo sapiens* are not of this kind. Instead they have been honed through the Darwinian process of natural selection. Today philosophers like Dennett, anthropologists like Boyer, and behavioural scientists like Hinde are making efforts to understand the selection mechanism which over the ages has brought forth and sustained this most curious and troublesome aspect of human behaviour. It is a complex picture.

Eric Kaufmann[1] says:

> The religious population has two demographic advantages over its non-believing counterpart. First, it maintains a 15-20 per cent fertility lead over the non-religious. Second, religious people in the childbearing 18-45 age range are disproportionately female.

Here is one factor which favours the survival of religions, however absurd their claims, however divisive their impact. Yet transmission of religious belief is also dependent upon rates of conversion and apostasy in each new generation. Here education has a key rôle to play. That education needs to be discerning and objective, not constrained to the point where it consists of little more than indoctrination as the means to assert over others a religious conviction which in fact is deeply flawed.

What have the Authors of Scripture Done?

In the ancient world it was the thesis of Jewish scripture that the first man was made by **God**. So Adam represented the true origin for mankind, made (as the Hebrew name suggests) from the dust of the earth. Then from Adam's rib the first woman was formed. She gave birth to Cain whose father was the serpent, then to Abel whose father was Adam.

Let us put ourselves in the place of those who worked from this curious hypothesis. Abel was entirely derived from the earth. But Cain was a demi-god. And Cain had killed Abel before Abel could father any children. Cain went on to have children himself, so the whole human race must now be descended through evil Cain from the serpent. The point is hardly difficult to grasp. And with the slaughter of Abel we have a putative example of Darwinian selection, selection in this case for evil at the expense of what was good. Here is one way to construe and account for what in Jewish thinking is known as *yetzer ra*, the evil inclination in mankind.

It seems that the authors of Greek scripture thought in this way. Or rather that they did so with one essential proviso which lay at the heart of their Gnostic convictions. For them the cosmos was inherently evil, a disaster they attributed to its being placed in the charge of an evil god. But they could not accept that there was no escape from an ethical trap so dreadful and final as this. So they appear to have held that although Abel had died without *physical* descendents (*ie.* his seed remained within him), he did have descendents in what they thought of as the *spiritual* sense. Abel, and perhaps Seth, were examples of those who inherited what Adam knew … and so made no mistake (or sin).

The gospel authors appear to have numbered themselves amongst those who *knew* of the good **God** with whom the *Genesis* story begins. And if they knew **God** it was implicit that they would know who was *not* God. They knew that the **lord god** was not **God**.

They held that it was *gnosis*, the knowledge of **God** and of how to distinguish good from evil, that could save a person from all that was evil in an evil world. This is what we mean when we say that their approach was '*gnostic*'. They did not consider themselves 'children' of **God** in the *physical* (or genetic) sense, but rather in the *spiritual* (or memetic) sense.

In the letter *1 John* we find expressed this Gnostic concept of inheritance:

1 Jn. 3:9	πᾶς ὁ γεγεννημένος **ἐκ τοῦ** **θεοῦ** ἁμαρτίαν οὐ ποιεῖ, ὅτι σπέρμα αὐτοῦ ἐν αὐτῷ μένει: καὶ οὐ δύναται ἁμαρτάνειν, ὅτι **ἐκ τοῦ θεοῦ** γεγέννηται.	Each one begotten **_from_** **God** does not make a mistake [*alt*: does not sin] because his seed remains within him. And he is not able to make a mistake because he has been begotten **_from_** **God**.
3:10	ἐν τούτῳ φανερά ἐστιν τὰ τέκνα **τοῦ θεοῦ** καὶ τὰ τέκνα τοῦ διαβόλου: πᾶς ὁ μὴ ποιῶν δι**ΚΑΙ**οσύ**νη**ν οὐκ ἔστιν **ἐκ τοῦ θεοῦ**, καὶ ὁ μὴ ἀγαπῶν τὸν ἀδελφὸν αὐτοῦ.	In this the children **of God** are revealed, and the children of the devil. Each one not 'making' <u>justice</u> is not **_from_ God**, and the one not loving his brother.

The good **God** of Gn.1:1 is denoted in Greek scripture as ὁ θεός [*the* god]. In the genitive case this becomes τοῦ θεοῦ [*of the* god]. So this passage alludes to the 'children' of **God**. Like Adam and Abel, these are the ones who make no mistake, they commit no 'sin'.

In contrast, the authors write to describe Cain and his behaviour on the basis that **God** is unknown to him. In his ignorance, Cain worships the impostor **lord god**, *alias* the evil serpent, who in the scriptural scheme is his own father. So Cain's god is the **lord god**, otherwise known as 'the **Person**' or 'the **Logos**', the second god, the one introduced into the narrative of scripture on the sixth day of the creation sequence.

This **lord god** is denoted in Greek not as ὁ θεός [*the* god] but as θεός [*a* god]. In the genitive case this becomes θεοῦ [*of a* god]... as in εἰκόνα θεοῦ [*image of a* god] at LXX Gn.1:27.

In the fourth gospel (*John*) it is said of this second god, now manifested as '*The Light*':

Jn. 1:11	εἰς τὰ ἴδια ἦλθεν, καὶ οἱ ἴδιοι αὐτὸν <u>οὐ</u> παρέλαβον.	He came to his own, and his own did <u>not</u> thoroughly receive him.
1:12	ὅσοι δὲ ἔλαβον αὐτόν, ἔδωκεν αὐτοῖς ἐξουσίαν τέκνα **θεοῦ** γενέσθαι, τοῖς πιστεύουσιν εἰς τὸ ὄνομα αὐτοῦ,	But as many as did receive him, he gave to them authority to become children ***of a god***, to those trusting in his name.
1:13	οἳ οὐκ ἐξ αἱμάτων οὐδὲ ἐκ θελήματος σαρκὸς οὐδὲ ἐκ θελήματος ἀνδρὸς <u>ἀλλ' ἐκ **θεοῦ**</u> ἐγεννήθησαν.	These were begotten not from blood, nor from will of flesh, nor from will of man, ***but from a god***.

Those alluded to here are 'children' of the second god. Consequent upon their ignorance, they are the ones entirely deceived. They are the ones who sin, the 'blind' who make every mistake in the book.

It is next important to realise that the authors of scripture, having set forth Cain in *Genesis*, have him reappear in the gospels, but now in the guise of Jesus. The authors write to have Jesus fulfil in every detail the predictions which at Gn.4:10-16 are made about Cain. The evidence is overwhelming that in the NT narrative Jesus *is* Cain. This explains why we find Jesus referring to himself in the gospels as '*son of the Person*'. It explains too why the *'father'* to whom Jesus prays is disclosed in the gospels to be the serpent, or Satan.

We live in an age enlightened by the ideas of Darwin, ideas subsequently justified by a vast realm of evidence assembled first from the fields of palaeontology and biology, and now from genetics as well. On this basis we know that the assumption of a singular origin for mankind must be false. From geology and cosmology we know too that the age of the earth must be around 4,500 million years. It follows that scripture must be fiction: it does not provide the platform upon which any religion can be soundly sustained, either now or in the future. Yet scripture stands worthy of study in its own right as an expression of Gnostic ideology. It is worthy of study too for the response it has produced ... the remarkable social phenomenon of a collective delusion enduring for almost two thousand years, itself the direct result of a widespread failure to grasp the deeper meaning of things written down in a bygone age.

Why did they Do It?

After the passage of so many centuries, it is hard to be sure just why the authors of scripture should have chosen to wrap up their message in such an unexpected way. Perhaps the first thing to say is that if their ideas were complex then it was always likely they would be expressed in a form correspondingly complex.

Yet it is one thing to have complex ideas and seek to explain them so that all may understand. It is another thing to have such ideas and to set them out in such a way that you know the majority of readers will be led badly astray. It is clear from what is said in the gospels that the authors always expected many to be led astray on account of what they wrote. It is clear too, from what is now our history, that what the authors expected to happen did actually happen: many *were* led astray.

Scripture presented the masses with a religious tradition which was predictably popular but which these Gnostic writers knew would reinforce mistaken aspirations and leave the majority of their readers trapped in a world of evil and self-delusion.

Why would the writers proceed in this way? In our age it is hard for us to understand what their motive could have been. One possibility is that they were instructed to do it. The social structures of the ancient world differed greatly from the popular democracies familiar today in the western world. Typically these structures took the form of a pyramid, with the educated and the religious leaders somewhere near the top and the king, or Pharaoh, at the apex. Many times throughout history rulers have sought to formulate the religion of their people, and so to keep control.

Then what happens if the Ptolemaic ruler of Egypt demands that the Hebrew scriptures be rendered into Greek? He gets what he wants. The resulting scriptures appear to say one thing to the majority. At the same time they present a different theme, even the opposite theme, to the writers themselves and to those in authority.

A second possibility is that the writers are philosophers who seek of their own accord to demonstrate what they maintain is the difficulty inherent in *any* attempt to access knowledge of God. So they write to exemplify this difficulty by teaching their students a lesson - which turns out to be a hard one. To this end, the texts of scripture are prepared with great care. They take the form of a 'mystery', a format with a sting in its tail. This 'sting' (the same term is used by security forces even today) is directed exclusively for any person who, in a spiritual sense, is somewhat greedy or careless. Such persons will be *induced* to think that what they want they can have.

In particular, those who fear personal annihilation at death will be *induced* to think that offences against others can all be forgiven and death itself overcome (here is Christian doctrine in a nutshell). Yet if in the end this does not happen, these persons will have no one to blame but themselves. For *they* were the ones who read from the scriptures and supposed that they knew what was said. Yet in fact they read with too little care, failed to distinguish good from evil, and so were left deluded.

All those falling for a sting such as this make a great mistake of presumption. They fail to check out the credentials of the god who extends to them attractive promises. It is the theme of scripture that such persons, in all their haste and carelessness, end up embracing as their god the impostor, Satan ... the intending *deceiver* of the whole world (Rv.12:9).

Such an explanation is consistent with what is asserted in the gospels:

Lk. 8:17	οὐ γάρ ἐστιν κρυπτὸν ὃ οὐ φανερὸν γενήσεται, οὐδὲ ἀπόκρυφον ὃ οὐ μὴ γνωσθῇ καὶ εἰς φανερὸν ἔλθῃ.	For it is not hidden, that it shall not become visible, nor secret that it might not become known, and might come into view.
8:18	βλέπετε οὖν πῶς ἀκούετε: ὃς ἂν γὰρ ἔχῃ, δοθήσεται αὐτῷ, καὶ ὃς ἂν μὴ ἔχῃ, καὶ ὃ δοκεῖ ἔχειν ἀρθήσεται ἀπ' αὐτοῦ.	Then watch out how you hear. For to each who has, to him it shall be given, and to each who does not have, even what he thinks he has will be taken away from him.

To the one who 'has' (this is the Gnostic reader), to him it shall be given. But to the one who {thinks he has, but in fact} does *not* 'have', even what he *thinks* he has will be taken away from him.

It is a theme of deep poetic justice.

Those who pay attention to scripture, those who notice the little things and go on to solve the whole mystery, these appropriately cautious persons gain access to the challenging truth. They learn to know what (in the narrative) Adam knows, that man is made from the dust and will return to dust, having no access to the life of the gods.

But those who rush in, those who fail to study scripture with care, such persons will be deluded by their encounter with it. Their inappropriate desire will be amplified by their shallow interpretation of what is written, and they will end by getting what they truly deserve. Deceived by Satan's easy promise, such persons will end in his clutches.

It appears to be the making of this primary distinction, the Gnostic distinction between the **spiritual** person and the merely **soulish** (or *psychic*), which scripture, in all its complexity, has been devised to achieve. Thus the letter to *Hebrews* has this to say of the **Logos**:

Heb. 4:12	ζῶν γὰρ ὁ **λόγος** τοῦ θεοῦ καὶ ἐνεργὴς καὶ τομώτερος ὑπὲρ πᾶσαν μάχαιραν δίστομον	For the **Logos** of God (is) alive and active, and sharper than every two-mouthed dagger
	καὶ διϊκνούμενος ἄχρι μερισμοῦ ψυχῆς καὶ πνεύματος, ἁρμῶν τε καὶ μυελῶν,	… and penetrating even to the dividing of Soul and Spirit, both of joints and marrow,
	καὶ κριτικὸς ἐνθυμήσεων καὶ ἐννοιῶν καρδίας:	and able to discern (the) considerations and notions of a heart.
4:13	καὶ οὐκ ἔστιν κτίσις ἀφανὴς ἐνώπιον αὐτοῦ, πάντα δὲ γυμνὰ καὶ τετραχηλισμένα τοῖς **ὀφθαλμοῖς** αὐτοῦ, πρὸς ὃν ἡμῖν ὁ **λόγος**.	And it is not a creature invisible in its countenance, but all things (are) naked and have had (their) neck twisted (round) <u>to the **eyes**</u> of that which (is) for us the **Logos**.

The **Logos** is manifested here as ὄφις [*the serpent*].

The Christian Church

We have only to read carefully in order to see that scripture follows the
Gnostic convention, structured throughout by its authors on the basis
that *two* gods exist in opposition. Then is it not a most remarkable fact
that throughout almost seventeen centuries which now have elapsed
since the Catholic church was first established in the era of Constantine,
so many have *denied* that there were two gods in scripture, insisting
upon a distorted interpretation which allows for only one?

The Roman Catholic church in particular must be held accountable for
the overwhelming absurdity of this position. For in asserting one god,
the Christian tradition to which this church first gave rise has fulfilled
the prediction made amidst the very gospels upon which it seeks to rely,
the prediction that 'the many' would take the deluded path which leads
only to destruction.

Mt.	εἰσέλθατε διὰ τῆς στενῆς	Enter in through the narrow
7:13	πύλης:	gate.
	ὅτι πλατεῖα ἡ πύλη καὶ	For broad (is) the gate and
	εὐρύχωρος ἡ ὁδὸς ἡ	spacious the way which
	ἀπάγουσα εἰς τὴν ἀπώλειαν,	leads to destruction, and
	καὶ **πολλοί** εἰσιν οἱ	***many*** are those entering in
	εἰσερχόμενοι δι' αὐτῆς:	through it.

Mt.	ἀμὴν γὰρ λέγω ὑμῖν ὅτι	For truly I say to you that
13:17	**πολλοί** προφῆται καὶ δίκαιοι	***many*** prophets and just men
	ἐπεθύμησαν ἰδεῖν ἃ βλέπετε	desired to see what you see,
	καὶ οὐκ εἶδαν,	and did *not* see,
	καὶ ἀκοῦσαι ἃ ἀκούετε καὶ	and to hear what you hear,
	οὐκ ἤκουσαν.	and did *not* hear.

Is it not truly amazing that this heedless institution should have missed
what has been done by those who wrote the gospels, that it should have
overlooked entirely those central features of scripture which provide for

what is set forth to be good *to be distinguished* from what is set forth to be evil?

Here is an organisation which has assumed the task of explaining the scriptures to the world. But it cannot explain them. The consequence is that literally billions of people have been led by it into a spiritual and logical trap first set to seduce the unwary in the age of classical antiquity.

The Christian church has followed *blindly* the example of Cain, embracing the figure of Satan as 'Father'. Failing to recognise its mistake, it goes on to deny even the possibility that it might be mistaken. But the evidence of the gospels speaks for itself. Here is the assertion that 'treasure' has been hidden:

Mt. 13:44	ὁμοία ἐστὶν ἡ βασιλεία τῶν οὐρανῶν θησαυρῷ κεκρυμμένῳ ἐν τῷ ἀγρῷ, ὃν εὑρὼν ἄνθρωπος ἔκρυψεν, καὶ ἀπὸ τῆς χαρᾶς αὐτοῦ ὑπάγει καὶ πωλεῖ πάντα ὅσα ἔχει καὶ ἀγοράζει τὸν ἀγρὸν ἐκεῖνον.	The kingdom of the heavens is like a treasure hidden in the field, which finding it a person hid. And from his joy he goes off and sells all that he has and buys that field.

And here the assertion that *nothing* is hidden which will not become known:

Mt. 10:26	μὴ οὖν φοβηθῆτε αὐτούς· οὐδὲν γάρ ἐστιν κεκαλυμμένον ὃ οὐκ ἀποκαλυφθήσεται, καὶ κρυπτὸν ὃ οὐ γνωσθήσεται.	Therefore do not fear them. For nothing is concealed that will not be revealed, and hidden that will not become known.

Much indeed has been hidden, hidden long ago. And it can still be found. For look, with this book *we have found it!*

We have shown that there is a message concealed within the message. We have shown that from *Genesis* through the gospels to *Revelation* there are '*things written within and backwards*', things '*sealed down with seven seals*'. We have shown too that what has been concealed holds immense significance for interpretation of the message as a whole: for it inverts the first impression completely.

And what does the Roman Catholic church have to say about this? Armed with what wisdom it has contrived to accumulate from seventeen centuries spent in the intensive study of scripture, it says[2]:

"There can be *nothing* hidden in the gospels"

Here is an organisation which has fallen far short of the mark set for it in scripture. One might say it has fallen at the first fence. For in claiming what it does, it remains after seventeen centuries sublimely unaware:

- That Jesus is portrayed in scripture to be evil Cain

- That the 'Father' to whom Jesus prays is Satan (the serpent)

- That the Eucharist (the core component of Catholic liturgy) is a re-enactment of the sacrifice attributed in scripture to Cain

- That its claim for man to be made in the image of God is merely repetition of the message first delivered by the serpent, the message by which (in the story) *Eve was deceived*

- That its claim for believers to 'live for ever' is a further repetition of the serpent's deceitful message

How could such a course, a course so obviously mistaken, have been followed by so many, and for so long? It is a good question. By taking the stance that it does, the Catholic church has aligned itself with all that the authors have set forth in scripture to be evil and ignorant.

And then, when so obviously it has missed the trick which cripples it so badly, it shows its ignorance all over again by seeking to deny that there is anything more to be learned than it already knows.

What have we shown in this Book?

We have shown, either directly or by implication:

- That scripture is fiction.

- That the claim of the Christian church(es) for the historicity of scripture is mistaken.

- That scripture is Gnostic in its underlying ideology, as equally in the methods employed for its composition.

- That in scripture two gods are set forth. One is good, the other evil. The evil god seeks to be recognised as the only god, in this way precluding the option for good.

- That scripture is structured in such a way that many will be deceived by its message. Yet at the same time it provides that those who take care, or those better taught, may grasp the nature of the 'mystery' and in this way avoid being deceived.

- That in the gospels John the Baptist is portrayed as good.

- Whereas Jesus is portrayed as evil (indeed he is Cain).

- That as with Isaiah before him, the apostle Paul is set forth to be a deluded prophet (or apostle).

- That Christian doctrine is confused and mistaken, initially on the notion of 'original sin', and then on nearly every other count.

- That the Christian tradition is that of those deceived. Failing to identify and to solve the mystery, failing even to recognise who Jesus is supposed to be, *it is axiomatic in scripture itself that those embracing Christ are those deluded by Satan's heady ploy.*

What are the Implications?

It seems that the Christian church has mistaken evil for good, light for darkness, bitter for sweet ... and Satan for God.

LXX	οὐαὶ οἱ λέγοντες τὸ πονηρὸν	Woe to those saying Evil is
Is.	καλὸν καὶ τὸ καλὸν πονηρόν	good and Good is evil,
5:20	οἱ τιθέντες τὸ σκότος φῶς καὶ	those putting Darkness for
	τὸ φῶς σκότος	light and Light for darkness,
	οἱ τιθέντες τὸ πικρὸν γλυκὺ	those putting Bitter for sweet
	καὶ τὸ γλυκὺ πικρόν	and Sweet for bitter.

It could hardly have made any greater mistake.

Judged by the yardstick of scripture itself, *is it not plain that the Christian church is inherently evil?* Of course this explains many things ... from armed crusades and ambitions for power ... all the way down to institutional child abuse by members of a celibate clergy. Recognising the evil inherent here, it seems reasonable that the influence of the Christian churches should henceforth be curtailed in the public sphere. For example:

- Public funding and financial privilege should not be extended by any civil state to any denomination of the Christian church.

- Representation in civil government should not be extended by any civil state to any denomination of the Christian church.

- The right to influence or to control state funded institutions (such as schools or hospitals) should not be extended by any civil state to any denomination of the Christian church.

Where corresponding privileges are afforded to non-Christian traditions which likewise draw a monotheist interpretation from Judaeo-Christian scripture, these too should be reviewed.

In the place of *all* these traditions should we not do well in our age to focus upon developing human communities which provide for us to work together and to care for one another without placing reliance upon the notion of a god, or gods … and free from the corrupting expectation for a personal life beyond death?

For scripture
(which is fiction but is highly instructive)
tells that:

Adam, forbidden by the **lord god** to eat from
The Tree for Knowing Knowledge of Good and Evil,
was never deterred from doing so.

Instead, he ate from it.

In this way he learned the truth:

about **God**
(good)

about the **lord god**
(evil)

and about himself
(dust)

---- o ----

1 Cor. 2:6	σοφίαν δὲ λαλοῦμεν ἐν τοῖς τελείοις, σοφίαν δὲ οὐ τοῦ αἰῶνος τούτου οὐδὲ τῶν ἀρχόντων τοῦ αἰῶνος τούτου τῶν καταργουμένων:	And we speak wisdom amongst those accomplished, yet a wisdom not of this age, nor of the rulers of this age, of those being made redundant.
2:7	ἀλλὰ λαλοῦμεν θεοῦ σοφίαν ἐν μυστηρίῳ, τὴν ἀποκεκρυμμένην, ἣν προώρισεν ὁ θεὸς πρὸ τῶν αἰώνων εἰς δόξαν ἡμῶν:	But we speak a godly wisdom within a mystery, hidden away, which **God** fore-ordained before the ages purposed for our glory,
2:8	ἣν οὐδεὶς τῶν ἀρχόντων τοῦ αἰῶνος τούτου ἔγνωκεν, εἰ γὰρ ἔγνωσαν, οὐκ ἂν τὸν κύριον τῆς δόξης ἐσταύρωσαν.	Which not one of the rulers of this age have known. *For if they knew, they would not have crucified the 'lord of glory'.*
2:9	ἀλλὰ καθὼς γέγραπται, ἃ ὀφθαλμὸς οὐκ εἶδεν καὶ οὖς οὐκ ἤκουσεν καὶ ἐπὶ Καρδίαν ἀνθρώπου οὐκ ἀνέβη, ἃ ἡτοίμασεν ὁ θεὸς τοῖς ἀγαπῶσιν αὐτόν.	But just as it has been written "Things which eye did not see and ear did not hear - and which did not ascend to (the) <u>heart</u> of a person ... which **God** prepared for those who love him".
2:10	ἡμῖν δὲ ἀπεκάλυψεν ὁ θεὸς διὰ τοῦ πνεύματος: τὸ γὰρ πνεῦμα πάντα ἐραυνᾷ, καὶ τὰ βάθη τοῦ θεοῦ.	Yet to us, **God** revealed (them) through the spirit. For the spirit investigates all things, *even the deep things of God*.

2:11	τίς γὰρ οἶδεν ἀνθρώπων τὰ **τοῦ ἀνθρώπου** εἰ μὴ τὸ πνεῦμα **τοῦ ἀνθρώπου** τὸ ἐν αὐτῷ; οὕτως καὶ τὰ **τοῦ θεοῦ** οὐδεὶς ἔγνωκεν εἰ μὴ τὸ πνεῦμα **τοῦ θεοῦ**.	For who amongst persons knows the things of the **Person** except the spirit of the **Person** which is in him? So also no one knows the things of **God** except the spirit of **God**.
2:12	ἡμεῖς δὲ οὐ τὸ πνεῦμα τοῦ κόσμου ἐλάβομεν ἀλλὰ τὸ πνεῦμα τὸ ἐκ **τοῦ θεοῦ**, ἵνα εἰδῶμεν τὰ ὑπὸ **τοῦ θεοῦ** χαρισθέντα ἡμῖν:	But we received not the spirit of the world but the spirit which is from **God**, so that we might know the things granted to us as a favour by **God**.
2:13	ἃ καὶ λαλοῦμεν οὐκ ἐν διδακτοῖς ἀνθρωπίνης σοφίας λόγοις ἀλλ' ἐν διδακτοῖς πνεύματος, πVευμΑτΙΚοῖς πVευμΑτΙΚὰ συγκρίνοντες.	Which things also we speak, not in teachings (which are) sayings of human wisdom but in teachings of a spirit, comparing spiritual things with spiritual things.
2:14	ψυχικὸς δὲ ἄνθρωπος οὐ δέχεται τὰ τοῦ πνεύματος **τοῦ θεοῦ**, μωρία γὰρ αὐτῷ ἐστιν, καὶ οὐ δύναται γνῶναι, ὅτι πVευμΑτΙΚῶς ἀVΑΚρίνεται:	But a Soulish person does not receive the things of the spirit of **God**, for to him it is foolishness. And he is not able to know (them) because it is examined spiritually.
2:15	ὁ δὲ πVευμΑτΙΚὸς ἀVΑΚρίνει [τὰ] πάντα, αὐτὸς δὲ ὑπ' οὐδενὸς ἀVΑΚρίνεται.	But the Spiritual (person) examines all things - and he himself is examined by no one.

Appendix 1

Mathematics of the Bread and Fish Concealed in the Gospels according to Principles configured in Chapter 1 of LXX *Genesis*

It is in Mark's version of the 'feeding of the five thousand' that Jesus speaks to his students as follows:

Mk.	ὁ δὲ λέγει αὐτοῖς, πόσους	But he said to them "How
6:38	ἄρτους ἔχετε; ὑπάγετε ἴδετε.	many breads do you have?
	καὶ γνόντες λέγουσιν, πέντε,	Go and see." And, knowing,
	καὶ δύο ἰχθύας.	they said "***Five*** … and ***two***
		fishes".

The passage hints strongly at the presence of a Gnostic riddle in the text because, when Jesus asks how many breads they have, we are told by the writer that '*knowing* they said **five** … and **two** fishes'.

If, in the narrative, the students '*know*' the answer then there must exist some rational basis for knowing it. Indeed the word **γνόντες** [*knowing*] is a participle of the verb **γινώσκω** [*I learn to know*], the Greek word from which we derive the English word '***Gnostic***'.

It seems reasonable to suppose that if we could establish the basis for the riddle then we too would *learn to know* what the students in the narrative are held to know. We too would be able to answer the question as quickly and easily as they seem able to do. But where do we look to find this extra knowledge?

In *Matthew*, in the midst of the sower parables, when the woman has just hidden yeast in three measures of meal, we find this useful clue:

Mt. 13:34	ταῦτα πάντα ἐλάλησεν ὁ ἰησοῦς ἐν παραβολαῖς τοῖς ὄχλοις, καὶ χωρὶς παραβολῆς οὐδὲν ἐλάλει αὐτοῖς:	All these things Jesus spoke in parables to the crowds, and without a parable he spoke nothing to them
13:35	ὅπως πληρωθῇ τὸ ῥηθὲν διὰ τοῦ προφήτου λέγοντος,	So that it might be fulfilled what was spoken through the prophet saying:
	ἀνοίξω ἐν παραβολαῖς τὸ στόμα μου, ἐρεύξομαι κεκρυμμένα ἀπὸ καταβολῆς [κόσμου].	"I shall open up my mouth in parables, I shall blurt out things hidden from (the) laying down [of world]".

Whatever may have been hidden in this textual treasure hunt, it seems to have been done at the *laying down of the world*. This points us to the creation sequence in the first chapter of *Genesis*. And, because the gospels were written in Greek, it points us to the Greek version of *Genesis*, almost certainly the Septuagint (LXX).

Let us return to *Mark* for the next clue in this treasure hunt:

Mk. 6:31	καὶ λέγει αὐτοῖς, δεῦτε ὑμεῖς αὐτοὶ κατ' ἰδίαν εἰς ἔρημον τόπον καὶ ἀναπαύσασθε ὀλίγον.	And he said to them "Come here privately into a desert place and rest a little".
	ἦσαν γὰρ οἱ ἐρχόμενοι καὶ οἱ ὑπάγοντες πολλοί, καὶ οὐδὲ φαγεῖν εὐκαίρουν.	For those coming and going were many, and they were not having leisure to eat.

| 6:32 | καὶ ἀπῆλθον ἐν τῷ πλοίῳ εἰς ἔρημον τόπον κατ' ἰδίαν. | And they went away in the boat to a desert place privately. |

The conjunction of *a desert place* with the *water* required for a boat to be used and the necessity to *provide food*, when taken together, brings to mind the scenario on Day 3 of the creation sequence:

LXX Gn. 1:9	καὶ εἶπεν **ὁ θεός** συναχθήτω τὸ ὕδωρ τὸ ὑποκάτω τοῦ οὐρανοῦ εἰς συναγωγὴν μίαν καὶ ὀφθήτω ἡ ξηρά καὶ ἐγένετο οὕτως	And **God** said "Let the water beneath Heaven coalesce into one assembly [*alt:* one synagogue] and let the dry appear" - and it happened thus.
	καὶ συνήχθη τὸ ὕδωρ τὸ ὑποκάτω τοῦ οὐρανοῦ εἰς τὰς συναγωγὰς αὐτῶν καὶ ὤφθη ἡ ξηρά	And the water beneath Heaven coalesced into their assemblies [*alt:* their synagogues] - and the dry appeared
1:10	καὶ ἐκάλεσεν **ὁ θεός** τὴν ξηρὰν γῆν καὶ τὰ συστήματα τῶν ὑδάτων ἐκάλεσεν θαλάσσας καὶ εἶδεν **ὁ θεός** ὅτι καλόν	And **God** called the dry 'earth', and the systems of waters he called 'seas'. And **God** saw it as good.

1:11	καὶ εἶπεν **ὁ θεός** βλαστησάτω ἡ γῆ βοτάνην χόρτου σπεῖρον σπέρμα κατὰ γένος καὶ καθ' ὁμοιότητα καὶ ξύλον κάρπιμον ποιοῦν καρπόν οὗ τὸ σπέρμα αὐτοῦ ἐν αὐτῷ κατὰ γένος ἐπὶ τῆς γῆς καὶ ἐγένετο οὕτως	And **God** said "Let the earth sprout a grassy plant spreading seed according to (its) kind and variety - and a fruit-bearing tree making fruit of which its seed (is) within it, according to (its) kind upon the earth". And it happened like this.
1:12	καὶ ἐξήνεγκεν ἡ γῆ βοτάνην χόρτου σπεῖρον σπέρμα κατὰ γένος καὶ καθ' ὁμοιότητα καὶ ξύλον κάρπιμον ποιοῦν καρπόν οὗ τὸ σπέρμα αὐτοῦ ἐν αὐτῷ κατὰ γένος ἐπὶ τῆς γῆς καὶ εἶδεν **ὁ θεός** ὅτι καλόν	And the earth brought forth a grassy plant spreading seed after its kind and variety - and a fruit-bearing tree making fruit of which its seed (is) within it, according to (its) kind upon the earth. And **God** saw it as good.
1:13	καὶ ἐγένετο ἑσπέρα καὶ ἐγένετο πρωί ἡμέρα τρίτη	And evening happened - and morning happened: THIRD DAY.

In the gospel we were looking for **five** pieces of *bread*. Let us advance the hypothesis that the reason we are looking for **five** pieces in *Mark* is that this number matches the quantity of *bread* concealed at Day 3 in *Genesis*, the first location in scripture where food becomes available. Thus we suppose that the construction in the gospel may be based upon a 'prototype' which already exists in LXX *Genesis*.

The gospel narrative is filled with those who are said to be blind. We still do not know what this '*bread*' looks like. But it could easily be some feature repeated in the text, a feature we are supposed to look for and to count. Let us analyse the passage for Day 3 (*ie.* LXX Gn.1:9-13) to discover what textual features occur just **five** times.

We find that the letter δ occurs **five** times. Next, with 24 letters in the Greek alphabet, there are 576 letter pairs (digrams) theoretically possible. Of these just 396 are actually used in the NT canon. And if we count the letter pairs in the passage for Day 3 in LXX *Genesis* we find just ten pairs which occur **five** times:

αλ, ασ/ας, αυ, εγ, εο, ησ/ης, θε, μα, νε, συ

As it turns out, we have here part of the information required to deduce what the authors intend when they use the term '*bread*'.

By analogy with the method used in algebra for the solution of simultaneous equations, what we need now is a second source of information to give us a second equation. For this, let us turn to the second feeding narrative in *Mark*, the one known for the 'feeding of the four thousand'. Here Jesus says to his students:

Mk. 8:2	σπλαγχνίζομαι ἐπὶ τὸν ὄχλον ὅτι ἤδη ἡμέραι τρεῖς προσμένουσίν μοι καὶ οὐκ ἔχουσιν τί φάγωσιν:	"I am queasy over the crowd because they have remained with me three days already and do not have anything to eat.
8:3	καὶ ἐὰν ἀπολύσω αὐτοὺς νήστεις εἰς οἶκον αὐτῶν, ἐκλυθήσονται ἐν τῇ ὁδῷ: καὶ τινες αὐτῶν ἀπὸ μακρόθεν ἥκασιν.	And if I send them away fasting to their household they will faint on the way: and some of them have come from afar."

As before, we find Jesus asking the students (disciples) how many pieces of bread they have:

Mk.	καὶ ἠρώτα αὐτούς, πόσους	And he was asking them
8:5	ἔχετε ἄρτουσ; οἱ δέ εἶπαν,	"How many breads do you
	ἑπτά.	have?". So they said
		"Seven".

As before, the students '*know*' without hesitation what the answer is.

It is three days since the crowd of five thousand was fed. We have worked on the basis that this first 'event' in the gospel corresponds in some way with the narrative in LXX *Genesis* for Day 3. If three further days have now elapsed in the gospel narrative then, following the parallel, that takes us forward in *Genesis* to the events recorded for Day 6. Here is the passage in question:

| LXX Gn. 1:24 | καὶ εἶπεν **ὁ θεός** ἐξαγαγέτω ἡ γῆ ψυχὴν ζῶσαν κατὰ γένος τετράποδα καὶ ἑρπετὰ καὶ θηρία τῆς γῆς κατὰ γένος καὶ ἐγένετο οὕτως | And **God** said "Let the earth bring forth a living soul after a four-footed kind, and creeping things and wild beasts of the earth after (their) kind": and it happened like this. |
| 1:25 | καὶ ἐποίησεν **ὁ θεός** τὰ θηρία τῆς γῆς κατὰ γένος καὶ τὰ κτήνη κατὰ γένος καὶ πάντα τὰ ἑρπετὰ τῆς γῆς κατὰ γένος αὐτῶν καὶ εἶδεν **ὁ θεός** ὅτι καλά | And **God** made the wild beasts of the earth after (their) kind, and the pastoral beasts after (their) kind, and all the creeping things of the earth after their kind. And **God** saw them as good. |

1:26	καὶ εἶπεν ὁ **θεός** ποιήσωμεν ἄνθρωπον κατ' εἰκόνα ἡμετέραν καὶ καθ' ὁμοίωσιν καὶ ἀρχέτωσαν τῶν ἰχθύων τῆς θαλάσσης καὶ τῶν πετεινῶν τοῦ οὐρανοῦ καὶ τῶν κτηνῶν καὶ πάσης τῆς γῆς καὶ πάντων τῶν ἑρπετῶν τῶν ἑρπόντων ἐπὶ τῆς γῆς	And **God** said "Let us make A PERSON according to our image and according to likenesses. And let them rule (over) the fishes of the sea, and (over) the birds of Heaven, and (over) the pastoral beasts, and (over) all the earth, and (over) all the creeping things which creep upon the earth"
1:27	καὶ ἐποίησεν ὁ **θεὸς** τὸν ἄνθρωπον κατ' εἰκόνα θεοῦ ἐποίησεν αὐτόν ἄρσεν καὶ θῆλυ ἐποίησεν αὐτούς	And **God** made 'THE PERSON'. According to (the) image of a god he made HIM. Male and female he made THEM.
1:28	καὶ ηὐλόγησεν αὐτοὺς ὁ **θεὸς** λέγων αὐξάνεσθε καὶ πληθύνεσθε καὶ πληρώσατε τὴν γῆν καὶ κατακυριεύσατε αὐτῆς καὶ ἄρχετε τῶν ἰχθύων τῆς θαλάσσης καὶ τῶν πετεινῶν τοῦ οὐρανοῦ καὶ πάντων τῶν κτηνῶν καὶ πάσης τῆς γῆς καὶ πάντων τῶν ἑρπετῶν τῶν ἑρπόντων ἐπὶ τῆς γῆς	And **God** blessed them, saying "Grow and multiply and fill the earth and LORD over it. And rule (over) the fishes of the sea, and (over) the birds of heaven, and (over) all the pastoral beasts, and (over) all the earth, and (over) all the creeping things which creep upon the earth"

1:29	καὶ εἶπεν ὁ **θεός** ἰδοὺ δέδωκα ὑμῖν πᾶν χόρτον σπόριμον σπεῖρον σπέρμα ὅ ἐστιν ἐπάνω πάσης τῆς γῆς καὶ πᾶν ξύλον ὃ ἔχει ἐν ἑαυτῷ καρπὸν σπέρματος σπορίμου ὑμῖν ἔσται εἰς βρῶσιν	And **God** said "Look, I have given to YOU [pl.] every grass spreading seed to propagate which is above all the earth, and every tree which has within itself fruit (having) seed to propagate. For you it shall be for eating.
1:30	καὶ πᾶσι τοῖς θηρίοις τῆς γῆς καὶ πᾶσι τοῖς πετεινοῖς τοῦ οὐρανοῦ καὶ παντὶ ἑρπετῷ τῷ ἕρποντι ἐπὶ τῆς γῆς ὃ ἔχει ἐν ἑαυτῷ ψυχὴν ζωῆς πάντα χόρτον χλωρὸν εἰς βρῶσιν καὶ ἐγένετο οὕτως	And to all the wild beasts of the earth, and to all the birds of Heaven, and to every creeping thing that creeps upon the earth (and) which has within it a soul of life, (I have given) every (kind of) green grass for eating". And it happened like this.
1:31	καὶ εἶδεν ὁ **θεὸς** τὰ πάντα ὅσα ἐποίησεν καὶ ἰδοὺ καλὰ λίαν καὶ ἐγένετο ἑσπέρα καὶ ἐγένετο πρωί ἡμέρα ἕκτη	And **God** saw everything that he made, and look : exceedingly good. And evening happened, and morning happened: SIXTH DAY.

Let us repeat our analysis, this time to discover what textual features occur just **seven** times.

Again we find the letter δ. And if we count digrams, we find four pairs which occur **seven** times:

ασ/ας, ην, ρα, σε

It seems unlikely that the letter δ would be used as a token for '*bread*'. It is difficult to see any sound reason for using it in this way. But if we put together the two lists of digrams then we have:

5 times: αλ, ασ/ας, αυ, εγ, εο, ησ/ης, θε, μα, νε, συ

7 times: ασ/ας, ην, ρα, σε

The common denominator is plainly ασ/ας. It is the only group found **five** times in the passage in *Genesis* for Day 3 and **seven** times in the passage for Day 6. In algebraic terms, it is the solution to a pair of simultaneous equations. Then could this be the token which these Greek writers use to stand for '*bread*'? And does it make any sense that they should do such a curious thing?

The word in Greek for bread is ἄρτος. If we take the first and last letters of this word then we obtain, as a potential shorthand notation for bread, the letter pair ας. So our mathematical 'solution' makes quite good sense. Could this be the convention amongst the writers of Greek scripture … that the digram ας (or ασ, where it occurs in the middle of another word) is considered by them as the secret token for 'bread'?

If we conduct the corresponding analysis looking for what occurs exactly **two** times in the text of LXX *Genesis* for Day 3, and **two** times in the text for Day 6, we find that there is no solution using single letters but that when we count digrams there are multiple solutions as follows:

αγ, χο, χθ, ημ, ιμ, ρο, στ, υλ

Could one of these be the token used by the Greek writers to stand for '*fish*'?

The word used in *Genesis*, and in the gospels, for '*fish*' is ἰχθύς. Then from the list above, the solution which makes the best sense is χθ. If we conclude that the writers have adopted, as a shorthand notation for fish, this characteristic central pair of letters from the word ἰχθῦς then we may be close to the conclusion we hoped for. The final test will be to see how much sense these hypotheses make when applied to the other riddles of scripture … and in particular to the riddles set forth in the gospels.

For a quick test, let us search the whole of the NT canon for any single verse which contains the digram ασ/ας repeated five times and the digram χθ repeated two times. We come up with just one result:

| Mk. 6:41 | καὶ λαβὼν τοὺς πέντε ἄρτους καὶ τοὺς δύο ἰχθύας ἀναβλέψας εἰς τὸν οὐρανὸν εὐλόγησεν καὶ κατέκλασεν τοὺς ἄρτους

καὶ ἐδίδου τοῖς μαθηταῖς [αὐτοῦ] ἵνα παρατιθῶσιν αὐτοῖς, καὶ τοὺς δύο ἰχθύας ἐμέρισεν πᾶσιν. | And taking the **five** breads and the **two** <u>fishes</u>, <u>looking up</u> into Heaven, he blessed and <u>he broke</u> the breads.

And he gave to [his] students so that they would set before them - and the two <u>fishes</u> he divided amongst <u>all</u>. |

Using a purely *mathematical* technique we appear have solved one of the important conundrums at the very heart of Greek scritpure. For we seem to have identified what the writers mean when they refer to '*bread*' … and to '*fish*'.

Then perhaps it is significant that in the gospel narrative the students (disciples) of Jesus are known by the Greek word μαθητὴς … a word plainly connected with the English word '***mathe***matics'.

Blindness and deafness are common afflictions for those who meet with Jesus in the gospel narrative. But for us as readers these conditions begin to resolve when we learn how to recognise those things which have been hidden in the text … hidden indeed *from the very laying down of the world.*

Mk. 7:32	καὶ **φέρΟυσΙΝ** αὐτῷ κωφὸν καὶ μογιλάλον, καὶ παρα**Κα**λοῦσ**ΙΝ** αὐτὸν ἵνα ἐπιθῇ αὐτῷ τὴν χεῖρα.	And <u>they brought</u> to him (someone) deaf and having a speech impediment, and <u>they appealed</u> to him that he might place to him the hand.
7:33	καὶ ἀπολαβόμενος αὐτὸν ἀπὸ τοῦ ὄχλου κατ' ἰδίαν ἔβαλεν τοὺς δακτύλους αὐτοῦ εἰς τὰ ὦτα αὐτοῦ καὶ **πτύσ**α**ς** ἥψατο τῆς γλώσσης αὐτοῦ,	And taking him away from the crowd privately, he threw his fingers into his ears and <u>spitting</u>, he touched his tongue.
7:34	καὶ ἀναβλέψ**ας** εἰς τὸν οὐρανὸν ἐστέναξεν, καὶ λέγει αὐτῷ, εφφαθα, ὅ ἐστιν, διανοί**χ**θ**η**τι.	And <u>looking up</u> into Heaven he sighed, and he said to him "Ephphatha!", that is "<u>Be opened up</u>".
7:35	καὶ [εὐθέωσ] ἠνοίγησαν αὐτοῦ αἱ ἀκοαί, καὶ ἐλύθη ὁ δεσμὸς τῆς γλώσσης αὐτοῦ, καὶ ἐλάλει ὀρθῶς.	And [immediately] his ears *were* opened up and the bond of his tongue *was* loosed and he spoke *rightly*.
7:36	καὶ διεστείλατο αὐτοῖς ἵνα μηδενὶ λέγωσιν: ὅσον δὲ αὐτοῖς διεστέλλετο, αὐτοὶ μᾶλλον περισσότερον ἐκήρυσσον.	And he charged them that they should tell no one. But as much as he charged them, they proclaimed (it) more abundantly.
7:37	καὶ ὑπερπερισσῶς ἐξεπλήσσοντο λέγοντες, καλῶς πάντα πεποίηκεν: καὶ τοὺς κωφοὺς ποιεῖ **ἀ**Κούε**ΙΝ** καὶ [τοὺσ] ἀλάλους λαλεῖν.	And they were hyper-abundantly astonished, saying "He has made all things well. Even the deaf he makes <u>to hear</u> - and [the] dumb to speak".

Chapter Notes

Preface

1. Most WG., *The Basic Catholic Catechism: Part Five, The Mystical Body of Christ*, 1990.
2. Hatt C., *English Works of John Fisher, Bishop of Rochester (1469-1535), Sermons and Other Writings, 1520-1535*, Oxford University Press, 2002, ISBN 978-01982 70119
3. Grayling AC., *What is Good ?*, Phoenix, 2004, ISBN 0-75381-755-1, p.94
4. For the record, it was on 23rd January 2001 that I was comparing the nominally parallel passages at Mt.15:39 and Mk.8:10 which cite respectively the different destinations μαγαδάν and δαλμανουθά . It occurred to me that these fictional place names were very likely made up in accordance with some rule not yet known to me, and that the Greek texts of the gospel had been composed to include a component somehow hidden from view, possibly relying upon the use of anagrams.

   I realised too that if this had been done then it should still be possible, for those who knew how, to recover the concealed component. This could yield incremental meaning which might then extend, interact with, or in some other way modify or correct, the first impression conveyed by the literal meaning alone of any particular passage.

1. Introducing Greek Scripture

1. Jobes KH. & Silva M., *Invitation to the Septuagint*, Baker Academic, 2000, ISBN 0-8010-2235-5, p.184.
2. Ratzinger (aka. Pope Benedict XVI), *Lecture at the University of Regensburg*, 12 Sep 2006.
3. Esler PF. (Ed.); Brown D., *The Early Christian World*, Vol.2, Routledge, 2000, ISBN 0-415-16497-4, p.1161seq.
4. Ginzberg L., *The Legends of the Jews*, Vol.1, Trans. Szold H., Johns Hopkins University Press, 1998, ISBN 0-8018-5890-9, p.71.

2. Culture and Doctrine: Then and Now

1. Esler PF. (Ed.); Logan AHB., *The Early Christian World*, Vol.2, Routledge, 2000, ISBN 0-415-16497-4, p.907.
2. Couliano I, *The Tree of Gnosis*, found at: http://themoonsfavors.blogspot.com/2007/12/tree-of-gnosis-ioan-couliano.html
3. Logan AHB., *Gnostic Truth and Christian Heresy*, T & T Clark, 1996, ISBN 1-56563-243-5, p.135.
4. At LXX Is.44:6 the same boast is attributed to Sabaoth.
5. Barker M., *The Great Angel: A Study of Israel's Second God*, Westminster/John Knox Press, 1992, ISBN 0-664-25395-4, p.174.
6. Esler PF. (Ed.); Logan AHB., *The Early Christian World*, Vol.2, Routledge, 2000, ISBN 0-415-16497-4, pp.915-921.
7. The cuckoo is a parasite which lays its eggs in the nests of other birds: the eggs vary in colour and sometimes resemble those of the bird whose nest has been selected. Once hatched, the young cuckoo turns out all the other fledglings (or eggs) which are left to perish on the ground. It is this behaviour which natural selection provides as the means for survival of the cuckoo species.
8. Libreria Editrice Vaticana, 2007 http://www.vatican.va/holy_father/benedict_xvi/audiences /2007/documents/hf_ben-xvi_aud_20070328_en.html
9. Esler PF. (Ed.); Logan AHB., *The Early Christian World*, Vol.2, Routledge, 2000, ISBN 0-415-16497-4, p.920.
10. Küng H., *The Catholic Church - A Short History*, Weidenfeld & Nicolson, 2001, ISBN 0-297-64638-9, pp.30-31.
11. Darwin C., *The Origin of Species*, Oxford University Press, 1996, ISBN 0-19-283438-X, p.3.
12. The current position in Britain is set out in *The Gift of Scripture*, Catholic Truth Society, 2005, ISBN 1-86082-323-8.
13. Torry M. (Ed.), *The Sermons of John Boys Smith: A Theologian of Integrity*, St John's College, Cambridge, 2003, ISBN 0-9501085-6-1, p.183 & pp.258-9.

3. The Key to Scripture's Plot: LXX *Genesis*

1. Barker M., *The Great Angel: A Study of Israel's Second God*, Westminster/John Knox Press, 1992, ISBN 0-664-25395-4, p.162, 165, 188.
2. *Trans*: Schaff P. et al., *City of God*, Buffalo: Christian Literature Co., 1887.

4. LXX *Genesis*: The First Seven Days

1. Barker M., *The Great Angel: A Study of Israel's Second God*, Westminster/JohnKnox Press, 1992, ISBN 0-664-25395-4, p.175.
2. Alter R., *The Five Books of Moses*, Norton, 2004, ISBN 0-393-01955-1, p.19.

5. The Book of Genesis of Heaven and Earth

1. Ginzberg L., *The Legends of the Jews*, Vol.1, Trans. Szold H., Johns Hopkins University Press, 1998, ISBN 0-8018-5890-9, p.105.
2. Barker M., *The Great Angel: A Study of Israel's Second God*, Westminster/John Knox Press, 1992, ISBN 0-664-25395-4, p.184.
3. *see* Jobes KH. & Silva M., *Invitation to the Septuagint*, Baker Academic, 2000, ISBN 0-8010-2235-5, p.213.
4. Ginzberg L., *The Legends of the Jews*, Vol.1, Trans. Szold H., Johns Hopkins University Press, 1998, ISBN 0-8018-5890-9, p.109.
5. Metzger BM. & Ehrman BD., *The Text of the New Testament*, Oxford University Press, 2005, ISBN 0-19-516122-X, p.26.
6. It is interesting to speculate on the methods which might have been adopted to make such a check. In modern times, computer analysis of the text makes it easy to verify, in a fraction of a second, the number of words in Greek *Genesis* with the power to spell the name of Cain.

6. The Book of Genesis of 'Persons'

No notes for this chapter.

7. From *Genesis* to the Gospels

1. With modern Greek fonts the lower case letter 's' appears as σ, or as ς where it comes at the end of a word. In the early Uncial texts of scripture there was no such distinction in form.

2. A rough equivalent to this scheme might be achieved in the English language by introducing the word *'presentable'* to embody the written form of the word *serpent* and the word *'spent'* to resemble its sound.

3. The Greek word used at Pr.23:1 is δυναστῶν, from which we derive the English word *dynasty*. This in turn may evoke the phrase used at Ac.19:9 where Paul resorts to: καθ' ἡμέραν διαλεγόμενος ἐν τῇ σχολῇ τυράννου [*reasoning daily in the school of a tyrant*].

4. It is perhaps significant that the poetic word ὄμμα is used here in preference to the more usual ὀφθαλμὸν [*eye*]. This provides that 'nothing should be brought to light'.

5. Alternate name for Satan, in Aramaic *'God-of-the-blind'*.

6. His failure is analogous to that of Jesus' students who in the gospels go fishing *at night* and are quite unable to catch any fish (*qv*. Lk.5:5; Jn.21:3). Night seems to be a token of good and of **God**, so we should not be surprised to learn that *at night* there are no fish around to be caught. Jesus, of course, is *'the light '*.

7. Surely refers to Elizabeth, barren until she conceives the infant who shall be named John (Lk.1:7, 1:13, 1:24).

8. The name means in Hebrew *'God-with-us'*.

9. Surely refers to Mary (who in the gospels is the mother of Jesus), whilst hinting simultaneously at the identity of the father.

10. At LXX Gn.3:15 the offspring of the woman are admonished to watch out for the serpent's *head*.

11. The beliefs of the Cathars are thought to have come originally from Eastern Europe and the Byzantine Empire.

8. John and Jesus

1. An alternate meaning for τροχὸν is the *coil* (of a serpent).

2. The name *Nazareth* seems to have been fictional: there is no evidence for a real-world settlement with this name and

location until about the fourth century CE, and no evidence whatever for the existence of any 'city' named *Capharnaum* (*qv*: Lk.4:31).

3. Narrative description of one subject under the guise of another suggestively similar.

4. It is unfortunate that the distinction so carefully drawn in Greek is not maintained in translation to Latin. Latin is not a language of scripture. It is imprecise, lacking any word for the direct article ('the'). So in Latin the pivotal distinction between ὁ θεός [**God**] and θεός [*a god*] is all but impossible to draw. Nor is it likely that Constantine would have wished to see it drawn.

5. Water from a river or spring is from the 'waters below' [*qv*. Gn.1:7]. In scripture this seems to be used consistently as a token of what is deemed to be good. But the 'waters above', along with thunder, lightning and hail, appear to be tokens of evil.

6. At Gn.8:7 Noah sends out a *raven* as the primary test for discovering whether the waters have dried up from the earth. Its carrion diet is 'opposite' to the cereal diet of the *pigeon* Noah sends out behind it. Does the contrast in the diet of the two birds match the contrast in the diets of Abel and Cain, the one a token of what is good and the other of what is evil?

7. It is of interest to note that at LXX Gn.14:14 we have:

> But Abram, hearing that Lot, his brother, was taken captive, counted his own who dwelt with him, three hundred, ten and eight of them, and pursued behind them as far as Dan.

9. The 'Father'

No notes for this chapter.

10. Cain and the Serpent at the Core of Scripture's Plot

1. Metzger BM., *Manuscripts of the Greek Bible*, Oxford University Press, 1991, ISBN 0-19-502924-0, p.36.

11. Jesus further portrayed as Cain

1. The name Gethsemani means in Aramaic '*oil press*'.

2. Brown RE., *The Gospel According to John*, Doubleday & Co (Geoffrey Chapman Ltd), 1966.

3. Carroll L., *TheHunting of the Snark*, Penguin Classics, 2006, ISBN 978-0140434910.

12. Paul: A False Apostle

1. The writer's first use of these words is at Lk.22:38 and Lk.23:55 respectively.

13. The Pauline Letters

1. Fitzmyer JA., in *New Jerome Biblical Commentary*, Ed. Brown RE, Fiztmyer JA, Murphy RE, Geoffrey Chapman, 2000, ISBN 0-225-66803-3, p.770.

2. Detering H., *The Falsified Paul: Early Christianity in the Twilight*, in *Journal of Higher Criticism* **10**, 2, 2003 … which may be found at: http://www.hermann-detering.de/FabricatedJHC.pdf

14. The Theme of Scripture Summarised

No notes for this chapter.

15. In Conclusion

1. Kaufmann E., *Breeding for God*, in *Prospect Magazine*, **128**, Nov 2006 … which may be found at: http://www.prospect-magazine.co.uk/article_details.php?id=7913

2. Observation made by the General Editor of the Roman Catholic *New Jerusalem Bible* in private conversation at Blackfriars, Oxford, UK on 24th April 2001.

422

Select Bibliography

Alter R (2004), *The Five Books of Moses*, Norton, 1064pp.

Armstrong K (2007), *The Bible: The Biography*, Atlantic Books, 302pp.

Avalos H (2007), *The End of Biblical Studies*, Prometheus Books, 399pp.

Barker M (1992), *The Great Angel: A Study of Israel's Second God*, Westminster John Knox Press, 253pp.

Bowler PJ (1990), *Charles Darwin: The Man and his Influence*, Cambridge, 250pp.

Brown D (2003), *The Da Vinci Code*, , 467pp.

Brown RE, Fitzmyer JA and Murphy RE [Eds] (1989), *The New Jerome Biblical Commentary*, Geoffrey Chapman, 1484pp.

Darwin C (1996), *The Origin of Species*, Oxford, 439pp.

Dawkins R (2006), *The God Delusion*, Bantam Press, 406pp.

Dennett C (2006), *Breaking the Spell: Religion as a Natural Phenomenon*, Viking, 448pp.

Ehrman BD (2005), *Misquoting Jesus: The Story Behind Who Changed the Bible and Why*, Harper Collins, 242pp.

Ellegård AE (1999), *Jesus: One Hundred Years Before Christ*, Century, 322pp.

Esler P [Ed] (2000), *The Early Christian World*, Routledge, 1342pp. (2 vols)

Freke T and Gandy P (1999), *The Jesus Mysteries*, Element, 423pp.

Gardner M [Ed] (1962), *The Annotated Snark: The Full Text of Lewis Carroll's "The Hunting of the Snark"* , Penguin, 126pp.

Ginzberg L (1937), *The Legends of the Jews, Vol. 1: From the Creation to Jacob*, Johns Hopkins, 424pp.

Goodman M (2007), *Rome and Jerusalem: The Clash of Ancient Civilizations*, Allen Lane, 639pp.

Grayling AC (2004), *What is Good?: The Search for the Best Way to Live*, Phoenix, 274pp.

Harris JG (1999), *Gnosticism: Beliefs and Practices*, Sussex Academic, 224pp.

Hinde RA (1997), *Religion and Darwinism*, British Humanist Association, 29pp.

Hinde RA (1999), *Why Gods Persist: A Scientific Approach to Religion*, Routledge, 288pp.

Humphrys J (2007), *In God We Doubt*, Hodder & Stoughton, 356pp.

Jobes KH and Silva M (2000), *Invitation to the Septuagint*, Baker Academic, 351pp.

Kahn D (1967), *The Code Breakers*, Scribner, 1181pp.

Küng H (2001), *The Catholic Church: A Short History*, Weidenfeld & Nicolson, 231pp.

Logan AHB (1996), *Gnostic Truth and Christian Heresy*, Hendrickson, 373pp.

Metzger BM (1981), *Manuscripts of the Greek Bible*, Oxford, 150pp.

Metzger BM and Ehrman BD (2005), *The Text of the New Testament*, Oxford, 366pp.

Noel G and Stanford P (1994), *The Anatomy of the Catholic Church*, Michael Russell, 209pp.

Ranan D (2006), *Double Cross: The Code of the Catholic Church*, Theo Press, 426pp.

Rowe D (2009), *What Should I Believe?: Why Our Beliefs about the Nature of Death and the Purpose of Life Dominate Our Lives*, Routledge, 294pp.

Simon B (2004), *The Essence of the Gnostics*, Chartwell, 240pp.

Singh S (1999), *The Code Book*, Fourth Estate, 402pp.

Skinner JR (1894), *Key to the Hebrew-Egyptian Mystery in the Source of Measures*, Kessinger, 387pp.

Torry M [Ed] (2003), *The Sermons of John Boys Smith: A Theologian of Integrity*, St John's College, Cambridge, 344pp.

Wansbrough H [Ed] (1985), *The New Jerusalem Bible*, Darton Longman & Todd, 2126pp.

Welsby DA and Anderson JR [Eds] (2004), *Sudan: Ancient Treasures*, British Museum Press, 336pp.

Yonge CD [Trans] (1993), *The Works of Philo*, Hendrickson, 924pp.

General Index

436

Index to Scriptural Passages